From Jihad to Politics

How Syrian Jihadis Embraced Politics

JEROME DREVON

Oxford University Press is a department of the University of Oxford.
It furthers the University's objective of excellence in research, scholarship,
and education by publishing worldwide. Oxford is a registered trade mark of
Oxford University Press in the UK and in certain other countries.

Published in the United States of America by Oxford University Press
198 Madison Avenue, New York, NY 10016, United States of America.

© Oxford University Press 2024

Some rights reserved. No part of this publication may be reproduced, stored in
a retrieval system, or transmitted, in any form or by any means, for commercial purposes,
without the prior permission in writing of Oxford University Press, or as expressly
permitted by law, by licence or under terms agreed with the appropriate
reprographics rights organization.

This is an open access publication, available online and distributed under the terms of a
Creative Commons Attribution–Non Commercial–No Derivatives 4.0
International licence (CC BY-NC-ND 4.0), a copy of which is available at
http://creativecommons.org/licenses/by-nc-nd/4.0/.

Enquiries concerning use outside the scope of the licence terms
should be sent to the Rights Department, Oxford University Press,
at the above address.

You must not circulate this work in any other form
and you must impose this same condition on any acquirer

Library of Congress Cataloging-in-Publication Data
Names: Drevon, Jerome, author.
Title: From jihad to politics : how Syrian jihadis embraced politics / Jerome Drevon.
Description: New York, NY : University of Oxford, 2024. |
Includes bibliographical references and index.
Identifiers: LCCN 2024012918 (print) | LCCN 2024012919 (ebook) |
ISBN 9780197765166 (paperback) | ISBN 9780197765159 (hardback) |
ISBN 9780197765180 (epub)
Subjects: LCSH: Jabhat al-Nuṣrah (Organization) |
Ahrar al-Sham (Organization) | Jihad—Political aspects—Syria. |
Islam and politics—Syria. | Islamic fundamentalism—Syria. |
Syria—Politics and government—2000-
Classification: LCC HV6433.S952 J334 2024 (print) |
LCC HV6433.S952 (ebook) | DDC 322/.1095691—dc23/eng/20240429
LC record available at https://lccn.loc.gov/2024012918
LC ebook record available at https://lccn.loc.gov/2024012919

DOI: 10.1093/9780197765197.001.0001

Printed on demand

À ma femme et ma petite fille, que son monde soit moins violent que le nôtre

Contents

List of Figures	ix
List of Tables	xi
Acknowledgements	xiii
Arabic Transliteration	xvii
Arabic Glossary	xix
Major Armed Groups and Coalitions	xxiii
1. Introduction	1
2. Creating an Insurgency	32
3. Expanding the Rebellion	76
4. Uniting the Armed Opposition	113
5. Politicising Jihad	163
6. Syria and the Future of Jihad	200
Annex: Methodology and Sources	213
Notes	219
Bibliography	231
Index	259

Figures

2.1	Territorial control in 2013	59
2.2	The division of armed opposition-held areas by 2017	61
3.1	Territorial control in mid-2012	77
3.2	Territorial control in 2013	79
3.3	Territorial control in 2014	80
3.4	Territorial control in 2015	82
4.1	The situation before the subjugation of three main armed opposition groups' strongholds	137
4.2	Initial Turkish observation points defined in 17 September 2018	142

Tables

1.1	Four ideal-type trajectories and influential examples in Syria	12
2.1	Armed groups' comparative features in the beginning of the conflict	71
3.1	Comparative characteristics of major armed opposition–held areas	90
3.2	Armed groups' comparative expansion	100
4.1	The main military operation rooms	122

Acknowledgements

I am grateful to numerous individuals who have contributed to this research in various ways. First and foremost, I would like to express my appreciation to the Syrians whom I interviewed over the years, who generously shared their understanding and experience of the conflict. Without their invaluable assistance, I could not have comprehended many dimensions of this conflict. I have also benefited greatly from the analyses published by Syrian researchers, who have authored detailed studies, reports, and newspaper articles from Syria itself. Their contributions are essential to any academic research on this topic. I would also like to extend my thanks to academics, journalists, think-tank and independent researchers, as well as friends, who discussed their perspectives and insights with me since I began this research. Their input has enriched this book. Special thanks go to Abd al-Qadir Kurabi, who kindly shared access to a variety of actors—especially Ahrar al-Sham's leaders—and provided analytical insights on northwest Syria. These discussions have helped to shape my analysis, but further research is still necessary to refine and amend specific aspects of the conflict.

I could not have undertaken this research without the participation of a number of leaders and members of Ahrar al-Sham, Hay'at Tahrir al-Sham (HTS), and other Syrian groups. They were willing to share their experiences, interpretations, and analyses, especially Khaled Abu Anas and Husam Tarsha. Many other Syrians loosely connected to Ahrar al-Sham or other Islamist actors, including Rami Dalati, Hassan Dugheim, and Abul-'Abbas al-Shami, also helped me understand Ahrar al-Sham, the Islamist social movement in Syria, and pre-2011 prison experiences. I am similarly grateful to the leadership of HTS—the former Jabhat al-Nusra, or Nusra Front—who welcomed several colleagues and myself to the Idlib province several times a year since 2019. Abu Muhammad al-Jolani, Abu Abdullah al-Shami, and Abul-Hassan al-Hamawi, the respective general commander, senior religious authority, and military leader of the group, generously shared their perspectives on the conflict with us as new events unfolded. This opportunity provided a welcome view into a very active local civil society. In Idlib, Walid Tamer was especially insightful in helping us understand local civil society developments.

This research was funded by the Swiss National Science Foundation (SNSF) as part of two early and advanced fellowships undertaken in Manchester and

Oxford, and a return phase in Geneva. I also received additional funding from the Project on Middle East Political Science (POMEPS) to conduct field research in Turkey. In Oxford, I was hosted by the School of Government and the Department of Political Sciences and International Relations. I learned from numerous discussions and workshops organised by Elizabeth Frazer and Jonathan Leader Maynard on Ideas and Political Violence, Stathis Kalyvas on MENA and conflicts, and Masooda Bano and Abdullah Bin Khalid Al-Saud on the future of Salafism. I wish to thank in particular Masooda Bano, Stathis Kalyvas, Jonathan Leader Maynard, Raphael Lefèvre, Kevin Mazur, and Andrea Ruggeri for their comments and suggestions. In Geneva, I was hosted by the Centre on Conflict, Development & Peacebuilding at the Graduate Institute of International and Development Studies (IHEID). I would like to thank Keith Krause and Oliver Jütersonke for providing all the resources and assistance I required, and for giving me the opportunity to present and discuss my research with colleagues. I benefited from many discussions with Jonathan Luke Austin, Matthew Bamber, Souhaïl Belhadj, Abdulla Erfan, Brian McQuinn, Bilal Salayme, and Robert Watkins. I also would like to thank Jeroen Gunning for his early encouragements and suggestions on armed groups' social structures.

I had the chance to present and discuss my research in multiple academic venues. Isak Svensson from Uppsala University offered me numerous opportunities to improve my work in several workshops and seminars associated to the project on "Resolving Jihadist Conflicts". Isak provided critical comments and suggestions and helped me reflect on broader questions related to conflicts and religion. Véronique Dudouet invited me to join the advisory board of the project on "Radical Islamist armed groups—(De)escalation paths and entry points for third-party engagement", funded by the Berghof Foundation, which similarly helped me refine many ideas that I elaborate in this analysis. Mona Kanwal Sheikh also invited me to events associated with her project on "Explaining Transnational Jihad—Patterns of Escalation and Containment", where I discussed several concepts that I developed in this book. Parts of this book were finally presented in workshops organised by the Conflict Research Society, Danish Institute for International Studies (DIIS), and the Folke Bernadotte Academy, the European University Institute, the Foreign & Commonwealth Office, the International Studies Association (ISA), the Mitchell Centre for Social Network Analysis of the University of Manchester, the Norwegian Defence Research Establishment (FFI), Paris Dauphine, and Uppsala Universitet and the Folke Bernadotte Academy. I notably discussed some of the ideas underpinning this book in Michael Gabbay and Mohammed Hafez's workshop on Armed Groups' Consolidation at the Naval Postgraduate School; Olivier Roy and Théo Blanc's seminar on Post-Salafism and Deradicalization at the European University Institute (EUI); Marc Lynch, Morten Valbjørn, and

Jeroen Gunning's TOI–POMEPS Workshop on Islamists in Warscapes; Michel Wyss, Vladimir Rauta, and Assaf Moghadam's workshop on Conflict Delegation and Proxy Wars in International Security; and the United Nations System Staff College (UNSSC) course on "Analyzing and Understanding Non-State Armed Groups" organised by Brian McQuinn. Discussing my previous book on Egypt at Stathis Kalyvas's T. E. Lawrence Program on the Study of Conflict at Oxford also helped me reflect on the introduction to the present book and its broader contribution to the literature. Last, I would like to also thank Sam Heller and the International Crisis Group (ICG) for inviting me to several workshops on Salafi Jihadi conflicts and engagement with these actors, before I joined the organisation.

Several friends and colleagues also carefully read and commented on either large sections of the book or the full manuscript. I would like to thank in particular Regine Schwab, Erik Skare, Alex Thurston, and Elizabeth Tsurkov. Stéphane Lacroix also had incisive questions and comments on Ahrar al-Sham, HTS, and Salafism more generally. Aaron Zelin's collection of primary sources (jihadology.net) is also an invaluable asset for any research on jihadis, and I would like to express my gratitude for his dedication and efforts.

In addition to the friends and colleagues mentioned throughout this acknowledgement, I have been fortunate, in the course of my research on armed groups' institutionalisation, to befriend Orwa Ajjoub, Aymenn Jawad Al-Tamimi, Amarnath Amarasingam, Obaydah Amer, Jean Nicolas Bitter, Lorenzo Bosi, Silvia Carenzi, Teije Hidde Donker, Leah Farrall, Hazim Fouad, Anand Gopal, Tore Hamming, Fouad Ilias, Patrick Johnson, Amr Jomaa, , Charles Lister, Aron Lund, Stefan Malthaner, Mike Marcusa, Fouad Gehad Marei, Broderick McDonald, Richard McNeil-Willson, Caelum Moffatt, Wassim Nasr, Thomas Pierret, Laila al-Refaai, Jonah Schulhofer-Wohl, Ben Smith, and Nagwan Soliman. Our rounds of discussions and chats, both in person and online, helped me improve this research and analysis of the Syrian conflict. They contributed to furthering my understanding of ongoing developments and informed the writing of this book.

I spent considerable time discussing the Syrian conflict and Jihadi groups with Patrick Haenni. Patrick helped me develop my ideas on the institutionalisation of religious authority as well as armed groups' choices in armed conflicts. We discussed new ideas on HTS and the pragmatism embraced by some Salafi Jihadi armed groups in parallel to our field research in Syria. My colleague Dareen at the International Crisis Group (ICG) also helped me refine some of my ideas on how HTS has evolved and generously shared information with me. Field research with Dareen, Noah, Patrick, and Tamas in Idlib was an exercise in camaraderie that helped us better understand the internal dynamics of the conflict. I would like to thank Humanitarian Dialogue (HD) for the initial opportunity.

I would finally like to thank my family, especially my wife, for being a constant source of support. My wife always supported my work even when it required intensive work and travels abroad. She was both patient and understanding, and kindly joined me when I had to spend extensive periods of time in Turkey. I would like to dedicate this book to our little daughter.

David McBride, editor-in-chief at Oxford University Press, helped my first book on Egypt come to fruition, and warmly supported the publication of this book on Syria, too. Academic publications take a notoriously long time to publish. This work was completed independently from my previous position of adviser for non-state armed groups at the International Committee of the Red Cross (ICRC). While I definitely benefited from many discussions with my ICRC colleagues, including Camille Allamel, Abbas Daiyar, Irénée Herbet, Ihcène Kiamouche, Ruben Stewart, Tamas Szenderak, and Fiona Terry, this book represents only my understanding of the Syrian conflict. It does not engage the ICRC as an institution or myself as a previous employee of this institution. Similarly, this work does not represent the views of my current employer, International Crisis Group (ICG).

The pre-press stage of this publication was supported by the Swiss National Science Foundation, which made possible the publication of this book in open access (Gold Open Access).

Arabic Transliteration

The transliteration of Arabic words and titles follows a simplified pattern. Diacritics are not included; Arabic words are not capitalised; Ayn and Hamza are differentiated; Arabic words and names mentioned in the *International Journal of Middle East Studies*' Word List are included accordingly; accepted English spelling is used for prominent Arabic names and figures (e.g., Gamal Abdel Nasser, not Jamal 'Abd al-Nasir).

Arabic Glossary

'almani	Secular
amir	Leader
'aqida	The Islamic creed
ash'ari	The mainstream religious creed (*'aqida*) endorsed by most Muslims
athari	A literalist religious creed (*'aqida*) in Islam
baghi	Extremism or rebellion (negative connotation)
bay'a	Allegiance, oath
bida'	Innovation in religion (negative connotation)
da'ish	(pl. *dawa'ish*) Pejorative name referring to the group Islamic State
da'wa	Preaching, religious proselytisation
fatwa	Religious ruling
fiqh	Islamic jurisprudence
fitna	Sedition
ghulu	Religious extremism in Islam (negative connotation)
hadina sha'biyya	Popular incubator
hadith	A recorded Prophetic tradition
hudud	The "limits" (literal meaning); Islamic penal punishments
ijtihad	Independent reasoning (source of Islamic jurisprudence)
indimaj	Unification (of armed groups)
irja'	Postponement (as in postponement of the application of Islamic law). Negative connotation. The murji is a Muslim committing *iraj'*.
isti'ana bil-kuffar	Appeal to the non-Muslims / the non-believers
istishhad	Martyrdom
jahiliyya	Ignorance; pre-Islamic time (negative connotation)
Jihad	Effort; struggle; war in God's path
Jihadi	A Muslim actively committed to the military dimension of jihad
kafir (pl. kafirun)	Non-believer / non-Muslim
al-khalifa	The Caliph
khariji	(pl. *khawarij*) Those who went out (literally); a heretical Islamic sect
al-khilafa	The Caliphate

kufr	Disbelief
madhhab	School of jurisprudence, differentiated in *hanbali*, *hanafi*, *maliki*, and *shafi'i*
mafsada	Corruption, negative public good
majlis al-shura	Consultative council
manhaj	The religious method
mashru' umma	the project of the Islamic nation
maslaha	Interest; public good
mithaq	Charter
mufti	Jurisconsult; highest religious authority in a state or a group
mujahid	(pl. *mujahideen*)A Muslim engaged in jihad
mukhabarat	The intelligence services
murabit	The Muslim on the frontline
al-qanun al-wad'i	Positivist Law
rafida (pl. *rawafid*)	The rejectors (derogatory term to describe *shi'a* Muslims)
sahwa	Awakening
sahwa	The Islamic revivalist movement, as in *al-sahwa al-islamiyya* or an anti–al-Qaeda armed reaction in Iraq during the 2000s supported by the American army (negative connotation)
al-salaf al-salih	The pious predecessors (the first three generation of Muslims)
Salafi	A Muslim who embraces the *Salafi* approach to Islam. Often dissociated in scholastic (*'ilmi*), activist (*haraki*), and Jihadi approaches.
al-salafiyya	Salafism
shabiha	Literally "ghost". Pro-government militias.
shahada	Testimony; martyrdom
shari'a	Islamic Law
shar'i (pl. *shari'in*)	Religious scholar giving religious edicts
sheikh	Religious scholar; notable
shirk	Associating something with God (negative connotation)
al-siyasat al-shar'iyya	Islamic Law-Guided Public Policy
sunna	The Prophetic tradition
taghalub	Domination
taghut (pl. *tawaghit*)	Despot; idol
takfir	Excommunication
takfiri	A Muslim inclined to excommunicate fellow Muslims (negative connotation)

tawheed	Oneness or unicity; divided in: *tawheed al-uluhiyya* (oneness of divinity), *al-rububiyya* (oneness of worship), and *al-asmat wal-sifat* (oneness of names and attributes)
al-'udhr bil-jahl	The excuse of ignorance
'ulama'	Religious scholars
umma	The Muslim community worldwide
usul al-fiqh	The principles of jurisprudence
al-wala wal-bara	Associating with the believers and dissociating from the infidels

Major Armed Groups and Coalitions

Some of the groups are called according to their Arabic name (e.g., Jaysh al-Islam, Jabhat al-Nusra), their English name (e.g., Free Syrian Army), or their English acronym (e.g., PKK, SDF). The choice follows the most common usage in the media.

Al-Qaeda: Tandhim Qa'idat al-Jihad
Ahrar al-Sham: Harakat Ahrar al-Sham al-Islamiyya, the Islamic movement of the Free Ones of the Levant
Faylaq al-Sham: the Sham (Levant) Legion
Free Syrian Army: al-Jaysh al-Suri al-Hur
HTS: Hay'at Tahrir al-Sham or the Committee for the Liberation of the Levant
Hurras al-Din: the Guardians of Religion
Islamic Front: al-Jabhat al-Islamiyya
Islamic State: al-Dawlat al-Islamiyya. The previous iterations were ISI, Islamic State in Iraq, and ISIS, Islamic State in Iraq and Sham.
Jabhat Fath al-Sham: the Front for the Liberation of Sham
Jabhat al-Nusra: the Front of Support for the People of Sham from Mujahidin from Sham in the Fields of Jihad or Jabhat al-Nusra li Ahl al-Sham min Mujahidi al-Sham fi Sahat al-Jihad
Jabhat al-Shamiyya: the Levant Front
Jaysh al-Fath: the Army of Victory
Jaysh al-Islam: the Army of Islam
Jaysh al-'Izza: the Army of Glory
Jund al-Aqsa: the Garrison of al-Aqsa mosque
National Liberation Front: al-Jabhat al-Wataniyya lil Tahrir
PKK: Kurdistan Workers' Party or Partiya Karkerên Kurdistanê
SDF: Syrian Democratic Forces or Quwwa Suriyya al-Dimoqratiyya
Southern Front: al-Jabhat al-Janubiyya
Suqur al-Sham: Alwiyya Suqur al-Sham, the Brigades of the Falcons of the Levant
Syrian Islamic Front: Jabhat Suriyya al-Islamiyya
Syrian Islamic Liberation Front: Jabhat Tahrir Suriyya al-Islamiyya
Syrian Liberation Front: Jabhat Tahrir Suriya
Syrian National Army: al-Jaysh al-Watani al-Suri
Syria's Revolutionary Front: Jabhat Thuwar Suriyya
Turkistan Islamic Party: Hizb al-Islami al-Turkistani
YPG: People's Protection Units or Yekîneyên Parastina Gel
Zinki Movement: Harakat Nur al-Din al-Zinki

1
Introduction

As non-violent protests spread throughout Syria in the midst of the Arab uprisings in early 2011, Islamist militants organised meetings in Syria and neighbouring countries. The militants anticipated that the peaceful demonstrations could not topple the regime and would soon turn violent. Rather than participate in the non-violent protests, they wanted to militarise opposition to the regime. Many had previous experience in jihad, having fought in conflicts such as Afghanistan in the 1980s, Chechnya in the 1990s, and Iraq in the first decade of the 2000s. A few had even already participated in the first military confrontation against the father of Syria's president in the late 1970s. The militants joined forces with non-Jihadi Salafis and activists to form the core leadership of Ahrar al-Sham, which soon became the leading Syrian armed opposition group.[1] Others formed Jabhat al-Nusra in early 2012 under the leadership of a former commander of the Islamic State in Iraq (ISI), Abu Muhammad al-Jolani, who later rejected the Iraqi group and pledged allegiance to al-Qaeda.[2]

The image was a familiar one. Since the consolidation of what became known as Jihadi Salafism by the end of the 1980s in Afghanistan and Pakistan, interconnected militants have conducted armed warfare in the name of jihad to replace Muslim regimes with their vision of an Islamic state.[3] Transnational Jihadi militants have promoted their politico-religious doctrines and contributed to the radicalisation and transformation of local conflicts from Chechnya to North Africa.[4] The foreign fighters helped to diffuse suicide bombings, the resorting to violence against civilians and religious minorities, and, increasingly, harsh governance over the civilians who had to live under their control. Al-Qaeda and then Islamic State in Iraq and Sham (ISIS, which became Islamic State or IS in 2014) built upon these networks to promote new affiliated groups worldwide and, at times, plan large-scale attacks against Western countries too.[5] The 9/11 strikes against the United States as much as the November 2015 Paris attack are the direct outcome of the radicalisation of local conflicts which, in addition to causing numerous Muslim victims, metastasised across Africa, Asia, and the Middle East.

The Syrian conflict shares similarities with previous local conflicts in which Jihadis took over. The Syrian army dissidents that formed the plethora of groups that coalesced into the Free Syrian Army (FSA) could never contain the Jihadi organisations that emerged from 2011 to 2012 onwards. Instead, Jihadis imposed themselves over the armed opposition and advocated for the re-establishment of the Caliphate, attracting foreign fighters from across the globe. They quickly caught Western countries off guard. The United States notably feared a repeat of the Soviet Union's 1980s war against Afghanistan, which had led to the formation of al-Qaeda. To weaken their military capabilities, the United States began to target their leaders and prominent commanders with special operations and drone strikes. The Operation Inherent Resolve military intervention launched against IS in 2014 involved a large air and ground campaign against the territories controlled by the Iraqi group. Despite destroying IS's territorial caliphate by 2019, Brett McGurk, the U.S. Special Presidential Envoy for the Global Coalition to Counter ISIL, continued to claim afterwards that one of the last provinces in the hands of the insurrection, "Idlib province [was] the largest al-Qaeda haven since 9/11."

But the Syrian conflict is also very different. The well-known scenario in which transnational Jihadis sway local groups did not happen. Instead, the conflict transformed the Jihadis themselves. While IS emancipated itself from al-Qaeda, rejected Osama bin Laden's organisation leadership over global jihad, and radicalised its ideas and practice, most of these militants actually rejected global jihad. The militants who formed Ahrar al-Sham, despite the participation of some of them in previous armed conflicts in the Muslim world,[6] were dismayed by the trajectory of the Jihadi social movement that al-Qaeda had monopolised by 2011.[7] They instead congregated around an Islamist project that would face the Syrian regime while presenting an Islamist alternative to both the Muslim Brotherhood and al-Qaeda, "the project of the Islamic nation" (*mashru' umma*), which became the group's initial motto.[8] The second group followed suit a few years later. Jabhat al-Nusra rejected transnational jihad in summer 2016. It became Hay'at Tahrir al-Sham (HTS) in January 2017 before it subjugated al-Qaeda remnants in the rebel-held province of Idlib in Syria, arrested their leaders and commanders, and explicitly prohibited them from launching attacks outside of Syria.[9]

The trajectories of the two groups are unique in terms of ideas and modes of organisation. Ideologically, the groups consciously distanced themselves from Salafi Jihadi jingoism during a conflict that witnessed the rise of ISIS/IS and its implementation of abhorrent practices—such as widespread mass killings and slavery—that even al-Qaeda considers repugnant.[10] ISIS/IS is the predictable outgrowth of the Jihadi social movement, which radicalised its theology and practices over the previous three generations. The multi-party armed conflicts that have fostered the emergence of the Jihadi social movement since the late 1980s have intensified internal ideological rivalries, simultaneously undermining the social movement's internal hierarchy and leadership.[11] In these conditions, ideological radicalisation is common even in non-Islamist cases.[12] But Ahrar al-Sham followed a surprising trajectory. Instead of radicalising to survive in a competitive environment, Ahrar al-Sham increasingly opposed the relentless violence resulting from the practical application of core Salafi Jihadi ideological principles. The group hence recognised the necessity and legitimacy of forging stronger ties to non-Salafi armed groups and foreign states, which Jihadis denounce as Islamically unlawful.[13] Ahrar al-Sham insisted on nurturing its popular constituency even if it entailed necessary adjustments to its ideological positions. Although Jabhat al-Nusra never went as far as Ahrar al-Sham ideologically, the former al-Qaeda franchise similarly rejected Salafi Jihadi teachings in the latest phase of the conflict, disavowed its intellectuals and religious scholars, and returned to the classic schools of Islamic jurisprudence before opening up to other Sunni Muslims and non-Muslim minorities.[14]

These groups' trajectories are also remarkable in terms of organisation. Most Jihadi groups do not create strong internal institutions.[15] Regardless of their organisational designs on paper, Jihadi groups often feature weak organisational structures that explain their leaders' predominance in their groups' ideological evolution and strategic choices.[16] The absence of institutional constraints on most Jihadi groups' leaders explains the hubris behind hasty decisions like bin Laden's 9/11 attacks, which went against the opinion of most of his own consultative council, according to its former mufti Abu Hafs al-Mauritani (2022) in an interview. Institutional weakness also contextualises the prominence of personal conflicts at the heart of many internal dissensions.[17] In contrast with most Jihadi groups, Ahrar al-Sham prides itself on a relatively strong institutional makeup that has acted as a real constraint on the group's successive leaders. Ahrar al-Sham preceded most Syrian armed opposition groups in institutionalising a collective leadership and internal religious authority. The group also recognised, early on, the necessity to articulate more complex political positions in its own political bureau. Ahrar al-Sham's organisational strength was central in its positioning at the centre of most cross-factional alliances and initiatives promoted by the Syrian armed opposition for the past few years. Jabhat al-Nusra also innovated organisationally. When the group transformed into HTS, it also established a political bureau to nurture ties to foreign actors including humanitarian organisations and U.N. agencies. Then, it promoted a technocratic government called the Syrian Salvation Government to rule the province of Idlib and normalise itself internationally.

By the final stage of the conflict, Ahrar al-Sham and, more important, HTS, had not only shed their Jihadi labels but were also seeking to create an entity aspiring to act as a functional state. In addition to the establishment of a local government by HTS, the former Jihadis established a military academy partially staffed with former Syrian regime officers to enhance their professionalism and standardise their training methods. They recognised the importance of a well-defined military doctrine and evan began exploring the doctrines of Western armed forces to develop a clear framework guiding their operations, tactics, and decision-making, according to HTS's general commander Abu Muhammad al-Jolani and military leader Abul-Hassan al-Hamawi.[18] The armed opposition is transforming into a more conventional force, blurring the boundaries between armed groups and a traditional army, as remarked by counterinsurgency theorists (Kilcullen, 2020; Biddle, 2022).[19] The initial phase of the conflict in which small factions and foreign fighters assumed prominent roles is now long gone, replaced by former Syrian Jihadis actively vying to act as statesmen.

The Syrian conflict raises two sets of questions. First, what factors have contributed to the success of Jihadis over their non-Jihadi competitors in the Syrian armed opposition? Were there specific reasons, such as ideology, that gave them an advantage or did they receive greater support from foreign actors? Second, why have some Jihadi groups rejected global jihad and adopted a more pragmatic approach over time, particularly after marginalising non-Jihadis? Were their leaders themselves responsible for this shift, or did other factors play a role in their decision-making? I argue that both questions have to do with Jihadi groups' ability to draw on wide domestic and international support networks, consolidate their organisational structures, and institutionalise their relations to other armed groups, the population, and foreign states. Exploring these questions offers valuable insights into the dynamics of the Syrian conflict and Jihadi groups' evolution more generally.

I have conducted extensive field research with Syrian armed opposition groups since the start of the Syrian conflict to gain a deeper understanding of these developments. I have interviewed key leaders, commanders, and members of Ahrar al-Sham, Jabhat al-Nusra/HTS, and other groups, whether allied or opposed, to comprehend how their positions have evolved over the past decade. Rather than relying solely on the tracts and communiqués published by these groups, I have engaged with them directly in discussions about the evolution of their positions over the years. Throughout my work, I have found that many individuals who were initially drawn to militancy and jihad, including some who previously supported bin Laden and al-Qaeda, came to realise its flaws. They opposed excessive violence and recognised the need to build closer ties with their population rather than imposing their ideas by force. In private conversations, they were eager to discuss political science and international politics and to deal with the world as realistic political actors, seeking a way out of the Salafi Jihadi deadlock, which, they thought, could never achieve its strategic objectives. My work was never purely academic, as I also interacted with diplomats, humanitarian actors, and civil society activists who were directly involved with these groups or wanted to engage with these actors. Since 2019, I have notably made multiple trips to northwest Syria, which is under the control of HTS and its supported government, to understand the group's military-political-religious development. This work has provided me with insights into its political and organisational evolution as they were unfolding.

I understand the two groups' trajectories as "politicisation." This concept refers to the development of realistic tactical and strategic objectives, durable alliances with other actors including foreign states and non-state armed groups, and normalisation of their interactions with the population. Jihadi Salafism is political, but the choice of the term "politicisation" seeks to capture armed groups' transformation into relatively mainstream political actors. Instead of dwelling on these groups' debatable "moderation," politicisation characterises armed groups that recognise their domestic and international positions and roles beyond a sole emphasis on theology or the military component of jihad.[20] This concept aligns with these groups' own understanding of the need to carefully balance political and military means and objectives.[21] It is congruent with Jihadi groups' internal debates on "Shari'a Politics" (*al-siyasat al-shar'iyya*), which is better translated as Islamic "Law-Guided Public Policy" (Hoover, 2019: 39). Medieval Muslim scholars such as Ibn Taymiyya, a major Salafi reference,[22] developed this concept to ground political actions within the constraints inherent with the Islamic tradition. Salafi armed groups have employed it to legitimise the need to be flexible in light of their external reality (e.g., al-Shami, 2014a; Ahrar al-Sham, 2017d; Hay'at Tahrir al-Sham, 2018e).

There is an unfortunate tendency to overlook armed groups' agency, particularly in Syria. Armed groups are often labeled as proxies merely responding to the wishes of their Western, Gulf, or Turkish sponsors. But reality is more complex. Foreign actors have played a significant role in the Syrian conflict, especially as Russia and Turkey took over the political-military momentum after 2017. But armed groups are rarely, if ever, the submissive tools of their sponsors. States' preferred groups often fail to be the most successful, forcing them to deal with armed groups that are more problematic. Additionally, states are often constrained by what they can impose on their supported groups, who often resist external demands.[23] I therefore seek to revive armed groups' agencies to present the evolution of their positions, especially how they navigate their relationships with foreign states, the population, and one another. I quote these interviews extensively to present these views to the reader, which are often neglected by a prevailing focus on interstate politics.

I challenge the widely held assumption that Jihadi groups always radicalise in armed conflicts. Instead, I argue that politicisation and radicalisation are the outcomes of internal and external institutionalisation processes that are not unique to Jihadi groups. These processes result from how Jihadis manage their internal dynamics and strategic relations to external actors. Understanding the conditions in which Jihadi armed groups institutionalise helps to contextualise these transformations. This approach contrasts with the Western emphasis on developing alternative narratives to "Jihadi ideology" and military-centric approaches.[24] By examining the cases of Ahrar al-Sham and Jabhat al-Nusra/HTS, I provide empirical evidence on how Jihadi groups emerge, expand, and politicise in armed conflicts. These cases offer valuable insights into the evolution of the Jihadi social movement and its prospects for normalisation.

Jihadi Internal and External Institutionalisation

This book addresses two important questions about the Syrian conflict. First, why did Jihadi groups quickly dominate the armed opposition while other organisations, such as those affiliated with the Free Syrian Army, failed to gain traction? Second, why did Ahrar al-Sham and then Jabhat al-Nusra, the two largest armed opposition groups, oppose al-Qaeda and ISIS/IS and politicise over time? While it is common to attribute these developments to the personal qualities of these groups' leaders, as if the successive leaders of Ahrar al-Sham and Abu Muhammad al-Jolani (the Nusra founder) were inherently more capable and pragmatic than other groups',[25] this explanation fails to account for the complex decision-making processes designed to mobilise fighters, establish resilient organisations, and manage relationships with other actors in an armed conflict. I therefore move the cursor away from armed groups' leaders and instead explore the broader institutional and relational dynamics that shape these groups' trajectories, drawing on a comparative analysis of Jihadi organisations during the Syrian conflict.

My first assumption is that Jihadi leaders are political actors who have to balance external and internal pressure to survive.[26] Jihadis navigate complex environments and interact with other actors with their own interests and preferences, including states, other armed groups, and the population. Some of these actors oppose the Jihadis, accept to ally with them, or merely seek some temporary accommodation. These external interactions impact Jihadis' own internal dynamics. In competitive environments where many armed groups share similar ideological views, Jihadis must stabilise their organisational structures to maintain their internal cohesion and their commanders' loyalty, and to avoid internal decay. Jihadi politicisation and radicalisation do not solely result from their leaders' independent cognitive processes or ideological beliefs. Politicisation and radicalisation are outcomes of the careful balancing act between these internal and external relational dynamics. This balance is achieved through internal and external institutionalisation processes that exist across the spectrum. The internal and external pressures that Jihadi groups face provides a deeper understanding of how these groups evolve and either politicise or radicalise over time.

My second assumption is that the main difference between Jihadis lies in their structuring networks and connections with other actors. Although the most evident difference between Islamist armed groups might be their potential affiliation with the Muslim Brotherhood, al-Qaeda, or IS (or their inclination towards a particular approach to Islam, like Salafism), there are more important factors to consider, especially how these groups organise. Despite sharing similar ideological views, Jihadis in Syria often had little else in common. Jihadi groups formed around various structuring networks, including foreign fighters, Syrian Islamists, former prisoners, foreign militants of the same nationality, or even one or several neighbouring villages.[27] While some groups maintained a hierarchical structure centred on a local strongman, others created a complex internal bureaucracy bringing diverse social networks together. The most successful groups' interconnection to a wider range of networks granted some access to more resources, information, and support. This networking capability is famously emphasised as the "strength of weak ties" (Granovetter, 1973), which suggests that new opportunities and information flow in loose social networks. However, being embedded in other networks can also constrain Jihadis. Armed groups might be tied to foreign actors, including states and other figures of authority. These ties imply additional responsibilities, commitments, and constraints. Foreign Jihadi ideologues, for instance, have occasionally managed to prevent the escalation of violence between Syrian jihadis (Hamming, 2020). Locally, an individual Jihadi may also be part of a prominent family, or an entrepreneur in a larger social movement, or simply the resident of a particular city. Belonging to a certain family can prevent local Jihadis from targeting local collaborators, which could ignite cross-family conflicts. More generally, local communitarian norms, including honour and family obligations, shapes armed groups' mobilisation and explains why some communities rebel while others abstain (Petersen, 2001) and how armed groups respond to certain obligations towards their supporting communities (Lacher, 2020).[28]

My focus on Jihadi institutionalisation seeks to understand how their organisational structures and connections with other actors consolidate over time. Institutionalism, as a field of study, explores how institutions—or "systems of rules that structure social interactions" (Hodgson, 2015: 501)—shape stable and recurring patterns of behaviour (Huntington, 1968: 12). Institutionalisation exists internally and externally. Internal institutionalisation is the "process by which organizations acquire value and stability" (Huntington, 1968: 12) and become "valuable in and of itself, and its goals become inseparable and indistinguishable from it" (Panebianco, 1988: 53). Jihadi groups can institutionalise themselves, much like political parties, when they are more than the whims of a few individuals. Institutionalisation follows a similar logic as the management of human resources by armed groups (Mironova, 2019), but in a more comprehensive manner. This process involves establishing more complex organisational structures, formalising decision-making processes, clarifying their ideological and political views, and creating an internal bureaucracy. Armed groups' internal institutionalisation plays a pivotal role in their overall success, enabling them to foster interunit cooperation, adaptability, division of labour, and specialisation (Biddle, 2022). In the political party literature, external institutionalisation concerns "external aspects [that] have to do with the party's [armed group, henceforth] relationship with the society in which it is embedded, including other institutions" (Randall & Svåsand, 2002: 12). Externally, Jihadi groups institutionalise when they stabilise their relations with (1) other armed groups, (2) the population, and (3) foreign states. External institutionalisation may take the form of cross-factional cooperation mechanisms with other armed groups—including shared operation rooms and alliance systems—that define their responsibilities, rights, and duties. It can also involve establishing a local administration over civilians, such as court systems or other adjudicating mechanisms. External institutionalisation may entail reinforcing cooperation with foreign states, potentially at a diplomatic level.

Jihadi groups' internal and external institutionalisation matter, since they establish new sets of norms and constraints on their behaviour. Most studies of Jihadi groups tend to overlook this dimension, preferring to focus on their individual leaders or ideologues instead.[29] But, when speaking about states, for instance, even seemingly personalised dictatorships can be constrained by rules and procedures that "change the underlying distribution of power within the ruling coalition" (Meng, 2020: 4). Institutions constrain and regulate behaviour by providing prescriptive guidelines and defining acceptable norms and conduct (Scott, 2013). As Huntington emphasised, institutionalised entities—states and non-states alike—acquire value and stability that is distinct from the role of their founding leaders only. Institutional strength does not solely depend on the longevity of a regime or an armed group, but rather on its autonomy and adaptability. Institutional strength is particularly evident in cases of leadership succession (Huntington, 1968: 14), since "leadership transitions [succeed] precisely because they have rules that can outlast the circumstances in which they were initially created" (Meng, 2020: 96).

While Jihadi groups may not reach the level of state institutionalisation, there is a similar logic in how rules and procedures influence their decision-making and resource allocation, enabling them to exist beyond their founding leaders. Jihadi groups that repeatedly lose their leaders would not survive without institutional strength, which facilitates leadership renewal and limits internal dissidence.[30] This is particularly evident in the case of Ahrar al-Sham, which lost most of its top-tier leaders in 2014 but was able to rebuild itself around clearer institutional norms that facilitated annual leadership elections thereafter. Ahrar al-Sham's own internal conflicts over strategy were subsequently channeled institutionally through a contest between its religious office and political bureau,[31] although this was followed by a phase of de-institutionalisation when the group was weakened by Jabhat al-Nusra's transformation into HTS. External institutionalisation exists in a similar manner. External institutional strength depersonalises armed groups' relations to one another, the population, and other states. It is reflected in the predictability and adherence to rules, procedures, and commitments underpinning their interactions with external actors.

It is easy to dismiss armed groups' internal structures, leadership composition, and bureaucratic systems as "cheap talk" that doesn't mean much in reality.[32] While smaller armed groups may exaggerate their complexity, larger armed groups rely on a set of consensual norms and procedures to maintain their internal cohesion and unity. These groups bring together militants with diverging views, who agree to work together based on a shared set of norms and procedures that they take seriously. These groups' success depends on their ability to uphold their institutional strength, which is particularly evident when they face internal dissidence. The heated debates that followed the successive splits of ISIS/IS from al-Qaeda, and then HTS from al-Qaeda, reflect the seriousness with which armed groups take the conditions of their allegiances, the prerogatives of their organisations, and the threats of dissent.[33] In interviews, armed groups' leaders acknowledge the importance of institutional norms and procedures in maintaining order and discipline within their groups, as well as in containing and even constraining dissident voices. This is not unique to Jihadis, as the Provisional Irish Republican Army (IRA), for example, successfully imposed a cease-fire by restructuring and manipulating its internal institutions to impose the views of its supporters.[34] Maintaining control, new internal structures, and the establishment of a more complex internal bureaucracy, including the creation of a political bureau to manage foreign relations, also impact these groups' functioning and trajectories, as well as their perceptions and interests. This does not mean, however, that there are no instances of dissent and even violence, including the purge of dissident voices within institutionalised groups. Some leaders may also attempt to subvert their groups' institutional norms by consolidating personal power instead.

I therefore differentiate internal institutionalisation and centralisation. Most research focuses on armed groups' centralisation or decentralisation to analyse their organisational structures, which informed previous debates on al-Qaeda's evolution as a centralised organisation versus a horizontal network of franchised groups.[35] I examine instead armed groups' internal institutionalisation, which consists in the consolidation of shared organisational norms, procedures, and practices. Armed groups can be highly institutionalised without full centralisation, even within the same country. Typically, they centralise their strategic decisions, political positions, and possibly financing at the leadership level. But, in practice, they also combine a mix of centralised special forces units, which undergo rigorous training and indoctrination, with more decentralised local units often fighting on a part-time basis that defend their territories.[36] This is similar to state armies, which also maintain both special forces and more local units like national guards. In Syria, large armed groups like Ahrar al-Sham and Jabhat al-Nusra institutionalised internally, creating a common group identity, centralised decision-making processes, and an internal bureaucracy to conduct military and non-military work. But they also spread out across geographically distinct areas, making it impossible to centralise all their military equipment nationally. Instead, they often gave general guidelines to their local commanders and a sufficient degree of autonomy to make tactical decisions. Larger groups like Ahrar al-Sham and Jabhat al-Nusra (and even some of those affiliated with the Free Syrian Army) additionally integrated independent local military units formed to defend specific areas, which occasionally switched their allegiances throughout the conflict based on their own priorities and preferences. These shifts in allegiance did not necessarily result in significant changes in these local groups' actual practices.[37] The main differences may have been the adoption of a new name, an increase in material support, and occasional restructuring and ideological indoctrination, though the latter became rarer over time.

Institutionalism is well suited to studying Jihadi groups for two reasons. First, it provides a nuanced understanding of armed groups' organisational dynamics. It can be challenging to distinguish between armed groups, cross-factional alliances, and shared operation rooms between armed groups. In the early stages of armed conflicts, armed groups may more closely resemble an alliance of independent entities merely sharing a name and a flag, rather than a fully integrated organisation. Examining institutionalisation processes, rather than theoretical organisational structures, allows for a better understanding of how armed groups organise in practice and how their modes of organisation change over time. This is crucial in moving beyond "black box" studies of armed groups that merely assume they are rational actors without delving into their internal dynamics and their impact. Second, institutional approaches examine the impact of external patterns of relations too. Jihadi groups are not isolated actors that evolve outside of their world. They interact with a wide range of actors, which impacts their political choices. Institutionalisation processes can constrain Jihadi groups' behaviours and ideas, regardless of their leaders' individual positions or stated ideological commitments.

This analysis draws upon Staniland's (2014) research on the impact of pre-war networks on armed group cohesion during conflicts. Staniland argues that the strength of pre-war ties between armed groups' leaders (horizontal ties) and their communities (vertical ties) informs the organisational strength of their groups. I take the analysis a step further in two directions. First, I focus on armed groups' institutionalisation during armed conflicts, rather than solely on their pre-war status. I argue that, in a conflict like Syria, many groups may rely on overlapping pre-war networks, yet distinct institutionalisation processes can result in vastly different organisational structures.[38] Second, I emphasise the importance of in-war strategic relations with other actors, such as the population, other armed groups, and foreign states, on Jihadi behavioural and ideological evolution.[39] Organisational cohesion does not automatically lead to these groups' politicisation. For instance, IS institutionalised internally and radicalised conjointly. Conflicts like Syria's involve numerous other armed groups and foreign states, and how Jihadi groups navigate these relationships ultimately influences their long-term trajectories. Jihadi politicisation is largely informed by the evolution of their strategic interactions with other actors, both domestic and foreign.

Institutional Trajectories in Syria: Jihadi Politicisation and Radicalisation

Before presenting the main arguments of the book, I want to introduce four ideal types featuring a combination of weak and strong armed groups' internal and external institutionalisation to better understand how armed groups' politicisation occurs. Jihadi groups' internal and external institutionalisation vary greatly, from non-existent to highly developed bureaucratic patterns. These institutionalisation processes play a crucial role in Jihadis' long-term trajectories. They also explain their radicalisation and politicisation, which cannot be attributed solely to ideological change. Jihadi groups' institutional trajectories exist in four ideal types based on a combination of strong and weak internal and external institutionalisation. Although armed group leaders can make deliberate decisions towards a specific trajectory, they cannot change course easily. Various pre- and in-war factors, along with the structural configuration of specific armed conflicts, determine the range of choices available to armed group leaders (table 1.1).

To operationalise armed groups' internal and external institutionalisation, I traced the evolution of Jihadis' organisational structures over time, particularly as they expanded across territories. To avoid overstretching, armed groups must become organisationally more complex to stabilise their internal decision-making processes, coordinate their brigades, and establish non-military functions like logistics, political representation, and internal courts to adjudicate the violations committed by their soldiers. Without institutionalising internally,

Table 1.1 Four ideal-type trajectories and influential examples in Syria

		Internal Institutionalisation	
		Weak	Strong
External institutionalisation	Weak	<u>Disappearance</u> Dissolution, criminality	<u>Radicalisation</u> Organisational encapsulation, societal isolation
	Examples in Syria		Islamic State, smaller actors like Jama'at al-Muslimun
	Strong	<u>Disintegration</u> Lack of organisational consistency, fragmentation along constituting units, alignment with foreign states	<u>Politicisation</u> Organisational consolidation, normalisation of their interactions with external actors
	Examples in Syria	Free Syrian Army groups	Ahrar al-Sham, Jabhat al-Nusra

armed groups can only remain small or divide. This is particularly the case in Syria, where most armed groups–held regions remained disconnected geographically throughout the conflict.

Additionally, I traced the emergence of shared institutional structures with other armed groups, including courts of justice to rule the population, factional alliances, shared military operation rooms, and coordination mechanisms with foreign states. The court system created by four armed groups in Aleppo after taking over the city is an example of external institutionalisation with the population; other examples include the Islamic Front as a factional alliance, the Fath al-Mubin operation room to synchronise military coordination between armed opposition groups, and the Military Operations Command in Turkey (Müşterek Operasyon Merkezi in Turkish, or MOM) as a mechanism of military coordination with foreign states. Not all external structures are created equal. While some primarily fulfilled media functions to justify to foreign countries that the armed opposition was united , others involved more intricate processes that delineated factional responsibilities, prerogatives, and compliance.[40] My analysis of Jihadi internal and external institutionalisation focuses, in line with Meng (2020), on the content of these institutional norms, analysing their implications in terms of decision-making and sharing of resources, more than their mere existence on paper.

The first scenario involves armed groups that do not institutionalise internally or externally. These groups are barely embedded in other networks, including social movements and localities, and struggle to develop strong organisational structures. As a result of their organisational weakness, they fail to establish a common identity and shared organisational norms and quickly lose relevance as groups. Without tight connections to other types of networks including local communities, they dissipate quickly over time. The most likely outcome is their disappearance, though individual members may join other groups or low-level criminal networks focused solely on short-term gains. Most of these groups disappeared in Syria, often under pressure from other factions that denounced them as bandits (*qita' al-turuq*).

The second ideal-type of armed group institutionalises externally but lacks internal institutionalisation. The lack of internal institutionalisation means that they barely share any common organisational structure and sense of belonging as groups, though they might share a name and a flag. Still, they remain strongly embedded in other networks, such as their localities, political groupings, or social movements, with they become increasingly associated with. In some cases, these groups become mere emanations of their local constituencies, lacking any distinctive ideological or normative specificities. They may even be instrumentalised by foreign states when their external ties to states predominate. These groups' external institutionalisation does not have to be very strong, as what matters primarily is their embeddedness in other networks and their responsiveness to them. What matters is that their external ties supersede organisational belonging, making these groups more responsive to external incentives and pressure than internal ones.[41] This makes it difficult for them to develop independent policies and apply them consistently, particularly when they are structured in sub-units that are strongly embedded in other networks, especially localities. When such groups exist across geographically distant areas, their internal fragmentation increases, hastening their disintegration into constituting sub-units. However, external embeddedness can also prevent their disappearance or transformation into criminal networks, given their ties to their communities or other groupings. External institutionalisation may nonetheless render these groups dependent on other actors, including other armed groups and states, without much remaining agency. Though not Jihadis, most groups affiliated with the Free Syrian Army (FSA)—which, after a phase of expansion, ultimately regrouped in their local communities or allied with Turkey—fit with this pattern.[42]

The third ideal-type refers to armed groups that institutionalise internally but not externally. This path is typically marked by rigorous ideological indoctrination, organisational centralisation, and the imposition of a clear internal hierarchy that serves as the foundation of their organisational cohesion. Unlike the second ideal-type, membership in the organisation takes precedence over other forms of belonging. This approach often leads to ideological encapsulation of the group, where group membership becomes ideologically justified as an end in itself, and external ties are seen as a threat.[43] This trajectory reinforces these groups' isolation from society, impedes the diffusion of new ideas, and reinforces their ideological radicalisation. Some groups might develop internal cult dynamics or be swayed by a strongman instead of institutionalising per se, with similar outcomes. Environmental isolation poses a real long-term threat that hinders their ability to obtain appropriate information and cultivate external support and allies. Their rejection of institutionalised alliances with other groups and states that do not entirely align with their views also means that they lack the ability to adapt to changing circumstances.

The most extreme case of the third type is epitomised by Jihadi groups that consider all non-members as apostates or non-Muslims, rendering the spilling of their blood lawful in their theological readings. This trajectory very much corresponds to IS in Syria, which excommunicated other factions, refused to ally with foreign states, ruled with harsh measures after imposing local hegemony, and executed dissidents. But it also applies to smaller entities that did not develop IS's bureaucracy but maintained the same combination of ideological indoctrination with a rejection of other actors, like the Group of the Muslims (Jamaʻat al-Muslimun) led by a Kuwaiti militant, Abu ʻOmar al-Kuwaiti, who later integrated IS before his execution by the group for "extremism", according to my interviews with several foreign fighters who had joined the group.[44]

In the last ideal-type, armed groups successfully institutionalise internally and externally. This strengthens their internal organisational cohesion while also normalising their external ties to other actors. Strong external connections facilitate the diffusion of new information, ideas, and support, which is critical for survival in rapidly changing environments. However, this ideal-type is not without potential tensions, as conflicts may arise between armed groups' institutional norms and external ties to other networks or actors. For example, accommodating the population or other states can contradict some of their ideological tenets, leading to internal resistance from more ideologically committed members. This ideal-type primarily fits with Ahrar al-Sham, and to a lesser extent Jabhat al-Nusra—which mostly politicised when it imposed its governance project over the province of Idlib from 2017–2018 onwards—during the Syrian conflict, which institutionalised their relations to other armed groups and the populations before nurturing ties to Turkey and other international actors.

My two guiding concerns—the victory of the Jihadis over non-Jihadi competitors and the politicisation of Ahrar al-Sham and, later, Jabhat al-Nusra—are therefore interrelated. The four ideal-types suggest that Jihadis can only radicalise or politicise if they are sufficiently institutionalised internally.[45] Armed groups that fail to develop a strong organisational component are more likely to lose internal coherence, fragment, and potentially disintegrate or transform into criminal networks rather than radicalise or politicise. To understand Jihadi politicisation, it is therefore necessary to examine, first, the factors that helped the Jihadis build strong organisations and institutionalise internally and, second, the evolution of their interactions—as they institutionalise externally—with one another, the population, and foreign states. It also means that the main difference between radicalisation and politicisation is relational, not ideological, as both represent contending attempts to navigate Jihadi groups' strategic relations with other actors.

As Jihadi groups strive to survive in competitive environments, they develop different types of interactions with their external environments. Jihadis radicalise when internal organisational cohesion takes precedence over any external ties or interactions. These groups reject normalisation with other actors and encapsulate themselves by defining the outside world as an enemy. Radicalisation often involves the imposition of severe punishment, such as death, to deter internal dissidence and enforce internal authority. The main challenge of radicalism is its sustainability. While some studies suggest that Jihadi groups have organisational advantages that attract better fighters and cadres (Kalyvas, 2018; Mironova, 2019) and solve important organisational dilemmas (Walter, 2017), their radicalism may lead to severing ties with external networks, which can impede their long-term ability to adapt to changing environments despite short-term gains.

In contrast to radicalisation, politicisation occurs when Jihadi groups are able to strike a balance between their internal organisational dynamics and their interactions with other actors. Achieving this balance is particularly challenging, because Jihadi groups must maintain internal cohesion while also making external concessions to foreign states or the population, which are necessary for survival in their environments. The main difficulty lies in justifying these concessions, which may contradict their core beliefs, to their members without losing their loyalty or risking defection to other groups. Group members may view these concessions as a form of betrayal and leave the group. Politicised groups may not necessarily moderate their ideological commitments, but they try to normalise their relationships with other actors that do not share their beliefs. Politicisation is a complex process that is largely driven by the type of concessions that Jihadi groups make both internally and externally. Internal concessions are contingent upon their organisational dynamics, including the level of control exercised over their followers and the presence of competing Jihadi groups. Externally, concessions depend on the characteristics of their civil societies, whose cohesion and strength helps civilians resist insurgents (Arjona, 2016; Kaplan, 2017; Krause, 2018; Svensson et al., 2022), and the types of relations and leverage exercised by external states and patrons. Jihadi groups' successful politicisation ultimately depends on their ability to balance their core beliefs with the need to adapt to changing circumstances and develop strategic external relationships. It is a delicate balance that requires careful consideration and management of internal and external pressures.

The armed opposition in Syria presents a relatively unique case of advanced internal and external institutionalisation. Not all other insurgencies are highly institutionalised, and some may rely on authoritarian dynamics centred on a strong leader to maintain their internal cohesion instead. The relationships among local armed groups may also not be highly developed, either. Syria stands out for the strong efforts of various armed groups to institutionalise, despite the challenges they faced. Even the Free Syrian Army regularly attempted to establish more formal structures over time, though it ultimately struggled to do so effectively (Baczko, Dorronsoro, & Quesnay, 2018). These efforts have internal and external causes. The intense factional competition among different groups in Syria forced them to develop stronger organisational structures in order to survive, as those allowed for better sharing of resources and power, and helped prevent the departure of sub-groups when the cost of defection was relatively low. Additionally, the presence of many groups in relatively small areas required them to collaborate in battles, share war spoils, debate the practicalities of governance, and ultimately institutionalise their relations to one another. Externally, the armed opposition faced a formidable opponent, with the regime receiving support from Iran-backed armed groups and later Russia. This environment required greater institutionalisation efforts by Jihadis than those linked to al-Qaeda in the Sahel, for instance, where Jihadi field commanders have a more prominent role than formal organisations (Thurston, 2020). However, while the level of institutionalisation in Syria may be unique, the underlying ideas behind it are relevant beyond this context.

The Main Arguments

Although the previous overview provides insights into how armed groups' internal and external institutionalisation underpin Jihadi politicisation or radicalisation, with a few important examples in Syria, it does not provide a detailed account of how this happened in practice during the conflict. For this, we have to situate the armed opposition in Syria's historical contexts, including lasting patterns of state construction that largely defined the type of armed opposition that could successfully mobilise the population and challenge the Baathist regime.

The first argument is about the militarisation of the armed opposition and the rise of Jihadi groups in Syria. The Syrian regime was unable to undertake reforms to quell the widespread protests and cater to the people's demands.[46] The regime's heavy reliance on the security services and the domination of a certain type of solidarity based upon a minority religious community eliminated any non-violent alternative. Given the absence of a peaceful solution, violent repression became the most probable choice for the regime. This decision was further compounded by the regime's international strategic alliance with Iran and Russia, which provided military support for violent repression and had no serious intention of ever abandoning the regime. These factors largely account for the militarisation of the opposition, resulting in the quick appearance of a plethora of armed groups with varied objectives.

The predominance of Jihadi armed groups in Syria was also a consequence of long-standing state policies. For decades, the Syrian regime prevented the development of a relatively autonomous civil society. In the absence of functional civil society, the armed groups that quickly dominated the uprising were those that could rely on social networks facilitating their mobilisation and coordination. Social networks embedded in larger social movements are particularly conducive to the emergence of armed groups, as they are structured around cohesive sets of ideas that foster alternative political projects to existing regimes. In Syria, Jihadi groups quickly marginalised non-Islamist entities thanks to their early reliance on interconnected networks of Islamist entrepreneurs embedded in both domestic and international networks. Despite their internal diversity, these networks quickly aligned themselves in opposition to the Syrian regime. This characteristic was decisive in presenting nation-wide political and military alternatives, as the armed opposition could consolidate only in geographically isolated regions situated on the periphery of the country. It also explains the growing external support for Jihadi armed groups, which were able to tap into their pre-existing support networks.

The previous arguments do not fully explain why some Jihadi groups performed better than others, nor how they politicised. Ahrar al-Sham was the most successful group during the early stages of the conflict. This group emerged from a larger Islamist social movement that had been developing in Syria and abroad for the past four decades despite being mostly dormant domestically. Although its early brigades were local, the group's reliance on networks of entrepreneurs associated with the Islamist social movement allowed it to establish coordination mechanisms early on and to expand throughout Syria's disconnected armed groups–held areas, in contrast to most other groups. Ahrar al-Sham exploited pre-war networks that overlapped with Jabhat al-Nusra's better than the latter, which was more elitist initially before being weakened by the split with IS in 2013. Ahrar al-Sham's strategy was to institutionalise its external ties to other armed groups in factional coalitions before institutionalising internally. This created a relatively consensual and de-centralised group that attracted an increasing number of independent military units and later, external state support. This pattern of development informed its political opening to other actors, including the population and other states, against the backdrop of pre-war debates on al-Qaeda, the negative legacy of the Iraqi conflict, and competition with Salafi Jihadi armed groups during the conflict. However, Ahrar al-Sham's politicisation was impeded by the killing of most of its leaders in 2014, which hindered internal decision-making processes and slowed its capacity to adapt quickly to changing circumstances. This led to the group's marginalisation vis-à-vis a contending group, Jabhat al-Nusra, whose internal institutionalisation was more centralised and ideologically infused. Eventually, Jabhat al-Nusra rebranded itself as Hay'at Tahrir al-Sham (HTS) and took over the province of Idlib in northwest Syria before politicising in its own ways.

The politicisation of Ahrar al-Sham and Jabhat al-Nusra / HTS contrasts with the trajectory of ISIS / IS. While IS is not my main focus, this framework of analysis also explains its trajectory during the conflict. As internal factional competition intensified, Ahrar al-Sham and Jabhat al-Nusra made a strategic choice to collaborate with each other and other armed groups—though this varied in time and place—before reaching out to foreign states. In contrast, IS isolated itself from the broader armed opposition. Rather than seeking cooperation, IS believed that establishing a monopoly over the armed opposition was key to its survival. IS therefore claimed that it had revived the historical Caliphate in 2014, insisting that all Muslims pledge allegiance to it. This allowed the group to claim superior authority, refuse to submit to the courts of justice formed by other armed groups, and even refuse to heed foreign Jihadi ideologues' advice.[47] IS's choice accompanied the integration of many smaller groups active in Syria, especially those formed by foreign fighters, as it consolidated and institutionalised internally. Externally, IS's approach involved fighting all other armed groups as well as foreign states while imposing harsh rules on the population. IS's radicalisation therefore reflected the challenges it faced when multiple groups and states got involved in Syria. Although this choice was informed by IS leaders' past experience in Iraq, it was not driven simply by its ideological commitments. Ideology rationalised more than caused IS's radicalisation.

My analysis of the politicisation of jihad and rejection of its globalism primarily focuses on Ahrar al-Sham and not Jabhat al-Nusra, the former al-Qaeda franchise. Ahrar al-Sham played a leading role in transforming the Syrian armed opposition, and its trajectory demonstrates the impact of internal and external institutionalisation processes on armed groups' politicisation. I discuss Jabhat al-Nusra mostly in comparison to Ahrar al-Sham, in order to understand the similarities and differences between the two groups, but without delving as deeply into the specifics of the former al-Qaeda franchise's evolution. Jabhat al-Nusra's politicisation after 2017, when it transformed into HTS, had early roots. Although Jabhat al-Nusra refused to deal with foreign states for longer than Ahrar al-Sham, and was also willing to directly confront other Syrian opposition groups, it similarly nurtured ties with other actors during the conflict, which informed the evolution of its behaviour, though to a lesser extent than Ahrar al-Sham. Jabhat al-Nusra's politicisation hence followed Ahrar al-Sham's own, though it became much more significant at a later phase, as discussed in chapters 4 and 5, when it established a civilian government in Idlib.

Ultimately, the political context that surrounded Syria after 2011 made possible the politicisation of Ahrar al-Sham and, later, former Jabhat al-Nusra as it became HTS. The alignment of Western countries against the Syrian regime, as well as its Iranian and Russian supporters, played a crucial role in these groups' politicisation. While pre-war discussions on the negative consequences of al-Qaeda's global jihad and how these groups institutionalised explain their politicisation, the willingness of Western countries to provide some leeway to Islamist armed groups not affiliated with al-Qaeda or ISIS was important to show them that alternative choices were possible. This was critical to allow a renewed focus on their national conflict, even considering the possibility of establishing ties with Western countries. However, the fact that ISIS/IS opted to wage an all-out war against Western countries demonstrates that certain actors chose not to adapt their strategy to this new political context.

The Politicisation of Jihad: Rationale, Scope, and Methodology

Jihad, as armed struggle, is inherently political. The legitimisation of armed opposition to Muslim domestic regimes or Western countries blamed for their foreign policy is not just an expression of inflexible theological commitments. These positions represent real political projects for the Muslim world, even if they are only loosely defined. Jihadis themselves are political actors (Thurston, 2020; Hamming, 2022), who "participate in local, national, and regional politics, and not just through intimidation but also through the management of strategic relationships" (Thurston, 2020: 2). However, my reference to "politicisation" as a process describes a phenomenon beyond mere violent opposition to political orders. It characterises armed groups' transformation into more mainstream political actors that, although they still legitimise and resort to violence, strive to actively balance political necessity with their military objectives and theological leanings. Politicisation emphasises the development of realistic tactical and strategic objectives; durable alliances with other actors, including foreign states and non-state armed groups; and normalisation of their interactions with the population. I prefer this term to "moderation," which depends on the specific context of each society and is debatable due to these groups' continued use of violence as well as the nature of some of their ideological beliefs. Politicisation reflects Jihadi groups' own discussions on the proper political and military means to achieve their objectives. These discussions often take place around the concept of "Shari'a Politics" (*al-siyasat al-shari'yya*), or Islamic Law-Guided Public Policy, which has long been associated with the medieval scholar Ibn Taymiyya, who is particularly popular among contemporary Salafis.

Politicisation contrasts with radicalisation, as understood in academic research as the adoption, maintenance, and intensification of violence. Radicalisation is a relational process resulting from militants' growing insolation from other actors, who increasingly perceive violence as an end in itself.[48] Armed groups that politicise do not embrace Western liberal democratic tenets but at least recognise the necessity and legitimacy of engaging with other actors that do not share their ideological beliefs or religious creed. They seek to achieve their goals through a more nuanced and pragmatic approach that recognises the importance of alliances, negotiations, and compromise, alongside the use of violence. This approach is necessary to establish their legitimacy in the eyes of their supporters, as well as to achieve their political objectives.

The politicisation of jihad falls along a spectrum. Some al-Qaeda affiliates have also occasionally engaged other actors. In the Sahel, for instance, Jama'at Nasr al-Islam wal Muslimin (JNIM), which is affiliated to al-Qaeda, has delegated some power to local judges, even suspending the implementation of harsh rulings in some instances to avoid antagonising civilian populations. This was initially communicated in a message of Abdelmalek Droukdel (2012), the head of al-Qaeda in the Islamic Maghreb, discovered in 2012. Al-Qaeda in Yemen but also Ayman al-Zawahiri (2013) himself, in his 2013 Guidelines on jihad, cautioned against excessive use of violence and instead recommended reaching out to local Muslim civilians. This is significantly different from the practices of most IS provinces. But al-Qaeda affiliates have never crossed the rubicon and still remain faithful to the organisation and its agenda, while Ahrar al-Sham and Jabhat al-Nusra rejected global jihad altogether and chose to openly engage with Western countries instead.

This research examines the politicisation of jihad beyond the confines of Jihadi Salafism. Salafis are not a monolithic group; there are real theological and political divergences among them.[49] Following the 1991 Gulf War, three main trends emerged: scholastic (*'ilmi*) Salafis, who focus primarily on religious teaching and research; politicos or activist (*haraki*) Salafis, who engage politically (including through political participation); and Jihadi Salafis (*al-salafiyya al-jihadiyya*), who legitimise violence against domestic Muslim regimes not implementing their conception of Islamic law and foreign countries that they denounce for supporting them (Wiktorowicz, 2006).[50] Each Salafi approach features varying degrees of transnationalism and actively engages in contentious debates surrounding the proper methodology to adopt, debating issues such as the legitimacy of jihad in various contexts, including Syria (Ismail, 2021). While these approaches have consolidated into distinct traditions structured around their own concepts and intellectuals, post-2011 developments suggest that these distinctions should be considered flexible. Regardless of their ideological commitments, changing environments can catalyse substantial transformations and revisions. For example, in Egypt, the opening of the political process has led former Jihadis to legitimise political participation (Drevon, 2015), while in Libya and Syria, former non-violent Salafis (including the so-called Salafi madkhalis, who are known for their loyalty to existing political orders and opposition to the Jihadis) have turned to armed violence (ICG, 2019a). These trajectories demonstrate the diverse political choices made in different environments. Therefore, this research focuses on Salafi groups that practically resort to violence, rather than exclusively examining Jihadi Salafis.

I take an inclusive perspective on the term "Jihadi," considering it as applying to a broad spectrum that encompasses various groups, with strictly Salafi Jihadi groups being only a sub-category along that spectrum. "Jihadi" is a label for a social movement composed of "(a) mostly informal networks of interaction, based on (b) shared beliefs and solidarity, mobilized around (c) contentious themes through (d) the frequent use of various forms of protest" [in this case, repertoires of armed violence].[51] Rather than focusing only on al-Qaeda and ISIS/IS, this term encompasses an array of groups tracing their origins to the Egyptian and Syrian militants who tried to change their regimes in the late 1970s. Egypt, in particular, played a significant role, as Egyptian militants would form the key ideologues and commanders of the Jihadi trend that expanded in the 1980s in Afghanistan and Pakistan, where Egyptian militants congregated with independent figures like Abdullah Azzam, later joined by individuals such as Abu Qatada and Abu Muhammad al-Maqdisi, who would reinforce the Salafi backbone of these groups.[52] Jihadi groups and religious scholars have embraced many perspectives, but they are linked to militants who engaged in conflicts such as Afghanistan in the late 1980s, Bosnia in the 1990s, Chechnya in the early 2000s, and Iraq in the 2000s. While there have been genuine differences of opinion and occasional conflicts among them, they maintain similar worldviews, sharing a general endorsement of violence—at least in theory—against Muslim regimes that fail to implement their understanding of Islamic Law.[53] Salafism plays a distinct role within Jihadism, with virtually all of the Jihadis embracing the Salafi approach to Islam. Al-Qaeda, for instance, has historically had Salafi membership but with a relatively more ecumenical approach focusing on opposition to Muslim regimes and their foreign supporters rather than strictly emphasizing Salafi beliefs. This is evident in their support for the non-Salafi Taliban in Afghanistan. On the other side of the spectrum, groups like the Groupe

Islamique Armé (GIA) in Algeria or Islamic State (IS) strictly insist on the need for Muslims to adhere to their understanding of the Salafi methodology.[54] I use the term "Jihadi", which these groups themselves use, to analyse the evolution of armed groups with shared lineage, who often remain interconnected in social networks – even if only loosely – who mobilise a similar constituency, and influence one another. Other organisations like Hizbullah, Hamas, and militants aligned with the Iranian-backed "Axis of Resistance" aren't "Jihadis" in this definition due to their belonging to a different social movement, though they have their own ideological project too.

My inclusive approach to Jihadism is because of the term itself. Ahrar al-Sham and HTS, along with some other minor groups, are now reluctant to use it (which was not always the case in 2011), even rejecting it and preferring instead the more neutral *mujahid* (literally "engaged in jihad"). Ahrar al-Sham promptly distanced itself from the term, vehemently rejecting any affiliation with al-Qaeda right from the start of the conflict, though its structuring networks overlapped with the Jihadi movement—though on the more "diluted" side of the spectrum—with whom it shared some views, as argued in chapter 5. Jabhat al-Nusra followed suit later on, severing ties with al-Qaeda and the Jihadi movement from 2016 onward.

My approach to the politicisation of jihad differs significantly from existing research on Islamist moderation or de-radicalisation. Rather than analysing groups that have disavowed violence (Ashour, 2009; Drevon, 2022; Matesan, 2020), I focus on armed groups that remain committed to the use of force. This approach is distinct from the moderation of mainstream non-violent Islamist movements, such as the Muslim Brotherhood, which have opted for political participation in semi-authoritarian regimes.[55] The choice of former Jihadis to renounce violence and of the Muslim Brotherhood to create political parties in several countries largely occurred when their domestic political systems supported these objectives.[56] The politicisation of jihad conversely happens as armed groups continue to fight domestic authorities.[57] However, there are notable parallels in my approach to Jihadi politicisation when compared to studies on the impact of political engagement within movements often associated with the Muslim Brotherhood. I similarly delve into the internal and external factors that shape these groups' choices, including their internal makeup and the structures of their political systems, and its impact on their ideas and behaviours. Some of the differences, in addition to these groups' continued use of violence, concern international incentives for politicisation. Foreign actors, including Western states, can set up a range of incentives and deterrents to encourage Jihadis to politicise. These may include targeted attacks on their leaders and commanders as well as international terrorist designations to either deter or punish them from aligning with global jihad, or, in much rarer cases, a degree of collaboration and support to encourage them to become more mainstream.

Ahrar al-Sham and Jabhat al-Nusra are key cases due to their scope and significance in the Syrian conflict. Ahrar al-Sham was one of the largest and most influential armed groups in Syria, mobilising a diverse range of fighters from various Salafi traditions, including those who had previously fought in foreign jihads. Its central positioning within armed opposition groups–led alliances and military operation rooms was partially due to its unique pattern of organisational expansion, which provides insights into the development of other armed groups. Jabhat al-Nusra, on the other hand, was the most successful al-Qaeda affiliate globally before rejecting bin Laden and al-Zawahiri's organisation to pursue its own agenda in Syria. The Syrian conflict is particularly significant due to the involvement of actors with diverse ideological persuasions, the participation of foreign fighters, and complex international interventions. Therefore, analysing the trajectory of Ahrar al-Sham and Jabhat al-Nusra, particularly as the latter transformed into HTS, sheds light on the broader Syrian armed opposition as a whole, including its most prevalent features and patterns of development.

I focus on Jihadis' social movement dynamics and institutionalisation processes as a response to a critical methodological gap in existing research, which I elaborate in the annex. Previous research relied heavily on easily accessible primary sources such as communiqués, tracts, magazines, books, and leaked internal communications, which can often exaggerate these groups' official claims and self-representation to their audience. Primary sources do not exist in isolation. Relying solely on written documents, without knowing their comprehensiveness and representativeness, can reify certain ideological debates that may have only limited real-time relevance in reality. While Jihadi groups most likely believe in the theological arguments they develop for internal and external consumption, these arguments may not necessarily be the cause of internal conflicts and disagreements. Such arguments cannot be isolated from the broader social movement and internal group dynamics that influence their evolution over time.

This research is based on extensive fieldwork and interviews conducted in Syria and Turkey since 2016. To gather primary data, I interviewed a substantial number of Ahrar al-Sham leaders, commanders, and members, including individuals who were involved with the group from its inception and others who joined later. These interviewees are either still active in Ahrar al-Sham or have left the group for various reasons. Additionally, I have conducted field research in the Syrian northwest province of Idlib since 2019 and coordinated with HTS to interview many of its leaders, including Abu Muhammad al-Jolani, and the group's military and religious leadership. To provide a comparative perspective, I have also conducted interviews with individuals active in other factions that have interacted with Ahrar al-Sham and HTS, either in alliance or opposition to them, to compare their organisational structures and strategic choices as well as their perspectives on the evolution of these groups. These individuals represent a broad range of armed factions discussed throughout this book, and their interviews were critical in understanding the relationships among the groups and explaining their comparative trajectories. I present additional information on the interviews and my methodology in the annex.

I made a concerted effort to extensively cite the perspectives of leaders from diverse armed opposition groups throughout the book, with a particular emphasis on Ahrar al-Sham and HTS. I want to provide the reader with a lucid understanding of these groups' political stances by allowing them to articulate their own views, which is rare in existing research. However, to ensure accuracy and balance, I diligently cross-referenced these quotes with accounts from a spectrum of sources. This means that I also interviewed civilians, humanitarian organisations, influential local figures, as well as dissidents and members of other armed groups, all of whom have had various levels of engagement with Ahrar al-Sham and HTS over the years.

Armed Conflicts, Jihadi Insurgencies, and Syria

I develop a relational approach to armed groups' trajectories in armed conflicts, drawing on institutional, social network, and social movement approaches. This dynamic understanding of armed groups' politicisation includes various fields of research that are examined mostly in isolation, from armed groups' alliances, mobilisation, relations to the population, and repertoires of violence. While existing research tends to focus on one set of issues, I integrate them in an encompassing analytical framework that studies them conjointly. The institutional approach to Jihadi groups' politicisation also examines ideational developments beyond existing rational choice approaches, which take political preferences for granted or analyse ideas instrumentally (e.g., Shapiro, 2013; Mironova, 2019).

There is little systematic research on armed groups' institutionalisation, with limited exceptions (e.g., Drevon, 2022). The closest research (Hoover Green, 2020) analyses specific dimensions of armed groups' institutions but not *armed groups as institutions*, as I argue. Many studies have nonetheless developed several important hypotheses on the pre-war and in-war factors underpinning armed groups' organisational cohesion and norms—which underpins their institutionalisation—during armed conflicts. Pre-war factors include the existence of strong pre-existing politicised networks (Staniland, 2014) and the recruitment of ideologically committed fighters (Weinstein, 2006). In-war factors include their bureaucratisation (Jackson & Amiri, 2019), ideology (Kalyvas, 2015; Mironova, 2019), the resort to specific repertoires of violence (Cohen, 2016), intensive political indoctrination (Hoover Green, 2020), foreign support (Seymour, 2014; Tamm, 2016), and material incentives to military commanders (Lidow, 2016). Additionally, new research programs analyse and compare, as this book does, how militant groups consolidate in armed conflicts (Hafez, Gabbay, & Gade, 2021).

Important dimensions of external institutionalisation also feature in existing research. Jihadi collaboration ranges from transactional cooperation to tactical cooperation, strategic alliances, and organisational mergers (Moghadam, 2017). First, cross-factional cooperation impacts their ideological and behavioural evolution, including their adoption of new conflict framing and repertoires of violence such as suicide bombing (Moghadam, 2008, 2017) and increased organisational capability (Bacon, 2018). Second, armed groups develop relations with other states.[58] Relations with states can increase their internal cohesion (Seymour, 2014; Tamm, 2016), inform their strategic decisions (DeVore, 2012), enable their willingness to commit to specific international norms and gain legitimacy (Jo, 2015), and enhance their ability to resist militarily (Szekely, 2016). Important research also analyses armed groups' foreign policy, including Hamas' (Seurat, 2022). Jihadi relations with the population are studied in the rebel governance literature,[59] which analyses the wartime institutions that emerge under armed groups' control (Arjona, 2016), especially the extent to which armed groups (1) try to impose new political systems on the population or rely on pre-existing institutions and (2) include other actors in governance (Stewart, 2020; Mampilly & Stewart, 2020; Furlan, 2020). Governance is particularly constraining on these groups when local communities and organisations are able to resist locally, including under Jihadis (Arjona, 2016; Kaplan, 2017; Krause, 2018; Bambers & Svensson, 2022; Jackson, 2021; Svensson & Finnbogason, 2020; Svensson et al, 2022).

Despite important exceptions, a substantial amount of research on Jihadis remains isolated from civil war research. Studies of Jihadi groups' ideological tenets, repertoires of violence, and alliances are often dissociated from similar research in non-Islamist settings, although important underlying factors exist in both cases. This is particularly true in empirical research of Jihadi groups and ideologues that do not consider recent developments in civil war studies, especially organisational research on insurgencies. While Jihadi organisations have specificities, they are ultimately armed groups faced with trade-offs, constraints, and opportunities that other armed groups similarly have to address. Jihadis' specificities can only be understood by de-exceptionalising them and comparing them to other types of armed groups. Cross-ideological comparisons expose some aspects of Jihadi groups' ideational frameworks that might set them apart without essentialising their core belief systems. Instead of taking ideas as a given or relegating them as epiphenomena contingent on material factors, the institutional approach of this book analyses how ideas emerge, consolidate, and transform in parallel to armed groups' institutional developments. My approach aligns with Lacher's (2020) and Thurston's (2020) important focus on the meso level, but with a thorough focus on armed groups' institutional dynamics instead of their communities or the choices of their commanders only. It also aligns with new research on insurgent bureaucratisation, as in the Taliban example (Jackson & Amiri, 2019).

I argue that a key specificity of Jihadi Salafism is the nature of these groups' interconnection to one another. Recent studies suggest that these groups' ideology help them solve organisational dilemmas (Walter, 2017), and add that Jihadis are better managers of human resources (Mironova, 2019), attract better cadres (Kalyvas, 2018), build strategic relations with the business community (Ahmad, 2017), ability to survive cycles of "Boom-Bust" (Ahmad, 2021), and have a different support structure (Toft & Zhukov, 2015). These arguments are actually interrelated. They are rooted in Jihadis' interconnection, which allows them to mobilise across diverse networks, attracting a wider range of human and material resources, including a variety of skills that local groups may lack. The sharing of worldviews and belief systems helps to nurture trust and limit internal divisions. Ideas and practices, including repertoires of violence such as suicide bombing, diffuse through these networks, potentially contributing to the radicalisation of groups willing to embrace some of these practices (Moghadam, 2008; Kilcullen, 2011; Bakke, 2014).

But Jihadi interconnection is also a challenge. The fragmentation of contemporary armed conflicts and the proliferation of armed groups pose a particular threat to Jihadi groups, as they share an overlapping constituency, structuring networks, and worldviews. Co-ethnic or co-ideological insurgents are more capable of appropriating one another's resources and supporting networks than insurgents that don't share many commonalities (Pischedda, 2020). True, co-ideological groups are also less likely to fight one another (Gade, Hafez, & Gabbay, 2019; Ahmad & Diallo, 2023 and tend to ally instead (Gade, Gabbay, Hafez, & Kelly, 2019; Blair et al., 2022; Balcells, Chen, & Pischedda, 2022). But insurgents sharing similar ideological commitments can also fight one another too for political (and not only theological) reasons (Hafez, 2019; Hamming, 2022), since achieving social movement hegemony is key to insurgent victory (Krause, 2017). More centrist groups generally prefer to balance or outbid one another (Hafez, 2017), or even defect to the incumbent, as they assess post-war rewards (Christia, 2012). Jihadi divisions are particularly enduring, since they usually lack strong external state sponsors (Kalyvas, 2018).

Ultimately, any insurgency has to grapple with its own set of dilemmas and paradoxes. Ucko's (2022) "Insurgent's Dilemma" is that modern insurgencies encounter a familiar challenge: once they achieve a certain level of success, they are met with a formidable military backlash that hinders their ability to consolidate their gains into strategic victories. Modern insurgencies are therefore developing new survival strategies that go beyond the traditional models that were effective during the Cold War, including pursuing local change instead of regime change, infiltrating the state, and building up ideational legitimacy. Balcells and Kalyvas (2022) add that identity and ideology play a crucial role in insurgencies' success as much as counterinsurgency responses do. The "Marxist paradox" is that revolutionary socialists tend to perform well in insurgencies, which are both longer and more deadly, but they fail to achieve more outright victories than do non-Marxists due to the stronger counter-revolutionary responses they encounter.

Jihadi politicisation is a response to their own paradox, namely that the features that empower them also prevent them from achieving a strategic victory. Their interconnection allows them to mobilise more effectively in armed conflicts than other local groups, recruit ideologically motivated members, and be militarily efficient. But these groups' ideological commitments and interconnection also alienate them from other states and the international community. Western states notably oppose negotiating with them, implement strict anti-terrorist regimes to de-legitimise and disrupt their activities, and often strike their leaders and commanders, making it virtually impossible for the Jihadis to achieve any lasting strategic victory. Additionally, these groups' interconnection reinforces their dependency on transnational militants and ideologues, who can threaten to withdraw their support and weaken their cohesion whenever Jihadis want to change. Socialising their members along strong ideological tenets also makes it challenging for them to renounce some of their core beliefs for more tangible gains without risking their defection. Thus, while their interconnection and shared worldviews help to mobilise resources, including human capital, across diverse networks, it also presents significant challenges. Jihadi politicisation, by engaging with a broader political landscape and normalising their relations with non Jihadis, is a response to these challenges in order to achieve at least some of their strategic objectives. Jihadi politicisation addresses the tensions inherent with Jihadi transnationalism that Mendelsohn (2018) highlighted, including its unease with other forms of identity (sub-national and national), the intricate challenges in fostering unity as a transnational movement, and the inherent conflicts arising from the pursuit of establishing separate states while balancing local and global commitments.

This is a unique study of the Syrian conflict. Most research examines longer historical trends underpinning the regime's historical construction and the consequences on its handling of the unprecedented uprising of the population after 2011 (Haddad, 2011; Van Dam, 2011, 2017; Belhadj, 2013; McHugo, 2014;

Rey, 2018; Daoudy, 2020). Rich testimonies of activists close to the insurgency (Hudhaifa, 2021), intellectuals (Khalifa, 2008; al-Haj Saleh, 2017; Bishara, 2022), journalists (Giovanni, 2016; Yassin-Kassab & Al-Shami, 2018; Yazbek, 2016; Malek, 2017; Abouzeid, 2018), and locals (Al-Faris, 2015; al-Dik & Bontemps, 2016; Pearlman, 2017; Hisham & Crabapple, 2018) are complemented by academic analyses of several themes. They include the role of foreign actors and the United Nations (Phillips, 2016; Wieland, 2021; Bellamy, 2022; Tol, 2022; Warrick, 2022), armed opposition groups' dynamics (Lister, 2015b; Abboud, 2018; Baczko, Dorronsoro, & Quesnay, 2018; Gade, Gabbay, Hafez, & Kelly, 2019; Gade, Hafez, & Gabbay, 2019; Schulhofer-Wohl, 2020a; Ibrahim, 2021; Schwab, 2021; Szekely, 2023), the competition between al-Qaeda and IS in Syria and beyond (Hamming, 2020), geography and sectarianism (Balanche, 2018), the impact of local community structures on the divisions of the armed opposition (Ghadban, 2022), armed groups' governance and foreign intervention (Mukhopadhyay & Howe, 2023), including the impact of local cease-fire (Sosnowski, 2023) and the U.S. proxy warfare (Plana, 2021), the pro-regime militias (Lund, 2015a; Leenders & Giustozzi, 2019, 2022; Üngör, 2020, 2024; Voller, 2022; Koontz & Waters, 2023) and state supporters (Charap, Treyger, & Geist, 2019; Hamilton, Miller, & Stein, 2020; Juneau, 2020; Borshchevskaya, 2021), the micro-sociology of the conflict (Sakhi, 2023) and wide-ranging thematic books (Paoli & Burgat, 2013; Hinnebusch & Zinti, 2015; Hinnebusch & Imady, 2018a; Phillips, 2020; Collectif, 2022).

Several studies have already covered several dimensions of Ahrar al-Sham and Jabhat al-Nusra's histories. Cross-factional research examines Jihadi armed groups comparatively in Syria, including how they consolidated and cooperated (Ibrahim, 2021; Schwab, 2021), their court system (Schwab, 2018), ideological differentiation (Schwab, 2023), relations to civilians (Bambers & Svensson, 2022), support of social networks (Gopal & Hodge, 2021), and transformation (Pierret, 2015a, 2015b; Almustafa, 2020, 2023). On Ahrar al-Sham, the most detailed articles examined its organisational reconstruction after the killing of its first-tier leadership in September 2014 (Abazeid, 2015a). This body of research develops important hypotheses on the impact of the group's early choices and prison debates on its subsequent trajectory during the war (Pierret, 2016; Abazeid & Pierret, 2018) to explain how the group became a "revisionist" actor (Heller, 2015). Other studies include Ahrar al-Sham's alliance systems (Lund, 2012, 2013a), de-escalation and dialogue (Göldner-Ebenthal & Elsayed, 2019), and general choices within the armed opposition (Lister, 2015b; Soliman, 2020; Drevon, 2020, 2021). These contrast with more trivial coverage of Ahrar al-Sham as a mere enabler of al-Qaeda's global jihad, to whom it would remain connected ideologically and organisationally in Syria (Cafarella, Heras, & Casagrande, 2016).[60]

Studies on Jabhat al-Nusra conversely include its contested relations with al-Qaeda and IS in Syria (Cafarella, 2014; Lister, 2015b, 2016c; Watts, 2016; Al-Tamimi,2016, 2017a, 2017b, 2018; Adraoui, 2019; Giustozzi, 2020; Zelin, 2023), de-escalation (Carenzi, 2020), governance (Haid, 2021; Furlan, 2022), local strategy (Cafarella, 2014), re-localisation (Adraoui, 2019), and transformation into HTS (Al-Tamimi, 2017, 2018; Heller, 2017b; Keser & Fakhoury, 2022; Zelin, 2022, 2023; Bakkour, 2023; Grant-Brook, 2023). Only little work has relied on field research with the group in Syria (ICG 2019c, 2020; Khalifa, 2020; Drevon & Haenni, 2021, 2022; Khalifa & Bonsey, 2021; Khalifa, 2023).

This research ultimately contributes to current debates on Jihadis and their political evolution in armed conflicts, offering a more nuanced understanding of the key factions that emerged in Syria. This analysis goes beyond the current focus on IS radicalism in Syria and other countries, providing a more comprehensive analysis of the broader political landscape affecting the Jihadi social movement.

Overview of the Chapters

The next three chapters provide an in-depth analysis of the comparative evolution of the major armed opposition groups in Syria, including their internal institutionalisation and the institutionalisation of their interactions with one another, the population (in chapters 2 and 3 specifically), and foreign states (chapter 4). These chapters analyse the reasons behind Ahrar al-Sham and then Jabhat al-Nusra's leading roles within the armed opposition while other groups struggled to gain momentum. Chapter 5 then incorporates these factors to examine how they shaped these groups' politicisation.

Chapter 2 provides a comprehensive analysis of the armed opposition's emergence. It examines the role of Islamist groups under the Syrian Baathist regime until 2011, and how the regime's repression led to the militarisation of the uprising and informed its early geography. The chapter then delves into the success of Ahrar al-Sham, which emerged as the most prominent group in the early stages of the conflict. It traces the evolution of Ahrar al-Sham from an aggregation of small military units that were particularly active in northwest Syria to its consolidation as the leading armed opposition group in Syria. The group's early coordination of its military sub-units was facilitated by its embeddedness in pre-existing Islamist and activist networks, which gradually facilitated its institutionalisation. What sets Ahrar al-Sham apart from other armed groups is its unique combination of several singular characteristics that allowed it to develop internal and external institutional foundations early on in the conflict without over-stretching. Meanwhile, Jabhat al-Nusra, which would become

Ahrar al-Sham's main contender for the leadership of the armed opposition later on, was much smaller initially and not as influential, despite its successful high-level attacks against regime targets.

Chapter 3 examines the expansion of the armed opposition throughout Syria, focusing on the challenges that armed opposition groups faced when attempting to institutionalise internally and externally (with other groups and the population) to survive after the opposition seized large parts of Syrian territory. While most groups existed in only one of Syria's distinctive armed opposition-held areas, without developing a presence throughout the country, Ahrar al-Sham and Jabhat al-Nusra were among the few groups that managed to spread to more than one region. Ahrar al-Sham's development was unique in that it formed in a bottom-up alliance system of many factions that institutionalised their ties to one another before institutionalising internally as a single organisational entity. This process established the group as a de-centralised entity that made decisions in consensus, strengthened its institutional makeup, and made it attractive for independent military units willing to join a larger group. This unique pattern of development also explains the group's local embeddedness in Syrian communities, particularly in the northwest.

Chapter 4 delves into the various efforts to unite and institutionalise the armed opposition (internally as well as externally, with other states) against the backdrop of increased international intervention in the conflict. The need to unify the armed opposition became critical to protect the areas under its control and bolster its credibility. However, most unification attempts were driven primarily by military necessity, leading to further polarisation around the two main contenders for leadership—Jabhat al-Nusra and Ahrar al-Sham. The chapter argues that the outcome of their conflict was largely determined by their diverging internal institutionalisation processes. Jabhat al-Nusra's emphasis on centralisation and discipline allowed it to maintain a stronger grip on power, ultimately leading to its consolidation as the dominant group in the last remaining Syrian province under opposition control despite Ahrar al-Sham's significant strength.

The final chapter explores how the institutionalisation of the armed opposition informed its politicisation. It traces Jihadi ideological revisionism from pre-2011 prisoners debates to the impact of the configuration of the conflict—including the domestic nature of the uprising and factional competition—to explains how new ideas emerged and consolidated in the armed opposition, especially in Ahrar al-Sham. The chapter then focuses on Ahrar al-Sham's institutional trajectory, examining the group's struggle to fully embrace the Syrian armed opposition's revolutionary agenda. Despite being one of the most successful armed groups in Syria, Ahrar al-Sham faced numerous institutional impediments that hindered its ability to fully realise its political aspirations. The final part of the chapter analyses the challenges posed by the rise of Jabhat al-Nusra (as it transformed into HTS), as well as the external subjugation of the armed opposition by Russia and Turkey.

The conclusion moves beyond the empirical study of the Syrian armed opposition to better understand Jihadi groups' evolution outside Syria. This chapter discusses the potential impact of the Syrian conflict on the evolution of the Jihadi social movement, especially in light of the territorial defeat of IS in Iraq and Syria. It examines the broader implications of the conflict for the evolution of Jihadi movements globally. This approach helps to re-evaluate the post-9/11 American policies towards Jihadi groups and their consequences.

2
Creating an Insurgency

One of the most notable features of the Syrian armed opposition is its internal diversity, with hundreds of armed groups emerging between 2011 and 2013. These groups were established by individuals with various rationales when the regime unleashed unrestrained violence to repress a popular uprising throughout Syria. Some were villagers trying to defend their localities, while others were soldiers who split from the army after refusing to repress popular protests. Still, some local activists went further and already wanted to topple the regime. Among them were several groups that embraced political ideas stemming from the Islamist social movement, including Ahrar al-Sham, which took an early lead among Jihadi-leaning armed groups. The range of groups that formed to face the Syrian regime was much more diverse than the dominant dichotomy between Islamist and secular entities.[1] This chapter analyses the militarisation of the Syrian opposition in 2011 and the reasons behind the rise of several Islamist actors—with a particular attention to Ahrar al-Sham—in comparison to other groups. It also provides an overview of pre-2011 Syria and its impact on the emergence of the armed opposition.

Syrian Islamists under the Baathist Regime before 2011

The success of any armed opposition is determined not solely by its choices once it decides to take up arms and fight. The circumstances that precede the outbreak of the war play a crucial role in shaping the prospects of any insurgency. Armed groups have to mobilise militants around them, develop underground networks, and liaise with one another to coordinate their actions and create enduring armed groups. Their ability to do so depends on many factors, including the presence of pre-existing politicised social movements (e.g., Staniland, 2014) featuring different degrees of transnationalism and cohesion (e.g., Gopal & Hodge, 2021).[2] Pre-war developments, which are increasingly relevant in civil war studies, have a major impact on wartime dynamics, though not in a deterministic manner. In Syria, the Islamist armed opposition did not emerge in a vacuum in 2011. Islamist armed groups—which ultimately took the lead—emerged on the periphery of a larger Islamist social movement that has flourished internationally for the past few decades despite being latent inside Syria before 2011. The Syrian component of the Islamist social movement has formed around a combination of formal and informal groups sharing a distinct collective identity and worldviews despite real internal divergences.

The Syrian Islamist social movement has its roots in the reformist movement of the 19th and early 20th centuries. The latter was very diverse internally, inclusive of many prolific Islamic associations such as Jam'iat al-Gharra, Jam'iat al-Hidaya al-Islamiyya, and Jam'iat al-Ulama in Damascus (Lefevre, 2013: 13).[3] After Syria's independence, the Islamic (inclusive of Islamists) movement was swayed by the Muslim Brotherhood, which successfully aggregated many early religious congregations into a single organisational structure. Originally a mainstream organisation that participated in Syria's political system, the Muslim Brotherhood engaged in political activities from 1947 to 1963 despite several coups that forced it to limit its political engagement. During the 1950s to early 1960s, the Brotherhood consistently sought to adapt to new political opportunities to mobilise its mostly urban constituency in the newly independent state.[4]

In 1963, the Baath Party took control of Syria. The coup preceded an internal leadership contest for control of the new regime, which subsequently consolidated as a neo-patrimonial regime that combined personal and bureaucratic loyalty to the new leader (Hinnebusch, 2019). The Baath Party, populist corporatism, state bureaucracy, and army and security forces formed the pillars of power in Syria (Hinnebusch, 2004: 75–82). Under Hafez al-Assad's rule, there was no room for internal challengers. The regime's repression targeted not only the Islamists but also its communists, nationalists, and socialist opponents. Although the regime started with a relatively narrow popular base, Assad's ascent to power paved the way for the "revolution from above" (Hinnebusch, 2004), which combined land reforms, nationalisation of the public sector, and investments in health and education (Balanche, 2009; Hinnebusch, 2012). The president's power was reinforced by concentric circles of authority bolstered by widespread corruption networks and clientelism. A cult of personality treated Assad as a demi-god who could not be publicly criticised (Wedeen, 2015), while the intelligence services permeated all levels of society (Glasman, 2013).[5]

Regime consolidation in Syria illustrates the contested role of the Alawi community. Multiple security services historically came under the control of Alawi figures, who systematically favoured Alawis over Sunni officers and generals regardless of formal hierarchy (Balanche, 2006b; McHugo, 2014). Despite being a minority, the percentage of Alawi officers has grown from 61% in 1997 (Courbage, 2007) to 80% in 2012 (Paoli, 2011).[6] The most well-trained and well-resourced brigades were recruited from this community, while other sections of the army were kept structurally weaker (Balanche, 2006b; McHugo, 2014).[7] But Alawi dominance alone does not fully capture the essence of the Syrian regime. Hafez al-Assad had to balance various social forces against one another. Many large Alawi families were also marginalised in favour of Assad, his clan, and his allies. The lower social classes among Syrian Alawis barely benefited from the regime's largesses (Paoli, 2011).[8] To sustain his regime, Assad instead established a broad network of alliances that combined state and traditional sources of power around a tight clique sharing a similar background, experience, and solidarity (Belhadj, 2013; Hinnebusch & Imady, 2018b; Daher, 2019). Sectarian domination was not necessarily the product of a pre-arranged plan but the outcome of a longer historical process (Van Dam, 2017) informed by the trusted social networks that stemmed from the same regions and continued to recruit one another while purging their opponents (Hinnebusch, 2015). The rural and minority background of this group became a mechanism to limit division and reinforce their cohesion (Haddad, 2011).

The Baath Party faced its most significant opposition from the Islamists, particularly the Muslim Brotherhood.[9] The hegemony of the Baath Party and the army marginalised all political actors, including the Brotherhood. When the Baathist military coup outlawed the organisation in 1964, the Brotherhood participated in strikes and mass protests throughout Syria, especially in the conservative city of Hama. This ban transformed the Brotherhood from a mainstream political party to a vilified opposition group. The end of parliamentarianism and increased repression forced the group to rethink its strategy and ideas. Internal divisions were compounded by its own leadership weaknesses and by the geographic antagonism between Damascus and the northern branches (Lefèvre, 2013: 88–96). The Brotherhood felt particularly threatened by Baathist policies that it viewed as antagonistic to Syria's Sunni-majority society and its foundations. As regime violence increased and rural minorities took over the state apparatus, the Brotherhood began to develop more sectarian and militant positions. Some of its ideologues and activists promoted jihad and opposed the Alawi community and democracy, such as Sa'id Ḥawwa. Hama, in particular, was a hotbed of opposition, as Baathist policies threatened its social and economic foundations.

By the late 1970s, various Islamist groups legitimised violence against the regime. Local attacks against regime forces flourished as riots and demonstrations accompanied the emergence of the Fighting Vanguard (al-Tali'a al-Muqatila) on the periphery of the Muslim Brotherhood. These groups targeted regime figures and conducted military training for a larger confrontation with the authorities. In 1979, an emblematic event was the killing of a large number of Alawi cadets in the Aleppo Artillery school, which intensified the conflict between the two sides and destabilised the regime's foundations. The regime responded with a massive crackdown on Brotherhood-affiliated groups and their Sunni supporters, resulting in the death of hundreds of demonstrators. The regime declared that membership in the Brotherhood was punishable by death in Syrian law. By 1979–1980, the Brotherhood had joined an armed conflict that it was not prepared for, and the regime ultimately crushed an ultimate uprising in the city of Hama in 1982. This event marked the end of the revolt against the regime, and up to 30,000 people lost their lives in the destruction of the city. The failure of the Islamists can be attributed to various factors, including their internal divisions, lack of preparation and foreign support, and indecisiveness (al-Suri, 1991; Lia, 2016).[10]

State repression effectively incapacitated the Muslim Brotherhood in Syria, forcing many of its leaders and members to emigrate to Jordan and Iraq. Some of its members remained involved in armed militancy, and by the late 1980s had settled in Afghanistan to fight against the Soviet invasion (Lefèvre, 2013: 137–147).[11] Among them was Abu Musab al-Suri, who would become a leading Jihadi intellectual in the following decade (Lia, 2009). Despite the crackdown, many militants and their offspring participated in the war after 2011 and joined various armed groups.[12] They framed their actions as a continuation of what they retrospectively referred to as the first revolution (Lefèvre, 2013: 137–147; Lia, 2009).

The forceful repression of the Brotherhood and its virtual organisational disappearance did not totally uproot the Islamist social movement in Syria. After the conflict with the Brotherhood ended, the Syrian regime had to accommodate religion (Pierret, 2013), similar to other states in the region (Cesari, 2014). The regime's economic liberalisation reinforced this choice, as it forced it to accept a growing role for apolitical associations that could provide basic subsidies to the population that the regime could no longer support.[13] By the late 1980s, the external rent provided by Gulf countries dwindled, and private capital fled the country. The diversion of resources for the conflict with Israel worsened domestic failures, particularly in the public sector. The economic downturn necessitated new investments and lower government spending, but the regime limited economic developments, constraining its prospects and autonomy (Haddad, 2011). Despite these challenges, Syria's political economy largely underpinned the regime's limited opening to several Islamist groups, which continued after the succession of Hafez al-Assad by his son.

Real constraints on Islamist movements did not curb the religiosity of the population nor prevent the emergence of new religious trends unaffiliated with the Muslim Brotherhood, which filled in the vacuum left by the organisation.[14] The Brotherhood itself became more inclusive in exile. The organisation called for a democratic opening in Syria and also reached out to former regime officials such as its former vice president Abdul Halim Khaddam in 2005. Although some

Brotherhood members were released from prison (Al-Haj, n.d.: 19), the group's influence within Syria remained a shadow of its former self of the 1970s. In the 1990s, non-political Islamic charities, educational institutions, and proselytising movements supplanted the Brotherhood and gained significant societal influence through a religious revival affecting large segments of society (Pierret & Selvik, 2009; Donker, 2013). As economic liberalisation failed to provide sufficient economic subsistence, Islamic charities grew in influence. Hafez al-Assad's regime had promoted a loyal form of Islam by supporting Quranic memorisation institutions and a network of loosely structured mosques, partially Islamising the public sphere. Instead of building Islamic institutions that could leverage influence inside the state (Pierret, 2013), the regime outsourced Islamic education to loyal clerics, contributing to the growth of these non-political Islamic groups (Pierret, 2013; Khatib, 2012).

However, domestic policies were not the only factors underpinning the growth of Salafi and Islamist activist networks in Syria. Two significant regional and international turning points also shaped the evolution of activist networks on the periphery of the Islamist social movement since the early 1990s. The first juncture coincided with the first Gulf War (Al-Haj, n.d.: 19; Mustafa, 2012: 4; Al-Haj, 2013: 3), in which new Islamist generations unaffiliated with the Muslim Brotherhood drew inspiration from the Sahwa (awakening) movement that emerged in Saudi Arabia. This movement was an Islamist response to the Saudi alliance with the United States. Its ideologues sought to articulate demands for political reforms in the country, the reassertion of the role of Islam in state and society, and their opposition to the presence of American troops during the war (Lacroix, 2011). While the roots of the intellectuals' dissociation from the Saudi regime originated in the Saudi neutrality during the conflict between the Muslim Brotherhood and the Syrian regime (Lacroix, 2011: 152), public criticisms materialised only after the first Gulf War. Jihadis, including Osama bin Laden, later embraced the Sahwa as well (Lacroix, 2011: 193–200).[15] This development paralleled the transformation of armed Islamist mobilisation from Afghanistan to Bosnia and later Chechnya (Hegghammer, 2010), which spurred numerous discussions among Syrian activist groups on jihad (Al-Haj, n.d.: 19). Khaled Abu Anas, one of the main founders of Ahrar al-Sham, recalled his early involvement in the Syrian Islamic revival.

> My involvement began in 1991. I was not religiously committed before that. We are from the post-Muslim Brotherhood generation who met on university campuses. I began my engagement with different books on Islam and listening to local sheikhs in Idlib. The Saudi influence was very strong in our lives as the beginning of the 1990s coincided with the Islamic revival (*al-sahwa*). I created the first group in Syrian universities to spread our Islamic activities.

We organised many meetings at the time. We were discovering the Salafi movement. We discussed many issues together. Some of us would prepare lectures on specific books and topics, which would then be discussed collectively. Most of the brothers were from Aleppo and I was the only one from Idlib. Our readings were very broad. We began with the foundations, Ibn Taymiyya and Ibn Qayyim.[16] Then we went to other sheikhs, including [Muhammad Nasir al-Din] al-Albani, [Abu Basir] al-Tartussi and others.[17] We tried to create a broad network throughout the country. As we only focused on the communists, the regime did not attack us. Then, we explored the concept of tawheed.[18] We started to emphasise jihad as well. We strived to transform the youths and create a new generation.

The second juncture that catalysed the expansion of Salafi and Islamist activist networks occurred in 2003, when the United States invaded Iraq. This event triggered non-violent Islamist protests in Syria and reignited internal debates on jihad among Syrian Islamists (Al-Haj, n.d.: 27; Mustafa, 2012: 4; Al-Haj, 2013). Although some individuals had discussed jihad in the 1990s, the rise of Jihadi Salafism gained momentum after 2003 in Middle Eastern countries (e.g., Drevon, 2016). Friends and students who were looking for the most appropriate response to what they perceived as a new threat to Islam embraced the Salafi Jihadi approach to Islam (Al-Haj, n.d.: 32). The regime indirectly supported the proliferation of Salafi Jihadi networks in their fight against American forces in Iraq, before clamping down on them in Syria. Numerous interviews with Islamists who remained independent or affiliated with Salafi armed groups during the uprising recognised that they initially embraced this approach to Islam for political more than theological reasons.[19] They perceived al-Qaeda, which virtually monopolised Jihadi Salafism after 9/11 (Drevon, 2017), as the only actor capable of facing the external threats to the Muslim world. Khaled Abu Anas also added that:

> Many of us come from Jihadi Salafism. This trend is a response to oppression. When Islam is under attack, jihad is a solution and a way out from the conundrum in which we are. That's why the youths embrace jihad. If you think about it, there are historically only two Islamist models: the Muslim Brotherhood and al-Qaeda. In these conditions, which one was the most relevant and convincing? The Brotherhood and its strategy of political engagement or al-Qaeda and armed struggle? Al-Qaeda was more attractive for those who wanted to do something.

During that period, a significant number of individuals exhibited a heightened religious commitment, actively seeking increased Islamist influence within Syrian universities. Ahrar al-Sham's first leader mentioned in an interview shortly before his death that (al-Jazeera, 2016):

> The university dormitories were small clubs in which we could discuss politics between different intellectual tendencies. Every year the Islamist trend was becoming more powerful.

To which Abul Talha al-Ghab, the first military leader of the group, added that:

> I became practising when I was at the university. I was looking for new references, which I obtained online. I was influenced by [the Muslim Brotherhood intellectual Sayyid Qutb's] In the Shade of the Qur'an (*fi zilal al-qur'an*) and Milestones (*ma'alim fil-tariq*). There was also a global change with the war on terrorism [after 9/11], which encouraged us to look at Islam more in depth in response.

It is worth highlighting that this line of reasoning is a prevailing sentiment among Jihadi groups of all orientations. In private interviews, they acknowledge the political motives for their adoption of this interpretation of Islam, rather than strictly theological ones. They do not merely contend that Jihadi Salafism is a more authentic expression of Islam's essence. Even the top religious authority of Jabhat al-Nusra, which was established by a network of ISI (Islamic State of Iraq, before the creation of ISIS) commanders before pledging loyalty to al-Qaeda, expressed a comparable view. According to Abu Abdullah al-Shami:

> Salafism spread in Syria under the influence of the war in Iraq in 2003. For many, the idea was to assess the force that could jihad in the region to resist the American invasion. Salafism was considered the way forward. Its popularity in the current conflict was further supported by the military victories achieved by Salafi armed groups. People follow the successful projects.

The relations between the Syrian regime and the Jihadi movement were complex and contentious prior to 2011.[20] Initially, the Syrian government cooperated with the United States against Jihadi networks in the aftermath of 9/11, participating in the rendition of suspects associated with al-Qaeda. According to a former CIA agent, "if you want a serious interrogation, you send a prisoner to Jordan. If you want them to be tortured, you send them to Syria" (Guardian, 2011). However, Syria's regional interests shifted after the U.S. invasion of Iraq in 2003 and forced departure from Lebanon in 2005, when the regime began to see Jihadi groups as a useful card in the region. This ambiguity led to some controversial interactions, such as the regime's support for the Palestinian armed group Fath Intifada that helped a new Jihadi group, Fath al-Islam, take over the Nahr al-Bared refugee camp in 2007 in north Lebanon (Rougier, 2007, 2015). Additionally, smaller groups like Jund al-Sham and unaffiliated militants launched sporadic attacks inside Syria. The Syrian regime also facilitated the transfer of foreign fighters transiting through the country to fight American forces and their allies in Iraq, including al-Qaeda–linked networks (Lister, 2015b: 31–50). Supporting the Iraqi insurgency was a way to destabilise the American occupation, which could have targeted Syria as well. The regime cracked down on these networks only when it was expedient to support negotiations with the American administration. Most Syrian armed groups and their supporters were subsequently jailed in Saydnaya, a notorious prison in the suburbs of Damascus. Many former prisoners went on to participate in the armed opposition, particularly in Ahrar al-Sham and Jabhat al-Nusra.[21]

The Salafi component of the Islamist social movement remained largely hidden from public view, and instead spread through discrete social networks on a small scale. In a private discussion in Idlib with four religious scholars associated with former Jabhat al-Nusra or close to the group, my colleague Patrick Haenni and I discussed the role of the Islamist social movement in Syria prior to 2011. Abu Abdullah al-Shami and Mathar al-Weis from HTS, along with Ibrahim Shasho, the minister of religious affairs for their supported government, and Anas Ayrut from the Sharia faculty at the University of Idlib, all concurred that there was no room for the public expansion of the Islamist social movement before the 2011 uprising. They explained that Syrians were especially hesitant to be associated with the Muslim Brotherhood due to their previous confrontations with the regime, and that there was a significant generational gap with the organisation, which was seen as out of touch with the younger generation.

While some Islamists assert that they lived in isolation prior to 2011 due to fear of arrest, others acknowledge that they were loosely connected in informal groups composed of friends, students, university graduates, and locals.[22] These groups were organised around specific religious preachers, mosques, or informal gatherings and were prevalent throughout Syria, with some areas in Aleppo, Hama, the suburb of Duma in Damascus, and rural areas showing particular activity (ICG, 2012; Abu Raman, 2013). The de-centralised and internationalised nature of the activist approach to Salafism was more conducive to its expansion in an authoritarian state like Syria, which was better equipped to suppress well-established organizations than an ideological trend disseminated through unstructured, loose social networks (ICG, 2012).[23] Despite its limited societal influence and public presence prior to 2011, Salafism and its militant variants are not just an imported phenomenon to Syria during the war. Militant Salafism is not exclusively a foreign phenomenon, although a competition between foreign actors has fuelled its growth since the early stages of the conflict (Pierret, 2016).

During the 2000s, many individuals in northwest Syria met privately to discuss a range of political and religious issues. Their internal debates spanned from the so-called caliphate of Abu 'Isa—a militant who claimed to have reinstated the historical caliphate amid the conflict in Afghanistan, which he ruled from his apartment in London (Jackson, 2014; Hussein, 2020)—to the concept of *irja* or postponement of the application of Islamic law in the Muslim world (Lav, 2012: 13–29) (ICG, 2017).[24] Although the Salafis, many of whom later became the nucleus of Ahrar al-Sham, shared some commonalities, such as their hostility towards the regime, they did not hold the same political outlook. While some Salafis preferred a more scholastic (*'ilmi*) approach to Islam that focused primarily on the study of religious creed (*'aqida*) without delving into political issues, others explicitly endorsed Jihadi Salafism and violence (ICG, 2017) and mobilised in support of armed resistance in Iraq in the 2000s. Two early leaders of Ahrar al-Sham, Khaled Abu Anas and Abu Abd al-Rahman al-Suri, reflected on their diverging views on Jihadi Salafism,[25] with Abu Anas suggesting that small activist networks were already contemplating the possibility of a war in Syria in the 2000s. Despite these differences, Syrian Salafis generally shared a strong opposition to the regime, which was widely viewed as religiously heretical (ICG, 2017).[26] Another early leader argued that:

> Many of our brothers went to Iraq to fight the American occupation. It was a very popular cause at the time. I personally thought that change was coming to Syria too. But I knew that it would be extremely difficult. I told the brothers that they should get prepared in Syria instead of going to Iraq.

But other Ahrar al-Sham founders like Abu Abd al-Rahman al-Suriconversely argued that Jihadi Salafism did not play a central role for all early Ahrar al-Sham leaders:

> I was a scholastic Salafi (*'ilmi*) before 2011. There was a lot of pressure on us. We could barely meet or organise. It was a very difficult situation. I come from a conservative family that is not necessarily Salafi. There was a wall between us and the regime. We would not help them, join the Baath Party, or anything like that. Being in that type of conservative family was risky in these conditions. Personally I began my involvement at a very general level. First, I started to read [Muhammad] al-Bukhari, then [Ibn Hajar] al-'Asqalani, Muslim [ibn al-Hajjaj] and others.[27] I assembled a large library in Idlib with religious books. People were warning against the Salafi Jihadi trend at the time. Then I met others and we had a lot of discussions on the trend. I therefore disagree with the claim that Ahrar al-Sham stems from Jihadi Salafism. Some were but not all of us. My literature is not Abu Muhammad al-Maqdisi and Abu Qatada.[28] I have not read them.

The Militarisation of a Popular Uprising(s)

In early 2011, the removal of the heads of Arab states in Tunisia and Egypt, Zine El Abidine ben Ali and Hosni Mubarak, respectively, inspired small-scale demonstrations across Syria.[29] The Syrian regime wrongly alleged that its foreign policy in support of regional resistance movements such as Hamas in Palestine and Hizbullah in Lebanon, the so-called axis of resistance formed with Iran, would shield it from protests, unlike pro-Western regimes like Egypt and Tunisia (Assad, 2011). The protesters proved the regime wrong when the arrest of schoolboys who had written anti-regime graffiti in Daraa inflamed popular indignation throughout the country. Daraa, a former bastion of the Baath Party that was marginalised by the regime's policies, became the epicentre of the early protests. The subsequent torture and assassination of a 13-year-old boy named Hamza al-Khateeb further fueled popular anger against the security forces throughout the country. While early protesters demanded prisoners' liberation and wide political reforms—not the downfall of the regime—the regime took only cursory measures, such as the reinstatement of a female teacher wearing the face veil in Banyas and some liberation of prisoners. These measures were too little, too late, particularly given the regime's increasing use of violence against demonstrators. The protestors considered Assad's first speech in March 2011, in which he spoke out against foreign conspiracies, and his failure to implement real measures, an affront (Marsh & Chulov, 2011). As violence escalated on the part of the regime, popular resentment intensified.

In the early stages of the Syrian uprising, protests began with small-scale demonstrations in Damascus that quickly spread to peripheral neighbourhoods, such as the eastern and southern suburbs of Duma and Midan.[30] As the movement grew, an increasing number of protesters gathered in Syria's cities around specific themes every Friday after congregational prayers. At this point, there were no signs of sectarianism. Local demands rather than sectarian claims (Rey, 2013) drove the protest movement, reflecting the strength of Syria's local identity and territorial crisis (Balanche, 2011). Demonstrators expressed local grievances against the backdrop of broader revolutionary demands. They often emphasised solidarity between Christians and Muslims to pre-empt the regime's attempts to portray the movement as a "Sunni threat" to Syria's religious minorities. Sunni rural areas were at the forefront, partially reflecting the regime's strategy of co-optation of certain groups (Haddad & Wind, 2014). But it would also be wrong to assume that only rural areas mobilised; urban areas also played a significant role in supporting the militarised revolution. Distinct armed groups emerged with a more urbanised perspective formed though some of these urban factions maintained connections to rural areas through familial networks (Sakhi, 2023: 84–113). The level of mobilisation of different cities, groups, or even neighbourhoods varied according to the nature of their local divergences and state-society relations before 2011 (Hokayem, 2017: 41; Mazur, 2021). By June 2011, hundreds of thousands of non-violent protesters had demonstrated in Syria's public squares. Demonstrations often occurred in informal or popular neighbourhoods where security control was feebler. Local coordination committees, the *tansiqiyyat*, played a crucial role in coordinating their activities locally and throughout Syria to give a sense of unity to the social movement and provide relief assistance and basic organisation (Abboud, 2018 63). The local protests combined nationwide themes with very local demands and reflected the grievances of certain regions and cities.

However, we also cannot isolate the conflict that began in Syria in 2011 from the structural factors underpinning Syria's domestic and international politics. While short-term triggers catalysed the demonstrations, the conflict has deep-rooted historical causes. The emergence of non-violent protests, the regime's response, and the militarisation of the opposition were not isolated events. A complex set of factors that define the available choices for both regime leaders and opposition groups largely contextualise the sequence of events after 2011. Even authoritarian leaders who rely on a small circle of decision-makers are influenced by a range of domestic and international factors that inform their actions. These factors are rooted in longer historical patterns of development.[31] For example, the resort to violence by the security forces is not only the choice of regime leaders or their subordinates. It also results from the nature of state-society relations across Syria before 2011 (Mazur, 2021), since the resilience of any regime depends on a combination of state organisation (from bureaucratic to patrimonial) and the degree of inclusiveness (Goodwin, 2001). Foreign countries and Syrian opposition groups initially overlooked these factors and mistakenly assumed that the regime could easily fall, as in Tunisia, Egypt, and Libya. By 2012, Western countries mistakenly became confident that Bashar al-Assadwould be quickly toppled.[32] Their assessment explained their reluctance to consider serious political discussions with regime supporters at the time, such as Russia, on a speculative replacement of Assad (Borger & Inzaurralde, 2015).

Multiple factors influenced the regime's response to the popular protests in 2011.[33] One of the most prominent is the nature of its elite and security apparatus (Barany, 2011; Lawson, 2015; Droz-Vincent, 2020).[34] Policing of protest varies according to regime types and traditions. Security establishments follow diverging procedures rooted in established traditions that structure their reaction to protest movements (e.g., Della Porta & Fillieule, 2004). Even inclusive democracies do not police waves of protest similarly (Della Porta, Fillieule, & Reiter, 1998). These differences are even more acute in an authoritarian regime. The regime's patronage networks for managing local communities across Syria largely determined its approach to the challenge posed by the protests in 2011, as well as the level and scope of violence in those communities (Mazur, 2021).

In 2011, the Syrian regime featured exclusive political structures. Only pro-regime protests had historically been organised by the regime. There were no independent political parties, unions, and other types of associations that could organise political protests, even in limited numbers, as in other countries such as Egypt and Jordan.[35] The security establishment was ill-prepared and untrained to manage large-scale social protests though the regime's structure prevented the split of cohesive military units, with only individual soldiers and conscripts leaving the army, rather than full battalions or divisions. Additionally, the security establishment lacked professionalism and institutionalisation, remaining mostly under the control of the ruling family and Alawi officers, which further hindered its ability to address the protests effectively. For instance, Atef Najib, a cousin of Bashar al-Assad, played a critical role in repressing the early protests in the south of the country in Daraa. Despite Western diplomats advising Assad to undertake reforms and punish his cousin for his actions, Najib was arrested for only a few days and subsequently released due to his mother's influence on Assad's mother (Dagher, 2019). Alawi officers generally felt threatened by the development of a protest movement in Sunni rural areas, as they believed their survival was inherently tied to the regime. The failure to address the protests was only compounded by the marginalisation of the Baathist old guard in the 2000s, which not only was more experienced but also enjoyed wider patronage networks throughout the country. Some of their pillars, including Assef Shawkat, died in a perplexing bombing on July 18, 2012, marking an early turning point in the conflict in favour of escalation (Dagher, 2014).

The regime's support base had also become increasingly narrow over time. By 2011, the regime relied mainly on certain segments of the Alawi community and the Sunni elite, while marginalising the Baath party and other central pillars that provided mobilisation and support (Hinnebusch & Imady, 2018b).[36] Bashar al-Assad had promoted a new class of bureaucrats loyal to him, but this only further entrenched the regime's reliance on a narrow elite centred on the Assad family and allied families like the Makhlouf. As the regime pursued neoliberal economic policies (Hinnebusch, 2012) in its "authoritarian upgrading" (Heydemann, 2007), it eroded the social contract it had previously maintained with the population (Hinnebusch, 2019). The regime had no coherent economic strategy, and instead focused on banking and tourism while neglecting traditional investments in agriculture and industry (Hinnebusch, 2012). This further marginalised large parts of the Sunni population, particularly in rural areas that were less integrated into state structures.

The regime's reliance on a social base that was antagonistic to the lower Sunni rural working class insulated it from immediate threats, but left it disconnected from significant segments of the population. Many working poor moved to the periphery of major cities, especially when drought plagued the country in the late 2000s (De Châtel, 2014), which armed groups later seized during the uprising. As a result, the regime lacked the means to respond to popular demands, and was unable to co-opt these marginalised groups as it had done in the past. The association of the Alawi community with the regime fostered the idea that their survival was tied to the regime's survival (Van Dam, 2017). Even when armed groups promoted non-sectarian agendas, the Alawi community remained stuck within this "loyalty trap" that hindered the emergence of an alternative (McLauchlin, 2018).

The weakness of Syrian civil society is a notable outcome of the two previous factors. The regime's reliance on a narrow base of support and the associated monopoly of the Baath Party over the regime state's structures had impeded the emergence of an autonomous civil society. Initial hopes that the so-called Damascus Spring that followed Bashar al-Assad's accession to power would enable the emergence of independent associations, gatherings, newspapers, and, potentially, political parties were rapidly quashed.[37] The Syrian regime never allowed a political opening, unlike semi-authoritarian regimes such as Egypt under Mubarak, where independent political parties existed despite occasional arrests and state pressure (Blaydes, 2010). Although some local associations were allowed to provide basic social services to alleviate the impact of economic liberalisation, associations focused on human rights were severely constrained. They were kept informal, under the leadership of some intellectuals who could not establish independent funding, coordinate, or even institutionalise (Abboud, 2015). Strong civil society is paramount to the cohesion of a protest movement. The weakness of civil society in Syria hindered the emergence of a cohesive leadership that could coordinate the protests and favour the choice of non-violence (Pearlman, 2011), though mobilisation can still occur to compensate civil society deficit (Pearlman, 2020). It also exacerbated armed groups' failure to overcome their divisions since pre-war networks are critical to armed groups' organisational cohesion (Staniland, 2014). As a result, the armed opposition fragmented, reflecting the fragmented social structure of the Syrian local communities that supported its growth (Ghadban, 2022).

Syria's regional alliance system was also critical in the regime's survival. The unwavering support of foreign allies—Iran and later Russia—shielded the regime from international pressure. Both countries were unlikely to restrain the regime or favour meaningful domestic change.[38] They are also authoritarian, and show little tolerance for domestic social protests, with Iran crushing its own domestic protests in 2009 and Russia three years later. They believed that any accommodation of the mostly Sunni opposition would undermine their position in the region. They feared that a new regime, or even a reformed one, would be less reliant on them and more aligned with Gulf and Western countries. Russia, in particular, has been consistently opposed to Western attempts at humanitarian interventions, citing violations of UN Security Council mandates.[39] Its vested geopolitical interests in Syria further cemented its support for the regime. As the opposition militarised, the regime consolidated external support against what it saw as an existential threat, which only further bolstered the backing of Syria's main allies (Phillips, 2016).

These four characteristics mean that militarisation was very likely, if not inevitable. The argument that the regime could have reformed itself and made the right decisions under the leadership of one man (Lesch, 2013) is not credible in a longer historical perspective. Historical processes largely set post-2011 developments (Saouli, 2018; Mazur, 2021). Non-violent transition was almost impossible, since the regime structures, which hindered political representation, could not be dismantled (Phillips, 2016; Van Dam, 2017; Balanche, 2018; Hinnebusch, 2019). The nature of Syria's regime and its tools to deal with a national-level challenge to its authority additionally offered next to no alternative to violent repression (Mazur, 2021). Unlike Egypt and Tunisia, Syria featured critical characteristics that obstructed a non-violent transition of power or any level of political opening and inclusion. The regime's historical reliance on security services mostly drawn from members of a minority religious community, the lower institutionalisation and professionalisation of the army, and an economic and political elite organically tied to regime survival was designed to protect the regime from military coups while keeping the mobilisation of key groups (Balanche, 2014b; Hokayem, 2017: 50). Although foreign support for the regime and later for various opposition groups ultimately bolstered violence on both sides, the regime's historical construction made violence the most likely option from the beginning.

Repression was brutal. The simultaneous uprisings of its population in different cities and regions caught the regime unprepared. Regime forces besieged rebellious cities, starting from Daraa in April and Baniyas and Homs in the next few months. Soldiers, snipers, and tanks fired at the demonstrators to quell popular protests and dissuade potential protestors, relying on its most loyal troops. The regime additionally gave free rein to unruly thugs connected to the regime, the infamous *shabiha* (literally "ghosts"), to brutalise popular neighbourhoods and sustain the repression of the protests (Lund, 2015a). Thousands of civilians disappeared in jail, where torture and executions were rampant, at an industrial scale. The deaths of thousands of them would only be announced in the next few years, officially as cardiac arrests (Barnard, 2019). During the first six months of the conflict, the opposition initiated only limited violence, with the main case being in the northwest city Jisr al-Shughur, where demonstrators seized weapons from a police station and clashed with the security forces.[40] At least 2,000 death and more than 10,000 arrests were reported by summer 2011.

Despite the emergence of local coordination networks inside Syria, a credible opposition movement was initially unable to consolidate due to the absence of territorial control. As a result, the organised Syrian opposition set up in exile in Istanbul. In April 2011, a conference was held in Istanbul, followed by numerous meetings that paved the way for the emergence of the Syrian National Council (al-Majlis al-Watani al-Suri) in August 2011. It became the National Coalition for Syrian and Revolutionary and Opposition Forces (al-I'tilaf al-Watani) in November 2012, which in turn formed the Interim Government in 2013. However, despite these efforts, the external opposition was plagued by numerous divergences of views, power contests for leadership, and limited local anchorage, which prevented them from shaping ongoing developments on the ground, especially as the uprising militarised. Their impact on the conflict was limited due to their inability to effectively coordinate with local actors and gain legitimacy among the Syrian population.

In response to the violent crackdown, locals began gathering weapons they either possessed or obtained through smuggling networks to protect themselves during demonstrations. Civilians sought to dissuade the security forces and, in some cases, shot back when attacked. Others organised low-scale armed attacks against army checkpoints, barracks, or convoys circulating in rural areas, which often gave them access to additional small arms and explosives.[41] These attacks were particularly common in rural areas where policing was more difficult, and the regime's presence was historically lower, allowing early armed groups to conceal themselves more easily. Occasionally, these attacks targeted specific individuals associated with repression. During the first months of the conflict, these armed attacks were not sophisticated. Their level of sophistication only grew over the next few months as the conflict continued, larger armed groups consolidated, and veterans of previous jihad came to Syria to help the nascent insurgency.[42] During the first year of conflict, however, the majority of the opposition remained non-violent, and armed resistance primarily emerged in response to the violent regime crackdown.

The characteristics of the regime also explain the organisational features of the armed opposition, especially its localism.[43] The weakness of civil society and the regime's indiscriminate repression drove early armed gatherings to rely on local social networks, including friends, acquaintances, and neighbourhoods, for structure and support. As a result, the armed groups that emerged during the first phase of the conflict were deeply embedded in their local communities, relying on these networks to build trust and gain support, as in other conflicts(Lewis, 2020). These local characteristics help explain the proliferation of hundreds of armed groups throughout the country between 2011 and 2012. Significant coordination and cooperation between these groups only emerged once they gained control of larger territories and received foreign support.

The emergence of the Free Syrian Army (FSA) in July 2011 did not fundamentally alter the dynamics of the conflict. The nature of the regime's repression and its legitimisation of violence shaped the formation of local factions that were deeply embedded in their communities. Some of these factions were composed of just a few dozen members recruited from among friends and neighbours, while others were manned by army dissidents. The label "Free Syrian Army" primarily intended to provide a unified political cover both inside and outside of Syria, as an organised opposition to the regime. The establishment of a unified organisational structure on paper reinforced the credibility of the opposition and sought to present a national alternative beyond their inherent localism. Although the Free Syrian Army quickly affiliated itself with the external opposition, direct command and control was more virtual than real. Violent networks emerged in parallel with non-violent protest movements, gradually intersecting with them as territories fell under their control (Donker, 2019).

Mobilising a Network of Islamist Entrepreneurs

Regime repression positioned Islamist activists at the forefront of mobilisation, as prominent entrepreneurs of the armed opposition. The non-discriminatory nature of state policies galvanised and united the latent Islamist social movement despite previous divergences of views. The severe suppression of the non-violent uprising decreased the significance of previous ideological debates. In contrast to countries like Egypt, where Salafis participated in the political process regardless of their pre-2011 positions on democracy (e.g., Drevon, 2015), state repression in Syria rallied them around the legitimisation of violence against the regime. Being closer to the Jihadi trend or the students of the creed became irrelevant once the uprising militarised in reaction to repression.[44] Notwithstanding previous political standpoints, Islamists who shared similar worldviews and ideological tenets sought to connect and create insurrectionary projects, even if they were only loosely connected beforehand. Their efforts contributed to the re-activation of the Syrian Islamist social movement and its partial transformation into a radical milieu, defined as the local environment that "shares [armed groups'] perspective and objectives, approves of certain forms of violence, and (to some extent) supports the violent group morally and logistically" (Malthaner & Waldmann, 2014: 979). The radical milieu is often associated with Islamists' conception of their popular incubator (*hadina sha'biyya*).

After violence escalated, particularly in northwest Syria, Islamist groups quickly expressed their commitment to the removal of the regime rather than its reform. As in non-Islamist conflicts, individuals' pre-existing identity and their need for action drives insurgent mobilisation (Bosi & Ó Dochartaigh, 2018). While Islamist actors aimed to protect their local communities from regime forces like non-Islamist actors, they also saw the new uprising as an opportunity to achieve long-standing strategic objectives of regime change and seek revenge for their earlier defeats in the 1980s. Khaled Abu Anas, the main founder of Ahrar al-Sham, elaborated on this point, stating that:

> We started one week before the revolution. Some of the youths were discussing the issue. We wanted to prepare militarily from the beginning. We did not want to participate in the non violent demonstrations so that we would not appear in public and be used as an excuse to justify repression by the regime. It was extremely difficult not to participate in these early developments and not to take the streets publicly. But we needed to travel to different cities and remain committed to secrecy. Then, I went to Saudi Arabia and we spoke about the next step with others. We agreed about our general guidelines. There was a good experiment in Libya and we were inspired by that.

It does not mean that all the Islamists embraced violence or that they were the only ones to do so. The Muslim Brotherhood, whose local infrastructures had been decimated by the previous military attempt to challenge the regime, was particularly hesitant and divided (Lefèvre, 2014, 2017; Conduit, 2019: 199–221). The organisation officially tried to dissuade the demonstrators from resorting to violence, as it favoured the coordination of small demonstrations that would quickly appear, dissolve, and be publicised in the media. Most of the group's initial support therefore focused on the provision of limited logistic support inside Syria in addition to the external coordination of the Syrian opposition abroad. Only a limited number of individual initiatives supported the militarisation of the uprising. According to a member of the Brotherhood political office, Samir Abu Laban:

> When the uprising started, we wanted the demonstrators to wait for six months. We wanted to see where the Arab revolutions were heading and thought that we should not join from the beginning. Then, we started to give local demonstrators what they needed in terms of resources, including cameras, money, phone numbers, etc. But we also warned them to calm down and not to resort to violence. Using weapons would make them lose control over the events.

The former head of the Syrian Muslim Brotherhood, Ali Sadreddine Al-Bayanuni (2018), confirmed that:

When the revolution started, the Muslim Brotherhood was sympathetic. But we evaluated that the regime would not surrender power easily. It could destroy all of Syria, all its cities. So the Brotherhood was very conservative in the beginning. Then, when the revolution spread throughout the country, it had to stand by it. Even when armed actions started, there was strong pressure from our popular bases to form our own revolutionary faction to fight. But as the Muslim Brotherhood, we decided not to form our own faction and to support other groups instead. Our members could simply join them.

But militarisation did not involve only Islamist actors. Many local groups embraced violence regardless of their political or ideological leaning. Although the regime blamed "radical" Islamists and foreign countries for the uprising, its repression was largely indiscriminate. The brutal suppression of non-violent protests by an unyielding regime influenced many non-Islamists to consider resorting to violence. Local groups of friends, neighbours, and families collectively deliberated about the next steps. The militarisation of the uprising served various objectives: to protect the demonstrations, dissuade the security forces, and confront regime forces (Baczko, Dorronsoro & Quesney, 2018: 94–95). The joining of many conscript soldiers who deserted the army and fled to the countryside seeking refuge and escaping forced conscription and individual fears reinforced the militarisation of the opposition (Albrecht & Joehler, 2017). Armed militants did not necessarily believe that they could topple the regime through violence, but the Western military support for the Libyan uprising influenced many proponents of violence who believed that a regional or international intervention could tilt the balance of power inside Syria.

The indiscriminate nature of repression explains the large diversity of armed groups created from 2011 onward. It also contextualises the similarity of their modes of organisation. The localism of nearly all the groups and the nature of their underpinning networks were largely determined by the nature of the legitimisation of violence. The early survival of armed groups depended on protecting information and preventing leaks to government forces, which explains the centrality of kinship networks and ethnically or religiously homogeneous areas (Lewis, 2017). Therefore, the vast majority of the early military units, both Islamist and non-Islamist, began locally in small groups of close friends, families, and acquaintances who gathered primitive weapons and some financial resources to attack regime forces. Given the level of trust required for armed mobilization, coordination was more likely to occur at a very local level than across different localities. While high levels of grievances contextualise the appearance of many groups willing to confront the regime, they usually only manage to unite when overlapping social networks can bring them together (Mosinger, 2018).

One of the main differences between Islamists and non-Islamists was the former's reliance on pre-existing social networks.[45] The Assad regime had long discouraged public criticism and undermined societal trust, making collaboration difficult prior to the uprising in 2011 (Wedeen, 2015, 2019; Ismail, 2018). The Islamists were comparatively better positioned due to their pre-existing and loosely connected social networks, which had been mobilised in the past. This allowed for easier coordination between different Islamist military units, especially in northwest Syria, as overlapping social networks enabled them to reach out to each other and form common fronts (Mosinger, 2018). The presence of influential rebel leaders with international experience was also pivotal for securing foreign support (Huang, Silverman, & Acosta, 2022). In contrast, non-Islamists and army defectors were more likely to be divided along urban-rural lines, family or neighbourhood rivalries, and other issues that are more salient in high-risk activities. Salafis, Islamist activists, and other religiously conservative Muslims were comparatively more interconnected through diverse social networks united by their antagonism to the regime and shared worldviews. The re-activation of the Islamist social movement provided a shared platform that facilitated early interactions between its components and eased concerns of betrayal, since members already knew each other's backgrounds and reputations prior to 2011. This was particularly important, as shared religious values can reinforce mutual trust in both violent (Ahmad, 2017) and non-violent contexts (Livny, 2020). Conservative families that shared some of their views also joined them, further facilitating initial coordination. As the founder of a local brigade that quickly affiliated with Ahrar al-Sham pointed out:

> All the groups started similarly around some local guy to whom people had loyalty. People who knew one another. I started to buy weapons in April 2011 to prepare early military work. I started to arm the youths around me. We asked money to merchants to gather weapons and financial resources. The early days of the revolution saw the creation of the first brigades later affiliated with Ahrar al-Sham with a clear Islamic identity.

Locally, non-Islamists express their frustration, retrospectively, at being unable to compete with the Islamists. The leader of a local faction that quickly affiliated with the Free Syrian Army in northwest Syria lamented that:

> The Islamists had a popular incubator (*hadina sha'biyya*) locally. They had influence in Aleppo, Hama, Homs, and Idlib. Even in my village there were families linked to the events of the 1980s [when Islamists and the Muslim Brotherhood fought the regime]. They hated the regime. We knew these families, and saw them opening the door to the Islamists. Some of them even

received support from Libyan armed groups, some of whom came here to support the beginning of the uprising.

Another local military leader of a group affiliated to the Free Syrian Army similarly recognised that:

> The Islamists had a different vision. I come from the army and can only think of military issues: how to take over a checkpoint, use an array of weapons, prepare a battle, etc. But the Islamists had a more encompassing view and were better at organising themselves. While we were focusing on local battles, they were preparing for what's next.

Militarisation nonetheless remained initially limited. The non-violent wave of protests during the early months of the uprising persisted and was not overshadowed by the armed resistance to the regime. Many individuals who would later play a significant role in the armed opposition initially continued to participate in the demonstrations. The emergence of the armed opposition occurred simultaneously with the wider protest movement, rather than in opposition to it (Donker, 2019). Although some core leaders of Ahrar al-Sham chose not to participate in the demonstrations and instead focused on military preparations, others initially supported non-violent protests but were later convinced that violence was the only way to achieve political change in Syria. Preparations for a broader armed confrontation were already underway, though they remained relatively limited in scale. These developments were significant in shaping the early infrastructure of Ahrar al-Sham, which was centred on several core groups situated in northwest Syria that would later be able to mobilise on a larger scale once violence became the dominant strategy of the opposition movement.

Northwest Syria was uniquely situated with its border adjacent to Turkey, which is critical to gather the foreign support that underpins the sustainability of any armed opposition (Salehyan, 2007). In contrast to other Syrian regions quickly besieged by regime forces, northwest Syria remained open to foreign supporters since early in the uprising. The continuous access to Turkey allowed early armed groups from the region to maintain ties with their families and acquaintances abroad, and to gather rudimentary support during the first few months of the uprising. This support was largely structured around personal networks, as local Syrians whose family members were studying or working abroad gathered limited financial assistance to procure basic weapons in preparation for the war. This early support was instrumental in laying the foundation for the eventual emergence of larger and more coordinated armed groups in the region.

The Emergence of the Brigades that Formed Ahrar al-Sham

Ahrar al-Sham became the most successful Islamist group during the early stages of the uprising. The nature of its early coordinating mechanisms gave it an advantage over the numerous other armed groups that appeared at the same time, including those with similar ideologies. These distinctive features not only propelled Ahrar al-Sham to the forefront of the conflict, but also played a significant role in shaping the group's political stance throughout the war.

In the early stages of the uprising in northwest Syria, interconnection between activist networks facilitated their rapprochement. The necessity to face repression drew the activists and other Islamists closer regardless of pre-2011 differences of views. Even Saudi Salafi religious leaders, who had previously opposed violence in the Muslim world, embraced jihad in Syria due to the new circumstances (Wehrey, 2012; Ismail, 2021). Local Islamists began to gather resources independently from business entrepreneurs and local contacts, with the aim of acquiring weapons for the small military cells that they had formed. They also held meetings to strategise before the full militarisation of the conflict. The local brigades that eventually formed the nucleus of Ahrar al-Sham brigades (Kata'ib Ahrar al-Sham) mobilised before the official existence of the Free Syrian Army (FSA) in July 2011. Abu Abd al-Rahman al-Suri recalled this period, stating that:

> We had a lot of meetings with other individuals who also created their own small groups. We wanted to coordinate our work and know one another better. I met Khaled Abu Anas, who created a brigade in Saraqib, through common friends. We discussed the revolution in general terms. We quickly realised that we were close in terms of ideas so we decided to continue our work together. He was closer to the Salafi Jihadi trend and I was closer to the scholastic (*'ilmi*) tendency but we had good prospects together. We wanted something Islamic in terms for the general direction of our movement.

Ahrar al-Sham owes its early success to the decentralised multi-network structure of the groups associated with the latent Islamist social movement that started to congregate. These groups were interconnected through various social networks, including student organisations, religious circles, activists, and Jihadi militants. This interconnectivity facilitated the mobilisation of a large number of individuals with access to financial resources and/or experience in warfare. In contrast, small local armed groups faced significant organisational and military challenges due to their lack of experience in conflict. The multiple ties to other activists and Jihadis provided a unique strength to the nucleus that formed Ahrar al-Sham. The group's early members coordinated their efforts in Syria, Turkey, and the Gulf. Some individuals had past experience in jihads, including in Iraq in the 2000s, which provided them with valuable knowledge and skills in armed struggle, including in manufacturing explosives.[46] As discussed in chapter 5, this experience also contributed to the group's early ideological development.

Ahrar al-Sham's creation preceded the liberation of prisoners by the Syrian regime from mid-2011 onwards. A common argument states that Islamist armed groups, including Ahrar al-Sham, were the direct outcome of the liberation of prisoners convicted for their association with the Jihadi trend or support for jihad in Iraq (Abazeid & Pierret, 2018: 67). A cynical explanation is that the regime wanted to tarnish the popular uprising and contribute to its militarisation (Lister, 2015b: 53–55; Dagher, 2019: 253). It would then be easier to legitimise repression as a fight against "Islamist extremism" and al-Qaeda. But Ahrar al-Sham started to coalesce before prisoners' liberation. Most early members deny the centrality of pre-2011 prison network in stimulating the group's quick expansion between 2011 and 2012, since most early cells were not associated with prison networks. However, the release of Islamist prisoners from Saydnayya prison did reinforce pre-existing dynamics on the ground. The prisoners often had connections with Islamists preparing for the armed opposition outside of prison. Upon their release, they were able to bolster the mobilisation of early Ahrar al-Sham cells by contributing their own connections and experience.

The characteristics of prison networks were indeed congruent with the proprieties of the activist networks and the Islamist social movement. Prisoners had often known one another for years, having been collectively socialised and sharing similar views and experiences.[47] When they returned to their hometowns throughout Syria, it was not difficult to contact one another based on prison affinity. The widespread and loosely connected prison ties facilitated contacts and coordination through wide geographic areas. The prisoners jailed for their support of the Iraqi insurgency in the 2000s were often acquainted with contacts willing to mobilise for a new jihad in Syria.

These interconnected networks facilitated the interactions between pre-existing military units and newly liberated prisoners. Two prominent leaders of Ahrar al-Sham were connected through shared contacts when they officially formed the group. Khaled Abu Anas from Saraqib met Hassan Abud, who was recently freed from prison. They discussed a military union against the regime from their respective localities. Abu Anas lead the group's military units around Saraqib, while Hassan Abud was responsible for northern Hama and the Ghab province. Abud was already a well-respected figure whose reputation was well-known among northwest Islamists. Abu Anas wanted him to lead the group, which he accepted despite his initial reluctance. They officially formed the Ahrar al-Sham Brigades (Kata'ib Ahrar al-Sham). Abu Anas recalled that:

> I met Abul-Kheir,[48] Abu Ayman al-Ghab and others who had a group around Aleppo. We wanted to name a general amir for the group. Abu Nuran from Saydnayya proposed the name of Hassan Abud, who was both well known and trustworthy. Hassan said he was not ready and could not do it. We sent other youths to convince him since we wanted somebody known. I told him to lead in the Ghab plains while I lead the remaining group. Then after a few months we could reassess. We wanted to prepare something new for the Muslim community (*umma*), something that would be different from both al-Qaeda and the Muslim Brotherhood.

Ahrar al-Sham's decentralised organisational structure was a key factor in its resilience. By operating across multiple geographic areas and core military units, the group was less vulnerable to regime repression. Even if some of the group's sub-units were destroyed or certain areas were reoccupied by the regime, Ahrar al-Sham as a whole was unlikely to be completely obliterated, as might have been the case with factions rooted in a single locality. This decentralised approach allowed Ahrar al-Sham to maintain a certain level of autonomy and flexibility, with each sub-unit having its own leaders and decision-making processes. This not only helped to protect the group from regime attacks but also made it more agile and able to respond quickly to changing circumstances. The decentralised structure allowed Ahrar al-Sham to draw on a diverse pool of resources and expertise from different regions, which helped strengthen the group's overall capacity. This stands in contrast to factions that were located in one geographic area only or those that relied heavily on a single source of support or leadership.

Ahrar al-Sham's early reliance on decentralised social networks influenced its organisational development and provided a strong foundation for its future success. Recognising the weaknesses of other Jihadi groups in institutional work, Ahrar al-Sham's initial leaders made a conscious effort to establish a more cohesive and consensus-driven decision-making process from the group's inception. The group's reliance on a decentralised network of supporters across multiple geographic areas and localities informed and sustained this choice. Unlike other armed groups centred on a few local strongmen, Ahrar al-Sham's decentralised structure required a stronger internal consensus to maintain cohesion. To ensure that all sub-groups were represented and shared power equally, Ahrar al-Sham's first consultative council (*majlis al-shura*) was composed of representatives from each sub-group who made strategic decisions by majority vote. This approach allowed Ahrar al-Sham to become a more attractive alternative to armed groups formed by local strongmen, which were often unable to share power and resources effectively.⁴⁹ While the group was not yet fully institutionalised, its early days set the stage for a resilient and adaptable organisation. Another early founder hence insisted that:

> We discussed the formation of one bloc. We would consult each other and continue to organise meetings to attract others. We all wanted to work in consensus. A general meeting with 7 or 8 people was organised in Abul-Kheir's house to design a general plan. We wanted to be popular, not closed on ourselves, open, and not limited to a particular geographic area. We would be open to new people and call everybody to join in.

Ahrar al-Sham's structuring networks shaped its early ideological views. According to Husam Tarsha, a head of international relations for Ahrar al-Sham, the group initially consisted of individuals who either (1) had left the ideas promoted by al-Qaeda views early on, like Hassan Abud, (2) were associated with the Jihadi trend but aimed to correct the excesses committed by al-Qaeda, like Khaled Abu Anas, or (3) had experience in various places of jihad, like Iyad al-Sha'ar, who was previously close to the so-called godfather of the Jihadi movement, Abdullah Azzam (Tarsha, 2018). This combination of various trends alongside local Syrian Salafis structured Ahrar al-Sham around a political project that combined jihad with reform. Previous ideological differences between activists, scholars, and Jihadi Salafis dissipated in favour of a more mainstream Islamist sensibility still associated with the Salafi approach to Islam.

Each sub-group of Ahrar al-Sham initially conducted independent armed attacks while taking collective responsibility on behalf of the group. These sub-groups maintained their ties with other social networks that engaged in various activities unrelated to Ahrar al-Sham. Some of them were integrated into local military councils and alliances, such as Liwa al-Tawheed in Idlib city, which regrouped local Islamist military units. They also participated in the establishment of independent courts of justice after the withdrawal of regime forces. This arrangement allowed Ahrar al-Sham to maintain its local embeddedness throughout the areas that were controlled by the armed opposition forces in northwest Syria without contradicting their affiliation to Ahrar al-Sham. For example, Abu Abd al-Rahman al-Suri led a local court of justice and explained that:

> We were carrying out our work independently because of geographic differences. But we could still conduct additional work on our own. For instance I created an independent court of justice in Idlib that was not linked to Ahrar al-Sham. I was also in Liwa al-Tawheed in Idlib, which included all the local Islamist groups.

Ahrar al-Sham's unique organisational structures challenge the common notion that Islamist groups only succeeded with foreign, often Gulf-based, assistance. The group was an early riser into the Syrian conflict, with ties to multiple networks outside of Syria that facilitated individual and state-supported assistance from a wide range of supporters, including families and friends residing abroad, mainstream Islamists, Gulf-based activists (Pierret, 2016), and even disillusioned Jihadi supporters who were disappointed with al-Qaeda's direction. These networks of support, along with regional developments in the Middle East that had given Islamist militant networks the upper hand for over two decades, gave Ahrar al-Sham a strategic advantage over other groups. Moreover, the group's wider networks of support acted as a self-perpetuating advantage. Foreign supporters, including states, were more willing to provide assistance to a group that was already known and successful. As state support for the opposition grew in the following years, Ahrar al-Sham emerged as a credible and effective group on the ground, reinforcing its already established position.

Ahrar al-Sham's unique configuration also contributed to its appeal for unaffiliated military units. By incorporating new brigades into its organisational structures able to coordinate the war effort across Syria, even with limited contacts in other regions,[50] the group provided a recognisable, successful, and enticing umbrella. Unlike local groups that were primarily based in one location and often hesitant to share power, Ahrar al-Sham's decentralised structures were more receptive to the inclusion of new brigades.[51] Additionally, the group's diverse social networks, which included student, local, regional, and international networks, made it more accessible through various weak ties. Positioned between the Free Syrian Army (FSA) and more radical groups, Ahrar al-Sham attracted a wide range of groups from both ends of the spectrum, such as small brigades formerly associated with the Free Syrian Army and more committed Islamists. As a result, an increasing number of small groups, not necessarily Salafi or Islamists, joined the group through their social networks. A member of its political bureau reflected on this phenomenon, stating:

> When the uprising happened in Tunisia, we started to congregate to think about our next step in Syria. We discussed that in Damascus university where I was based and organised a few small demonstrations. The answer was very violent. Small groups therefore appeared everywhere with limited armament. They started to get closer and ally to form something bigger. My group did not join Ahrar al-Sham simply because of the group's ideas. It was primarily because Ahrar al-Sham was more organised and had a clearer agenda. Others had a poor reputation locally. We did not know everybody in Ahrar al-Sham but people from our group knew some of their leaders from their time in prison before, so it was easier.

Abu Khaled, who would later head Ahrar al-Sham's political bureau, added that:

> In the first phase, we were participating in demonstrations before joining Ahrar al-Sham when it was just a brigade (*katiba*). It was in reality the first armed brigade ever created, before the Free Syrian Army. Abu Abdullah al-Hamawi [Hassan Abud], who was known from prison, played a prominent role. We knew him through a common friend of the group. We were initially wondering what to do next, and that was the best possibility. We trusted him and his project.

The gradual strengthening of interactions between Ahrar al-Sham's constituent units fostered a growing sense of internal solidarity and a shared purpose. As the conflict with the regime progressed, increased coordination became necessary, as did the sharing of new war spoils. Initially, the group relied on a system of coordination between local units that made strategic decisions by consensus, but as cross-cell interactions became more frequent, a sense of belonging to a single political project solidified. As one of Ahrar al-Sham's early leaders observed:

> Initially, we carried out our military operations individually and claimed responsibility as Ahrar al-Sham. Then, Abu Abdullah [Hassan Abud] tried to make it a real union. So when people in the Ghab plains got spoils of war, Abu Abdullah decided to spread them among Ahrar al-Sham's units. That was the real beginning of Ahrar al-Sham as a group. The discourse changed after that. There were more exchanges. We could tell one another what we needed, and people would give it. It made us an attractive alternative to others. That was also the case vis-à-vis Jabhat al-Nusra. Jabhat al-Nusra was not widely known, including its leadership. People were more apprehensive. On the other hand, Ahrar al-Sham leaders were known in terms of histories, background, and families. It was easier to solve issues between us.

The Early Geography of the Conflict

The non-violent uprising that began in Syria quickly spread throughout the country, yet the geography of the conflict also hindered efforts to unite armed opposition-held areas in the years that followed. The regime's historical consolidation did not merely inform its response to the popular uprising and the choice to quash the protest with considerable violence. It also shaped the geography of the conflict at country and city levels.[52] These policies were historically designed to prevent internal dissent and protect core strategic interests, more than promote national integration and economic development per se. They were critical once the armed conflict started. Long-term historical patterns of developments affected the overall geography of the conflict—especially the disconnection between opposition-held areas—by determining to a large extent the regime's short-term tactical choices.

The uprising of the Syrian population in urban and rural areas significantly destabilised the regime. Within two years of the conflict, the regime lost control over most of the country. The existence of complementary types of grievances, from national-level grievances to local issues reflecting more narrow group-level grievances—which stemmed from the nature of state-society relations before the uprising (Mazur, 2021)—fuelled the growth of the protest movement. The uprising galvanised large segments of the Syrian population, even though they were not necessarily pursuing the same objectives. The Syrian conflict features a predominantly political schism between the regime and the opposition, with a myriad of smaller-scale issues intricately intertwined with this overarching divide. These encompass a spectrum of local and social concerns that, by and large, align with the broader political fault lines. As of mid-2013, Syria fractured, as delineated in the following map that highlights the intricate web of fronts separating opposition groups from the regime (see figure 2.1). This fragmentation underscores the erosion of the regime's authority over significant swaths of the country, which contributed to its growing dependence on external military forces, notably non-state armed groups hailing from Lebanon and Iraq.

The protest movement in Syria's major cities gained momentum as weekly demonstrations drew increasing numbers of supporters. The sectarian makeup of the regime's security apparatus limited its ability to suppress the protests. The regime lacked enough reliable troops to quell the unrest across the entire country, and in some areas, repression only encouraged further violent mobilisation by severing local intermediary structures that channeled grievances (Mazur, 2021). To address this challenge, the authorities decided to prioritise certain areas, which were later referred to as "useful Syria" after the regime resorted to militarization and repression to maintain control (Qutrib, 2016). Despite the regime's insistence that every inch of the country was a red line, Assad acknowledged in 2015 that territorial control over specific regions was necessary for regime survival, given the shortage of manpower to confront the opposition throughout the country (Samaan & Barnard, 2015).

The regime's strategic interests were centred on the cities, territories, and communication routes linking Damascus to the central region and the Alawi stronghold in the coastal areas near Latakia. Despite the Alawi heartland's weak integration into the Syrian state (Balanche, 2006a), maintaining ties to Damascus was critical to preserving the regime's structural backbone. Syria's

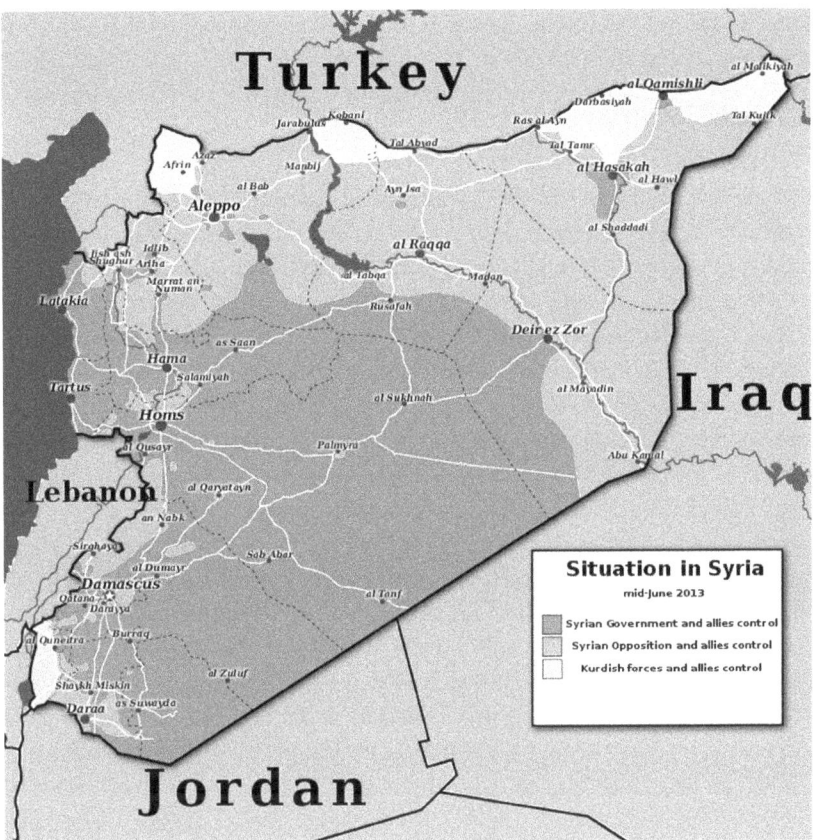

Figure 2.1 Territorial control in 2013
https://commons.wikimedia.org/wiki/File:Situation_in_Syria_(June_2013).svg

Russian ally shared this priority, as evidenced by its emphasis on the Tartus naval base, which provides strategic access to the Mediterranean Sea, complemented by the Hmeimim air base constructed during the war. These areas are home to most of Syria's urban population, including the economic elite. Despite opposition forces occupying the majority of Syria's territory by 2013, they never managed to seize the regime's strategic backbone. The regime's military priorities were therefore focused on preserving these areas, even as the opposition gained ground elsewhere in the country.

The need to maintain Syria's structural integrity informed the regime's military priorities. As the opposition gained control of parts of Syria's countryside, regime forces focused on securing the primary communication routes between Latakia and Damascus, especially around Homs. Certain areas near Damascus were particularly concerning, as they could potentially isolate the city from the rest of

Syria. To address this threat, the regime initially concentrated its efforts on a few key areas, including the Badiya, Daraya, Madaya, Zabadani, and the periphery of Homs. Regime forces were especially wary of the strategic link between Homs and Lebanon, which could provide support to local armed groups and create strategic depth. Only the eastern side of Damascus, in the Ghouta, remained outside of regime control until 2018. The regime also employed a strategy of local accommodation in Druze areas of Suweida to neutralise religious minorities and prevent them from siding with the opposition (Hokayem, 2017: 55).

Syria's cities faced varying challenges during the uprising, depending on their historical community structure and the regime's control strategy. There are two main patterns of city structure in Syria: mix-cities, where Sunni, Alawi, and potentially Kurds coexist (e.g., Lattaqiya, Banyas, and Homs), and cities that are more internally cohesive but externally encircled by communities more closely associated with the regime (Balanche, 2011, 2018). Aleppo features a hybrid pattern of both internal divisions and external encirclement. Damascus and Aleppo were relatively unaffected by the uprising compared to other Syrian cities, largely due to the regime's heavy presence and economic largesse before 2011 (including tourism and economic liberalisation). The regime's control prevented mobilisation, which was mainly limited to the suburbs. The core centre of Damascus was never directly threatened, while Aleppo—which is more closely associated with the business elite—remained under regime control during the war except for the more informal eastern districts, which were controlled by the opposition from July 2012 to the end of 2016. This division showed that local divisions were not only political but also socio-economic. Hama, a historically oppositional city to the Baath Party, remained under regime control throughout the conflict. Although massive protests occurred in the beginning of 2011, the city was never seized by the opposition.

But other cities in Syria experienced a different trajectory during the uprising and embraced the revolution. Homs was its major epicentre. Armed groups seized control of parts of the city early on, with Baab al-Amr neighbourhood being a focal point. The regime responded with a harsh siege that lasted for three years, from May 2011 to May 2014, before local armed groups were forcibly evacuated. Homs posed a significant threat to the regime due to its connection to northern Lebanon and its location near the highway linking Damascus to Aleppo. Two other cities were also lost by the regime until now. The first city to be controlled by the mainstream opposition, before their expulsion by ISIS/IS, was the eastern city of Raqqa. The second city was the provincial city of Idlib in the northwest, which remains in the hands of the mainstream armed opposition in 2024.

The regime's ability to maintain control over Syria's central cities and structural backbone allowed the armed opposition to control territories only in the periphery of the country. It also prevented armed groups from controlling continuous geographical areas, as opposed to distinct and disconnected territories, and hindered their ability to unite as a single body. This led to the development of distinct armed groups that mostly existed in isolated parts of the country. These features mean that issues such as the resort to foreign fighters and armed groups' connections to foreign states varied across regions.[53] The territorial evolution of the conflict by 2017 is illustrated in the following map, which shows the consolidation of four main armed opposition strongholds: (1) the northwest, (2) the east, (3) the Damascus periphery, and (4) the south, along with isolated pockets, particularly around Homs (figure 2.2). With the exception of the neighbourhoods situated in the periphery of Damascus, these areas maintained external access to foreign supporters, which provided some level of strategic depth to local armed groups. External support enabled them to maintain their

Figure 2.2 The division of armed opposition-held areas by 2017
https://commons.wikimedia.org/wiki/File:Situation_in_Syria_(September_2017).svg

territorial hold by providing logistical support, access to new weaponry, and a safe haven for some of their commanders and leaders, although the nature and consequences of this external support varied overtime.

Northwest Syria was the first region to be largely controlled by armed opposition and the last region to remain outside of regime control. Local armed groups seized control of its borders by mid-2012, paving the way for extensive external support through Turkey. Northwest Syria was not strategically significant like other regions. It is home to mostly Sunni Muslims that the regime neglected and did not trust since the Baathist regime took over, especially after the wide region stretching from Hama to the Turkish border rebelled against the authorities in the late 1970s. The main threat to the regime was the region's geographic proximity to the Alawi stronghold in the coastal areas, but a natural barrier in the form of a mountain range and limited communication axes hindered the armed opposition's expansion to this region.

Eastern Syria was the second major armed opposition stronghold, with the city of Raqqa being the first provincial capital to fall under full armed opposition control in 2013, when regime forces withdrew due to the armed opposition's military pressure. Eastern Syria is more rural and tribal than the strategic backbone in the west, with a population of 3.5 million inhabitants before 2011 between the governorates of Deir el-Zor, Hassaka, and Raqqa. The region's northern border with Turkey is home to most of Syria's Kurdish population, which critically shaped the armed opposition's trajectory in the area and later informed Turkey's involvement. The strategic importance of eastern Syria lies mainly in the presence of oil and gas, which account for most of Syria's production.

Apart from the periphery of Damascus, which directly threatened the capital city, the Daraa governorate in the south was the last region seized by armed groups. The Syrian uprising began in this governorate, historically a stronghold of the Baath Party. The early development of the uprising in the region was underpinned by the structure of these dense local social networks (Leenders, 2012). Throughout the phase of armed opposition control, the south remained connected to Jordan, which imposed tight control over external support, in contrast to Turkey. Jordan feared a domestic backlash, which prevented the relatively uncontrolled flow of foreign fighters witnessed in the north. Additionally, the south's local societal makeup was more cohesive than in the northwest, which limited internal clashes between armed groups with only a few exceptions.

The armed opposition was confined to specific provinces throughout the entirety of the conflict, with local dynamics influenced by each region's unique history, geography, and regime policies shaping the type of armed opposition that could emerge and consolidate. Although the presence of extensive front lines with the regime presented a threat, due to a lack of sufficient manpower to simultaneously face the armed opposition throughout the country, these divergences also reinforced the internal diversity of the opposition and obstructed the creation of a strong nationwide alternative to the regime. However, geographic diversity was not the only challenge faced by the Syrian opposition.

Comparing Armed Groups' Specificities

During the first two years of the Syrian conflict, many armed groups emerged alongside Ahrar al-Sham. However, most of these groups were short-lived and only a limited number of entities survived.[54] Many of these marginal military units didn't last more than a few weeks or months, and some didn't even leave any written evidence of their existence.[55] To understand the development of Ahrar al-Sham in comparison to the most notable armed opposition groups, this retrospective analysis highlights specific and shared patterns of development with the main other actors.[56] By examining the choices of Ahrar al-Sham's leaders in light of the conflict's constraints and opportunities, this comparison suggests that Ahrar al-Sham was unique in featuring the most favourable characteristics for organisational survival during the first phase of the conflict. Understanding the processes of armed groups' consolidation in armed conflicts is crucial to show how militants, irrespective of their particular ideological leanings, encounter diverse choices that shape their trajectories over time (Hafez, Gabbay, & Gade, 2021).

The dichotomy between arguably secular groups affiliated with the Free Syrian Army and Islamists does not adequately capture the early days of the plethora of armed groups that formed in Syria.[57] Early armed groups differed primarily in terms of their local embeddedness, geographic reach, and the type of relationships between their sub-units. As most military units began locally, these factors suggest that the most significant factor influencing the survival, consolidation, or division was their comparative modes of organisation. Organisational factors that facilitated coordination and integration across different localities were critical to armed groups' early trajectories. These factors largely shaped the evolution of armed groups and their prospects of survival in the beginning of the conflict. These factors were ultimately largely informed by the type of pre-war networks on which armed groups' early mobilisation relied upon, which also informed their capacity to garner external support and establish connections with supporters and, later, state sponsors, as argued by Gopal & Hodge (2021).

Several military units emerged under the Free Syrian Army label, which gained prominence early on in the conflict. These insurgent organisations formed for specific battles, often to defend or seize a city before moving elsewhere. One of them, Liwa al-Tawheed, emerged during the battle of Aleppo in the summer of 2012. It aggregated many small units that were established early on around villages, neighbourhoods, and groups of acquaintances. The group synchronised their efforts to seize the city of Aleppo, but it did not rely on clear pre-existing social networks. Liwa al-Tawheed did not survive the death of its charismatic leader, Abdul Qader Saleh, in November 2013. Its sub-groups joined other fronts and movements, illustrating the failure to create lasting institutional structures beyond personal or sub-group loyalty. Another organisation, Liwa Khalid ibn Walid, was formed in the Homs governorate by army deserters starting in the summer of 2011 to defend the city of Homs during a siege imposed by the regime. Parts of the Liwa were included in the al-Faruq Brigades (Kata'ib al-Faruq) in the neighbourhood of Bab Amr, where the regime siege was particularly prominent, before expanding elsewhere. The third group, Ahfad al-Rasul, expanded throughout Syria by aggregating many units composed of locals and army deserters with some level of external support. Despite their successes, these insurgents struggled to create lasting institutional structures beyond their immediate fighting units, which limited their ability to provide a coherent alternative to the regime.[58]

These groups' main weakness was to outstretch quickly in absence of wide supporting networks and shared ideological leanings. These organisations grew too quickly and without building internal resilience, causing splits along personal and local divides, followed by sub-units joining other groups as foreign support diminished. Unlike Ahrar al-Sham, which consolidated its position by relying on the Islamist social movement and ideological proximity, these large early insurgents gathered primarily for military reasons without strong underpinning networks. Loyalty remained based on sub-groups structured around particular geographic areas or prominent individuals. As a result, they were unable to survive external rivalries between countries that started to support their favourite factions.[59] Instead, they dissolved as organised groups and reconstituted themselves in other larger entities.[60] These groups epitomise cases of "mismanaged expansion that undermines social relationships and strains processes of socialization and control" when armed groups vie "to seize territory and bring in new social blocs" to seize new places (Staniland, 2014: 41).

Only a small number of these groups managed to consolidate and maintain relative cohesion throughout the entirety of the Syrian conflict. These groups primarily remained in their hometowns and did not expand throughout Syria like the groups that outstretched or like Ahrar al-Sham or Jabhat al-Nusra, which allowed them to avoid overstretching and maintain their early geographic strongholds. Their ideological leanings were unclear, but they often included conservative Muslims and Islamists without well-defined ideological identities. Unlike other groups, these local groups remained embedded within a relatively narrow geographic area, with some expanding to other areas for a limited time before shrinking back to their strongholds. Their regions were not reoccupied by the regime, allowing them to consolidate without facing the organisational challenges associated with unchecked expansion. They brought together allied families, clans, and local strongmen around a strong local identity, which helped to maintain local anchorage over time. The most notable of these groups were located in the Idlib province, as it remained under the control of the armed opposition the longest. Although these groups were not necessarily dissociated from the Islamist social movement, their local identities and embeddedness took precedence over other affiliations.

Two out of three of these factions did, in a subsequent phase of the war, partially integrate or ally with Ahrar al-Sham considering the nature of its strategy of alliance in the region.[61] These groups are the Nour al-Din al-Zinki movement (Harakat Nur al-Din al-Zinki, Zinki Movement thereafter), Suqur al-Sham (Alwiyya Suqur al-Sham), and Jaysh al-'Izza (the Army of Glory). They are all based in northwest Syria. The Zinki Movement originated in the countryside of Aleppo in late 2011 and played a significant role in the Battle of Aleppo. Despite joining and leaving many cross-group alliances, including Ahrar al-Sham later in the conflict, the Zinki Movement maintained its local embeddedness and organisational cohesion throughout the entire conflict.[62] The group was initially a part of Liwa al-Tawheed before reasserting its independent existence. The Zinki Movement emerged as a coalition of local brigades around a local leader, which did not spread randomly but remained in contiguous areas to preserve its internal cohesion. The group aimed to protect its local constituents by providing basic social services and security and defending its members against external attacks, which limited organisational dissension (Hussein, 2017g).

Suqur al-Sham is an armed group that emerged early in the conflict in the Zawiyya mountains. It has had a fluctuating relationship with Ahrar al-Sham. It was involved in the initial discussions for its creation but, although Suqur al-Sham joined and left Ahrar al-Sham several times, it maintained its coherence and independence as a distinct group over time. During the early stages of the conflict, Suqur al-Sham expanded its presence in different parts of the country, but eventually, it consolidated its territorial control in the Zawiyya mountains only. Internal tensions over resources, such as foreign support and war spoils, rather than purely ideological differences, contributed to some subfactions defecting to the Islamic State (IS) (Chivers, 2015).[63] Over time, Suqur al-Sham significantly declined in its size and influence, shifting from being one of the largest opposition groups to a more localised entity centred on its original strongholds. Ahrar al-Sham leaders attribute Suqur al-Sham's limited integration into their organization to factors such as the group's strong local identity and issues with its leadership.

The last faction remained more isolated during the conflict. Jaysh al-'Izza was formed in north Hama by army deserters from all of Syria in alliance with local residents.⁶⁴ The group historically gathered local brigades present in northern Hama around Latamneh and Tamina around a defected officer, Jamil al-Saleh, and army dissidents (Puxton, 2017). The group's consolidation accompanied its organisational evolution from Liwa Shuhada al-Tamina (the Legion of the Martyrs of Tamina) to Tajamu' Kata'ib wa Alwiya al-I'za (the Gathering of the Brigades of Glory) in 2013 and Jaysh al-'Izza (the Army of Glory) in 2015. The group's limited geographic expansion combined with the supervision of army officers kept it closer to embeddedness with its local constituency (Muhammad, 2019).

Ahrar al-Sham shares several features with another major Salafi armed group, Jaysh al-Islam (the Army of Islam), despite several key differences. Jaysh al-Islam, like Ahrar al-Sham, has roots in the Islamist social movement, but with a more limited geographic focus on the Ghouta area near Damascus.⁶⁵ A religious preacher, Zahran Alloush, formed the group by teaming up with fourteen other individuals after his release from prison in mid-2011, mobilising pre-2011 religious proselytisation (*da'wa*) networks in Duma, Alloush's hometown, which initially hesitated to join the group and engage in violence but eventually gave it a distinct Salafi scholastic (*'ilmi*) religious identity as they joined the group.⁶⁶ However, unlike Ahrar al-Sham, Jaysh al-Islam was based in a small, besieged area, which hindered its coordination and interaction with other parts of Syria. The group was also formed around its charismatic leader and lacked the multifaceted leadership structure of Ahrar al-Sham. Despite real ideological differences, some of its early units might have integrated with Ahrar al-Sham had they been based in the northwest.⁶⁷ Faylaq al-Rahman (the Mercy Corps), a smaller group that emerged from the Zayd Sufi congregation, also shared Jaysh al-Islam's localism and pre-existing religious networks but did not become a major actor in the conflict.

In contrast with other groups, Jabhat al-Nusra⁶⁸ emerged from a pre-existing armed group when a commander of the Islamic State in Iraq (ISI), Abu Muhammad al-Jolani, and several of his associates moved from Iraq to Syria in 2012. Syrians active outside the country created the group, in contrast with Ahrar al-Sham's consolidation around local Islamists only sporadically supported by activists from abroad. Al-Jolani proposed the formation of Jabhat al-Nusra to ISI as a project that would avoid repeating the mistakes of ISI in Iraq, given the different nature of the Syrian jihad as a domestic struggle rather than a reaction against foreign occupation (Atun, 2016a).⁶⁹ In an interview conducted in Idlib, al-Jolani argued that:

> When the war started in Iraq in 2003, there was a strong popular sentiment in the region against the U.S. invasion. Our thinking was simple at the time, and we went to fight there. We were not as aware as we are today. We were later taken

by surprise by the extreme ideology that emerged in prisons in Iraq, the culture of extremism (*ghulu*). In 2011, when the Arab spring and the Syrian revolution started, it was time to come back and join the struggle.⁷⁰

Jabhat al-Nusra leaders also emphasised the negative impact of harsh governance measures on the population in Iraq and sectarian warfare against Shia Muslims, aligning with Ahrar al-Sham's early criticisms of al-Qaeda. Abu Maria al-Qahtani, the group's first religious leader (*mufti*), specifically cited extremism (*ghulu*), indiscriminate killings, and excommunication as practices that alienated supporters in Algeria and Iraq and caused internal divisions (Al-Qahtani, n.d.). However, Jabhat al-Nusra still considered itself Salafi in religious creed while rejecting accusations of indiscriminate excommunications (Jabhat al-Nusra, n.d.). Another of the group's highest religious authority, Sami al-Uraydi, a close associate of Abu Muhammad al-Maqdisi, who left Jabhat al-Nusra when the group renounced its ties to al-Qaeda, insisted that Jabhat al-Nusra was Salafi yet willing to fight alongside all Syrian factions without excommunicating the population (Uraydi, 2012).The group aligned with al-Qaeda leader Ayman al-Zawahiri's guidelines for jihad in 2013, which emphasised collaboration with other armed groups and minimizing civilian casualties but diverged on the issue of foreign operations. While al-Zawahiri emphasised targeting the far enemy – Western countries –, Jabhat al-Nusra insisted that it would not conduct foreign operations.⁷¹ Abu Abdullah al-Shami, the group's current main religious authority, reflected on its early positioning, stating:

> ISI [IS previous name] became very violent in Iraq from 2006 to 2011. Its behaviour negatively impacted peoples' perception. We opposed extreme violence. I oppose it in Islamic law but also in terms of political and popular perceptions. In the beginning, we were linked to al-Qaeda through ISI but we agreed with both of them that we would only be involved locally. Our only focus was the Syrian revolution. We wanted to fight Bashar and his supporters, nobody else. So when the non-violent demonstrations militarised, many people who were in Iraq thought that they should do something in Syria as well. They felt part of this movement. Jabhat al-Nusra was part of the revolution from the beginning, although the group is not all the revolution. The problem is that we were not treated as an outcome of a local process. We were seen as al-Qaeda. But al-Qaeda has different faces. al-Qaeda in 2004 in Iraq is not like al-Qaeda in 2011 in Syria. And it is also not like al-Qaeda in 2001 in Afghanistan.

Compared to Ahrar al-Sham, which consolidated around decentralised local brigades, Jabhat al-Nusra adopted a top-down approach to mobilisation. Early group leaders initially gathered in Damascus before spreading throughout the country, using their pre-existing networks to recruit individuals and orchestrate high-level bombings against regime forces.[72] The group's early members solicited individual allegiances (*bay'a*) and personal recommendations (*tazkiyya*) in a top-down process of mobilisation and ideological indoctrination. They also coordinated with newly liberated prisoners, although most Islamist prisoners joined other groups, according to former prison leaders.[73] During the first phase of the war, Jabhat al-Nusra's spectacular armed attacks did not require mass mobilisation.[74] The group's subsequent mobilisation only occurred in a relatively controlled manner, including among Islamist activists. Although the group remained relatively small in number during this phase, it had a notable military impact. Abu Abdullah al-Shami elaborated on some of the differences between Jabhat al-Nusra and Ahrar al-Sham:

> In the beginning of the revolution, we knew people across the regions. For example, we knew somebody in Hama who knew somebody from Deir al-Zur who was close to us. We expanded on this basis. In contrast with Ahrar al-Sham, though, we did not keep pre-existing factions intact. If you do that, you can sanctify their regionalism. So we took people individually, trained them, and usually sent them back to their regions. The process was more centralised.

In addition to primarily Syrian groups, foreigners also established small brigades in the beginning of the conflict. These groups primarily formed in north and northwest Syria thanks to its proximity with the border with Turkey, although Jordanians reached the south of Syria and Lebanese militants the province of Homs as well. The groups included contingents from an array of countries, including Chechnya (Ajnad al-Kawkaz, Junud al-Sham), Central Asia and China (Hizb al-Islami al-Turkistani, the Turkistan Islamic Party), Gulf countries (Suqur al-'Iz), Libya (Kata'ib al-Muhajireen, Liwa al-Umma), and Morocco (Harakat Sham al-Islam).[75] Most of them enjoyed cordial relations with Ahrar al-Sham. Some of these groups had a well-defined identity and objective before joining the conflict, while others were formed specifically for it. One such group that pre-existed the Syrian conflict is the Turkistan Islamic Party, which has its origins in the Islamic Movement of Oriental Turkistan that was created in 1997 under the Taliban regime, to which it likely pledged allegiance (Mantoux, 2017). The Turkistan Islamic Party (TIP) arrived in Syria in 2012 and evolved into a formidable military force by 2015, according to two of its leaders and military commanders.[76] Although some groups remained largely independent, others successfully integrated themselves into particular localities and recruited Syrian locals as well. That was the case with Kata'ib al-Muhajireen (the Brigades of the Immigrants), which became Jaysh al-Muhajireen wal-Ansar (the Army of the Immigrants and the (local)

Supporters), when it allied with local Syrians drawn from Jaysh Muhammad and Usud al-Sunna. Some groups became famous for mobilising European combatants, such as Majlis Shura al-Mujahideen created by the Absi brothers in the north of Syria that was particularly prominent for recruiting many Belgium, Dutch, and French citizens (Van Ostaeyen & Van Vlierden, 2017).[77] The foreign groups subsequently played an important role in the split between Jabhat al-Nusra and ISI, when the latter aggregated most foreign brigades in its ranks, as argued in the next chapter.[78]

The militarisation of the uprising further marginalised the Muslim Brotherhood, which was previously considered the main opposition to the regime in Syria. Despite the group's notable political role in exile, its organisational structures were moribund inside Syria (Lefèvre, 2013: 170–179; Díaz, 2017: 76–103; Conduit, 2019: 134–152). The Brotherhood did not form its own faction in Syria and mainly operated abroad, where the exiled opposition was trying to establish a political alternative to the regime (Lund, 2013c).[79] Although some individual initiatives, such as the Commission for the Protection of Civilians, provided logistical support to military groups, the Brotherhood's efforts lacked organisation and success in co-opting other groups (Lefèvre & El Yassir, 2014; al-Musa, 2020). After September 2012, the Muslim Brotherhood provided assistance to the Shields of the Revolution (Duru' al-Thawra), but their military coordination lacked efficiency and internal discipline. The Brotherhood was perceived as an old organisation incapable of addressing the challenges faced by the armed opposition, and many groups accepted its support without endorsing its demands. In the case of Ahrar al-Sham, one early leader insisted that:

> Individuals from the Muslim Brotherhood reached out to us as new territory was liberated. They said that they could help us on condition. They wanted to change the name of our groups and impose strict terms and conditions on our actions. We refused it. If they wanted to help, they could do it for God, without conditions. They tried many times, with all the factions.

The last category of armed groups, which evolved in parallel to the primarily Sunni Arab groups,[80] is the dominant Kurdishroup. The Kurdish Democratic Union Party established the YPG (People's Protection Units) along the withdrawal of regime forces from broad Kurdish areas (Caves, 2012; ICG, 2014; Allsopp & van Wilgenburg, 2019). I do not examine this group in-depth considering that its organisational construction occurred independently from Sunni Arab armed opposition groups, which are antagonistic to Kurdishclaims of autonomy or potential claims of independence. The YPG is organically associated with the Turkish-based PKK, from which many prominent leaders and cadres stemmed when the Kurdish Democratic Union Party (PYD) emerged in Syria in

2003. It adopts a similar ideology based on Abdullah Occalan's ideas, although it subsequently tried to downplay organisational ties to the mother organisation.

The accompanying table compares key features of several groups and their impact on their early trajectories (table 2.1). These features include armed groups' local embeddedness in Syrian communities, the presence of an Islamist agenda, their territorial expansion, and whether they lost control of their localities to the regime. These hypotheses synthesise important findings from existing research in civil war studies and serve as alternative explanations to my argument on armed groups' underlying networks and institutionalisation.

This comparison highlights Ahrar al-Sham's unique characteristics in comparison to other Syrian armed opposition groups. Ahrar al-Sham featured a hybrid pattern of development, which combined other groups' essential features. Its first military units benefited from the local embeddedness of factions that emerged through a bottom-up process throughout Syria. However, unlike factions that were only based in one main stronghold, Ahrar al-Sham emerged in several places simultaneously in areas that were not besieged by the regime and remained well-connected to foreign supporters. As a result, Ahrar al-Sham did not rely on a single strong leader. The group's embeddedness in activist networks associated with the latent Islamist social movement, ideological proximity, and gradual bottom-up consolidation allowed it to avoid over-stretching, which led to the disappearance of other groups. Ahrar al-Sham's cross-factional consolidation eventually distinguished it from Jabhat al-Nusra as well, which also partially exploited shared prison and international supporting networks but for a more elitist—and therefore limited—mobilisation. These complementary characteristics have enabled Ahrar al-Sham to build internal cohesion based on decentralised organizational structures united by core ideas.

Ahrar al-Sham Takes the Initiative

Ahrar al-Sham's singular trajectory in the beginning of the conflict facilitated its external institutionalisation with other actors as well. The group's early characteristics facilitated its expansion, the consolidation of shared ideas, and the establishment of preliminary organisational structures that contrasted with most other groups' reliance on a single geographic area, leader, or military necessity. These features positioned Ahrar al-Sham at the forefront of numerous initiatives proposed by armed groups inside Syria to lead the armed opposition by the end of 2013. They underpinned the group's attempts to institutionalise externally with other actors despite real obstacles.

Ahrar al-Sham's organisational configuration made it a critical broker of the armed opposition in Syria. Its extensive ties to wide decentralised networks inside

Table 2.1 Armed groups' comparative features in the beginning of the conflict

	Local embeddedness	Islamist leanings?	Pre-existing networks	Presence in wide geographic areas	Strategic location lost to the regime	Future of the group
Ahrar al-Sham	Yes	Salafi (all trends)	Yes	Yes	No	**Institutionalisation of cross-factional ties**
Jabhat al-Nusra/ISIS	Initially limited	Salafi Jihadi	Yes	Yes	No	Substantial expansion
Jaysh al-Islam (Jaysh al-Islam)	Yes	Scholastic Salafi ('ilmi)	Yes	No	No	Independent, joining other alliances
Foreign brigades	No or little	Mostly Salafi Jihadi	Abroad	No	No	Independence of some, the majority joined IS
Al-Tawheed / al-Faruq	Yes	Partially Islamist for Taweed	Limited	Yes	Yes	Split along constituting units
Faylaq al-Rahman	Yes	Sufi	Yes	No	No	Independent, joining other alliances
Suqur al-Sham (Suqur al-Sham)	Yes	Partially Islamist	Limited	Only initially, then no	No	Independent, joining other alliances
Zinki Movement (Zinki Movement)	Yes	Partially Islamist	No	No	No	Independent, joining other alliances
Ahfad al-Rasul	Yes	No	No	Yes	No	Split along constituting units
Jaysh al-'Izza	Yes	No	No	No	No	Independent, joining other alliances

[a] The three groups are described as "partially Islamist," since they included local Islamist and non-Islamist figures around political programmes that made some references to Islam without being overtly Islamist.

and outside Syria facilitated the flow of resources and people, and strengthened its interconnection with a plurality of actors. Unlike the factions affiliated with the Free Syrian Army, which quickly split and reconfigured due to their localism and organisational inability to transform into a lasting national alternative, and more elitist Jihadi groups like Jabhat al-Nusra, which initially did not attempt to become an alternative to other groups, Ahrar al-Sham gradually became the leading armed opposition group. Local gatherings and congregations of army deserters lacked the same connections, while Jabhat al-Nusra remained focused on covert military actions and abstained from proposing political initiatives.

To illustrate its attempts to institutionalise externally, Ahrar al-Sham established its political bureau outside Syria early on. This move aimed to strengthen its ties to external actors and develop new ideas.[81] Ahrar al-Sham's political bureau would be critical in opposing a potential international designation as a proscribed group in the following years (Tarsha, 2018).[82] Recognising that insurgencies cannot be won solely through military means, Ahrar al-Sham's leaders understood the importance of developing their political positions and nurturing ties with other groups. They sought to present new proposals to unite the opposition and expand their political understanding. Husam Tarsha, head of Ahrar al-Sham's international relations, recalled that:

> The political branch of the group preceded the transformation of Ahrar al-Sham from brigades to movement, when we unified with other groups. It was an important step that allowed us to put our ideas together. When we created a political office, the idea was to publicise who we are and what we stand for. It aimed at presenting our movement abroad with accurate information regarding our positions. We suffered from misrepresentation and so it is important to facilitate the representation of our movement abroad.

Ahrar al-Sham's consolidation as a congregation of several armed brigades influenced its approach to institutionalising ties with other armed groups as well. The group's trajectory led it to prioritise establishing larger fronts that could coordinate the political positions and armed attacks of the main armed groups, paving the way for a potential organisational integration. The scattered geography of the conflict made a top-down approach unfeasible, where one armed group could simply absorb all other factions throughout Syria. Instead, coordinating with other factions on a relatively equal basis before creating shared organisational structures was more suitable. Ahrar al-Sham initiated several proposals to unite the opposition inside Syria through successive fronts that could coordinate and unify the main armed groups operating in the country. One of the first attempts was the creation of Syria's Revolutionary Front (Jabhat Thuwar Suria) in 2011,[83] which gathered mostly Ahrar al-Sham and smaller

Islamist groups active at the time (Lund, 2012: 39–41). Although this front did not achieve its objectives, it was part of Ahrar al-Sham's early learning curve.

The creation of fronts highlights two significant internal and external challenges that affected many opposition groups, including Ahrar al-Sham, and hindered their external institutionalisation efforts. The first internal challenge relates to developing realistic political positions that group members can comprehend and agree upon. Members fighting on the front lines may hold more radical political views than their leaders, because they may not fully appreciate the necessity of political realism (Shapiro, 2013). According to Tarsha, the relative failure of the Syria's Revolutionary Front helped Ahrar al-Sham realise that it needed to be more responsive to the expectations of its sub-brigades and engage in thorough consultations rather than imposing proposals from the top-down:

> Our ideas were not always aligned with our popular support on the ground. People loved the revolution and were very zealous. The leader has to evolve alongside his soldiers but we were pushing for an ideological development that was initially too quick. We needed to take the time for our supporters to evolve alongside us. The second issue concerned other armed opposition groups. Some of them wanted to capture the direction of the revolution and did not endorse our move.

Khaled Abu Anas added that:

> We created Syria's Revolutionary Front in the beginning. I believed that it was a good idea but it had some negative repercussions. I was more aware of how things were perceived on the ground than the brothers outside Syria. They announced many things on TV which could then be used against us inside. Some brigades would stop supporting us and take distance. We could not do that so we withdrew.

The second issue faced by opposition groups during the conflict was cross-group differences. The diversity of the armed opposition posed a challenge to the consolidation of fronts, as groups often had ideological divergences or differences in administrative choices. For instance, after the creation of the Syria's Revolutionary Front, armed groups established the Syrian Islamic Liberation Front, which brought together large Islamist-leaning factions such as Suqur al-Sham, Kata'ib al-Faruq, Liwa al-Islam (later Jaysh al-Islam), and Liwa al-Tawheed. Armed groups also held discussions to unite the Syrian Islamic Liberation Front and Ahrar al-Sham–led Syria's Revolutionary Front, given their geographic and ideological proximity. However, these discussions failed due to diverging views on the legitimacy of parliamentarian democracy, which was supported only by the Syrian Islamic Liberation Front. As a result, Ahrar al-Sham established the Syria Islamic Front (al-Jabha al-Islamiyya al-Suriyya) to unite with smaller factions instead.[84] According to Tarsha, the failure of the union between the two fronts was due to the following:

> We disagreed with other Islamists on the reference to democracy, as we wanted to avoid a confusion between recognising people's authority, which is in our fundamental principles, and democracy as an ideology and frame of reference that stems from the Western intellectual, political, and ideological traditions, which we disagree with. We believe that Syrians can choose their leaders in the system of the "people who loosen and bind" (*ahl al-hal wal-'aqd*), which is part of the Shura (consultative) system in Islam. However, mentioning democracy from the beginning was an issue. Our priority is the liberation of the land, not what comes after. Why present and impose that in the first place? There will be a time for this after the liberation of the country. We instead wanted to bring all the factions together. In addition, there were also other reasons that explain the failure of the initiative, including that it was too quick, without a real structure and internal regulations. It was just a media announcement while we sought to sort out the details first and then move forward.

During this period, Ahrar al-Sham had a complex relationship with the local population. While the group refrained from imposing harsh regulations associated with the Islamic penal punishments (*hudud*) in the territories under its control, it did contribute to the radicalisation of public discourse in Syria. Ahrar al-Sham was among the actors that introduced an Islamist discourse that was not prevalent at the start of the Syrian uprising, which fuelled the sectarianisation of the conflict framed by pro-regime and pro-opposition actors alike.[85] Ahrar al-Sham leaders used the pejorative term *nusairy* to describe Alawis,[86] and believed that in a post-Assad Syria, only (Sunni) Muslims could control the presidency and main sovereign ministries.[87] However, Ahrar al-Sham did develop a more moderate discourse on minorities over time (Lund, 2013a: 22). For example, its 2013 charter (Ahrar al-Sham, 2013) called for respect for religious minorities as an integral part of Syrian society. Nonetheless, Human Rights Watch (2013) denounced Ahrar al-Sham for participating in an armed attack in which Alawi civilians were killed, although this attack did not reflect the group's general military approach.

Ahrar al-Sham consolidated as the largest Syrian armed opposition group by 2013, surpassing both more radical Islamist factions and mainstream Free Syrian Army groups. What set Ahrar al-Sham apart was its ability to consolidate numerous military units under a single organisational umbrella, which enabled it to spearhead multiple initiatives aimed at uniting the armed opposition, distinct from the mainstream Syrian groups based in Istanbul. This internal institutionalisation and structural configuration enhanced its appeal and attracted growing external support, including from regional states such as Turkey and Qatar. Some of the group's members' pre-2011 ties in Qatar also played a role in securing its backing, as argued in chapter 4. This self-reinforcing dynamic gave Ahrar al-Sham a significant advantage over other groups in leading the opposition against the Syrian regime.

Conclusion

In personal interviews, Ahrar al-Sham leaders and members often emphasise that the group's early successes were not due solely to its military prowess, but also to its clear political views and objectives. They argue that this bolstered the group's credibility and attractiveness to Syrians seeking an alternative to the Assad regime. Yet others argue that many Syrians joined Islamist armed groups like Ahrar al-Sham because they were better resourced, better organised, and active in key battles, and because these groups were more aligned with their values (Mironova, 2019: 67–84). But they do not fully account for why Islamist groups like Ahrar al-Sham were able to gain such prominence and support in the early stages of the conflict.

The early success of Ahrar al-Sham in the Syrian armed opposition can largely be attributed to its unique characteristics. In the absence of autonomous and strong civil society, Ahrar al-Sham's initial entrepreneurs created local military units like most other armed groups. Ahrar al-Sham's main peculiarity was its early internal and external institutional trajectory. The group's pre-2011 activist networks and association with a largely latent social movement helped to strengthen the ties between its constituent units and fostered trust and cooperation. Building their group step by step, Ahrar al-Sham leaders avoided over-stretching and instead developed real institutional capabilities through a decentralised organisational structure based on consensual decision-making, in contrast with the brigades that attracted substantial foreign support without building real institutional capabilities and collapsed when external support switched sides or ceased. This approach facilitated the integration of a large number of individuals with previous experience in insurgency, which fostered the group's initial learning curve. Ahrar al-Sham's trajectory also contributed to the external institutionalisation of its ties to other groups through a succession of alliances that marked its strategic approach to the unification of the opposition. Jabhat al-Nusra was comparatively much smaller initially, focusing on planning spectacular armed operations that did not require large organisational structures.

3
Expanding the Rebellion

The characteristics of the Syrian regime before 2011 played a significant role in the militarisation of the uprising and the localism of the armed opposition. But, as the conflict intensified, armed groups had to transform from an irregular insurgency into more conventional forces.[1] They realised that remaining isolated local military units would not be sufficient to confront the regime and provide a viable alternative to the population. The need for larger, more organised and co-ordinated groups was crucial to effectively challenge the regime. While smaller brigades could only remain localised, larger groups were capable of consolidating themselves and expanding to other regions. However, the enduring geographic separation of armed opposition–held areas posed a significant challenge, as the opposition failed to gain control over contiguous territory on a national scale.

The fragmentation of Syria, with armed groups controlling disconnected areas, had a significant impact on the internal and external institutionalisation of the armed opposition. Each region under its control featured unique characteristics that shaped the emergence and survival of multiple groups during the early phase of the conflict. These characteristics influenced the type of armed group that could thrive in each area, as well as the nature of cross-factional interactions and the stability of local orders. This chapter analyses the armed opposition across Syria, with a particular focus on the northwest, and examines the key factors that contributed to Ahrar al-Sham's rise to dominance by 2014.

The Evolution of the Front Lines and Its Consequences

Armed opposition groups began to seize territory in irregularly scattered areas of Syria in 2012. Local civilians loosely grouped together in a patchwork of military units armed with limited weaponry seized these areas, reflecting the regime's inability to maintain control over these territories under popular pressure. While most of the territories were located along Syria's borders with Iraq, Jordan, Lebanon, and Turkey, locals also took over pockets in cities such as Damascus, Homs—particularly in Rastan—and northern Hama. Borderlands often connected populations situated on the other side of the border, providing logistical support for the armed opposition. In the summer of 2012, a coalition

From Jihad to Politics. Jerome Drevon, Oxford University Press. © Oxford University Press 2024.
DOI: 10.1093/9780197765197.003.0003

of civilians, local military units, and more organised armed groups seized control of the border crossings of Baab al-Hawa and Baab al-Salama between Syria and Turkey. Control over the border with Turkey was crucial for the armed opposition's sustainability and expansion in north and northwest Syria. The capture of the border controls in 2012 was a turning point for the Syrian armed opposition, enabling it to achieve substantial victories by mid-2013 (figure 3.1).

The regime was ill-prepared to face simultaneous insurrectionary uprisings in numerous areas of the country. While the army's leadership and its most well-equipped fighting units remained loyal to the regime for various reasons, including the peculiarities of officers' integration in Syrian cities (Khaddour, 2015), conscripts and low-level officers began to desert and flee to rural areas under armed groups. Others stayed in the army but were not considered loyal enough to be sent effectively to the front lines. Assad eventually recognised that the regime was spread

Figure 3.1 Territorial control in mid-2012
https://commons.wikimedia.org/wiki/File:Situation_in_Syria_(August_2012).svg

too thin and had to prioritise certain territories, surrendering several regions to the opposition due to limited manpower (Samaan & Barnard, 2015). This was especially the case in the Kurdish areas, which were transferred to the Kurdish YPG as the regime withdrew its troops (ICG, 2014). Meanwhile, a coalition of armed groups from northwest Syria moved towards the province of Raqqa in the east of the country, capturing the regional capital city in March 2013. This was a significant victory for the opposition, as it allowed them to establish a foothold in the east.

Victory breeds victory. Armed opposition groups gained an advantage by capturing a significant amount of weapons from the regime's stockpiles as they captured military bases. As their military momentum picked up, they started to receive more external support from countries aligned with the opposition.[2] Adding to this, previously neglected rural areas that had suffered from drought in the late part of the first decade of the 2000s began to shift towards insurrectionary control from 2012 onwards. These dynamics further lengthened the front lines with regime forces, which were difficult to man effectively. The losses in the east were particularly significant, given the presence of oil resources and the border with Iraq, which ultimately helped ISIS to expand in the region. By 2013, the armed opposition controlled nearly all of the border with Turkey and Iraq, as well as large areas around Damascus.

The armed opposition's territorial gains forced the regime to prioritise its control over "useful Syria" over the years. These areas include Damascus, Hama, Homs, Aleppo's wealthiest regions, and the Alawi heartland, encompassing most of the population and strategic locations. The regime's lengthy front lines and limited manpower prevented it from confronting armed opposition groups across the country. Some sources indicate that the regime had only 20,000 to 25,000 troops at its disposal, in addition to 100,000 irregular forces and 60 Shia militias, comprising roughly 30,000 combatants (Lister, 2016a). These factors forced the regime to rely heavily on local militias and foreign troops, primarily non-state armed groups from Lebanese, Iraqi, and Afghan militias, to bolster its weak military (Eisenstadt, 2018; Schneider, 2018).

Regime forces, increasingly supported by external allies, particularly Iran and Hizbullah, concentrated their efforts on the central and densely populated areas of the country. In the spring of 2013, regime forces, aided by foreign militias, launched a successful attack to reclaim the strategically important town of Qusayr. The Lebanese group provided notable support during this operation (Blanford, 2013). Qusayr was a crucial supply line for the armed groups based in Homs, which had been under siege by the regime. The town was strategically positioned between the capital and the Alawi heartland, a coastal region bordering the Mediterranean Sea. Regaining control of Qusayr increased the pressure on the armed groups located in Homs and ultimately led to a series of retreats by the armed groups in control of parts of the city (figure 3.2).

Figure 3.2 Territorial control in 2013
https://commons.wikimedia.org/wiki/File:Situation_in_Syria_(June_2013).svg

In 2014, the armed opposition divided. Previously, Syrian armed opposition groups had been intermingled throughout opposition-held areas. But the split between ISIS and Jabhat al-Nusra, later followed by ISIS's war against all the opposition, dissociated areas controlled by the former from those controlled by remaining groups.[3] ISIS primarily established itself in the east of the country, along the border of its strategic stronghold in Iraq, which was further strengthened by the seizure of the Iraqi city of Mosul in June 2014. The mainstream opposition, including Jabhat al-Nusra, was mostly located in the northwest, the south, and limited pockets around Damascus and Homs. The front lines stabilised and stopped shifting substantially, as they had done in the previous few years. Although regime forces seized limited geographic areas in strategic locations, particularly in Damascus, the military situation stabilised (figure 3.3).

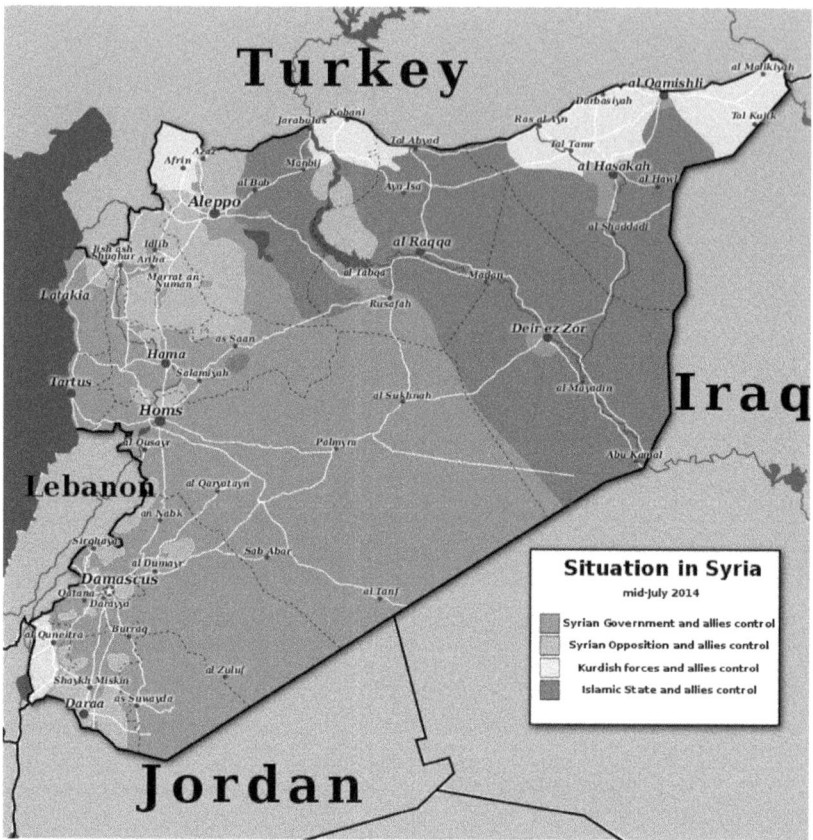

Figure 3.3 Territorial control in 2014
https://commons.wikimedia.org/wiki/File:Situation_in_Syria_(2014).svg

The evolution of the front lines posed significant challenges to the armed opposition, as it was unable to capture and hold contiguous territory from which it could launch an expanded offensive against the regime. While the victories achieved between 2012 and 2015 resulted in the consolidation of five distinct regions under rebel control, this was not enough to achieve a strategic victory. The largest rebel-held zones were located in the northwest, where a multi-factional coalition held sway, and in the east, which was under the control of IS. The two other significant areas were in the south of the country, along the border with Jordan, and in the Ghouta periphery of Damascus. In addition, an isolated pocket of rebel-held territory survived in the north of Homs. These regions evolved independently from the Kurdish-dominated areas. Coordination between them was difficult due to the localised nature of most armed groups. To achieve a strategic victory, the rebels needed to unify and coordinate their efforts, putting pressure on the regime from multiple fronts simultaneously. This was a daunting challenge given the fragmented nature of the opposition, but it was essential to achieving their goals.

In 2015, the opposition made its last significant gains. The mainstream opposition consolidated its position in northwest Syria by capturing the provincial city of Idlib in the spring of 2015, thanks to a large military coalition.[4] At the same time, ISIS declared the creation of a Caliphate and solidified its territorial control over half of the country, before suffering significant losses due to Western military assistance to the Kurdish YPG when it became the Syrian Democratic Forces (SDF) as it integrated smaller independent military units. The SDF regained control over significant areas previously held by ISIS along the Turkish border (PeÇanha & Watkins, 2015). External military intervention also helped the SDF consolidate control over most of northern Syria along the border. The situation started to appear bleak for the regime, which faced a potential threat to its Alawi heartland in the coastal region near the Russian military naval facility of Tartus. Alas, a Russian military intervention in September 2015 halted the insurrectionary advance and ultimately turned the tide in favour of Assad and Syria's regional allies (Delanoë, 2018) (figure 3.4).

In 2015, the Russian intervention in Syria marked a significant turning point in the conflict.[5] After Iranian general Qassem Soleimani's visit to Moscow in the summer, Russia launched a sudden military intervention aimed at stabilising the Assad regime and countering perceived Western attempts to replace him. This accompanied a diplomatic effort to subvert the U.N.-sponsored political process.[6] Russia's intervention primarily involved providing anti-aircraft defence systems in Syria to deter foreign attacks and deploying sophisticated reconnaissance and targeting equipment to systematically weaken the mainstream armed opposition while claiming to attack ISIS. To undermine popular support for the armed opposition, Russia carried out a campaign of systematic punishment against civilian and humanitarian infrastructures. The Russian campaign occurred in three stages: stabilising western Syria, capturing Aleppo, and neutralising ISIS in the centre and east of the country. Ultimately, Russia re-seized the offensive and forced the armed opposition to regroup in only one region, the northwest. Despite the relatively low number of Russian troops permanently settled in the country (only 4,000 to 8,000), Russia relied on locally trained paramilitary forces and Iranian-supported militias, while also engaging special forces, military police, and private military contractors in later phases. Though the Russian intervention was relatively cheap in terms of material contribution, it reinforced Russia's credibility as a state ally and provided an opportunity to test military equipment and improve military innovations.

The transformation of the Syrian conflict into a conventional war with stable front lines, territorial control, and battles presented a significant challenge for

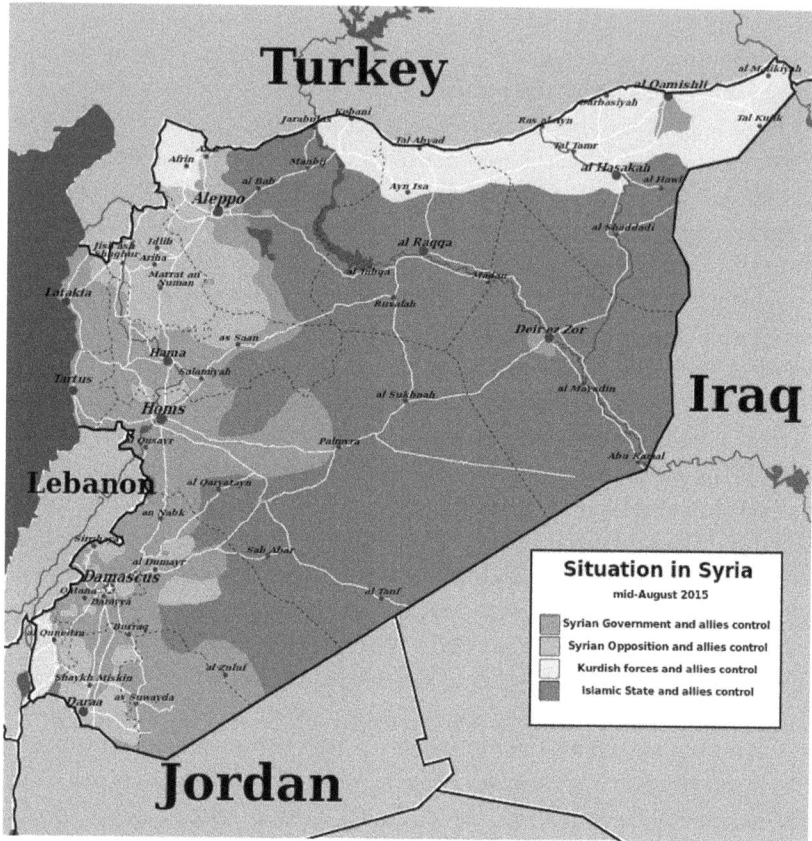

Figure 3.4 Territorial control in 2015
https://commons.wikimedia.org/wiki/File:Situation_in_Syria_(August_2015).svg

the armed opposition.[7] The early military units that emerged in 2011 and 2012 were ill-equipped to manage large front lines. Therefore, the armed groups had to transform into more professional military forces capable of deploying heavy weaponry, coordinating on a large scale, and securing external military support. Moreover, the armed opposition had to establish a credible political alternative to the regime that could provide basic governance structures and services to the local population. Territorial control involved new functions such as policing, coordinating with foreign organisations, providing essential services, and restraining factional competition. The stabilisation of local governance meant that thousands of armed groups could not continue to operate independently and had to unite within their regions and coordinate with other areas. These choices required different strategies, ranging from factional coordination, alliances, and local hegemony to the potential unification of all the armed opposition examined in the next chapter. At the same time, the regime relentlessly targeted civilian infrastructures to prevent the consolidation of polities that could present alternative visions for the country's future (Martinez & Eng, 2018).

Armed Groups and Jihadis Outside Northwest Syria

The geography of the Syrian conflict largely shaped the development of the armed opposition. While the conflict is often portrayed as a war in which hundreds of armed groups competed for survival and leadership, this approach overlooks the significant differences between armed opposition–held territories. Studies of armed groups' alliances and competition in civil wars (Christia, 2012; Woldemariam, 2018) typically assume that armed groups coexist homogeneously within a country or ally with each other cross-nationally (Bacon, 2018). Only a few studies examine how different types of factional competition or modes of organisation in distinct areas of a country impact armed groups' governance (Arjona, 2016; Lacher, 2020; Parkinson, 2023). In Syria, armed groups were not equally present throughout opposition-held areas. Each region presented a unique set of structural constraints and opportunities that influenced armed groups' consolidation during the conflict. These characteristics determined armed groups' modes of organisation and the nature of the factional orders that developed over the years. A key factor in shaping the development of the armed opposition was the type of order established in different parts of armed opposition–controlled Syria, whether unipolar and hegemonic, bipolar, or multipolar.

Apart from Idlib province in the northwest, there were five major areas held by armed groups across Syria. The first two were isolated pockets in the north of Homs and the suburbs of Damascus, while the other three were located in the country's periphery to the south, east, and along the northern border with Turkey.[8] These regions varied greatly in size, with the eastern area covering half of Syria, including desert terrain, and the northern Homs enclave being relatively small. Foreign access to these areas also differed significantly: besieged enclaves had limited access, the south was under close Jordanian supervision, and the IS-controlled border with Iraq provided substantial access to American-provided spoils of war, particularly after the capture of Mosul in 2014.

While the armed opposition in Syria resorted to violence across the country, the nature of armed occupation–held territories determined the conditions under which local armed groups could institutionalise both internally and externally. Externally, factors such as external access, territory size, and strategic importance informed the number of groups that could develop and survive in each region. These factors also informed their patterns of interaction, alliances, and competition, and affected their relations with the local population. Internally, these features contextualise armed groups' ability to institutionalise themselves and maintain internal cohesion, particularly in the aftermath of the killing of prominent leaders or commanders. This perspective recognises the agency of armed groups while also situating their choices within the environmental and organisational conditions in which they emerged and developed.

During the first few months of the uprising in Syria, two armed opposition pockets emerged in al-Ghouta and the north of Homs. These regions shared some crucial characteristics, including the fact that local residents expelled regime forces with minimal external assistance and managed to keep them out for nearly six years. These areas also had few foreign fighters, and their inhabitants relied on smuggling networks to establish a subsistence economy that helped them survive the prolonged siege imposed by regime forces and their allies. These territories therefore did not witness the same degree of internal factional diversity as the northwest, as the formation of new groups was limited. Despite these similarities, armed groups in these two regions developed along two distinct patterns.

In the Ghouta, in the suburbs of Damascus, Jaysh al-Islam tried to impose a hegemonic model. Strategically located on the periphery of the capital and just a few kilometres from the presidential palace, the region posed a significant threat to the regime's survival. Despite a bitter siege accompanied by severe regime attacks, including the use of chemical weapons (Human Rights Watch, 2013; United Nations Secretary-General, 2013), local armed groups managed to expel regime forces by the end of 2012 and dominate the region for nearly six years. The region had limited access to the rest of the country through the desert of 'Otayba until the regime imposed a siege in 2013. The strategic importance of a region under siege required stronger internal unity to stabilise the front lines and the economy of the enclave, which Jaysh al-Islam sought to impose. The group started to dominate the area in 2013 by relying on local pre-war Salafi networks and group leader Zahran Alloush's extensive family ties in the Gulf, which bolstered the group financially and militarily (Lund, 2016).[9] Private assistance was later complemented by state support from Saudi Arabia when parts of the ruling family decided to increase their support to the Syrian opposition in 2013 (Black, 2013; Oweis, 2013). Although Jaysh al-Islam initially tried to expand into other Syrian regions, with up to 40% of its constituent brigades based outside of Ghouta, it ultimately focused only on the local enclave, especially after local Salafis joined in, according to the group's former spokesman.[10] To externally institutionalise its dominant role, Jaysh al-Islam created military and judicial power structures that could abolish competing local courts and security forces and unify the enclave under its sway. The group notably spurred the creation of the Unified Judicial Council and the Unified Military Command Council, which were inclusive of most other factions while remaining under Jaysh al-Islam's ultimate domination (Lund, 2016, 2017; Schwab, 2018).

Other groups, including Ahrar al-Sham and Jabhat al-Nusra (and beforehand ISIS), could never contain Jaysh al-Islam in the Ghouta. The first group that Jaysh al-Islam crushed was ISIS.[11] Jaysh al-Islam engaged in a fierce conflict against ISIS, justifying a robust military response between 2013 and 2014 due to accusations of extremism and violence against the opposition. Jaysh al-Islam launched a wide military campaign against the group and countered ISIS's execution of militants by carrying out its own executions of ISIS personnel. Ahrar al-Sham and Jabhat al-Nusra conversely remained in the province, but with limited influence. Ahrar al-Sham played a limited role in the region due to its geographic isolation from its stronghold in the northwest, where most of its early brigades were based. According to a prominent Ahrar al-Sham leader, Hassan 'Abud initially managed the connection to the group's brigade in the Ghouta through a Skype contact ,. Meanwhile, Jabhat al-Nusra was unable to establish a significant presence in the region as it clashed with Jaysh al-Islam's forces. Other armed groups in the Ghouta were mainly confined to the area, especially after the expulsion of ISIS in 2014.[12] Jaysh al-Islam's dominance in the Ghouta forced other armed groups, including ideologically opposed factions, to form alliances to counterbalance its military power. The creation of new factions was even prohibited by the Unified Military Command Council in 2015, which is a common strategy used by dominant groups to prevent the emergence of challengers. In 2016, the Ahrar al-Sham leadership outside of the Ghouta had to accept its integration into Jaysh al-Islam, but the local branch of Ahrar al-Sham instead allied with other groups in the Jaysh al-Fustat alliance to balance Jaysh al-Islam's power (Al-'Omari, 2016; Ahrar al-Sham, 2016a).[13]

Despite Jaysh al-Islam's military dominance, the group failed to fully control local civil society institutions, many of which remained independent. Moreover, Jaysh al-Islam's economic hegemony was closely tied to its military power, yet the group struggled to control the tunnel economy that was crucial to the enclave's survival while under siege. Jaysh al-Islam's weakness in controlling the tunnels, combined with the death of its leader, Zahran Alloush, in December 2015, intensified factional competition and weakened the group (Lund, 2016, 2017). This eventually led to the regime's partial reconquest of the enclave and its division in 2016.[14]

The Rastan-Talbiseh enclave stood out for its relatively balanced relations between local factions. In 2011, the region rose up against the regime and expelled its forces with the help of army defectors. Later, the expulsion of rebel forces from the old city of Homs in 2014 further strengthened the local armed groups.[15] As in the Ghouta, foreign fighters were virtually absent in the region. The enclave remained under siege for six years, occupying a strategic location between

Damascus and northern Syria, but its small size limited its potential as a long-term threat to the regime. The number of groups was also limited in the region. Despite the presence of Ahrar al-Sham, which was particularly influential in the area, other groups such as Jabhat al-Nusra and Free Syrian Army factions were also present. While there were occasional armed confrontations involving Jabhat al-Nusra when it attacked factions it deemed suspicious,[16] there was no single group that dominated the enclave like Jaysh al-Islam did in the Ghouta. Competition between groups was relatively contained, compared to in other armed opposition–held areas. Overall, the Rastan-Talbiseh enclave had limited prospects for the armed opposition, given its geographic isolation and small size.

The regime could not besiege the last two regions due to armed groups' continued control over the border, although Ahrar al-Sham and Jabhat al-Nusra did not play a major role in these areas. In the south of the country, local armed groups bordered Jordan, which closely regulated the border and closely monitored the armed opposition. There were Jordanian foreign fighters initially, especially in Jabhat al-Nusra's local leadership, but they left for the province of Idlib in 2014. Local groups instead coalesced in 2014 to form the Southern Front (al-Jabhat al-Janubiyya) to institutionalise their relations to one another and with external actors. The objective of the Southern Front was to centralise Arab and Western support, mostly provided by Jordan and the United States, through the Military Operation Command (MOC) in Amman, which contrasts with the divided support for the armed opposition elsewhere. The Southern Front did not have a clear organisational hierarchy for internal command and control. Instead, it relied primarily on ad hoc joint operation rooms to coordinate armed operations with the MOC in Amman. But the centralisation of military support from abroad had a clear downside. When Jordan froze the front lines and U.S. funding stopped in 2017 (Sadaki, 2016), the Southern Front did not have the ability to survive on its own.[17] The alliance weakened, and would never recover until all the south of the country was seized by the regime once again a few months later.

The south of Syria, with its more cohesive social fabric and centralisation of external support, saw a relatively marginal role of Islamist armed groups, as compared to other regions. This is reflected in local groups' official embrace of more pluralistic and democratic objectives (Lund, 2014a; ICG, 2015; Lister, 2016e). Unlike other regions, Ahrar al-Sham never managed to establish a significant presence in the south, due to its focus on other Syrian regions. The main Islamist alternative was Jabhat al-Nusra, which, despite having a primarily local membership, had to be more flexible and coordinate with the Southern Front. It also had to submit to shared courts of justice. Some foreign commanders, especially the Jordanian Abu Julaybib, nonetheless contributed to Jabhat al-Nusra's gradual distancing from the locals, especially when the group lost its eastern stronghold and regrouped in the south (Abazeid, 2014). A former Jabhat al-Nusra commander denounced the group's Jordanian leader in the south for his despotism and micromanagement, which caused issues related to sharing spoils of war, little internal accountability, and IS infiltration (Abu Sayyaf, 2015). IS had only a sporadic presence in the south before co-opting local factions, such as Liwa Shuhada al-Yarmouk, which pledged allegiance to the group (Al-Tamimi, 2015b).[18]

Ahrar al-Sham and Jabhat al-Nusra's attempts to establish a foothold in eastern Syria were short-lived. In early 2013, Ahrar al-Sham played a key role in the opposition's capture of Raqqa, the first provincial capital to fall. The group took control of important assets in the city, including its central bank, but it quickly became apparent that it was ill-prepared to govern a city of that size.[19] Despite collaborating with other groups, Ahrar al-Sham was unable to replace state institutions. The group was not manned by local fighters but by military brigades coming from other Syrian regions, with limited exceptions. The group was also unable to effectively confront ISIS, both militarily and ideologically. Ahrar al-Sham commanders signed local agreements with ISIS to avoid direct confrontation, and did not attempt to assert dominance over the group.[20] Ahrar al-Sham's leadership later acknowledged that its fighters were not willing to fight another Islamist armed group, regardless of their actions.[21] This lack of response to ISIS ultimately led to Ahrar al-Sham's expulsion from Raqqa, despite being one of the largest groups. Jabhat al-Nusra also tried to resist ISIS. Both groups fought over the control of Raqqa and the oil fields in the east. But ISIS ultimately prevailed and expelled Jabhat al-Nusra.

The consolidation of ISIS's hegemony (later renamed IS) occurred in 2014, after the group expelled Ahrar al-Sham and Jabhat al-Nusra.[22] This was facilitated by its decision to regroup its forces along its Iraqi border, which allowed for easy transfer of troops and military equipment between the two countries, after the Syrian opposition expelled the group from the northwest.[23] An early prison campaign had already allowed the Iraqi group to gather its cadres previously detained in Iraq (Lewis, 2013; Arango & Schmitt, 2014). Geographic contiguity with Iraq was critical. Controlling both sides of the border enabled the group to transfer troops and military equipment easily between the two countries and consolidate local control, which was further bolstered by its adroit tribal outreach (Dukhan & Hawat, 2014). ISIS also benefited from the capture of Mosul, which provided the group with weapons and money for its Syrian military campaigns. Despite its ineffectual local rule, ISIS was adroit in isolating and targeting each of its local opponents (Rosenblatt & Kilcullen, 2019). The group also seized oil resources from Jabhat al-Nusra and integrated most foreign fighters into its ranks, who could easily be moved across fronts, were more ideologically committed, and could not leave IS once in its territory (see also Mendelsohn, 2019). ISIS also used foreign fighters to subjugate local tribes without concern for triggering broader tribal conflicts or inhibiting local ISIS members from participating in the fighting due to local power dynamics according to local observers.[24] ISIS proclaimed itself to be a state, denied the legitimacy of all other groups, and imposed local taxes and governance to institutionalise its local authority (Revkin, 2020). Additionally, the group imposed its hegemony over a contiguous territory, allowing it to institutionalise itself internally and create mobile military forces that could be easily moved and recomposed, in sharp contrast with the localism of most other armed groups.[25]

In the north of Syria, the Kurdish YPG marginalised Arab armed groups as it imposed its hegemony over a large territory on the border with Turkey.[26] The YPG's early rise, bolstered by its organic ties to PKK in Kurdish-populated areas, facilitated its quick ascendancy as the dominant military force before any alternative contenders could emerge.[27] The group established checkpoints and seized local administration with relative ease when the regime withdrew, with minimal clashes. The YPG's external institutionalisation occurred through the creation of successive local administrations, starting with the Democratic Autonomous Administration, the Democratic Federation of Rojava, the Democratic Federation of Northern Syria, and the Autonomous Administration of North and East Syria. The objective of these changes was to sustain the group's claims to inclusiveness as territorial control expanded, despite persistent authoritarian practices. To distance itself from being seen solely as a Kurdish force, the YPG created the Syrian Democratic Forces (SDF) when the United States decided to support the group militarily, particularly after the battle of Kobane, which began in 2014. Despite this move, the Kurdish group retained effective administrative and military control over the province, knowing that lasting U.S. support was necessary for stabilisation.[28]

The comparison between the armed opposition's strongholds highlights the diverse contexts in which different types of armed groups operated. In northern Homs, Ahrar al-Sham and Jabhat al-Nusra established balanced relations with other groups. In contrast, they played a relatively marginal role in the south, due to the unique geographic characteristics and local fabric of the region. In the east, ISIS (later IS) expelled all other groups and imposed harsh local rules to prevent internal dissidence, leaving Ahrar al-Sham and Jabhat al-Nusra without a foothold in the area. In the Ghouta, despite Jaysh al-Islam's imposition of relatively tight control over other groups, hegemony was not absolute.

Ahrar al-Sham, Jabhat al-Nusra, and ISIS/IS were the only groups able to expand and maintain a presence in multiple regions.[29] Jabhat al-Nusra initially formed cells throughout Syria, mobilising locally as armed groups' control consolidated. After the split with IS, Jabhat al-Nusra lost most of its soldiers but maintained a presence in most areas. IS, on the other hand, gathered most foreign brigades and fighters despite its expulsion from the northwest and the

Ghouta periphery. Although IS subsequently managed to create local cells or co-opt sub-factions elsewhere, it never posed a substantial existential threat to other regions. In contrast, Ahrar al-Sham managed to expand throughout Syrian regions through a more bottom-up process, as discussed in the last sections of this chapter. The consolidation of only two groups that were able to expand throughout Syria ultimately polarised the opposition, as argued in chapter 4. Moreover, the comparison illustrates how local civil society was repressed by IS and tightly controlled by the YPG in the two areas of real hegemony. In other regions, civil society sustained its existence according to the characteristics of the regions and the evolving balance of power between local armed groups.

Ahrar al-Sham and Jabhat al-Nusra were uniquely able to expand throughout opposition-held territory while maintaining organisational control over their sub-units, though their control over these sub-units was not absolute. While both groups did not experience the same level of expansion, overreach, and loss of control as did the early groups associated with the Free Syrian Army mentioned in the previous chapter, they still encountered situations where they had to delegate their decision-making to their local units. One of the most challenging aspects was the management of their relations with other factions. While it was relatively easy for both groups to give instructions to their sub-units regarding fighting or not fighting the regime, dealing with other groups posed more significant problems. As previously observed, certain sub-groups within Ahrar al-Sham, for example, refused to merge into Jaysh al-Islam in al-Ghouta despite orders from their central leadership. Others refused to fight ISIS when their leaders asked them to. But even Jabhat al-Nusra, with its stronger discipline, faced similar issues. Group commanders recognised that they had to delegate tactical decisions to their sub-groups in other regions—the "blocs" (*qawati'*) headed by a military and a religious leader—without micromanaging them, or that some of their units were under the direct influence of Abu Muhammad al-Maqdisi in Jordan and never fully under control, at least before 2016, according to former HTS commander Abu Maria al-Qahtani in an interview.[30] A group dissident, Saleh al-Hamawi, added:

> Enforcing discipline within our group was simpler before 2013. Our leaders were strong and well respected. Our members still revered the organisation (*haybat al-tandhim*). But some individuals were already more focused on fighting for their specific territories and were resistant to moving across different areas. I had to motivate them by appealing to their commitments, their respect for the leadership, and their religious beliefs. The split with IS had a detrimental effect on our group's cohesion. The public disagreements and debates among our leaders undermined our credibility and eroded the trust within the organisation.

Table 3.1 Comparative characteristics of major armed opposition–held areas

	Creation of new groups	Internal institutionalisation[a]	External institutionalisation	External support
Ghouta enclave	Limited, then forbidden	Limited centralisation and localism	Failed hegemony of Jaysh al-Islam	Divided
Homs enclave	Limited	Localism	Pluralist	Limited
South	Constrained by Jordanian control	Localism	Unity on paper under the Southern Front	Cohesive (under Jordan supervision)
East	Forbidden by IS hegemony	Centralisation and localism	Hegemony of IS	Cohesive (from IS's Iraqi stronghold)
North	With YPG consent	Centralisation and localism	Hegemony of the YPG / SDF	None initially, then cohesive under Western control

[a] This feature emphasise whether local armed groups developed centralised military forces that did not stem from specific localities, reflecting an effort to institutionalise internally.

Finally, the comparison between these regions and their dominant armed groups also illustrates the relationship between armed groups' networking structures and modes of organisation. Armed groups are more capable of restructuring their organisational structures when they establish hegemony in a contiguous geographic area. Factional competition is less of an issue, and different military brigades—including those consisting of foreign fighters—can co-exist with local groups focused on defending their communities. This increases the military efficiency of the dominant group. In contrast, in regions where factional competition is present, armed groups face limitations in their ability to change their organisational structures, as suggested in the next section on the northwest (table 3.1).

Armed Groups' Strategies in the Northwest

Northwest Syria stood out from other armed opposition–held territories due to several salient characteristics of the Syrian conflict, including a large number of contending groups, foreign fighters, and competition between foreign countries. This region's geography, bordering Turkey, played a crucial role in differentiating it from other areas. Turkey quickly embraced the uprising against Assad's regime and did not closely supervise the armed opposition before 2017, as Jordan did in the south. The strategic depth provided to the armed groups was critical in ensuring durable access to unsupervised support networks. Private supporters of the armed opposition were later supplanted by states that supported competing factions and developed competing agendas.[31] The next section argues that the characteristics of the northwest were particularly conducive to Ahrar al-Sham's strategy of alliance-based expansion.

The characteristics of northwest Syria sustained the unique diversity of its armed opposition, with barriers to forming new armed opposition groups being relatively low. Local groups mushroomed before switching allegiance between different organisational umbrellas or developing their own independent support networks from a variety of supporters.[32] The diversity of external support networks exacerbated existing divisions in the province, which was already marked by important local, social, and urban divides. Moreover, northwest Syria never enjoyed the strategic importance of Damascus and central Syria for the regime, which had to prioritise other front lines. The region is inhabited by a large Sunni majority, who were viewed with hostility by the regime and had no significant access to resources. While parts of northwest Syria posed a potential threat to Syria's Alawi heartland and Russian military installations in the region, this threat materialized only in a later phase of the conflict, after 2015.

The characteristics of northwest Syria illustrate the range of choices available to local armed groups as the war transformed. The previous chapter presented armed groups' early emergence from the local gatherings that outstretched quickly to those that remained centred on their localities as a main strategy of survival to the elitist mobilisation of Jabhat al-Nusra and the more insular foreign-led brigades. Early underpinning networks informed armed groups' subsequent choices as the war became more conventional when larger front lines with regime forces stabilised and armed groups started to govern the population in their territories. Contrasting the choices of other groups is important to the subsequent analysis of Ahrar al-Sham's specificities. It illustrates why Ahrar al-Sham was particularly efficient in an area where a very large array of groups emerged due to the low costs of joining the armed opposition independently.

Armed opposition groups in the northwest followed two distinct patterns of institutionalisation, both internally and externally. Prior to 2017, no armed group was able to establish complete dominance. Externally, armed groups developed shared structures of governance that partially underpinned their institutionalisation with the population, as argued at the end of this section. Internally, armed groups faced two main choices: either (1) expand their organisational capacity by expanding further while simultaneously institutionalising their group, or (2) consolidate in a limited geographic area only and institutionalise external cross-factional alliances with other groups to adapt to changing local necessities and threats.

The first pattern of development, organisational expansion combined with internal institutionalisation, was quite rare. Only a limited number of groups were able to expand their organisation within and across regions without dividing along constituent sub-units. One notable case besides Ahrar al-Sham is Jabhat al-Nusra, which expanded across Syria by mobilising a small-scale elitist social network of entrepreneurs partially based on pre-existing ties. The group then started to recruit more extensively locally, too. The transformation of the war shifted Jabhat al-Nusra's priorities from planning spectacular attacks against regime forces situated behind front lines to traditional ground warfare, requiring a larger personnel. The group preferred to recruit individual members who were vetted, rather than pre-established factions, although some factions were occasionally included. In such cases, the integration of new factions imposed a tighter indoctrination in Jabhat al-Nusra's religious and military training camps as well as the centralisation of resources according to the group's highest religious authority.[33] Jabhat al-Nusra's ability to maintain organisational cohesion and expand without dividing into sub-units is noteworthy, given the fragmented nature of the Syrian conflict. This pattern of development was relatively rare, and it allowed Jabhat al-Nusra to become a significant player in the conflict before and after its split with ISIS in 2013.

Jabhat al-Nusra's split from ISIS in 2013 can be attributed to various factors, with the primary one revolving around power dynamics. The crux of the matter was that Jabhat al-Nusra's leadership staunchly resisted ISIS's attempts to regain control over the group. ISIS had grown concerned that Jabhat al-Nusra was becoming too influential within Syria, and that its leader, al-Jolani, was proving too independent and difficult to manage. In addition to internal power struggles, there were also strategic differences between the two groups. Jabhat al-Nusra was reluctant to orchestrate armed attacks against the mainstream Syrian opposition based in Istanbul, which ISIS demanded of the group, and adopted a more pragmatic approach in its overall dealings with other insurgent factions.[34]

The outcome of the split between Jabhat al-Nusra and IS was largely determined by the former's ability to integrate foreign fighters into its organisational structures as it institutionalised. Prior to the split, IS commanders launched their own initiative to gather the allegiance of a large number of foreign-led brigades and fighters. The IS leadership used ambiguous arguments to convince their followers that they remained committed to al-Qaeda and its leader, Ayman al-Zawahiri, while also promoting their claims to statehood (Doornbos & Moussa, 2016a). In addition to these alluring claims, IS relied on the promotion of foreign commanders into its organisational structures. For instance, Amr al-Absi, who led the foreign-manned Majlis Shura al-Mujahideen, became IS's local leader in Aleppo, where he bolstered the group's presence around a core number of foreign fighters. Similarly, Abu 'Omar al-Shishani from Jaysh al-Muhajireen wal-Ansar became IS's military leader in Syria. Half of the group joined IS, including many of Shishani's followers (Hussein, 2015). Many Uzbek nationals also chose to join IS (Hussein, 2017e). As a result, the allegiance of most foreigners to IS nearly obliterated Jabhat al-Nusra when the split occurred. According to Jabhat al-Nusra's leaders, the group lost more than 70% of its resources and personnel. A former Jabhat al-Nusra commander added that 25% of group members remained, half of the group joined IS, the remaining proclaimed their neutrality while waiting for an answer from al-Qaeda. The latter included members who would later form Jund al-Aqsa (Abu Sayyaf, 2016b).

Jabhat al-Nusra managed to survive by institutionalising its own external ties to al-Qaeda. Jabhat al-Nusra and al-Qaeda were previously indirectly subordinated through IS's own allegiance to al-Zawahiri. But the allegiance was not direct. After splitting with IS, Jabhat al-Nusra's leader, al-Jolani, believed that the group needed to pledge public allegiance to al-Qaeda to maintain the loyalty of his soldiers and save the group. He explained in an interview:

> When we broke off with al-Baghdadi, we didn't have any good options. We were going to be wiped out by them so I gathered my inner circle to take a quick decision. I told them that I was considering pledging allegiance to al-Qaeda. They advised me against it, and some described it as a suicidal move. But no one was able to provide me with an alternative. We had no other option but to pledge allegiance to al-Qaeda in order not to lose everyone to ISIS. But I conditioned my pledge of allegiance to al-Qaeda on the idea that we will not use Syria as a launching pad for external operations, nor let others use it for that. I wrote this to Zawahiri and he agreed to it, and if you recall my response to Zawahiri after our delinking decision you will see that I never changed my position on that.[35]

Jabhat al-Nusra's survival was due not only to its institutional ties to al-Qaeda but also its focus on local anchorage as the group pursued its strategic partnerships with other insurgents, particularly Ahrar al-Sham.[36] As Jabhat al-Nusra adopted successive campaigns of recruitment, which gradually relaxed membership criteria, it further integrated with the mainstream opposition and fought alongside their troops. More importantly, Jabhat al-Nusra became more assertive in reaching out to the local population in its external institutionalisation efforts. The group briefly claimed that it would establish an emirate in the northwest after losing its eastern stronghold, a move interpreted as a response to IS's state-building aspirations after the promotion of more radical figures in the group such as its new religious leader Sami al-'Uraydi (Abazeid,

2014).[37] Jabhat al-Nusra also established its own courts of justice (Dar al-Qada) and provided social services under the general service management (Idarat al-'Ama lil-Khadamat). According to Saleh al-Hamawi, a former leader who left the group in 2015 due to disagreements with al-Jolani:

> Many people were leaving us in favour of IS in 2014, especially when it proclaimed the creation of the Caliphate. Some of them disagreed with IS, especially its excessive violence, but still believed that creating an Islamic state was important. Our only solution was to have our own governance. This started with the declaration that we created an emirate, which many groups pushed back against, up to the creation of Dar al-Qada. But we had an understanding with other groups, including Ahrar al-Sham, that we should not impose the Islamic legal penal punishments (*hudud*) because we were still at war. And in reality this helped us survive, and people stopped going to IS and remained with us.

Jabhat al-Nusra's ability to navigate its relationships with opposition groups was crucial for its survival. While it was strategic in its collaboration with mainstream opposition factions, the group also dismantled factions that it deemed antagonistic. Jabhat al-Nusra notably targeted the groups it viewed as hostile or too closely aligned with Western countries, such as the Syrian Revolutionaries Front of Jamal Maarouf and the Hazm movement (Lund, 2014c; Lister, 2016c).[38] This approach enabled Jabhat al-Nusra to avoid antagonizing the opposition as a whole while playing a role in the eviction of IS from northwest Syria, as will be discussed in the next chapter.[39]

The second group that managed to expand organisationally and to institutionalise internally is Faylaq al-Sham. Faylaq al-Sham is an alliance of nineteen brigades disseminated throughout Syria, though mostly in the north and northwest, that formed in March 2014. Most of its constituting brigades are present in the northwest. Initially, these brigades were associated with the Commission for the Protection of Civilians (CPC) and the Shields of the Revolution, which were particularly present in the northwest and enjoyed partial support from the Muslim Brotherhood during the first year of the conflict. However, Faylaq al-Sham has consistently distanced itself from the Brotherhood, which initially refused to endorse the alliance (al-Musa, 2020). Faylaq al-Sham sought to facilitate external support from states such as Saudi Arabia, which were hostile to the Muslim Brotherhood (Lefèvre & El Yassir, 2014). Faylaq al-Sham formed alongside the consolidation of larger formations in 2014, partially in response to the growing threat posed by IS in the region (al-Musa, 2020). The group was nonetheless a marginal entity when it formed, with limited manpower and military efficiency. Faylaq al-Sham was later encouraged by Turkey to unite smaller brigades and former Syrian army officers to increase its military efficiency. Its organisational expansion is therefore not comparable to Ahrar al-Sham and Jabhat al-Nusra, which were in dominant positions when they expanded. Faylaq al-Sham only grew in importance in the following years thanks to Turkish tutelage, especially during the formation of the Jaysh al-Fath operation room.[40] Turkey specifically encouraged smaller groups to join Faylaq al-Sham to improve its military efficiency and coordination. The group's external ties to Turkey explain why the group has been considered its political card as well as a conduit for financial and military support to the opposition with little independent political projects of its own.

The second major pattern of development was to consolidate and institutionalise locally without substantial expansion to other areas. In contrast to the groups mentioned in the previous chapter that rapidly expanded and outstretched organisational capacity before disintegrating, several local groups consolidated in limited geographic areas without significantly expanding outside of it. These groups maintained the strong local embeddedness from their early days, which sustained the provision of most recruits and support. They primarily expanded in a limited fashion in geographically contiguous areas based on interconnected local ties. As the conflict transformed into a conventional war, these groups institutionalised and evolved from brigades to legion (*liwa*) or movement to reflect their consolidation and functional differentiation beyond mere military functions, including the provision of local services, policing, and judicial courts in their areas.[41] Three groups that have managed to survive the longest with a distinctive identity despite vague ideological commitments are Suqur al-Sham, Zinki Movement, and Jaysh al-'Izza.[42]

Local groups' survival rested on a flexible approach to the institutionalisation of their external ties to other groups. These groups joined and left a plurality of alliances created for specific battles, to achieve unity, or simply to expel IS from their localities. For instance, Zinki Movement joined Liwa al-Tawheed in 2012, Jabhat al-'Asala wal-Tanmiyya in 2013, Jaysh al-Mujahideen in 2014, al-Jabhat al-Shamiyya in 2015, HTS in 2017, and the Syrian Liberation Front (Jabhat Tahrir Suriyya) and the National Liberation Front (al-Jabhat al-Wataniyya lil-Tahrir) in 2018.[43] Suqur al-Sham intermittently joined and left Ahrar al-Sham, as well as the Syrian Islamic Liberation Front in 2012, Jaysh al-Fath in 2015, and the National Liberation Front in 2018. These groups' choices of external partners and alliances were mostly based on the evolution of their priorities in northwest Syria. In all cases, they kept their organisational cohesion and geographic localism intact. The persistence of localism explains, more than does a superficial consideration of their ideological commitments, their ability to gather support from a range of actors stretching from committed Islamist groups to Western countries depending on changing local and regional dynamics. Zinki Movement, for instance, received support from all parts of the spectrum. Support ranged from the CIA-run program to Jabhat al-Nusra when the group became HTS after severing ties with al-Qaeda, as argued in the next chapter.[44]

Local groups occasionally attempted to create larger, institutionalised organisations through cross-factional alliances, but these efforts were often unsuccessful.[45] For example, al-Jabhat al-Shamiyya, composed mostly of remnants of Liwa al-Tawheed, attempted to merge with Jaysh al-Mujahideen to form a unified organisation (*indimaj*) rather than just coordinating under a larger nominal umbrella (al Jabhat al-shamiyya, 2016). While geographic proximity facilitated a merger, a key obstacle was the allocation of resources. To prevent the usual splits that occurred after a limited period of time, the two groups agreed that any members or sub-groups that split would do so individually without any weapons. Additionally, all groups joining the alliance would abandon their previous names and logos, and agree to punish any violation of the agreement. The aim was to discourage organisational splits and prevent groups from prioritising their local or organisational interests over the new larger entity. Despite the written agreement, it was not fully implemented, and many sub-groups left the alliance in a similar manner to how they initially joined, with mostly remnants of Ahrar al-Sham in Aleppo and former Liwa al-Tawheed remaining.[46] Al-Jabhat al-Shamiyya would only become a relatively strong player in northern Aleppo a few years later, when it set up in the north of Aleppo and gained new financial resources locally.

Foreign brigades in Syria that did not join ISIS or Jabhat al-Nusra pursued a similar approach to cross-factional institutionalisation. These groups were often organised along national lines, such as Chechens, Moroccans, Central Asians, and East Asians. Unlike larger groups such as Jabhat al-Nusra and Ahrar al-Sham, they were not strongly embedded locally and remained relatively isolated. Some of them, often created their own bases where they lived outside large population centres. After the split between ISIS and Jabhat al-Nusra, these foreign brigades in northwest Syria generally sought to avoid involvement in factional conflicts. They evolved independently, but often cooperated with other armed opposition groups on an ad hoc basis for military battles and shared operation rooms. A few foreign-manned brigades, including Harakat Sham al-Islam, Jaysh al-Muhajireen wa al-Ansar, Katiba al-Khadra, and Harakat Fajr al-Sham al-Islamiyya, sought to institutionalise their ties to one another by forming an alliance called Jabhat Ansar al-Din (the Front of the Partisans of Religion) in 2014.[47] However, these groups had limited political and military influence, and they became an epiphenomenon of the war once most foreign fighters and brigades joined IS. The Turkistan Islamic Party is one of the few exceptions, retaining some influence in its local stronghold of Jisr al-Shughur due to its stronger manpower (Mantoux, 2017).[48]

One of the most controversial groups was Jund al-Aqsa, which was accused of secretly aligning with IS.[49] After declaring its neutrality when IS and Jabhat al-Nusra broke ranks (Kujan, 2016), the group assisted Jabhat al-Nusra's attacks on other factions, such as the Syria Revolutionary Front and Hazm. The group also engaged in factional conflicts by killing numerous leaders of other factions and helping IS members move in and out of Idlib province (Abu Sayyaf, 2016b). As a result, Jund al-Aqsa faced severe backlash from various opposition groups, especially Ahrar al-Sham. Ahrar al-Sham accused the group of excommunicating its members (Ahrar al-Sham, 2016n), while the Syrian Islamic Council denounced them as heretics (*khawarij*) like IS for killing and excommunicating fellow Muslims (al-Majlis al-Islami, 2016). This led to calls for Jund al-Aqsa's eradication by an array of religious scholars close to Ahrar al-Sham and other groups (n.m, 2016b).

The choice between (1) organisational expansion and institutionalisation or (2) limited consolidation combined with the institutionalisation of cross-factional ties also impacted armed groups' evolving modes of organisation. In absence of hegemony, the first type of groups could reconfigure more substantially over time. Embeddedness in a plurality of social networks and localities gave them the opportunity to create relatively independent and centralised military forces that could be used across geographic areas. This decision was important to limit the feedback mechanisms stemming from their local communities, while emphasising the primacy of group belonging (including through ideological indoctrination). Jabhat al-Nusra was more successful than Faylaq al-Sham in that regard. Faylaq al-Sham primarily remained an agglomeration of locally embedded armed groups with only limited centralised components. In the second case, the local groups that relied on cross-factional alliances also created more professional military forces. But their military forces remained more closely tied to their local communities because of the limited geographic spreading of their groups. Over time, their military forces were usually composed of a certain number of better trained full-time professional soldiers who coordinated with part-time local fighters mobilised on a case-to-case basis.[50]

In absence of hegemony, non-military affairs were conducted in multiple ways.[51] Local councils that usually remained independent spread in armed opposition–held areas, although local families with factional backing often contended with one another for influence, too.[52] Councils typically coalesced through the involvement of notable individuals and various revolutionary groups following an ad hoc approach to secure external support. One of the key notable challenges was the existence of multiple governance structures lacking clear mechanisms for their establishment.[53] Despite gaining increased legitimacy over time, these councils grappled with issues such as the absence of a taxation system, difficulties in resource extraction, and a heavy reliance on external support. Furthermore, they faced hurdles related to a lack of technical capacities and accountability mechanisms (Humanitarian Dialogue, 2014).

In absence of external supervision, local councils varied substantially.[54] A limited number, as in Saraqib, imposed taxes that granted them a relatively significant autonomy vis-à-vis armed groups. Other local councils were too weak and swayed by local armed groups using their own source of support and organisational strength, or relied on international support to leverage some level of independence vis-à-vis local armed groups. Older conflicts between families often impacted local factional divides between major factions (e.g., Heller, 2016c),[55] which detrimentally affected the cohesion of armed opposition–held areas by entrenching factional influence. Only in one case, outside the northwest in Daraya, a local council imposed itself over local military groups (Hyyppä, 2023). Local councils enjoyed more independence during the first phase of the conflict, since armed groups did not initially focus on territorial control and civilian administration, which changed in a subsequent phase (Quesnay, 2017). But international support also created internal resentment, as some cities gathered more funds while others suffered from their association with Jabhat al-Nusra, which impeded support, since the group was internationally listed for its association with al-Qaeda.[56] Jabhat al-Nusra's general service management was relatively minor in comparison to Ahrar al-Sham's own services, which conversely benefited from the group's local anchorage and ability to mobilise an array of social networks, as argued in the previous chapter.[57]

Armed groups played an active role in local courts and services, which was a key aspect of their external institutionalisation and ties to the population.[58] In 2012, armed groups established the Shari'a committees (al-Hay'at al-Shar'iya) in Aleppo as an alternative to the local Unified Judicial Council. This heightened the resentment of the local groups that tried to establish independent judicial institutions but failed to impose themselves due to a lack of military power. According to a former Ahrar al-Sham leader, this step meant to assure the collaboration of all the factions in the new circumstances, especially in the field of security, though the commission also endeavoured to supervise schools and the economy as well (Al Shari', 2012). Factional courts were structured according to local balance of power (Schwab, 2018). The factions created their own courts and detention facilities where they effectively controlled territory and shared responsibility in urban areas where multiple factions cohabited. For example, a four-faction committee consisting of Ahrar al-Sham, Jabhat al-Nusra, Liwa al-Tawheed, and Suqur al-Sham formed in Aleppo ('Abd al-Haj, 2013).

Jabhat al-Nusra later left the four-faction committee in Aleppo when it pursued its own strategy of territorialisation, establishing its own independent court system, Dar al-Qada. Jabhat al-Nusra condemned factional quotas that prevented accountability of powerful individuals linked to the factions, as well as the absence of an independent executive force (Dar al-Qada, 2014). It is noteworthy that Jabhat al-Nusra's first ruling targeted one of the group's own commanders (Jabhat al-Nusra, 2015b) to signal that the new institution would not cover for its members as other groups' courts did. Despite this move, Jabhat al-Nusra was accused of numerous excesses, including killing individuals for apostasy and occasionally applying Islamic penal ordinances (*hudud*), albeit not in a systematic manner.[59] But Jabhat al-Nusra's reassertion continued to participate in the Islamic committee in Idlib city with five other factions, primarily under the dominance of Ahrar al-Sham.

The profusion of competing judicial orders impeded the unification of the court system. According to a former judge, each faction continued to apply its own rulings and procedures based on different juridical foundations.[60] More secular groups affiliated with the Free Syrian Army supported the Unified Arab Code, a set of rules proposed by the Arab League to formalise Islamic law (Jami'a al-Duwal al-'Arabiyya, 1996), while Islamist groups generally considered the positivisation of Islamic law anathema to their core religious beliefs (al-Zarier, Rateb, & Adely, 2017).[61] The atomisation of local order led to contradictory fatwas on religious norms (for instance, should breaking the fast during the month of Ramadan be penalised?), although the harsher physical penalties associated with the Islamic penal punishments (*hudud*) were generally not implemented because of the war ('Abd al-Haj, 2013). Individuals often exploited this situation to demand additional judicial rulings from other courts when they failed to win a first case.[62] Formerly trained Syrian judges were seldom used. Competition between different courts, the absence of a highest judicial body to adjudicate cases, and the absence of an executive force independent from the factions eroded the credibility of the courts, as recognised by Ibrahim Shasho, a former Ahrar al-Sham judge who would later become the minister of justice of the government supported by Jabhat al-Nusra's next utterance.[63] It also exacerbated factionalism as local Syrians close to particular factions used their assistance to protect themselves. Ultimately, the courts not associated with any specific faction were relegated to the role of mere record-keepers of judicial incidents rather than being effective in resolving them; their lack of enforcement capability hindered their capacity to bring about meaningful solutions (Sakhi, 2023: 114–149). A local leader of a faction affiliated with the Free Syrian Army regretted that:

> There were a lot of tensions between the groups. Which flag can we use, the Syrian revolutionary flag or the black *ra'ya* [a black flag used by Jihadis]? What law should we implement? Each group had its own court system. The Jihadis penetrated society with their courts, not with the provision of social services. They were quite pragmatic and popular. More importantly, they had an executive force that could implement their rulings (table 3.2).

Table 3.2 Armed groups' comparative expansion

Groups	Internal institutionalisation	External relations with other groups	Geographic continuity	Future
Ahrar al-Sham	Institutionalisation of cross-factional ties to consolidate organisationally	Institutionalisation of cross-factional alliance	No	One organisational division, then joining the National Liberation Front
Jabhat al-Nusra	Organisational expansion and internal institutionalisation	Institutionalisation of cross-factional alliance, forced dismantlement of some factions	No	Expansion and domination, creation of HTS
IS	Organisational expansion and internal institutionalisation in one contiguous region	Armed confrontation with all the opposition	Most of the group regrouped in one area, with minor branches elsewhere	Hegemony and territorial downfall
Suqur al-Sham	Consolidation in a limited area	Institutionalisation of cross-factional alliances	Yes	Inclusion in the National Liberation Front
Zinki Movement	Consolidation in a limited area	Institutionalisation of cross-factional alliances	Yes	Suppression by Jabhat al-Nusra (HTS by then)
Faylaq al-Sham	Limited organisational expansion initially, which then increased with external state support	Institutionalisation of cross-factional alliance	No	Inclusion in the National Liberation Front
Smaller Jihadi brigades	Consolidation in a limited area	Institutionalisation of cross-factional alliances	Yes	Mostly independent
Pro-IS foreign brigades	Joining IS	Armed confrontation with all the opposition	Yes in IS territory	In IS

Ahrar al-Sham's Unique Strategy of Alliance

Ahrar al-Sham emerged as the leading armed opposition group aside from IS and Jabhat al-Nusra, which initially suffered from its split with Baghdadi's group. Ahrar al-Sham's unique approach to its internal and external institutionalisation played a key role. Ahrar al-Sham's strategy was to externally institutionalise its relationships with other armed groups to facilitate their integration into its own organisational structures, particularly in northwest Syria, which remained its centre of gravity throughout the conflict.[64] By consolidating in a bottom-up process of factional aggregation and incorporating pre-existing groups into its organisational structures—what Hafez, Gabbay, & Gade (2021) call "cooperative consolidation" in other contexts—Ahrar al-Sham managed to expand into disconnected territories and avoid significant splits. In contrast, Jabhat al-Nusra relied on a top-down, centralised approach to mobilisation, a "competitive consolidation" that outcompeted other groups. It also focused on recruiting and socialising individual fighters in different regions before centralising their resources, including weaponry.

The previous chapter argued that Ahrar al-Sham's early success was due, in part, to its embeddedness in the latent Islamist social movement. Unlike other armed groups, Ahrar al-Sham was formed by interconnected locals who were not besieged, did not rely on one geographic location or strongman, and did not form for one particular battle. It emerged as a coordination of independent military units that gradually institutionalised through the establishment of shared organisational structures, which facilitated the integration of new brigades. These unique characteristics not only reinforced Ahrar al-Sham's credibility and attractiveness within Syria, but also made the group more appealing to foreign supporters, including private donors and states. Ahrar al-Sham positioned itself as a critical broker of the armed opposition, promoting influential political and military initiatives inside Syria.

Ahrar al-Sham's early development had a significant impact on its strategy of expansion as the conflict in Syria unfolded. As the armed opposition seized larger territories, the consolidation of larger armed groups became necessary. Ahrar al-Sham's ability to expand across disconnected geographic areas was quite unique among Syrian armed groups, and was facilitated by its embeddedness in the Islamist social movement. This embeddedness allowed Ahrar al-Sham to establish contact with independent Islamist military units that were seeking to join a larger entity to adapt to the new realities of the conflict. Additionally, other military factions looking for the support of a larger group were drawn to Ahrar al-Sham due to its decentralised organisational structures and its ability to broker across multiple social networks, including prison, university, and militant networks. Abd al-Salam Hussein (al-Jazeera, 2016) retrospectively argued in a documentary before his death:

> The movement of Ahrar al-Sham emerged when all the brothers who headed smaller groups united. We knew one another. We were in prison together. We knew their histories, methodologies, and objectives. Since we agree about the tools and objectives, why should we remain dissociated and claim that all we want is Islam?

Ahrar al-Sham implemented a strategy of alliance formation with other groups. The purpose was to institutionalise cross-factional relations before institutionalising internally as a new entity. After the failure of the Front of Revolutionaries mentioned in the previous chapter, Ahrar al-Sham leaders created the Syrian Islamic Front (al-Jabhat al-Islamiyya Suriyya) in December 2012. The Syrian Islamic Front gathered Ahrar al-Sham (as Kata'ib Ahrar al-Sham—Ahrar al-Sham Brigades) along with Liwa al-Haq in Homs; Harakat al-Fajr al-Islamiyya in Aleppo and its countryside; Jama'at al-Tali'a al-Islamiyya in the Idlib countryside; Kata'ib Ansar al-Sham in Latakia and its countryside; Katibat Mus'ab bin 'Omayr in the Aleppo countryside; Jaysh al-Tawhid in Deir al-Zor; and Kata'ib Suqur al-Islam, Kata'ib al-Iman al-Muqatila, Sarayat al-Maham al-Khassa and Katibat Hamza bin Abd el-Mutallib in Damascus and its countryside.[65] The alliance aimed at facilitating the organisational unification of these groups, which could become a credible actor including vis-à-vis Western countries (Lund, 2013a: 17). Leading negotiators argued that, although they shared similar ideas, the main impediment was posed by the difficulty in coordinating across disconnected areas and the need to attract the largest possible number of factions (Lund, 2013a: 16). In the next few months, the Damascus factions united as Katibat Hamza bin 'Abd al-Mutallib and then joined Kata'ib Ahrar al-Sham, Harakat al-Fajr al-Islamiyya, and Jama'at al-Tali'a al-Islamiyya as the Islamic movement of Ahrar al-Sham (Harakat Ahrar al-Sham al-Islamiyya).

Although the groups that formed Ahrar al-Sham shared a common goal of replacing the Syrian regime with an Islamic state, they were not necessarily aligned ideologically. Some smaller groups were considered more ideologically committed than Ahrar al-Sham's early units. Ahrar al-Sham leaders later argued that, in light of the factional competition with groups like Jabhat al-Nusra, it was better to integrate more "radical" entities into their group in order to better control and assimilate them. Some of these groups played a notable role in Ahrar al-Sham's ideological revisions, as discussed in chapter 5.[66] Ahrar al-Sham leaders nonetheless recognised that the incorporation of these units posed significant challenges. Some of these groups also played a key role in the competition between Ahrar al-Sham and Jabhat al-Nusra, which ultimately led to the incorporation of some Ahrar al-Sham brigades into the latter. Ahrar al-Sham's head of international relations, Husam Tarsha, explained that:

> The idea was to co-opt the groups that were more radical to moderate them inside our movement. They did not have the prison experience and ideological revisions that we undertook during our imprisonment. Integrating them was a challenge but we believed that these people were better inside our movement than with our competitors like Jabhat al-Nusra.

Ahrar al-Sham's transformation from a coalition of brigades to a movement was driven by the necessity to expand its activities beyond conventional military work in newly conquered territories. The group established administrative, political, social, and religious offices to support its core tasks. Ahrar al-Sham placed great emphasis on its political bureau, which developed new positions on a range of domestic and international issues and fostered ties with foreign actors. This characteristic set Ahrar al-Sham apart from other Jihadi groups, which never featured political offices. In 2013, the group published a new charter (*mithaq al-haraka*) to clarify its objectives and approach, with the aim of providing a blueprint for other groups to follow (Ahrar al-Sham, 2013). While calling for a state ruled by Islamic Law yet respectful of religious minorities, the charter stressed the importance of institutional work to conduct an array of missions beyond military operations, including politics, media, religious proselytisation (*daʿwa*), and education. Ahrar al-Sham's leadership structure reflected its bottom-up consolidation, with the leaders of each constituent unit joining a consultative council (*majlis al-shura*) that made strategic decisions. The constituent units ceased to use their pre-joining names to promote the consolidation of a shared group identity. Unlike most other groups, the leader's prerogatives were institutionally constrained, with the integration of new members to the council requiring a vote and strategic decisions requiring council approval. The leader's role was primarily administrative, including the nomination of new commanders and reorganisation of the group's internal bureaucracy. Although Ahrar al-Sham subsequently opened up to other factions and foreign countries, the charter already indicated that the group presented itself as rather inclusive. As Khaled Abu Anas argued:

> I disagreed that we moderated during the war. The first proof is our initial description of ourselves. We mentioned that we were a popular movement that was independent. Second, we did not use an Islamic name that could be used against us. We did not, we do not, want people to judge Islam based on us or our behaviour. We therefore decided not to use an Islamic name for the group and explicitly told our sheikhs not to have a Salafi Wahabi discourse.

The consolidation of Ahrar al-Sham as a movement proved to be highly attractive to other factions due to its unique internal features. The group's bottom-up approach made it more internally consensual and inclusive than most other groups, simplifying the admission of new sub-groups based on their size, representativeness, and the skills of their leaders. This made it easy for new factions to pledge their allegiance to Ahrar al-Sham and benefit from the joining of a larger armed group without significant internal reconfiguration. In contrast to Jabhat al-Nusra or IS, Ahrar al-Sham did not impose strict ideological commitments or regulations on new members. As Khaled Abu Anas noted:

> Our work relies on the creation of institution. This is necessary in order not to sanctify the individuals but also renew our group over time. We therefore created institutional offices—including administrative, military, financial, and social—with their own responsibilities and functions. People are chosen based on their abilities but organisational norms have changed over time. For instance, we did not use sub-factional quotas for the joining of the consultative council initially. There were influential people that should be in the council regardless of the strength of their groups. So we took them in. But then we needed a vote to include any new member.

Ahrar al-Sham expanded its efforts to institutionalise its alliances with other groups by creating the Islamic Front in November 2013. This umbrella organisation brought together key members of the two main Islamist alliances in Syria: the Syrian Islamic Liberation Front (which included Liwa al-Tawhid from Aleppo, Suqur al-Sham from Idlib, and Jaysh al-Islam from Damascus) and the Syrian Islamic Front (which included Liwa al-Haq from Homs, Ansar al-Sham, and the Kurdish Islamic Front). Under the leadership of Suqur al-Sham's Abu 'Isa al-Sheikh, the Islamic Front replaced the Syrian Islamic Front and established new leadership, including Ahrar al-Sham's Hassan Abud as the head of the political office, Jaysh al-Islam's Zahran 'Alloush as the head of the military office, and Abul-'Abbas al-Shami as the head of the religious office. The goal was to unify these disparate groups into a cohesive organisation that would operate under a single name and identity, shedding their previous names and affiliations.

The Islamic Front was one of the most ambitious attempts to unite the Islamist armed opposition under a single group, although it was defunct after only a year. One major reason for its relative failure was timing. In 2014, a large-scale confrontation between mainstream armed groups and IS plagued the opposition all over Syria, resulting in the expulsion of IS to the east of the country. This led to short-term military priorities taking precedence over everything else, obstructing ongoing initiatives in favour of factional unity. Instead of consolidating under the Islamic Front, short-term alliances formed to face the threat of IS. Additionally, even within the Islamic Front, there were internal divisions regarding opposition to IS (al-Shami, 2014b), with some groups being reluctant to fight it actively. Moreover, institutionalising ties and sharing power among armed groups that had already begun consolidating in different areas proved more challenging than agglomerating smaller military units. Rather than unifying all their organisational structures, the groups maintained their names and internal structures. As Khaled Abu Anas recalled:

The Islamic Front was our best hope but the conditions were difficult. It was only a relative victory. The union failed because we were too fast. For instance, we wanted only to use the name Islamic Front and no longer the names of the constituting groups. We needed time for that. Second, the fight with IS exacerbated the lack of trust inside the alliance. There were additional issues. The head of Jaysh al-Islam, [Zahran] Alloush, would be military leader though he is in a small area under siege and we were most prominent in the north. Also, how do you share resources? Everything went to us before, while now it had to go to the Islamic Front. Similarly, we disagreed about the repartition of the seats in the new consultative council which would be based on the same number of seats for each group regardless of their size. All of that was not fair.

Others argued that geography also imposed different priorities on the components of the Islamic Front. An Ahrar al-Sham leader contended that:

Jaysh al-Islam is based on Duma and Ghuta. My personal understanding is that, as a group located so close to Damascus, they thought that their region was critical politically. They therefore preferred to unite their own region, which would then be a card to play if the revolution succeeded in Damascus.

The failure to consolidate the Islamic Front into a cohesive organisational merger, rather than just a coordinating alliance, also explains why Jabhat al-Nusra did not join the new entity. Despite al-Qaeda leader al-Zawahiri's advice for Jabhat al-Nusra to join the alliance, the group ultimately chose not to. There were discussions among armed opposition groups, including Ahrar al-Sham and Jabhat al-Nusra, that considered a limited merger between the two groups. Jabhat al-Nusra's leading religious scholar, Abu Abdullah al-Shami, provided insight into the discussions, stating that:

The consultative council of the two groups discussed a potential union in Aleppo. It only included other factions subsequently. We initially agreed about everything. We chose the leader, religious scholars, etc. Ahrar al-Sham then told us that they wanted to have more factions inside the union. We convened three rounds of meeting before Ahrar al-Sham came up with the international terrorist listing. We told them that it was not an issue as we only had a local focus. We said that we would renounce al-Qaeda in case of a broader union. Then the Islamic Front became a project. Abu Khaled [al-Suri] said we could join the Islamic Front instead of the initial union. We told him that we first had to sit with all the factions to assess them and clarify what they stood for. We wanted to sit with Jaysh al-Islam, as we had reservations regarding their links to the Saudis, Suqur al-Sham, and Liwa al-Tahweed. We wanted to understand them more. We sat with most of them, aside from Suqur al-Sham, before the announcement of the Islamic Front. We said that we would join the Islamic Front if it was a true union. But it was only a media operation. Even their logo was not consistent since each group wrote Islamic Front before adding the name of the faction underneath.

Jabhat al-Nusra's position is noteworthy for two reasons that contextualise its response to subsequent proposals for unity discussed in the next chapter. Abu Abdullah al-Shami's stance exemplifies Jabhat al-Nusra's insistence on carefully vetting potential allies and its deep suspicion of certain armed groups' ties to foreign countries deemed hostile. Additionally, Jabhat al-Nusra prioritised a genuine organisational merger and reconfiguration of groups, rather than a looser coalition that could only consolidate gradually. This position reflects Jabhat al-Nusra's centralised trajectory, in contrast to Ahrar al-Sham's more bottom-up approach to internal institutionalisation.

Despite Jabhat al-Nusra's refusal to join the Islamic Front, Ahrar al-Sham managed to further institutionalise internally under its own umbrella. Liwa al-Haq, Suqur al-Sham, and the Kurdish Islamic Front were absorbed into the group despite the Islamic Front's failure to unite all the Islamist factions. Their integration was facilitated by territorial contiguity in the northwest. Liwa al-Haq did not join Ahrar al-Sham previously when the group remained under siege in Homs, while Suqur al-Sham had long entertained close relations to Ahrar al-Sham and its leaders in northwest Syria.

Ahrar al-Sham's Internal and External Characteristics

Ahrar al-Sham adopted a two-dimensional structure during its internal institutionalisation as a movement.[67] The group retained the local embeddedness of its brigades across Syria, allowing them to maintain their local ties and structures even after joining the group. Additionally, Ahrar al-Sham integrated some of these brigades' leaders in its central leadership based on their size, significance, and specific skills. This unique combination of local embeddedness and vertical integration enabled the group to centralise decision-making processes, elaborate coherent political and religious positions, and gather external financial and military support while maintaining its local structuring. This approach made Ahrar al-Sham an attractive option for independent brigades seeking to strengthen their positions by joining a larger group.

Ahrar al-Sham's decentralised structure meant that the group had to balance accommodating its local sub-groups with maintaining internal cohesion. Most constituting brigades maintained the possibility to reassert their independence or join other groups since alternatives existed, requiring Ahrar al-Sham to be responsive to internal demands and expectations, but also share power with important sub-units. According to the group's communiqués, the main tools to impose discipline were to punish individual commanders in Ahrar al-Sham's internal courts (Ahrar al-Sham, n.d.e), or in some cases, to expel specific sub-groups that failed to abide by the group's orders or that committed excessive violations (e.g., Ahrar al-Sham, 2015e). Some leaders or commanders were also paradoxically promoted to virtually powerless positions as a means of marginalisation. Despite efforts to maintain internal cohesion, there were complaints that powerful leaders or commanders were not always disciplined, due to the need to balance different trends within the group.[68]

Ahrar al-Sham's decentralised structure positioned it favourably to establish external ties with foreign supporters of the armed opposition. The group's ability to integrate a wide range of brigades dispersed throughout Syria, despite its stronghold in the northwest, strengthened its appeal, in contrast with many groups affiliated with the Free Syrian Army that repeatedly fragmented and split. Although Ahrar al-Sham was not an official recipient of the foreign support provided through the shared military coordination set up in Turkey (the MOM)—explored in the next chapter—it did acquire control of some of their weapons when the Islamic Front seized control of the border at Baab al-Hawa (Lund, 2013b). As an efficient Islamist armed group that was not affiliated with al-Qaeda, Ahrar al-Sham was more easily engaged and supported outside established channels than groups like the al-Qaeda affiliate Jabhat al-Nusra. Unlike Jabhat al-Nusra, which could only gather support indirectly through spoils of wars, the seizure of assets owned by other factions, and occasional deals with foreign countries (Hassan, 2017), Ahrar al-Sham was a more attractive partner for foreign supporters looking for a reliable partner in the Syrian conflict.

Over time, the changing nature of the military fronts necessitated internal restructuring within Ahrar al-Sham. The group's early leaders, especially Abu Talha al-Ghab, recognised the need to create a specialised central force with specific skills that could be more effectively deployed throughout the country. Although this force was not immediately established, Ahrar al-Sham's strategy of alliances provided an opportunity to implement the idea (Ahrar al-Sham, 2015h). By integrating Suqur al-Sham, a leading armed opposition group in the early stages of the conflict from al-Zawiyya mountains that was already interconnected with Ahrar al-Sham leadership in familial, local, and regional networks, Ahrar al-Sham thought that it could transform it into its central military force. This move would have allowed Ahrar al-Sham to dissociate local brigades responsible for manning the front lines from a more professional military force that could better fight regime forces throughout the country. The agreement reached between

Ahrar al-Sham and Suqur al-Sham in the summer of 2015 delegated this responsibility to Suqur al-Sham. According to an Ahrar al-Sham leader:

> The idea was that Suqur al-Sham would become the central military force of Ahrar al-Sham as Jaysh al-Suqur. Abu 'Isa al-Sheikh is a good man and he was strong in his region. But the movement did not support him, unfortunately, and it never really happened. Abu 'Isa also felt isolated from remaining leaders. He was not like them so he decided to leave.

The establishment of a central military force faced obstacles from within Ahrar al-Sham itself. The decentralised nature of the alliance system that formed the basis of the movement meant that power was dispersed among various leaders and brigades, leading to competition and potential conflict. This was exacerbated by the loss of the group's core leadership in September 2014, which created further power vacuums.[69] The formation of a central force would have required significant changes to the group's internal power dynamics, potentially giving more power to the central force and altering the balance of power among the group's various brigades.

As Ahrar al-Sham institutionalised internally, it sought to signal a shift away from exclusively pursuing military objectives. The group tried to present a comprehensive alternative to the Syrian regime. With the acquisition of new territories, the group recognised the need to improve its external institutionalisation, which included establishing local governance structures capable of providing social services and enforcing law and order. Ahrar al-Sham's wide-ranging social networks enabled it to become a central actor of the armed opposition. Its presence was felt across a broad spectrum of Syrian society, allowing it to mobilise individuals with diverse skills and experiences. Besides the integration of new military brigades, other Syrians who had established local groups to conduct basic humanitarian work or participated in conciliation offices or courts of justice also joined the group. Many of these individuals had never taken up arms but were linked to Ahrar al-Sham through overlapping social networks. They joined the group because of its credibility and broader vision, which many other military brigades lacked. They include urban youth, students who joined the uprising early on, and civil society actors according to my interviews with a range of Ahrar al-Sham bureaucrats.[70]

The group's external institutionalisation differed significantly from that of other actors, beyond ideological considerations. Despite ideological differences, armed groups like IS and the YPG monopolised political order in their respective territories by establishing monopolistic institutions under their direct control. They replicated state entities and prevented the consolidation of competing armed groups with whom they would have to share power and responsibilities.

Their local authority, interactions with their constituencies, and flexibility varied in time and place, but their hegemonic aspirations were relatively constant features. Although hegemony can be authoritarian in nature, many locals expressed satisfaction at having a single authority with a relatively clear chain of command.[71] Even foreign NGOs managed to find some modus operandi with IS until 2014, by using their court systems on specific occasions and paying taxes, according to numerous interviews with humanitarian workers.[72]

Ahrar al-Sham's approach to its external institutionalisation was distinct from that of other armed groups elsewhere, owing to the multi-party nature of the armed opposition in its northwest stronghold. Rather than imposing its authority over other factions, Ahrar al-Sham sought to manage and balance them. The group collaborated with other factions to police armed opposition–held areas, replacing previous initiatives that were not connected to local armed groups. This approach was a response to the weakness of these initiatives led by civil society activists, who were unable to implement their decisions without the support of an executive force. But collaborating with other factions had its drawbacks. While factional consensus allowed for greater inclusivity and representation, it was less efficient than single-group hegemony. Moreover, sharing power among different armed groups could potentially entrench factionalism over time, as previously mentioned.

This strategy of balancing different factions also explains the group's reluctance to confront other armed groups when necessary, such as ISIS. Ahrar al-Sham and other factions played a key role in capturing Raqqa, with Ahrar al-Sham seizing former centres of power and the central bank in the city (al-Sharq al-Awsat, 2013). Ahrar al-Sham and ISIS were the strongest contenders at the time. But the armed opposition was inexperienced in governance and struggled to provide basic services and security, which allowed ISIS to gain a foothold, selectively attacking individual groups one after the other before taking over the city (Rosenblatt & Kilcullen, 2019). Despite having the potential to eliminate ISIS early on, Ahrar al-Sham and others chose not to confront the emerging threat. This decision was partly motivated by the fear that some group members would be reluctant to fight fellow Muslims, as revealed in interviews with leading Ahrar al-Sham members featured in a documentary. The group's religious authority at the time, Abu 'Abd al-Malek al-Shar'i, acknowledged in a recorded lecture to soldiers that some members were not ideologically inclined to shed Muslim blood, unlike ISIS, which excommunicated non-members.

> People were not going to fight a group whose banner bears "there is no god but God" [the Muslim testimony of faith]. They are not used to it. The second problem is our mentality. This mentality implies that we only fight the disbeliever. But that's wrong.[73]

Ahrar al-Sham additionally engaged in the provision of social services. The group supported bodies such as the Islamic Commission to Administer the Liberated Areas (al-Hay'at al-Islamiyya li Idarat al-Mataniq al-Muharara) (Ahmad, 2015) to deliver social services. Social provisions (especially bread delivery) strengthened the group and helped it expand in certain areas. Ahrar al-Sham leaders additionally fostered their ties to civil society and the growing number of professional unions that formed after expelling regime troops. Ahrar al-Sham leaders also understood the necessity to collaborate with NGOs and international institutions to strengthen local support. This position helped the group indirectly assist its local constituency, in contrast with Jabhat al-Nusra, whose resources were more limited. Ahrar al-Sham protected to a large extent local civil society against factions that imposed stricter regulations locally.[74] There was occasional local resistance to the group, which forced it to accept local compromises. For instance, Ahrar al-Sham agreed to conduct municipal elections in 2016 in Saraqib under local pressure, and share power without resorting to violence (Gopal, 2018). Ahrar al-Sham was therefore more lenient with the local population, which was helped by its primarily local membership. Accommodating local demands meant that, although demonstrations occurred against Ahrar al-Sham and other armed groups, they never reached the antagonism against Jabhat al-Nusra as the latter successively dismantled factions and occasionally used violence locally against its opponents (Bambers & Svensson, 2022).

The willingness to include a wide range of individuals with varying beliefs ultimately proved detrimental to the group. Many other armed groups regret that, at some point, one merely had to be Sunni to be able to join Ahrar al-Sham.[75] On the other hand, the inclusion of more committed Islamist militants hindered the group's ability to take clear stances on important issues, such as adopting the Syrian green revolutionary flag and the Arab penal code, which aligned with mainstream non-Islamist components of the armed opposition, and were accepted only after 2017. Notably, Egyptian religious scholars who had joined Ahrar al-Sham opposed these choices, and their allies promoted stricter local judicial rulings, such as limited applications of Islamic penalties.[76] Ahrar al-Sham's rapid expansion bolstered claims that the group was more radical than initially claimed (Hassan, 2016b), and that its actual strength was exaggerated (Hassan, 2016a).

Ahrar al-Sham institutional trajectory reinforced these divisions and never fully resolved them. The group's internal institutionalisation, particularly the dominant role of its leadership council, made it increasingly difficult to undertake internal reforms. Various factions within the group instead acted as internal lobbies, especially following the death of the group's top-tier leaders in September 2014.[77] Decision-making was further complicated by the need for consensus among members of the leadership council, which inhibited the adoption of swift responses to evolving events. As a result, the group's leadership became a revolving door of different leaders, each with limited power and prerogatives. These entrenched structures proved difficult to change over time, as different power brokers were resistant to losing their influence. As a result, weaker leaders were successively appointed after 2014, perpetuating the group's internal divisions.

As a whole, these characteristics explain why Ahrar al-Sham became the leading armed opposition group by 2015, whose presence in various regions of Syria and its Islamist political project that was amenable to collaboration with foreign countries, set it apart from other groups like IS and Jabhat al-Nusra. Western states were reluctant to classify the group as a "terrorist" organisation like al-Qaeda and IS, although the United States remained sceptical of the group (Hubbard, 2015) despite calls by the country's former ambassador to Syria Robert Ford to engage it (Ford & El Yassir, 2015). This situation changed in September 2014, when a significant number of the group's top leaders were killed in an explosion, raising concerns about the group's future. Despite this setback, Ahrar al-Sham's institutional foundation and foreign support enabled its survival and continued expansion in the following year. But the process of organisational reconstruction was accompanied by the entrenchment of a strong internal divide that eventually hindered its decision-making processes.[78]

Conclusion

The Syrian regime's historical consolidation contributed to the unique geographic fragmentation of the armed opposition. Rather than being able to establish a stronghold and expand from there, armed groups emerged concurrently in different regions of Syria and struggled to connect with one another. To survive, successful groups had to carefully balance internal cohesion, prevent dissent, and avoid overextending themselves. Only a select few, including Ahrar al-Sham and Jabhat al-Nusra, were able to expand and institutionalise across multiple regions. Others attempted to assert their dominance in a particular area or to build cross-factional alliances with neighbouring groups instead. Establishing hegemonic control, as seen with groups such as IS, Jaysh al-Islam, and the YPG, was a common strategy to consolidate political and military power and mitigate internal fragmentation.

Ahrar al-Sham was one of the most successful groups during the initial phase of the war in Syria, with its historical stronghold being in the northwest. This region was characterised by diverse support networks and a significant number of foreign fighters, leading to the proliferation of numerous armed groups. Ahrar al-Sham emerged as a coalition of Islamist brigades that institutionalised their relationships with one another before institutionalising internally as they became a movement. This mode of development contributed to Ahrar al-Sham's institutional trajectory, de-centralised structure, and local embeddedness in Syrian communities. It positioned the group advantageously during the intermediate phase of the conflict, although the features that enabled Ahrar al-Sham's success at the time eventually hindered its ability to defeat its more cohesive competitor, Jabhat al-Nusra, in the new phase of the war.

4
Uniting the Armed Opposition

The formation and expansion of the armed opposition presented two key challenges that justified the need to unite all the groups under a single umbrella. First, armed groups had to enhance their military capability to defend their territories and seize new ones, rather than being a collection of weakly organised local factions that could not confront the regime and its foreign supporters. Second, they had to establish new relationships with foreign states to become credible actors eligible for significant external financial, political, and military backing. As support for the regime grew, armed groups had to undergo a significant qualitative transformation to continue capturing new territories. Short-term military victories alone were no longer enough. Moreover, armed groups had to balance military and political priorities to adapt to the changing environment. If they could not unite the armed opposition, they had to at least institutionalise cross-factional relations to coordinate their efforts short of a meaningful organisational unity. While the previous chapter primarily explored armed groups' comparative choices through armed opposition–held areas, this chapter focuses on the impact of external actors on the armed opposition and its unification. It concludes with the polarisation of the armed opposition around Ahrar al-Sham and Jabhat al-Nusra by 2016 and the latter's subsequent takeover.

Synchronising the Rebellion Outside and Inside Syria

The early days of the insurgency were relatively precarious. Between 2011 and 2012, the armed groups lacked sophistication and primarily relied on a limited number and type of weapons obtained through smuggling markets. They later supplemented these with spoils of war obtained from regime troops. Cross-factional coordination was weak and primarily based on local dynamics. As mentioned in earlier chapters, large fronts formed in Aleppo and Homs around coalitions of local groups, composed of neighbours, acquaintances, and army deserters who had very local or personalised loyalty to individual commanders that did not last. Although small group coordination occurred in the countryside, it was not formalised under larger umbrellas. Local armed groups coordinated guerrilla hit-and-run attacks against regime checkpoints, gatherings, and moving targets.[1] During this phase of the conflict, foreign countries were only sporadically involved.

Relations between armed opposition groups, regardless of ideological or strategic divergences, were not initially antagonistic despite the lack of institutionalisation. Armed groups of all persuasions collaborated based on shared interests and immediate military priority. It was common, for instance, to see Jabhat al-Nusra before the split with ISIS partnering with mainstream factions affiliated with the Free Syrian Army in specific military battles. One of Jabhat al-Nusra's strengths was its use of car bombs against regime targets, which opened the way for other groups' ground troops to storm in. Car bombs played a critical role against fixed targets such as military bases and prisons besieged by opposition forces. In areas under armed groups' control, different factions set up their own headquarters and checkpoints, including inside the border control of Baab al-Hawa next to Turkey (Kurabi & Drevon, 2018). Initially, they were not preoccupied with establishing local governance structures, which remained mostly under civilian control (Quesnay, 2017). Ideological differences did not cause significant internal clashes and divisions, and individuals frequently switched memberships in different groups based on local needs (ICG, 2012; Baczko et al., 2018: 183). Syrians or foreigners with particular skills notably assisted different groups.[2] Interestingly, even ISIS members could leave the group without being punished, unlike the group's subsequent policy of jailing or executing deserters. This informally allowed for a relatively good reputation of armed groups like Jabhat al-Nusra before the split with ISIS (Lister, 2016c).

Although the armed opposition was already internally diverse before foreign states started to meaningfully engage the opposition, external intervention exacerbated internal tensions. While foreign states claimed to seek to unite and institutionalise the opposition by promoting hierarchical command and control, their practical support for contending groups contradicted this objective. From 2012 onwards, foreign involvement widened as European and regional states provided limited military and non-military support to various armed groups in order to increase pressure on the regime. Unlike in Libya, they did not aim to provide decisive military support to topple the regime, but rather sought to reinforce the opposition to compel the regime to negotiate with its opponents (Phillips, 2016: 125–146).[3] However, the involvement of foreign sponsors only reinforces factional alliances by punishing reluctant factions when sponsors do not compete with one another (Popovic, 2018), which was not the case in the early years of the Syrian conflict.

The initial attempts to institutionalise external support into a cohesive organisational structure that could unify the armed opposition in Syria repeatedly failed (O'Bagy, 2013; Lister, 2016e). These efforts began with the formation of the Higher Revolutionary Council in February 2012 and the Joint Command in September 2012. Mutual suspicion between Qatar and Saudi Arabia, which favoured their own allies inside and outside the initiatives, plagued these coordinating structures. The most promising attempt to coordinate external support came in December 2012 with the formation of the Supreme Military Council, which was designed to amend and unify the previous organisational structures. The Supreme Military Council was composed of a 30-member council led by a Chief of Staff officially commanding military fronts all over Syria and channelling Western and Arab support to vetted groups as armed groups started to control more territory in the north. Despite these efforts, the Supreme Military Council continued to suffer from previous shortcomings, including difficulties in imposing command and control over the factions, monopolising financial and military support, and institutionalising relations between local factions and the exiled military leadership. Many local groups continued to leverage independent support from various states, including those supportive of the Supreme Military Council, as well as non-state actors, which further divided the armed opposition. Even the subsequent creation of the Military Operations Command in Turkey (Müşterek Operasyon Merkezi in Turkish, or MOM) to coordinate northern factions did not substantially alter these dynamics.

The United States provided external assistance to parts of the armed opposition.[4] General David Petraeus first raised the idea in 2012, before beginning the training of several factions in 2013 (Mazzetti, Goldman, & Schmidt, 2017). Starting in 2013 and continuing until 2017, over $1 billion was spent on providing light weapons, training, salaries, and TOW anti-tank weapons, but no game-changing surface-to-air missiles (Chivers & Schmitt, 2013; Balanche, 2017). The United States selected certain armed groups within the opposition, subjecting them to vetting for support based on their reliability and lack of affiliation with proscribed armed organisations. But this approach encountered numerous challenges, as many armed groups disagreed with the U.S. argument that they should fight ISIS only, preferring to fight the regime as well (Stein, 2022). There were also tensions with Turkey, which sought collaboration with specific groups, notably Ahrar al-Sham, though the United States identified issues with partnering with it because of its ideological leanings (Stein, 2022: 79). Tensions between the United States and Turkey also grew due to the latter's alleged support for Islamist groups and the former's increasing support for the Kurdish YPG through the Pentagon (Solomon, 2017). The U.S. support had limited impact and effectiveness, with the exception of a successful coordination between Turkey and Saudi Arabia in 2015. Early hopes that the Müşterek Operasyon Merkezi (MOM) in Turkey could coordinate logistic support and assist the armed opposition also dissipated. Moreover, the slow approval of plans and supplies fueled corruption among armed groups and led to exaggerated claims of their real strength, with many groups inflating their numbers to their external sponsors. Additionally, the United States micromanaged the provision of supplies by asking for intricate details about weapon use in specific battles, particularly with regard to the TOW anti-tank weapons provided after 2014 (Bauer, 2019). Opponents to the United States' support for the opposition also insisted that some weapons ended up in the hands of armed groups like Jabhat al-Nusra, which used the support for vetted factions as a reason to dismantle them.[5]

The U.S. program did not aim to achieve an opposition victory, but rather to create a military stalemate that would force the regime to negotiate a political solution. In the words of William Burns, the U.S. deputy secretary of state at the time and current head of the CIA, "the argument for doing more in 2012 to bolster the opposition was never [...] about victory on the battlefield. It was about trying to demonstrate to Assad and his outside backers that he couldn't win militarily" (Burns, 2019: 327). This became clear to the Syrian opposition when the Barack Obama administration refused to strike the regime militarily to its use of chemical weapons against civilians (Chollet, 2016; Rhodes, 2018; Warrick, 2022). The United States began targeting Jabhat al-Nusra figures instead (Lund, 2014f), before the beginning of a massive military campaign against ISIS later on. These political decisions suggested to the regime and its supporters that Western countries had no real intention of intervening decisively in Syria. It reinforced the argument of Islamist armed groups that the revolutionaries could not rely on Western military support. This, in turn, strengthened the growing role of Islamist groups in the armed opposition, as they were less reliant on Western countries.

It is instructive to draw parallels between the United States support for the insurgency in Syria and the Mujahideen in Afghanistan in the 1980s. A particularly insightful perspective comes from Michael G. Vickers (2023), who served as the Under Secretary of Defence for Intelligence after his time in the U.S. Army Special Forces and the CIA. Vickers played a pivotal role in furnishing support to both the Mujahideen in the 1980s and some Syrian factions in the ongoing conflict. He posits that the United States faced three primary options in Syria: (1) to deploy a conventional force to directly confront the Assad regime; (2) to launch an air campaign in addition to the support provided to opposition groups in Afghanistan against the Taliban in 2001; or (3) to back Syrian mainstream opposition factions through the provision of "arms, ammunition, training, intelligence, and strategic and operational advice" (Vickers, 2023: 374), which partially happened. The United States' support in Syria faced two critical shortcomings according to him. First, it arrived significantly later than in Afghanistan, with military assistance commencing ten days after the onset of the Soviet invasion compared to a prolonged twenty-month delay in Syria. Second, the supply of weaponry was always much more limited. In Afghanistan, the United States provided more support within a single month than it did over the entire twenty-month period in Syria. Vickers instead argued that a more robust approach could have involved deploying greater airpower and supplying advanced weapons such as MANPADS to effectively counter Assad's air force.

Foreign involvement in the conflict in Syria created a sense of unity only in the south. In February 2014, the majority of armed groups became affiliated with the Southern Front, which institutionalised their interactions by coordinating financial and military support through the Military Operations Command (MOC) in Jordan. As described in the previous chapter, the Southern Front was one of the most successful examples of coordination during the Syrian conflict, thanks to unified support from Amman. This allowed the front to monopolise one channel of support, alleviating competition between foreign actors and limiting its negative repercussions on local factions, as in the northwest. Even Jabhat al-Nusra, which initially held a position of strength in the region, was contained by the Southern Front and had to coordinate with its local institutions (Abazeid, 2014). However, the cost of this foreign-enforced unity was the near-exclusive reliance of the armed opposition on Jordan and the United States. Over time, Jordan's interests changed, and it ultimately ended its support for the southern armed groups. When this happened, local groups no longer had any meaningful alternative, and the armed opposition ended in the region.

Foreign support for Free Syrian Army groups and the growing divide with Islamist armed groups explain the latter's attempts to establish their own alternative. The Islamists were cautious of internal competition with foreign-supported groups and attempted to create alternative fronts to counterbalance them. Notable initiatives in this regard were the Syrian Islamic Liberation Front and the Syrian Islamic Front, which aimed to institutionalise cross-Islamist interactions and potentially unite the Islamist factions in a single alternative to the Free Syrian Army. It is worth noting that the Syrian Islamic Liberation Front included important factions that were officially affiliated with the Supreme Military Council supported by Western countries, including Liwa al-Tawheed, Jaysh al-Islam, and Suqur al-Sham. This dual membership suggests that the Supreme Military Council could not monopolise armed opposition-based initiatives and that key factions that had previously been aligned with the Free Syrian Army were distancing themselves from the umbrella organisation (Lister, 2016e). The Syrian Islamic Liberation Front and Syrian Islamic Front were later overshadowed by the Islamic Front, which Ahrar al-Sham promoted to externally institutionalise cross-Islamist interactions before uniting them under a common organisational umbrella.

Still, Islamist groups themselves also began to fight one another. In addition to sporadic conflicts over resources and supporters, armed groups started to embrace more clearly defined identities and projects. The resulting divergences escalated into ideological arguments and factional warfare. The conflict began in 2013, when ISIS attempted to reassert control over its local affiliate, Jabhat al-Nusra, and attacked prominent Islamist commanders, including those from Ahrar al-Sham. The group's seemingly random—rather than systematic—attacks antagonised most Syrian groups.[6] After the gruesome torture and killing of an Ahrar al-Sham local leader, Abu Rayyan, the group escalated its resort to violence, allegedly killing a more prominent Ahrar al-Sham commander named by al-Qaeda leader al-Zawahiri to alleviate internal tensions between Jihadis, Abu Khaled al-Suri (Lund, 2014g). Internal clashes over territorial control and resources then translated into ideological arguments and factional warfare. Although ISIS initially claimed that it did not oppose other Islamist factions, tensions worsened after it claimed that it was a state to which all other factions should pledge allegiance. ISIS excommunicated the groups affiliated with Ahrar al-Sham–supported Islamic Front for collaborating with the military coordination body in Turkey (MOM), striving to establish an inclusive civilian body, and expressing a willingness to nurture ties to other states (Al-Hay'at al-Shari'yya, 2014). Internal hostilities began to dominate cross-factional relations. Armed groups started to institutionalise their ties to one another by forming new alliances that prioritised the internal fight against ISIS, such as the Jaysh al-Mujahideen alliance created in the countryside of Aleppo to expel the Iraqi group (Lund, 2014d). The confrontation with ISIS destabilised the opposition and imposed a change of priority. It paralleled the growing decentralisation of the Free Syrian Army (Lister, 2016e). After calling for ISIS to repent and cease to excommunicate the armed opposition (Abu Khalid, 2013), Ahrar al-Sham started to mobilise against it as well (Ahrar al-Sham, 2014).

As Islamist groups began to gain influence, Ahrar al-Sham experienced a notable upswing in external support from various states, most notably Qatar in cooperation with Turkey. Qatar started to send much larger military shipments in coordination with Turkey from an array of sources, including Libya. Qatar's choice to support Ahrar al-Sham largely resulted from the group's own efforts, as it was transforming into a movement—and not only a coalition of military brigades—between 2012 and 2013, to expand its political engagement. Ahrar al-Sham notably sought to nurture diplomatic connections, exemplified by meetings with figures such as the U.S. ambassador Robert Ford and other Western diplomats in 2013, as well as the authoring of two op-eds to major Western newspapers, mentioned in chapter 5. Ahrar al-Sham aimed to make a strong international case that it was an "acceptable" recipient of foreign military support, which mattered particularly for Qatar, as it did not want to appear to be supporting a listed "terrorist" group. The shift towards political and diplomatic activities paralleled a significant increase in military aid from this country. Additionally, individuals who closely collaborated with Ahrar al-Sham and the Müşterek Operasyon Merkezi in Turkey explain that Ahrar al-Sham did, on occasion, obtain weapons from the MOM, despite not being an official part of the internationally supported mechanism. These acquisitions typically occurred indirectly and occasionally under various aliases, while avoiding any reference to Ahrar al-Sham as a group.[7]

However, foreign countries like Qatar did not propel Ahrar al-Sham's success per se; rather, Qatar recognised Ahrar al-Sham's inherent strengths and its potential as an alternative force and decided to support it. While numerous other factions associated with the Free Syrian Army received substantial military backing and political endorsement, often surpassing what Ahrar al-Sham received, they failed to establish themselves as leaders of the Syrian opposition. In the case of Ahrar al-Sham, Qatar understood that the group was already a formidable player on the ground, with a presence in most opposition-controlled areas. Additionally, it had a more palatable political image compared to groups like Jabhat al-Nusra at the time: Ahrar al-Sham, a Salafi armed group, was not affiliated with al-Qaeda and displayed a willingness to engage with foreign partners, making it a more attractive partner for foreign countries.

The expulsion of IS from northwest Syria and the stabilisation of the front lines in 2014 sparked the most promising effort to institutionalise the armed opposition by unifying the remaining groups. With the most uncompromising component of the armed opposition confined to eastern Syria and Jabhat al-Nusra temporarily weakened, factional tensions abated. In the summer of 2014, the largest groups discussed an initiative aimed at unifying the armed opposition in a single structure. The initiative, "Hold Fast" (Wa 'Itasamu), aimed to establish a Revolutionary Leadership Council (Majlis Qiyadat al-Thawra) that would be inclusive of both Islamist and non-Islamist factions (Lund, 2014e). This council was designed to unify the opposition's judiciary, military, and political organisational structures into one cohesive body that would represent all forces and gain international recognition. Despite its initial promise, the process ultimately stalled when an explosion decimated the collective leadership of Ahrar al-Sham in September 2014 (Lund, 2014e).[8] According to the head of international relations in Ahrar al-Sham, Husam Tarsha, two initiatives were actually competing at the time:

> We wanted to unite all the factions in a common structure, which would have represented all the political forces in one single umbrella. Five large factions initially congregated for the project under the council of the five. We contacted everybody, including the coalition (*al-i'tilaf*) and the Islamic Council. It took six months without being revealed to the public. Unfortunately, another initiative supported by independent preachers competed with this initiative. They released their initiative before us with a similar content. They claimed to have united 103 factions and a preparatory committee of 30 individuals. We

entered the discussions to allow it to succeed but the killing of our leadership in September ultimately killed the initiative.

The failure of the Revolutionary Leadership Council initiative and the expulsion of IS from armed opposition–held territories paralleled Jabhat al-Nusra's gradual reassertion of its position vis-à-vis local factions that it accused of being corrupt or supported by the United States. The United States designated Jabhat al-Nusra as a terrorist group in December 2012, followed by the United Nations Security Council, which listed the group under the 1267 sanction regime against al-Qaeda and ISIS in May 2013. The impact of this classification was limited initially, as Jabhat al-Nusra continued to collaborate with most armed groups. However, in September 2014, the United States began to strike a network of commanders linked to Jabhat al-Nusra. U.S. officials denounced these commanders as the "Khorasan" group or network, despite doubts that such a group actually existed (Hussain, 2015). Journalists who met individuals close to this network argue that al-Qaeda had sent some commanders to persuade Jabhat al-Nusra's sub-factions that had joined IS or were leaning towards the Iraqi group to return to the fold of al-Qaeda (Doornbos & Moussa, 2016b). However, the United States maintained that these commanders were planning foreign attacks from Syrian territory. This reinforced Jabhat al-Nusra's fears that external military support for the armed opposition could ultimately be diverted in an internal war against its soldiers, despite the Syrian opposition's initial reluctance to disavow Jabhat al-Nusra (Zelin, 2012b).

Jabhat al-Nusra took the offensive and defeated specific groups that it considered corrupt or long-term strategic threats, such as Division 30, Jamal Maarouf's Syria Revolutionary Front (Jabhat Thuwar Suriyya),[9] and the Hazm movement in 2014 and 2015. Hazm rose to prominence in January 2014 until its dissolution in March 2015. It was an alliance of small factions, with several previously affiliated with Kata'ib al-Faruq. The group received support from the CIA, which provided covert support including TOW anti-tank weapons and training in Qatar. By October of the same year, following U.S. airstrikes targeting Jabhat al-Nusra, the latter seized Hazm's bases and weaponry, claiming it as a preemptive measure amid concerns that these resources might be turned against it. Most of Hazm's fighters then joined other groups, including al-Jabhat al-Shamiyya. The Syrian Revolutionaries Front, comprising over ten small military brigades, conversely emerged in December 2013 as a counterbalance to other factional alliances, notably the Islamic Front spearheaded by Ahrar al-Sham. Despite its early prospects in becoming one of the largest groups in the northwest, it faced numerous accusations of profiteering at checkpoints and prioritising involvement in smuggling operations over active engagement in combat.[10] The group grew in influence with external backing from Saudi Arabia, which opposed Syrian Islamists. In October 2014, Jabhat al-Nusra confronted the Syrian Revolutionaries Front, alleging corruption within its ranks, leading to its dissolution, with very little intervention from other factions to protect it (Sly, 2015).

By targeting only specific groups, Jabhat al-Nusra was more astute than IS's exclusivism, since it continued to emphasise its alignment with Syrian armed groups' revolutionary agenda and willingness to collaborate with other factions. These decisions accompanied the empowerment of more radical figures, especially Jordanians, and the marginalisation of more reformist figures. One of them, Saleh al-Hamawi, later resigned and complained about Jabhat al-Nusra's weaker institutional structure with little clear political direction (Hamawi, 2015).

After the summer 2014 initiative failed to unite the opposition, a series of shared military rooms emerged, comprising prominent armed groups that agreed to coordinate specific military battles. These military rooms were based on increasingly sophisticated cross-factional coordination mechanisms, where armed groups negotiated their material contributions to specific battles and the distribution of spoils of war. In addition, they established adjudication mechanisms and courts to resolve factional disputes over resources.[11] Over time, these groups recognised that if organisational unity could not be achieved, more institutionalised military coordination was still possible.

The most successful institutionalisation of cross-factional military coordination formed at the time. In March 2015, armed groups in the northwest created Jaysh al-Fath (the Army of Conquest) with the goal of seizing the provincial city of Idlib (see also Schwab, 2021: 159–162). The coalition emerged during a time of Qatari, Saudi, and Turkish rapprochement, which facilitated the institutionalisation of cross-factional military coordination (Ignatius, 2015; Lister, 2015c). The alliance included prominent Islamist factions such as Ahrar al-Sham, Jabhat al-Nusra, Jund al-Aqsa, Faylaq al-Sham, Ajnad al-Sham, Liwa al-Haq, and Jaysh al-Sunna, with Ahrar al-Sham and Jabhat al-Nusra as the dominant actors. Jaysh al-Fath gave the armed opposition a unique opportunity to control northwest Syria. It received substantial logistical and military support from foreign countries that had previously supported contending actors on the ground. The coalition's success illustrated the regime's inability to protect military fronts prior to the 2015 Russian intervention. A leading member of Ahrar al-Sham's consultative council specified:

> Previous shared military rooms occurred in an ad-hoc basis without a clear system. We merely checked who wanted to participate in specific battle and then we proceeded with the operation. Jaysh al-Fath was different. There was a system and regulations that did not exist beforehand. We agreed about what would happen from the beginning. We named a military leader, chose who

would rule Idlib afterwards, and determined the spoils of war according to the contributions of each faction.

The more institutionalised Jaysh al-Fath coalition significantly altered the military dynamics on the ground. By synchronising external support from multiple states that had previously held antagonistic agendas, the military coalition seized the city of Idlib on March 28, followed swiftly by the expulsion of remaining regime forces from Syria's northwest. This military momentum led to the decision to replicate the model elsewhere, resulting in the formation of a division of Jaysh al-Fath in the Qalamoun region within the next few months. Subsequent shared operation rooms included Fatah Halab and Ansar al-Shari'ia, established in spring and summer 2015 to seize the remaining parts of Aleppo before their replacement by Jaysh Halab in 2016. The operation rooms were based on localism and immediate military priorities. Instead of attempting to unite all the armed opposition, as in the past, they agreed to coordinate on significant military operations to achieve local military objectives. However, the rationale of the operation rooms quickly shifted from offensive actions to merely defending newly conquered areas. While Jaysh al-Fath initiated an offensive phase, the Russian military involvement that began in autumn 2015 reversed the momentum and forced armed opposition groups to defend their gains more than to expand them (table 4.1).

The shared military operation rooms highlighted Ahrar al-Sham's central role as a broker between factions associated with the Free Syrian Army (including Islamist-leaning groups) and more hard-line Islamists. Ahrar al-Sham's presence in most armed opposition–held areas and cordial relationships with the majority of Syrian armed groups reassured mainstream armed groups that were wary of military collaboration with Jabhat al-Nusra.[12] Additionally, Ahrar al-Sham and mainstream groups legitimised Jabhat al-Nusra's wide participation in shared military operation rooms, giving the group international cover. Many factions and international organisations viewed Ahrar al-Sham as a guarantor of their security and protection locally.[13] Even humanitarian actors occasionally

Table 4.1 The main military operation rooms

Operation room	Place	Period
Jaysh al-Fath	Idlib	Early 2015
Ansar al-Shari'a	Aleppo	Mid to End 2015
Jaysh Halap	Aleppo	February 2016, then December
Fatah Halab	Aleppo	April 2015 to January 2017

relied on Ahrar al-Sham to protect their local employees and resources.[14] While Ahrar al-Sham did not prevent Jabhat al-Nusra from dismantling several groups, it acted as a counterbalance to Jabhat al-Nusra's perceived hegemonic ambitions.

The successes of the military operation rooms presented new challenges for the Syrian armed opposition. While the shared military coordination helped achieve important military objectives, close collaboration with Jabhat al-Nusra drew increased international criticism that the opposition was aligning with al-Qaeda. The group's ties to al-Qaeda burdened the armed opposition, as the regime and its allies exploited the allegiance to al-Zawahiri to discredit the opposition and portray them as no different from IS. Despite Jabhat al-Nusra's denial of planning foreign attacks (Lister, 2015a), external pressure prompted Ahrar al-Sham to distance itself from the group's external affiliations. For instance, Abu Jaber al-Sheikh, Ahrar al-Sham's leader in 2015, insisted on the group's opposition to Jabhat al-Nusra's external affiliation to al-Qaeda in his interview with al-Jazeera (al-Sheikh, 2015). Besides, Western states imposed strict conditions on the provision of specific weapons, such as anti-tank weapons, which had to be reported and videotaped before further provisioning (Barnard & Shoumali, 2015).[15] Some weapons, such as anti-aerial weapons (MANPADS), were not provided at all.[16] It was clear that military collaboration alone would not suffice; a clear political project was needed to alleviate international fears. A former Ahrar al-Sham leader expressed his frustration, stating:

> The idea of Jaysh al-Fath was proposed to liberate Idlib but I thought at the time that it was a mistake. I wanted to free Idlib for the interest of the revolution and the city, but I feared that Jabhat al-Nusra would use Jaysh al-Fath for itself. We should not have allied with them. They had their own objectives and, internationally, the operation was perceived as if al-Qaeda was taking over a Syrian city. You could see that in international coverage of the operation!

Ideological and political divergences among the factions further exacerbated tensions and complicated efforts to establish governance post-territorial control. The seizure of Idlib raised contentious questions about local governance, including the role of the factions and the place of Syrian civil society. While institutionalised military collaboration was relatively easy to establish with cohesive foreign support, governance post-territorial control proved to be more difficult. The coalition tried to prevent internal factional fighting by imposing its sole control over some areas where non-affiliated groups could not operate (Jaysh al-Fath, 2016b). The components of Jaysh al-Fath debated the imposition of military rule versus the creation of a civilian administration in Idlib. Ahrar al-Sham favoured a civilian administration with a factional quota which was subsequently established in the provincial city given the group's stronger military forces. But other independent religious preachers and groups opposed the entry of the Syrian opposition from abroad, arguing that Islamic Law should be applied immediately in the city.[17] Ahrar al-Sham insisted in public communiqués that the coalition included many groups with their own policies and projects, not just Jabhat al-Nusra, and that it respected citizens' basic rights (Ahrar al-Sham, 2016e). A small Salafi Jihadi outfit, Jund al-Aqsa, which was more aligned with IS's views without being organisationally affiliated, blamed Ahrar al-Sham for refusing to enforce Islamic Law in the city and inciting Jaysh al-Fath to fight IS (Jund al-Aqsa, 2015). The group left the alliance, and other more mainstream factions, such as Faylaq al-Sham, Zinki Movement, and Suqur al-Sham, joined the alliance instead (Jaysh al-Fath, 2016a). These changes preceded multiple assassinations against other armed groups, which many blamed on Jund al-Aqsa (Abu Sayyaf, 2016b). Ahrar al-Sham attempted to balance its position by clarifying both the Islamist credentials of the alliance and its position on the U.N. plan, Turkey, and the United States and Russia (al-Nahhas, 2015a). The inclusion of new groups paved the way for the promotion of Jaysh al-Fath as a possible institutional framework for the armed opposition.

The Bi-Polarisation of the Armed Opposition around Ahrar al-Sham and Jabhat al-Nusra

The game-changing Russian involvement in the Syrian conflict preceded several attempts to revive the moribund political process. The first of these attempts was a series of meetings that began in Vienna in October 2015, followed by a conference in Riyadh, Saudi Arabia, two months later. Despite the hostility of the Syrian regime and Russia, the Saudi meeting aimed to unify the political positions of the Syrian opposition, resulting in the formation of the High Negotiations Committee, which included Ahrar al-Sham but not Jabhat al-Nusra. This committee aimed at representing the opposition and developing a shared political program. The subsequent failure to relaunch the Geneva process led to direct negotiations between the United States and Russia for a country-wide ceasefire that would receive international support. While a partial ceasefire was implemented from February to July 2016, the escalation of violence in the summer of 2017 led to a new deal between the United States and Russia in September of that year to implement a new cease-fire. Alas, this cease-fire barely lasted a week.

However, international discussions on the political process were not the main drivers of violence in 2016. The Russian military intervention that started in September 2015 reversed the gains made hitherto by the armed opposition, shifting the balance of power on the ground. The city of Aleppo was a key battleground in the conflict, serving as a symbolic, economic, and political objective for both sides. The opposition had partially controlled Aleppo since 2012. The regime launched an offensive to retake the city in October 2015, with the support of foreign allies primarily from Iran and Lebanese Hizbullah. Over the next few months, the regime forces reconquered a series of strategic towns around Aleppo, gradually isolating the armed opposition–held areas from their strategic connection to Turkey. By the summer of 2016, regime forces had successfully severed armed groups' supply routes and besieged them, while the counterattacks launched by the armed opposition failed to yield any significant results due to the wide power imbalance. The Battle of Aleppo occurred in tandem with the U.S. elections, providing a strategic window for Russian involvement. Russia, committed to asserting control over the city, viewed the city's capture as a symbolic declaration that the opposition was incapable of victory. By the end of the year, the regime's foreign allies had exerted massive military pressure, forcing armed groups to evacuate the city under a cease-fire agreement. Turkey played a pivotal role in negotiating the surrender of East Aleppo, facilitating the evacuation of both civilians and fighters from the eastern sector. As a result, the city of Aleppo was firmly under the control of the regime by the end of 2016.

Aleppo was lost for internal and external reasons. Internally, the opposition's military commander who led armed groups' forces in Aleppo, Abu al-'Abd Ashida, insisted that the fall was largely caused by internal divisions among the factions, including fights over supplies and their repartition, and their failure to fully commit to the defence of the city (Ashida, 2016a).[18] He blamed smaller armed groups for trying to control pieces of territory that they could not properly defend as well as their weaker religious indoctrination. These divisions were exacerbated by the regime's policy of mass targeting and the international community's reluctance to engage with the opposition and prevent them from collaborating with Jabhat al-Nusra. While these internal weaknesses were real, Aleppo was also lost for external reasons. Aleppo simply could not remain in opposition hands with isolated Turkish backing. As the main backer of the opposition, Turkey could not compensate for the reduction of Gulf and international support for the armed opposition. Turkey could not, in isolation, secure Aleppo considering the combination of Iranian and Russian military support for the regime's military reconquista. Turkey instead decided to prioritise the use of Syrian armed opposition groups in its own operations in the north of the country against the Kurdish YPG. Some Syrians blame the transfer of opposition troops from Aleppo to the north as an underlying reason for the fall of the city, though this represents only parts of the picture.[19]

These political and military developments increased pressure on the armed opposition to unite. With the failure of the 2014 initiative and internal disputes within Jaysh al-Fath, the need for organisational unity became a political necessity to present a coherent external political representation. It was also a military necessity imposed by Russian support for the regime, as the loss of Aleppo to the regime made it essential for the opposition to unite. While organisational unity was previously viewed as an opportunity to achieve new victories, it had now become a defensive mechanism to cope with significant external threats. This shift in perception was due to the serious nature of the threats facing the opposition, including the military might of the regime's foreign allies and the need to present a united front in the face of international pressure.

While armed groups still occupied other Syrian regions, the primary focus of the unification of the armed opposition centred on the northwest by 2016. This region had become the main stronghold of the armed opposition, benefiting from the most reliable external support. The imbalance between armed opposition–held territories worsened as the opposition lost ground in other areas, leading them to regroup in the northwest. As explained in detail later in this chapter, successive attempts were made to unite the armed opposition in the northwest, driven by the multi-factional order that had consolidated in the region by 2016. The northwest region's unique characteristics prevented the imposition of a single group's hegemony, making consensus-based political and military unity the only viable option. As such, the process of unification required extensive negotiations and a willingness to compromise among the various factions.

The armed opposition polarised around Ahrar al-Sham and Jabhat al-Nusra by 2016. The Free Syrian Army was merely a patchwork of local gatherings without real prospects, despite the military efficiency of some of them. The localism of Free Syrian Army armed groups prevented their transformation into a nation-wide alternative. The only groups that could realistically unite the opposition after the expulsion of IS were Ahrar al-Sham and Jabhat al-Nusra, the groups that managed to expand significantly throughout discontinuous geographic areas around recognisable political projects. There were real ideological differences between them. Ahrar al-Sham embraced a relatively more flexible approach to other groups and Syrian civil society, while Jabhat al-Nusra was initially more ideologically committed to more narrow religious and political views. Despite the latter's public reassurances that it would not set harsh structures of governance while the conflict continued, many actors were suspicious of Jabhat al-Nusra. They notably denounced its philosophy of domination (*taghalub*) against the armed opposition.[20]

But ideological divergences was not the most salient difference between Ahrar al-Sham and Jabhat al-Nusra. Ahrar al-Sham was the product of a series of institutionalised mergers and alliances, resulting in a group characterised by a balanced distribution of internal power, making it more amenable to factional negotiations, though this also led to a lack of ability to make quick and decisive decisions. On the other hand, Jabhat al-Nusra consolidated in a top-down concentration of power, with more solid control held by its leader and his close associates. Despite being weakened by the split with IS in 2014, Jabhat al-Nusra maintained strong internal discipline and cohesion, which allowed for expanding recruitment and local embedding over the previous few years (Lister, 2016c). These contrasting organisational patterns influenced the respective groups' approach to the unification of the armed opposition and its practicalities.

Ahrar al-Sham and Jabhat al-Nusra had diverging views on the unification of the armed opposition. Ahrar al-Sham advocated for a broad merger of all the groups, while Jabhat al-Nusra was more cautious and preferred to unite only with factions it trusted. A major obstacle to the unification of these groups was Jabhat al-Nusra's relationship with al-Qaeda. Ahrar al-Sham insisted that Jabhat al-Nusra must officially break off from al-Qaeda to avoid being designated as an international terrorist group, whereas Jabhat al-Nusra was concerned about the potential negative impact on its internal cohesion if it severed ties with al-Qaeda. Several prominent commanders and sub-factions would ultimately leave the group when it eventually broke with al-Qaeda, which had been one of Jabhat al-Nusra's leaders' biggest fears. Abu Abdullah al-Shami, the group's highest religious figure, argued:

> We didn't want to face the issue that we faced when we split with IS. Everybody was scared of what could happen. For me, what mattered what the interest of the Syrian jihad and not the interests of al-Qaeda. But there were strong voices against it. [al-Qaeda leaders] Sayf al-Adl and Ayman [al-Zawahiri] opposed it. People who later joined Hurras al-Din[21] were sitting in their houses before vehemently opposing this decision. They were sending wrong information to Ayman [al-Zawahiri], who was afraid that what happened with IS was occurring again.

In early 2016, a group of religious scholars close to several Islamist factions, including Ahrar al-Sham and Jabhat al-Nusra, launched the first initiative (Mubadarat Ahl al-'Ilm) to unite the armed opposition under a consultative council (*majlis al-shura*) that would govern the areas under armed groups' control.[22] The initiative failed due to two primary reasons. First, the factions demanded that Jabhat al-Nusra break off its ties with al-Qaeda before joining the new entity, while Jabhat al-Nusra argued that the creation of a new group would cancel any external allegiance. Second, Jabhat al-Nusra mistrusted many factions and demanded that they clarify their positions on issues such as the political process, the application of Islamic Law, and the protection of foreign fighters (Bajis, 2016). While these conditions allowed Jabhat al-Nusra to be responsive to the initiative without committing to it, it also signalled to its members that the group would not compromise on its core commitments. Given the popular pressure to unite, no faction wanted to appear publicly as the main obstacle to organisational unity. Jabhat al-Nusra thus proposed a more limited merger with only the factions in Jaysh al-Fath, but this plan was rejected, as it failed to address Jabhat al-Nusra's position on al-Qaeda, as noted by the head of Suqur al-Sham Abu 'Isa al-Shaykh (al-Shaykh, 2016d).

Pressure from Ahrar al-Sham and other opposition groups informed the decision of Jabhat al-Nusra to renounce its ties to al-Qaeda. Ahrar al-Sham and its allies insisted that organisational merger was impossible as long as Jabhat al-Nusra kept its allegiance to al-Qaeda. They believed that any new entity inclusive of Jabhat al-Nusra would be listed as a proscribed organisation by foreign countries. After heated internal debates, Jabhat al-Nusra recognised that its ties to al-Qaeda would continue to hinder organisational unity (Lister, 2016c). The ties to al-Qaeda also allowed Russia to justify exemptions to cease-fires and continue to strike large areas in armed opposition–held territories, including where Jabhat al-Nusra was weak or absent. The United States had independently targeted many prominent Jabhat al-Nusra leaders in drone attacks and could not oppose Russia's claims, though it rejected Russia's claims that Ahrar al-Sham was similarly a terrorist organisation (Nichols, 2016). Jabhat al-Nusra's embeddedness in the opposition, which was a strength to the group's survival, had become a real burden on everyone else. Although the opposition understood that Jabhat al-Nusra pledged allegiance to al-Qaeda in 2013 to survive the split with ISIS, they were now pressuring the group to renounce it.[23] Ahrar al-Sham was adamant that no unification could occur as long as Jabhat al-Nusra remained committed to Zawahiri's organisation. While Ahrar al-Sham managed to avoid international designation as a proscribed group linked to al-Qaeda, the group was aware that its military collaboration with Jabhat al-Nusra dismayed Western countries, including the United States. Despite the group's divergences with al-Qaeda and ISIS, repeated efforts to engage with Western countries were obstructed by its military collaboration with Jabhat al-Nusra, which precluded real Western military support (Hubbard, 2015).

Jabhat al-Nusra engaged in extensive internal consultations to reach a consensus on breaking ties with al-Qaeda.[24] This decision was not taken lightly, as the group was concerned that some members might defect and refuse to join a new organisation. To ensure that the rupture was Islamically acceptable, the group engaged in internal discussions with al-Zawahiri's envoy in Syria, Abul-Khayr al-Masri, who was also the deputy leader of the organisation. Abul-Khayr was incidentally released by Iran as part of a prisoner swap with al-Qaeda in Yemen, exchanging him for a diplomat captured there, prior to his journey to Syria in late 2015 (Callimachi & Schmitt, 2015). Jabhat al-Nusra was able to justify the break by citing al-Zawahiri's previously publicised position that the interests of the Syrian jihad take precedence over those of al-Qaeda as an organisation. Additionally, Jabhat al-Nusra argued that the difficulty of maintaining regular contacts with al-Zawahiri meant that it had the right to make decisions based on rapidly changing circumstances. According to Abu Abdullah al-Shami:

> You have to understand the nature of our contacts with al-Qaeda. We would interact with them intermittently. We would send a message and receive an answer three months later. But the situation in Syria was changing on a daily basis. By the time we received their answer, the situation would be totally different. I have the interest of the revolution at heart more than the interest of al-Qaeda. Our connection to al-Qaeda became an impediment to a full merger but we needed to renounce al-Qaeda in an acceptable jurisprudential [*fiqhi*] manner. When Abul-Khair came to Syria after an exchange of prisoners with al-Qaeda in Yemen, he understood the nature of the revolution and supported us.

Jabhat al-Nusra rebranded in the summer of 2016, changing its name to Jabhat Fath al-Sham and renouncing its allegiance to al-Qaeda.[25] The group initially insisted that it remained committed to its Salafi beliefs and the foundations of jihad in Islamic law (Jabhat Fath al-Sham, 2017b). Jabhat Fath al-Sham was only an internal rebranding without organisational expansion (Atun. n.d.). But the decision was internally contested by some prominent members, who left the organisation.[26] There were also rumours that many others would have also left had the split not occurred (Lister, 2016d). Notable debates contested the group's continued ties to al-Qaeda, with some accusing Jabhat Fath al-Sham of trying to mislead Western countries by claiming to have renounced its ties while maintaining a secret allegiance. But the group's subsequent actions suggested that it was more concerned with deluding internal al-Qaeda supporters than Western countries. Despite this controversy, other groups such as Ahrar al-Sham praised Jabhat Fath al-Sham's creation, though they lamented that it came too late (Ahrar al-Sham, 2016m; Tajamu' Ahl al-'Ilm, 2016a). Al-Qaeda central and its ideologues were furious with the decision. The Salafi Jihadi ideologue Abu Muhammad al-Maqdisi lamented:

> HTS tricked us. [Abd al-Rahim] Atun [aka Abu Abdullah al-Shami] sent me a message saying that they were facing a possible alliance of the US and Russia against them, and that they needed to change the name of their group. He said the change was not real, and that a secret allegiance would remain. He added that Abu Faraj al-Masri [a close associate of Ayman al-Zawahiri] and Abul-Khair [al-Masri, the number 2 of al-Qaeda] accepted it tactically. But once it became public, Sayf al-Adl contacted me. He was furious and said that the group lied and had no right to take this decision. So I withdrew my support. While

Atun said that the decision would be withdrawn if al-Qaeda refused, they did not rescind their decision and preferred to maintain the split with al-Qaeda.

The loss of Aleppo in late 2016 accelerated discussions on unification among the opposition groups. After one year of Russian intervention in the conflict, the opposition realised that it could not win the war against the combination of Russian air support and foreign ground troops. This realisation put pressure on the groups to resume previous discussions on unity, especially since Jabhat al-Nusra's ties to al-Qaeda had officially disappeared. In December 2016, two unification processes occurred simultaneously. The first process involved factions more closely aligned with the Free Syrian Army as well as Faylaq al-Sham, Jaysh al-Islam, and Ahrar al-Sham. The second process involved Jabhat Fath al-Sham, Ahrar al-Sham, Suqur al-Sham, and Liwa al-Haq. The second alliance placed conditions on non-collaboration with the Turkish military operations in the north. Jabhat Fath al-Sham did not want to be sidelined by the first initiative and strongly favoured the second initiative. But this deepened internal divisions within Ahrar al-Sham over its strategic priority, reflecting long-standing hesitations and disagreements of the previous few years (Rida, 2016b). As a result, Ahrar al-Sham was unable to make a consensual decision, which further complicated the unification process.[27]

After a series of uncertain negotiations, Ahrar al-Sham's leader Ali al-'Omar initially agreed to join Jabhat Fath al-Sham in a new entity, but the group's consultative council opposed the decision and backtracked. Many leaders and commanders, especially those who felt closer to the revolutionary groups, refused to join Jabhat Fath al-Sham in the new alliance. They believed that granting military control to Jolani while severing ties with Turkey was equivalent to committing suicide, as this move would hasten the demise of the movement under international terrorist listing (Al-Shaykh, 2016a). Conversely, foreigners and individuals favouring a more military-focused approach were more inclined to join HTS. Intense debates ensued over the institutional formation of the new entity, including the consolidation of sub-brigades, centralisation of weapons, appointment of commanders, and the future of smaller factions that were not willing to accept superior authority (Al-Atrash, 2017). Only a newly formed sub-faction of Ahrar al-Sham, Jaysh al-Ahrar, joined Jabhat Fath al-Sham alongside other smaller factions, forming a new entity called Ha'yat Tahrir al-Sham (HTS).[28] An Ahrar al-Sham leader who was close to Turkey but still advocated for joining HTS described his thought process:

> Our internal position was difficult at the time. We were faced with very strong internal divisions. Our sheikhs were supportive of a broader union and the street was pushing for it. Outside, there was a real threat from Jund al-Aqsa. We

had to make a decision accordingly. We could have controlled Jabhat al-Nusra. They could be in charge of the military while we would have controlled internal security and the consultative council. They could have ended the threat posed by Jund al-Aqsa. So we can say that I agreed about the general principal of union (*indimaj*) but mostly diverged on the detail. I insist. We could have controlled them and our bases would not have left us.

The localised nature of the armed opposition shaped the nature of interfactional competition when unity failed. Neither Ahrar al-Sham nor Jabhat Fath al-Sham had the ability to effectively deter their sub-units from leaving, or to exert control over the other group. This was particularly evident in the case of Ahrar al-Sham, which historically had a less centralised and ideologically cohesive structure than Jabhat al-Nusra. Consequently, the cost of desertion was very low for the local sub-units. A prominent military commander lamented at the time of the split with Jaysh al-Ahrar in early 2017:

The killing of our leaders in 2014 had a major impact on us. We were becoming a conglomeration of local groups with many internal issues. We were stabilising when the split with them occurred. Our internal divisions weakened our ability to resist initially. Those who kept the revolutionary line stayed with us while those who were more inclined toward Jabhat al-Nusra joined them and fought us.

Ahrar al-Sham and Jabhat Fath al-Sham strived to present themselves as the most legitimate Islamic group, hoping to gain broad support. This struggle played out in a flurry of online statements, with each side claiming that sub-brigades were defecting to the other group.[29] Some larger sub-units countered with their own statements reaffirming their loyalty to their respective groups or conversely supporters stressing the importance of unity with Jabhat Fath al-Sham (n.m. 2016.c). Meanwhile, Jabhat Fath al-Sham consolidated support by swaying previously independent religious scholars who blamed Ahrar al-Sham for the failure to unite the armed opposition (al-Muhaysani, 2016). Ahrar al-Sham sought legitimacy through institutions such as the Islamic Council.

The difficulty in imposing control over all the sub-groups forced Jabhat Fath al-Sham to emphasise its own domestic Islamic legitimacy as well. The group was closer to the Consultative Council of the People of Science (Majlis al-Shura Ahl al-'Ilm), a Salafi alternative to the Islamic Council.[30] But the council still denounced Jabhat Fath al-Sham's next iteration, HTS, for attacking other factions (Majlis Shura Ahl al-'Ilm, 2019a). Many members of the council also resigned over time. HTS was initially unable to unify judicial and religious rulings in the occupied province as an alternative to the Islamic Council, which was based mostly abroad but was more inclusive of both Salafi and non-Salafi influences. Unlike the Islamic Council, which was backed by many Islamist factions, the Consultative Council of the People of Science did not have widespread factional endorsement.

HTS therefore gathered Jabhat Fath al-Sham, Jaysh al-Ahrar (formerly in Ahrar al-Sham), the Zinki Movement, and Ansar al-Din, Jaysh al-Sunna, and Liwa al-Haq under a single organisational umbrella. Responsibilities were shared among constituting groups. Former Ahrar al-Sham leader Abu Jaber al-Sheikh was named general commander, Jabhat Fath al-Sham's al-Jolani became the military leader, and the head of Zinki Movement's Shahab al-Din assumed the function of head of the consultative council. HTS additionally integrated most of the independent Islamist religious preachers who had proliferated during the Syrian conflict under its umbrella, including many scholars who were in the Consultative Council of the People of Science (Hay'at Tahrir al-Sham, 2017c). Their integration aimed at controlling independent religious voices to ultimately restrain their influence on the ground by institutionalising their role and functions inside the new group.

After a low-level confrontation with HTS, Ahrar al-Sham absorbed several factions previously aligned with the Free Syrian Army to protect them. These smaller groups felt threatened by HTS, which they denounced for attempting to dominate the opposition (*taghalub*). Ahrar al-Sham became a protective umbrella organisation for these factions, arguing that it could unite all remaining factions, protect them, and create a general council to decide on political, military, religious, and judiciary affairs (Ahrar al-Sham, 2017f). The new groups that joined Ahrar al-Sham were Suqur al-Sham, the Jaysh al-Islam affiliate in the north, a faction of al-Jabhat al-Shamiyya, Jaysh al-Mujahideen, and Fastaqim group (Ahrar al-Sham, 2017c; Suqur al-Sham, Jaysh al-Islam, Jaysh al-Mujahideen, Fastaqim, Jabhat al-Shamiya, 2017). Independent religious scholars encouraged this decision, asking Ahrar al-Sham to protect these factions and integrate them into the group's consultative council (Zayn al-Din, Harush, & 'Aloush, 2017). Alas, the integration of these groups into Ahrar al-Sham's organisational structures was more symbolic than real, as they did not immediately get a seat in its consultative council.[31] The polarisation of the armed opposition was only the beginning of a looming internal military confrontation.

The inability to achieve broader unity resulted in the division of northwest Syria into two main poles. Ahrar al-Sham's continued strength posed a threat to HTS, which feared that foreign countries, particularly Russia, could pressure Turkey to use a group like Ahrar al-Sham as a possible conduit to act against it. As a result, military hegemony over northwest Syria became the only means for HTS to impose a new regional and international reality that other actors would ultimately have to accept and manage (Heller, 2017b). Since unity could not materialise through cross-factional negotiations, it had to be imposed militarily. The subsequent internal power struggle was therefore not the result of irreconcilable ideological differences, but the outcome of a logic of survival between two groups competing to lead the armed opposition in northwest Syria.

In July 2017, the internal conflict between Ahrar al-Sham and HTS began, with the outcome being determined by these groups' respective organisational structures and local dynamics (Abazeid, 2017; Haid, 2017b). Ahrar al-Sham was rooted in its local communities, but its military forces were de-centralised and still in the process of centralisation. HTS further weakened Ahrar al-Sham by creating sub-groups in areas where Ahrar al-Sham had its strongest military presence, putting pressure on group members not to engage in factional fights to preserve these localities (Abazeid, 2017). Some Ahrar al-Sham sub-groups had to remain neutral or even declare allegiance to HTS for protection (Ahrar al-Sham, 2017e). HTS was also ideologically more prepared, having indoctrinated its fighters well in advance of the conflict. It made effective use of its central military force and foreign fighters to seize strategic locations, particularly the border of Bab al-Hawa with Turkey and the roads leading to the Shia villages of Fu'a and Kafaria, which held significant political and economic value.

The External Subjugation of the Armed Opposition

The antagonism between Ahrar al-Sham and HTS was superseded by regional power politics between Turkey and Russia. After a bilateral cease-fire agreement signed in December 2016, they conducted talks in January 2017 in Astana, marking the beginning of the Astana process, which gradually started to prevail—in practice—over the Geneva U.N. track. The main achievement of the multi-partite negotiations occurred in March and May 2017, when Iran, Russia, and Turkey established four "de-escalation zones" throughout Syria, including the largest zone in Idlib and the others in an enclave in the north of Homs, the Ghouta in the periphery of Damascus, and in the south of the country. The purpose of these zones was to facilitate humanitarian access by officially ceasing fighting and designating checkpoints and monitoring centres manned by foreign troops from the three countries to guarantee the cease-fire. Although the deal was initially not accepted by the regime or the armed opposition, it ultimately imposed a new dynamic that no armed opposition group, or even the regime, could directly challenge. However, the implementation of the Astana process remained contentious, since it was ambiguous enough to be interpreted differently by the parties, particularly Russia and Turkey (ICG, 2019c). The Sochi agreement later introduced additional details clarifying the two countries' understanding of the situation in Idlib. Notably, the agreement outlined the establishment of a de-militarised zone designed to create a clear separation between Syrian armed opposition groups and regime troops. Other key provisions included the mandatory withdrawal of heavy weapons from the front lines, the withdrawal of proscribed armed groups (including HTS), the facilitation of unrestricted civilian movement on the M4 and M5 highways, and the implementation of joint Russian-Turkish patrols along these strategic routes.

The three countries supporting the opposing sides of the conflict transformed it from open warfare to conflict management. This occurred against the backdrop of a retreating Trump administration, leading to a sidelining of Western countries and the Geneva process. The new phase claimed to launch a plan in which Syria's constitution would be amended, and the regime reformed. But these official objectives were interpreted more cynically by Astana opponents, who viewed the new phase as a tactical move to dissociate and systematically neutralise each active military front. The regime proved unable to face all fronts simultaneously due to the dearth of ground troops, so disconnecting each geographic area was necessary to allow the regime to strike each front individually while maintaining stability elsewhere.

Despite their diverging visions and preferences, the interests of the three countries—Iran, Russia, and Turkey—converged for the first time. Iran chose to disengage from direct military confrontation with the opposition while cementing its gains in the region and ensuring the regime remained in power in Damascus. The transformation of the conflict would enable Iran to consolidate its economic and political role in Syria by participating in its reconstruction and embedding itself in strategic areas. Russia's vision was more ambitious than Iran's. While Iran wanted to disengage from direct military confrontation with the opposition, Russia aimed to reduce its military engagement in Syria while preserving the regime in Damascus. Against the backdrop of Russia's own antagonism with Western countries, the stabilisation of Syria would be a significant victory for Russia, allowing it to reassert its regional role by demonstrating its reliability to pro-American regimes after more than two decades of gradual marginalisation. Russia was able to impose its preferred outcome through a combination of political support for the regime, particularly in the U.N. Security Council; military reconquista;, and a disinformation campaign. This was a real reversal of fortune after nearly two decades of perceived Western hegemony and support for political change in the region.

For Turkey, the Syrian conflict shifted from being a political card to becoming a matter of national security. Turkey ultimately agreed to manage the conflict with Iran and Russia—despite its support for regime change since 2011—for domestic and regional reasons (ICG, 2016). Substantial Western military assistance to the Kurdish YPG / SDF in the north of Syria in a common fight against IS infuriated Turkey, which had fought the PKK for three decades.[32] The deadlock reached by negotiations with the PKK by 2015, partially caused by Turkish domestic policies and an escalation by underground Kurdish groups that launched attacks inside Turkey, positioned the two actors in a direct confrontation.[33] As the United States began providing military support for the PKK-tied YPG / SDF, Turkey became increasingly concerned about a scenario similar to the consolidation of an autonomous Kurdish region in north Iraq after 1991. This outcome could de-stabilise the regional order and encourage the Kurdish population in Turkey to support a similar move in their own country. Although Turkey did not essentially modify its posture toward the Syrian regime, it gradually evaluated the "Kurdish threat" in northern Syria as a more immediate national security concern, which necessitated a stronger engagement with Russia in conflict management.

Turkey's primary objective was to prevent the formation of a contiguous autonomous Kurdish region in northern Syria under an entity linked to the YPG, and ultimately the PKK. The YPG began to capture large swathes of the north of the country with significant American air support and special forces on the ground after the siege of the Kurdish city of Kobani by IS and massive U.S. airstrikes against the so-called caliphate. This imposition of a new Kurdish-led order on a third of Syria created a new strategic threat to Turkey. Kurdish forces effectively controlled northeast Syria and its oil resources by the end of the Battle of Raqqa against IS in October 2017. To counter this Kurdish breakthrough, Turkey launched a new military campaign called the Euphrates Shield (*dar' al-frat*) from August 2016 to March 2017, which officially aimed to fight both IS and the Kurdish YPG in the west of Kobani. The campaign relied on a combination of local Syrian armed groups provided with Turkish weaponry and Turkish air support to take control of the northern Syrian cities of Jarablus, al-Rai, and al-Bab by spring 2017. The military operation was followed by the Olive Branch campaign (*ghasn al-zaytun*) launched in early 2018 to seize the Kurdish-inhabited areas farther to the west and decisively sever Kurdish zones in northern Syria with the acquiescence of Russia.

Russia pursued a pragmatic approach in its negotiations with other countries, taking into account their respective priorities. Russia's responsiveness to Turkish fears was not only important for its international position. It was also a strategic move to weaken NATO by partially dissociating a critical member from the alliance in the Middle East. As part of the agreement between Russia and Turkey, Russia sold the S-400 missile system to Turkey, which not only undermined Western military assistance but also pushed an American red line due to the risks associated with integrating the system into NATO's military defence system (Has, 2019). Additionally, Russia engaged in talks with Jordan and Israel regarding the southern part of the country, while cooperating with the United States on issues related to northeastern Syria.

The tensions between Turkey and the United States, stemming from Turkey's deepening ties with Russia, transcended the Syrian conflict. The United States expressed apprehension that the warming relations between Turkey and Russia, fostered by Vladimir Putin's support for Turkish president Recep Tayyip Erdogan during the attempted coup in the summer of 2016, would lead to Turkey's acquisition of the S-400 missile defence system from Russia. This posed a significant concern for the United States and NATO, as the deployment of the S-400 could potentially compromise the security of NATO's defence capabilities. Ultimately, Turkey procured the defence system but refrained from deploying or actively using it.

Russia's approach to conflict de-escalation brought the armed opposition to submission step by step. The campaign started in 2017, when the Astana process defined four "de-escalation zones" located in (1) the greater Idlib area (which includes parts of Latakia and Aleppo under opposition control), (2) the Rastan pocket next to Homs, (3) the eastern Ghouta next to Damascus, and (4) the southern regions under armed opposition control. By separating each opposition-held area and addressing the concerns of each key state with strategic interests in each of them, Russia paved the way for a succession of military operations that allowed the Assad regime to reassert control over three of the four de-escalation zones.

The military operations followed a similar pattern. Russian forces negotiated so-called reconciliation processes with local groups that were willing to reintegrate into the state and recognise the sovereignty of the regime. Claiming to be a guarantor, Russia suggested that some former armed groups could play a role as local forces, receive amnesty, and regulate their status with the regime without fear of retribution. When local actors were reluctant to cooperate, they were pressured into submission or given an escape route to the northwest, where they could resettle. By isolating these four zones and treating them separately, Russia prevented a joint military escalation of the armed opposition. Prior to this strategy, the opposition's main military strength was its presence on large front lines with the regime that were difficult to defend given the dearth of ground troops. The de-escalation and isolation of the four regions allowed the regime to focus all its military strength on one front at a time, while other fronts were hesitant to engage in renewed military confrontation for fear of de-stabilising their own region. This strategy even proved effective against armed groups like Ahrar al-Sham and HTS, who were present in different regions but ultimately could not escape the Russian trap (figure 4.1).

The stance of the armed opposition in relation to Turkey varied. Ahrar al-Sham expressed its support for a safe zone in the north under Turkish influence (Ahrar al-Sham, 2015b). The Islamic council and the Salafi-leaning Consultative Council of the People of Science also praised Turkey for the creation of a safe

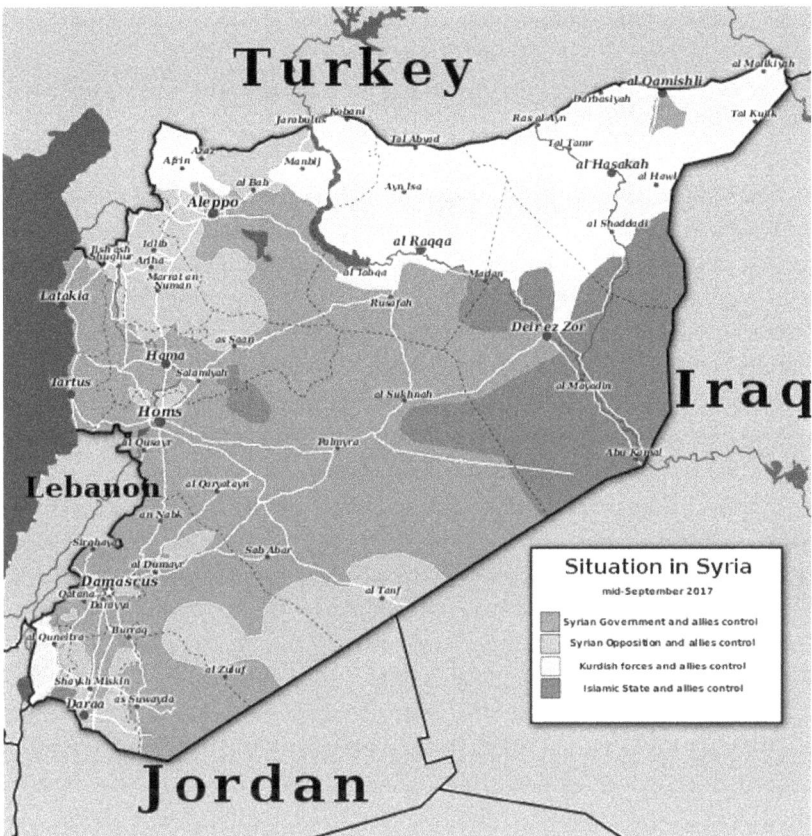

Figure 4.1 The situation before the subjugation of three main armed opposition groups' strongholds
https://commons.wikimedia.org/wiki/File:Situation_in_Syria_(September_2017).svg

zone, particularly if it could help unite factions under a united army (al-Majlis al-Islami, 2019; Majlis Shura Ahl al-'Ilm fi al-Sham, 2019b). But the Salafi scholars also distanced themselves from what they called the "factions of the Pentagon," whom they considered corrupt, and instead aligned themselves with the "sincere factions" that could create a local administration (Tajamu' Ahl al-'Ilm, 2016b). While most other groups endorsed this position, Jabhat al-Nusra had previously argued that its conception of Islamic Law prevented its participation and withdrew from the region several years before (Jabhat al-Nusra, 2015a). Then, when the group became Jabhat Fath al-Sham in 2016, it strongly opposed the operation while acknowledging a divergence of opinion among religious scholars. Jabhat Fath al-Sham blamed the United States for its support for the PKK and the American collaboration with Russia in fighting them.. Jabhat Fath al-Sham considered any collaboration—even mere coordination—with foreign military forces in the north to be unlawful (Jabhat Fath al-Sham, 2016a).

The response of the armed opposition to the Astana process similarly differed. Those with closer ties to Turkey were invited to participate and generally did so. Ahrar al-Sham conducted internal discussions about the pros and cons of participation before ultimately deciding against attending, believing that it would not lead to a substantial cease-fire. Alas, the group emphasised that it opposed any internal confrontations between supporters and opponents of the process and urged mutual respect for the decisions of each group (Ahrar al-Sham, 2017b). Turkey was furious, thinking that Ahrar al-Sham was not a reliable partner. Simultaneously, various factions including Ahrar al-Sham, Jaysh al-Islam, Faylaq al-Rahman, al-Jabhat al-Shamiyya, Jaysh Yarmuk, Jaysh Idlib al-Hur, and Jaysh al-Nasr continued to express appreciation for Turkey, while assigning blame to Russia and Iran for the ongoing situation (Ahrar al-Sham, Jaysh al-Islam, Faylaq al-Rahman, al-Jabhat al-Shamiyya, Jaysh Yarmuk, Jaysh Idlib al-Hur, Jaysh al-Nasr, 2017). In contrast, HTS was more adamant against the Astana process, viewing it as an attempt to achieve politically what could not be won militarily. The group condemned the process as treacherous to God and his messenger, and accused the Russians of exploiting internal divisions among the factions (Ha'yat Tahrir al-Sham, 2017i, 2017p; Ha'yat Tahrir al-Sham, 2018d).

The regime's subjugation of the de-escalation zones began with the armed opposition stronghold of Ghouta in February 2018. Ghouta was a key bastion of the armed opposition under the leadership of Jaysh al-Islam. The regime's military reconquest occurred through heavy bombardment and ground assault, which effectively split the pocket in two and led to its fall by April 2018. The regime's use of chemical weapons added further pressure to local armed groups and their supporters, despite their military ability to resist. During the negotiations, the Russians attempted to incite defections and reconcile with each group in their area. They demanded that each group submit its heavy weapons and accept only the military presence of the regime. Jaysh al-Islam eventually agreed to a cease-fire with some control over its weapons and the creation of a Russian control post at the entrance of the area. They also acknowledged the return of the regime's civilian administration and services, according to the chief of staff of Jaysh al-Islam (Bayraqdar, 2018). The Russians ultimately brought the region to submission through a combined strategy of siege and violence, including the use of chemical weapons by the regime (Atlantic Council, 2018).[34] As a result, Jaysh al-Islam moved to the north of Aleppo instead of Idlib to avoid living under HTS. Turkey imposed certain conditions on the group's number of weapons and soldiers, but overall conditions in the area were different from those in Ghouta, since the group was no longer strongly embedded locally (Hussein, 2018a).

The Syrian regime's campaign to retake control of armed opposition–held areas was swift and effective. Employing a combination of negotiation and coercion, the regime – with Russia's assistance – secured the surrender of some insurgents while compelling others into exile to Idlib in the north with the looming threat of extreme violence for those who resisted (including the resort to chemical weapons in the suburbs of Damascus). The Damascus suburb was quickly followed by the northern Homs enclave, both of which quickly surrendered. The armed groups who opposed reconciliation with the regime were evacuated to northwestern Syria.

In June and July 2018, ground and aerial military pressure on the armed groups facilitated a relatively quick move toward the Jordanian border. The south had long been under the sway of external backers, who stopped supporting the armed opposition in the area, facilitating its submission under Russian conditions (Al-Jabassini, 2019). The capture of the south was significant, since it had been a stronghold of the opposition and the epicentre of the Syrian initial uprising. Complicating matters, the existence of the de-escalation agreement had temporarily halted the conflict, leading to a hesitancy among armed opposition elsewhere, especially in the northwest, to reactivate the northern front to relieve the pressure on the south.[35] Such a move might have provided a pretext for the regime and Russian forces to intensify their bombardment of the region. The regime and its foreign allies, especially Russia, struck an accord with Israel to deter the involvement of Iranian-backed forces in the province. Then, the regime secured control over the border with Jordan, encircled Daraa city, and negotiated with Russia the surrender of remaining armed opposition groups. Under the tutelage of Russia, agreements were brokered with local opposition groups, enabling recently reconciled areas to retain autonomy despite the Syrian regime's reclaiming of control. These accords sought to facilitate the integration of former opposition fighters into local forces aligned with the Syrian regime. However, this is marred by a darker reality. The reconciliation process, despite regime assurances of safety, took a grim turn with the arrest of hundreds of individuals. Some individuals faced forced disappearances or met their demise through torture, starkly contrasting the promised security for those settling their status through reconciliation.

At the same time, some negotiations did occur between the different parties. The multi-party war extended throughout the region, up to Iraq and the Gulf. For instance, in 2017, Qatar and Iran brokered a complex multi-party agreement involving Ahrar al-Sham and HTS on one side, and Kata'ib Hezbollah in Iraq on the other.[36] The so-called four villages deal aimed to secure the release of 26 members of the Qatari royal family who had been kidnapped in Iraq in exchange for hundreds of prisoners held by the Syrian regime. The terms of the agreement involved an exchange of population between two Shia-besieged villages located in northwestern Syria, Fouaa, and Kfarya, for two Sunni-besieged, Madaya and Zabadani, that had been held by armed opposition groups within regime-controlled areas. Ahrar al-Sham nonetheless emphasised that the expulsion of people from Fouaa and Kfarya was not its demand, but rather a directive issued by the regime (Jabhat Tahrir Suriya, 2018). Additionally, Qatar paid a substantial ransom to various parties involved in the negotiations, including Ahrar al-Sham, HTS, and Kata'ib Hezbollah. Saudi Arabia referred to the deal to denounce Qatar for supporting terrorism, and started to be-siege its Qatari neighbour at the time (ICG, 2023b).

The front lines across Syria reached a relative stabilisation point by July 2018, with the regime forces managing to seize control of three out of four de-escalation zones. The remaining armed opposition groups were either concentrated in the Idlib province located in the northwest or in the Turkish-held areas in the north. Many groups who lived in the areas newly seized by the regime therefore had to relocate there, where they joined forces with the local armed groups who already controlled these regions. This exodus brought the remaining armed opposition groups under more direct Turkish influence, regardless of their previous ideological or political divergences.

Merging Remaining Opposition Forces in Political-Military Statelets

The subjugation of the armed opposition in 2017–2018 marked a crucial turning point in the Syrian conflict. By July 2018, the front lines had largely stabilised, with the remaining armed opposition groups congregated in the north and northwest of Syria under the tutelage of Turkey. The Sotchi talks, which began in October 2017, spurred the establishment of Turkish military observation points throughout the Idlib province on the front lines with regime-held areas (ICG, 2018, 2019c). The talks also de-limited a de-escalation zone in Idlib and required the departure of so-called radical groups from areas closer to the front lines. Although the terms were flexible, the growing Turkish military presence forced all the groups to accommodate Turkey as the last true backer of the armed opposition. Even HTS, which previously attacked armed groups too close to Turkey and refused to be associated with it, had to find its own modus operandi (ICG, 2019c). But these armed groups were not simply Turkish proxy forces. While some groups lost most of their agency, others managed to maintain sufficient room for manoeuvre in this new environment.

The Turkish position on the Syrian conflict significantly transformed by 2018 and 2019 (ICG, 2020). Initially, the conflict was primarily a political tool to gain regional influence. With the 2011 uprisings favouring political movements closer to Turkey, the country sought to leverage the conflict to reinforce its influence in the region, particularly in case of a political transition. But, as the armed opposition faltered, the conflict became primarily a security issue for Turkey. In addition to opposing the establishment of an autonomous foreign-supported Kurdish entity in northern Syria, Turkey increasingly aimed at (1) limiting the flow of refugees and (2) preventing the infiltration of militants, which could weaken its political leadership at home (figure 4.2).

The Turkish-backed armed forces are mainly located in the northern areas along the border with Turkey, which are marked in light green on Map 7.1.[37] These forces initially operated in Operation Euphrates Shield against ISIS and Kurdish forces, and officially formed the Syrian National Army (al-Jaysh al-Watani al-Suri) in December 2017. While the new army was intended to serve as the basis for a national army, it remains a symbolic organisational umbrella for pre-existing groups. The three main military components of the new army (the Victory Bloc, Sultan Murad, and al-Jabhat al-Shamiyya) became three legions, later supplemented by a fourth additional legion. Ahrar al-Sham's forces in northern Syria joined the third legion, while its exiled forces from Homs joined the fourth legion. Turkey provides direct financial and training support to the national army, which it has used to further its own objectives in the north of the country, particularly against the Kurdish YPG.[38] Despite Turkey's involvement, persistent factional infighting and a lack of internal reorganisation have severely hindered the operational cohesion of the national army, resulting in a series of internal divisions, mergers, and disputes (e.g., Al Nofal, 2022). As a result, Turkey has not effectively disciplined the new army or asserted real control over its internal components. Some of these groups were subsequently used as a conduit to mobilise foreign fighters to other conflicts, such as Libya and Azerbaijan, fuelling criticisms from Syrian actors who are otherwise supportive of Turkey (Tsurkov, 2020; Wehrey, 2020).

The Syrian National Army, directly trained and supported by Turkey, represents only a limited component of the armed opposition in the north of the country. The majority of remaining groups are located in the province of Idlib. The loss of the three other armed opposition–held territories eliminated the comparative advantage the opposition had in exploiting the weakness of regime ground troops. Although regime forces continue to face a shortage of soldiers, the concentration of military strength in one area alleviated this disadvantage. The so-called reconciliation process with former armed groups who agreed to stay in their regions after their seizure by regime forces helped the latter forcibly conscript new troops among former armed groups by threatening them with prison sentences.

The final phase of the conflict presented the greatest challenge yet, requiring a more comprehensive internal and external institutionalisation of the armed

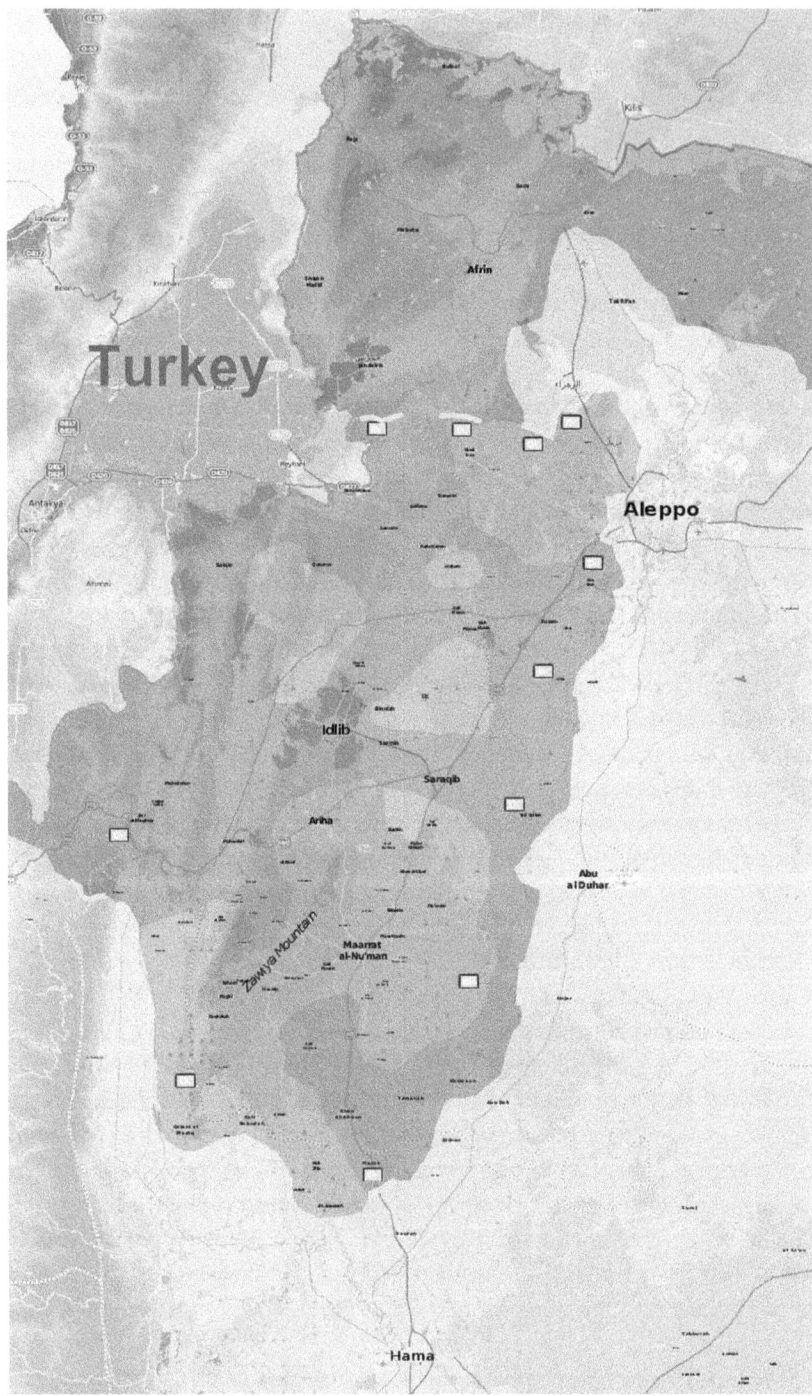

Figure 4.2 Initial Turkish observation points defined in 17 September 2018
https://upload.wikimedia.org/wikipedia/commons/thumb/1/18/Turkish_Observation_Points_in_Idlib.svg/800px-Turkish_Observation_Points_in_Idlib.svg.png

opposition. To succeed in this new environment, it needed a single political-military project to balance the military and political necessities of the conflict while representing the region both regionally and internationally. The existence of two groups broadly aligned with two conflicting political projects was unsustainable. Many armed groups were reluctant to deploy their best troops and heavy weaponry to the front lines, fearing a loss of power vis-à-vis their rivals. While shared military operation rooms previously consolidated to respond to immediate military threats posed by regime forces, they did not fully institutionalise the collaboration of armed groups' specialised units in the long run. The only durable solution was the consolidation of a structured entity similar to an army, with a unified chain of command, specialised units, and additional local de-centralisation. This step was particularly crucial given the speed with which other fronts, particularly in the south, fell under the regime's military assault. The new international configuration also meant that victory would not be purely military. The armed opposition required significant external support from not only Turkey but also Western countries to resist a full-scale regime assault. The armed opposition could make any full-scale regime attack extremely costly, but it could not prevent it. Thus, unifying political authority was a necessary step in this direction.

The institutionalisation of a unified armed opposition nonetheless faced the reality of northwest Syria. The region's internal diversity and the arrival of factions exiled from other regions posed significant challenges. Although the number of groups had shrunk by 2017–2018, with a limited number of significant actors largely affiliated with two contending poles, the divide between Ahrar al-Sham and HTS still largely hindered their merger. Their ideational proximity shaped the nature of competition between them, which was more threatening than it would have been between ideologically opposed groups that do not cater to the same constituency (Pischedda, 2018). HTS's fears were fueled by real threats that Turkey could encourage other groups to fight it as part of the Astana process (Heller, 2017c). HTS also suffered from financial instability. According to a former leading Jabhat al-Nusra member, Ali al-Arjani, the group had previously relied on spoils of war and seizure of resources from other factions (Al-'Arjani, 2019). But the group did not have stable financial incomes even as it became the leading armed group when it established HTS.

A HTS religious scholar at the time, who was previously affiliated with Ahrar al-Sham and was later excluded from HTS itself, Abu al-Fath al-Farghali, presented three main reasons for the internal confrontation between the two groups, where he stood in favour of HTS. He argued that (1) Ahrar al-Sham's civilian project was a threat to HTS, (2) HTS needed to control the border with Turkey and expel Ahrar al-Sham from it, and (3) HTS's perceived hegemony would allow the group to force Turkey to rely on it as an intermediary instead of other groups.[39]

Ahrar al-Sham tried to respond to its inability to push back HTS. The group suffered significant losses in terms of military equipment and economic resources when Jaysh al-Ahrar split, as well as lucrative economic incomes when the border control of Bab al-Hawa with Turkey was lost to HTS. Despite the participation of multiple groups seeking protection against HTS's hegemonic aspirations, the sheer number of groups does not necessarily equate to military efficiency, particularly against a more disciplined contender. Ahrar al-Sham's past trajectory of institutionalised alliances with other groups positioned it as a critical broker between different networks and groups. But the group was organisationally impotent from 2014 to 2017 and failed to deter HTS. The group seized the opportunity of a prisoner exchange with the regime to appoint a new leader, Hassan Sufan, who had previously played a prominent role in prison. Sufan criticised the multiple deficiencies of the group and undertook some internal reforms upon taking over in October 2017.[40] One of the significant changes Sufan implemented was the resumption of his predecessor 'Ali al-'Omar's efforts to establish centralised military forces not solely based on specific localities. According to former Ahrar al-Sham leader and member of its consultative council, Abu Yahiyya al-Hamawi:

> We have developed three different types of military forces: the commandos (*mughawir*), the special forces, and the frontline patrols (*ribat*). They have different levels of training and specialisation. The commandos are the most well equipped and trained. They are, along with the special forces, centralised and not based on geography like before. They were built two and a half year ago [early 2018]. We were starting to train and equip them when HTS took over, which explains why we were unable to fight initially. Although we lost the first battle, we were much better in the second phase since preparation was underway.

HTS conversely lost momentum following the initial joining of several prominent groups and independent religious preachers. Despite making initial gains against Ahrar al-Sham, HTS's unification project failed to merge all the groups and impose a new reality on regional states and the international community. Despite HTS's military strength, Ahrar al-Sham's politico-military project remained a sword of Damocles that regional actors, such as Turkey, could potentially back against the group. Moreover, many sub-groups, including Zinki Movement, Jaysh al-Ahrar, Ansar al-Din, several brigades of foreign fighters, and prominent religious preachers such as Abd al-Razzaq al-Mahdi and Abdullah al-Muhaysini, left HTS. They opposed interfactional conflicts, the targeting of individual scholars, and blamed HTS for not abiding by its internal regulations (Shehab al-din, 2017; Majlis Shura Jaysh al-Ahrar, 2017; Jabhat Ansar al-Din, 2017). HTS hence re-centred around Jabhat al-Nusra's core and its closest allies. The group's main comparative advantage was the presence of a movable central military force that could be deployed throughout the Idlib region to strike contending factions.

The factional clashes that took place between 2017 and 2018 exposed the localised nature of the armed opposition. Throughout the entire conflict, most military units remained strikingly localised, with only a few armed groups having centralised military forces. Local brigades frequently changed alliances along with the transformation of the armed opposition. The consolidation of two antagonistic poles around Ahrar al-Sham and HTS accompanied an online war of communiqués asserting some of their local sub-groups' renewed allegiance, neutrality in internal wars, declaration of independence, or switch to other groups. This phenomenon reflected the low cost of switching given the bi-polarity of the armed opposition (Seymour, 2014). Even sub-factions of Ahrar al-Sham and HTS occasionally claimed neutrality in the larger fight between the two groups (e.g., Sarayat al-Tamkin, 2018). Over time, many sub-groups joined Zinki Movement, Jaysh al-Ahrar, and, more significantly, Faylaq al-Sham (al-Khatib, 2018) to protect themselves. Faylaq al-Sham's official position of neutrality (Faylaq al-Sham, 2018) and strong ties to Turkey gave assurances that its sub-groups would not be attacked by either side.

During the last phase of the conflict, villages also expressed their positions on the interfactional conflict. Some villages insisted that local inhabitants loyal to HTS should split, give their weapons, and publicise their departure. Otherwise, they should leave the village (al-Majlis al-'Askari li Baldat Kafruma, 2019; al-Majlis al-'Askari fi Kafr 'Uyud, 2019; Thuwar Kafr Halab, 2019). Other local communities where Ahrar al-Sham was particularly strong, as in the Ghab plains, openly stood in favour of the group against HTS (Majlis Shura Sahl al-Ghab, 2017). This phenomenon also illustrates to a large extent how factional belonging and geography became associated over time. That was less the case for HTS, which reflects the group's weaker local embeddedness considering its stronger emphasis on centralisation and lesser reliance on geography.

There is a complex interplay among armed groups, sub-groups, and local communities in northwest Syria. While larger groups such as Ahrar al-Sham had to balance competing demands from foreign supporters and their sub-brigades, local communities similarly had to navigate the shifting dynamics of the armed opposition. They decided to align with one faction or another for a range of reasons, from the need for protection against another group to ideological considerations and pragmatic concerns. For many villages, aligning with the dominant faction in their area allowed them to ensure their safety and prevent attacks from the opposing side regardless of any ideological alignment. Joining HTS, though, was problematic due to the group's political views and past association with Jabhat al-Nusra. This was particularly true in areas with a strong revolutionary history, such as Saraqeb and Ma'arat al-Nu'man. Some of these local communities were also reluctant to align with HTS, because doing so could result in losing external support from foreign countries, as the group is listed as an organisation proscribed for its—now inexistent—connection to al-Qaeda.

The armed opposition's failure to institutionalise cross-factional military cooperation, which the polarisation between Ahrar al-Sham and HTS exacerbated, contributed to the opposition's loses between December 2017 and spring 2018. Regime forces took advantage of the factional conflict between Ahrar al-Sham and HTS to launch renewed attacks on south east Idlib. The regime reportedly facilitated the transfer of IS cells to the area to further de-stabilise the opposition and create additional enemies to face simultaneously, according to interviews with HTS security officials and open source intelligence.[41] The regime aimed at reconquering the strategically important Abu al-Duhur Airbase, which had been under opposition control for years. Defending the area was particularly challenging due to the flat geography and lack of air defence capabilities. Despite the armed opposition's efforts, the regime and its foreign allies, including ground troops from Hizbullah, successfully recaptured the airbase by January 2018.

In early 2018, Ahrar al-Sham and Zinki Movement resumed their fight with HTS. Ahrar al-Sham had partially recovered from the previous confrontation and formed a new alliance with Zinki Movement called the Syrian Liberation Front (Jabhat Tahrir Suriya). The goal of the front was to coordinate the two groups' political positions and unify their organisational structures. A lesson from the previous failure of the Islamic Front to consolidate the armed opposition motivated the two groups' decisions to use only the name Syrian Liberation Front thereafter. The alliance, however, did not alter the groups' strong local embeddedness throughout northwest Syria. Ahrar al-Sham remained dominant in the Ghab plains and the Zawiyya mountains, while Zinki Movement retained its strongholds in western Aleppo. The Syrian Liberation Front was well-positioned to act as a counterweight to HTS's influence in the province, and the groups aimed to bolster themselves militarily by replicating HTS's centralisation. A leading member of Ahrar al-Sham emphasised the importance of centralising their military forces, stating:

> Inside Ahrar al-Sham, we are united by our ideas but we remain grounded geographically. Our members remain in their villages and cities, where they stem from. People are always more willing to defend their own land as it is part of who they are. We have nonetheless created centralised military force on two different levels. First, the special forces have specific training and specialisation. Their mission is to train local members on specific military technical skills. The

second force, the commandos (*mughawir*), is centralised at a higher level. They possess all the skills and abilities. We do not see this force as a deterrent or a tool against other Syrian groups. It is aimed at the regime. They would help local fighters fight better.

The conflict between HTS and the Syrian Liberation Front resumed in early 2018, sparked by the assassination of an HTS commander. The ensuing clashes lasted for several months and demonstrated that neither side held a significant advantage over the other in military terms. The Syrian Liberation Front managed to recover from the loses inflicted by HTS the previous year. Despite intermittent cease-fires brokered by religious scholars and independent factions, the conflict persisted. The proximity of Zinki Movement to Turkish-controlled areas made HTS wary of the Syrian Liberation Front's position in the northeast.

The factional fighting also created an opening for al-Qaeda supporters who had previously been affiliated with Jabhat al-Nusra and refused to sever ties with al-Zawahiri's organisation. In February 2018, several sub-units that were formerly affiliated with Jabhat al-Nusra formed a new organisation, Hurras al-Din (Guardians of Religion) (Tandhim Hurras al-Din, 2018).[42] The new organisation included small factions like Jaysh al-Badiya, Jaysh al-Malamih, and Sarayat Kabul, which remained faithful to al-Qaeda (Jaysh al-Badiya, 2018; Jaysh al-Malamih, 2018; Sarayat Kabul, 2018). The group claimed independent organisational belonging and neutrality in the factional clashes. It initially tried to form an alliance "for the support of Islam" (Hilf Nusrat al-Islam) with the former Jund al-Aqsa, by then renamed Ansar al-Tawheed (Tandhim Hurras al-Din & Ansar al-Tawheed, 2018), though HTS later encouraged the latter to leave the formation (Ansar al-Tawheed, 2020). Hurras al-Din instead established its own military operation room to coordinate attacks against regime forces, "incite on the believers" (Harid al-Mu'mineen) with smaller groups (Ansar al-islam, Jabhat Ansar al-Din, & Tandhim Hurras al-Din, 2021).

After the factional clashes ended, Ahrar al-Sham resumed its strategy of alliance formation by joining the National Front for Liberation (al-Jabhat al-Wataniyya lil Tahrir, 2018), a new front formed in May 2018 with Turkish backing and structured around Faylaq al-Sham. The aim of the umbrella group was to institutionalise all the armed opposition internally and externally, and establish a government that would dissolve all groups under a common politico-military project. Ahrar al-Sham saw the National Liberation Front as a means to achieve this goal. According to Husam Tarsha, looking back on the situation, this was a necessary step to bring all the armed opposition under a unified banner.

> We want to create a new government in both Idlib and the north. The purpose would be to unify all the structures of governance under some regional

agreement. We need a united army to survive the onslaught. This situation cannot remain like this for ever. Others will impose their will on us ultimately.

But HTS was more successful in institutionalising a governance project to rule Idlib province. The group took advantage of an initiative proposed by independent academics and intellectuals to unite local administration. HTS used the initiative to form the so-called Salvation Government, which could facilitate humanitarian aid and gain regional and international recognition without being officially under HTS control.[43] An independent Islamist activist, Rami Dalati, said that he initially proposed the concept of an independent government to both Ahrar al-Sham and HTS. But others say that the HTS leadership itself discussed the creation of an independent government that HTS leader al-Jolani eventually adopted. Nevertheless, Dalati maintained:

> I proposed the idea of creating an independent administration to both Ahrar al-Sham and HTS. Ahrar al-Sham leader was not convinced but Jolani was more open to the idea. He did not want to focus on bread, humanitarian help, and assistance. He wanted to focus on the military. We thought that its members could be selected among Syrian intellectuals and academics. They would not be the servants of Jolani, especially for civilian issues. It was not a real concern for him as he primarily focused on the military dimension of the conflict.

The Salvation Government's success hinged on its ability to exert control over Idlib province. Its main contender was the National Liberation Front, inclusive of Ahrar al-Sham by then. With the Front controlling half of the province, the imposition of the Salvation Government as the de facto authority that other countries would have to recognise was not possible. The National Liberation Front remained a potent alternative in case Russia and Turkey agreed to eliminate HTS and install an alternative. The Astana agreements still called for the elimination of "terrorist" groups, and the National Liberation Front presented a viable option to Turkey that was not provided by local armed groups such as Jaysh al-'Izza or Suqur al-Sham. Ibrahim Shasho, a former minister of justice and religious affairs in the Salvation Government who switched his allegiance to HTS after leaving Ahrar al-Sham, recognised:

> The problem with Ahrar al-Sham, contrary to local groups like Suqur al-Sham, for instance, is that they have a comprehensive project (*mutakamil*). They do not merely care about their local areas but deal with political, social, and military domains complementarily.

The last military confrontation was therefore difficult to prevent. In January 2019, a series of clashes erupted between Zinki Movement and HTS in Idlib province. While HTS claimed that the Zinki Movement refused to hand over members accused of killing an HTS member to a court, the real rationale of the fight lay elsewhere. HTS opponents insisted in private discussions that HTS's true motivation was to seize control of Zinki Movement's areas and lucrative economic resources, as the group's territory is situated between the regime and the northern regions.[44] Others add that Jolani would have felt betrayed by Zinki's leader when the group decided to leave the HTS alliance, despite HTS's strong support for Zinki when it integrated the group.[45] The conflict quickly spread throughout the province, with HTS ultimately prevailing against Zinki Movement. Despite Ahrar al-Sham's alliance call for a general mobilisation against HTS (al-Jabhat al-Wataniyya lil-Tahrir, 2019a), HTS contained Ahrar al-Sham in the south of the province and exploited the opportunity to mobilise against Ahrar al-Sham territories in the Ghab plains. HTS ultimately prevailed against Zinki Movement, Ahrar al-Sham, and Suqur al-Sham in the Jabal Zawiyya. The group seized their heavy weapons and imposed their submission to the Salvation Government, though some of the weapons were later restituted to them. Many locals affiliated with Ahrar al-Sham in the Ghab plains moved to Turkish-controlled territory in the north but later returned to Idlib to defend the province.[46] Zinki Movement was effectively expelled from the province (Hay'at Tahrir al-Sham, 2018g) and subsequently restructured and integrated into the national army under Turkish patronage. Turkey changed its leadership and started to provide salaries (al-mudun, 2017) before dissolving it into Faylaq al-Majd and the National Army (Zinki, 2019).

The outcome of the military confrontation was largely influenced by the different institutional trajectories of the two sides. Ahrar al-Sham and Zinki Movement were localised groups that lacked the ability to effectively combat a more centralised internal competitor, despite Ahrar al-Sham's belated attempts to establish centralised military forces, which were too late to prevent its initial loss of economic resources in 2017. Their military capabilities against the Syrian regime were insufficient to withstand internal competition, particularly in comparison to HTS's centralised control over resources and stronger internal discipline. Moreover, HTS shrewdly refused to treat the Syrian Liberation Front as a unified entity and instead dealt with its sub-factions independently to weaken them one by one. Following the battle, a commander from Ahrar al-Sham expressed his regret, stating:

> HTS came to our villages with heavy weapons. They did not hesitate to hit us, even if it threatened the civilians. Our fighters are local. They did not want to

endanger their communities and decided to stop the fight for this reason. They were not willing to fight HTS as much as HTS was willing to fight them.

Foreign fighters divided during the military confrontation. Many foreign fighters insisted on their neutrality, refusing to be used for inter-factional issues and power struggles as they had been in previous conflicts in Afghanistan and Chechnya (Abu Saleh al-Uzbiki, Abd al-Rahman al-Masri, Abu Safiya, 2017; Nukhbat min al-Muhajideen al-Muhajarin fi Ard al-Sham, 2017; Katiba al-Boukhari, 2018). Other foreign fighters and foreign-manned brigades conversely issued statements in support of HTS (n.m, 2019), while Ahrar al-Sham and the National Liberation Front tried to reassure foreign fighters that they would protect them (al-Jabhat al-Wataniyya lil-Tahrir, 2019b).[47] The largest group of foreign fighters, the Turkistan Islamic Party, which is usually perceived as neutral, claimed that it was pushed into confrontation in self-defence against Ahrar al-Sham–aligned armed groups (Hizb al-Turkistani al-Islami, 2018). Other groups denounced the intervention, including the alliance of Ahrar al-Sham and the Zinki Movement (Jabhat Tahrir Suriya, 2018) and Jaysh al-Ahrar (Jaysh al-Ahrar, 2018). Even individual foreign fighter members of HTS opposed it (Hussein, 2018b). According to an Ahrar al-Sham military commander:

> The two sides were exhausted but we still managed to keep many strongholds. Unfortunately [Abu Muhammad] al-Jolani had more resources. He controlled the border control of Baab al-Hawa and therefore managed to integrate many fighters who left other Syrian regions since he paid them more. Then, he used the Turkistan Islamic Party against us. We thought we could win against him, but didn't expect the Turkistan Islamic Party to turn their back on us.

HTS's military victory resulted in the imposition of the Salvation Government over all areas previously controlled by various factions, including Ahrar al-Sham. Although Ahrar al-Sham and its ally Suqur al-Sham were permitted to remain in the province, the end of factional conflict limited their ability to manoeuvre, as the HTS-supported government imposed near-hegemonic governance.[48] The Salvation Government centralised the court systems previously under partial control of various armed groups, took control of the local prisons, and implemented gradual administrative change throughout the Idlib province. According to a former prime minister of the Salvation Government Basam Sahiouni and his minister of interior, some of the local judges previously chosen by factions remained in their positions.[49] The Salvation Government was a means of institutionalising local administration while maintaining plausible deniability of its relationship with HTS. The relationship between the two entities is more ambiguous than straightforward. HTS initially retained control of security in the province and maintained its internal prisons and courts for security and political issues, particularly those involving IS cells, and it forbade the creation of new factions by insisting that any individual splitting should leave without weapons, nor should they establish a new group (Hay'at Tahrir al-Sham, 2018e). The Salvation Government had more leeway in the fields that HTS could not entirely control, or was not willing to (Drevon & Haenni, 2020).

Ahrar al-Sham's isolation paved the way for HTS to mature politically. HTS presented itself as the answer to popular demands for institutionalising the revolution (Ha'yat Tahrir al-Sham, 2017q, 2019d). The group blamed the United States for calling for human rights and liberty while supporting oppressors, allowing Iran, and aiding the PKK (Ha'yat Tahrir al-Sham, 2017o). After denouncing other factions for collaborating with Turkey, HTS signalled its willingness to collaborate with its neighbour. Despite initially refusing to cooperate with Turkey in the north, HTS leader al-Jolani later supported Turkey's war against the YPG, whom he considers enemies of the revolution (Syria TV, 2019). This was a significant shift for a Jihadi group, which normally oppose collaboration with states that do not fully implement Islamic Law. In its communiqués, HTS emphasised that its main enemies were the regime and Russia, rather than Turkey (Hay'at Tahrir al-Sham, 2017j).

Similarly to Ahrar al-Sham, HTS also faced challenges from more radical groups. The first group was Jund al-Aqsa, which, without being organisationally affiliated with IS, did not oppose the Iraqi group and claimed to be neutral in its conflict with other Syrian factions. More worrying perhaps, Jund al-Aqsa also orchestrated assassinations of commanders of other factions in northwest Syria, especially Ahrar al-Sham. Following a confrontation between Jund al-Aqsa and Ahrar al-Sham, Jabhat al-Nusra's next occurrence Jabhat Fath al-Sham brokered an agreement stipulating a cessation of hostilities, the release of prisoners from both factions, and the consolidation of its control over disputed areas. Additionally, it established a court to solve their disagreement. Despite Jabhat Fath al-Sham extending its acceptance of Jund al-Aqsa's allegiance into the group, the latter failed to adhere to the terms of the agreement in practice. This non-compliance ultimately led to Jabhat Fath al-Sham severing ties with Jund al-Aqsa (Jabhat Fath al-Sham, 2017a). Later, when Jabhat Fath al-Sham became HTS, it warned Jund al-Aqsa against excommunicating other factions and urged it to submit to shared courts of justice to solve murder cases (Hay'at Tahrir al-Sham, 2017g). As Jund al-Aqsa refused to heed HTS's orders, HTS decided to clamp down on the group militarily. Some of its members negotiated a way out to Raqqa to avoid a bloodbath with HTS, where they joined IS. Others formed a new group, Ansar al-Tawheed, which remains in northwest Syria but under tight HTS control. A HTS security official argues that:

> Ansar al-Tawheed's leaders now accept our lead, and coordinate with us on security and military developments. Their more radical members were either expelled or arrested. The group has integrated one of our military brigade (*liwa*), which means that they only conduct military activities under our supervision. They cannot launch independent military operations without our agreement.

But the most significant threat came from former Jabhat al-Nusra leaders who formed the pro-al–Qaeda splinter group, Hurras al-Din. When HTS detained their most prominent leaders in an attempt to restrain the pro al-Qaeda organisation, several HTS sub-factions complained and threatened the leadership. They demanded the establishment of independent courts of justice with impartial religious scholars, such as Abu Qatada, based in Jordan (Hay'at Tahrir al-Sham, 2017a. See also Hay'at Tahrir al-Sham, 2017b, 2017e; al-Urduni, no date). These factions claimed that they would leave HTS if their demands were not met. The nature of the threat posed by Hurras al-Din was therefore not quantitative, but qualitative. Although the al-Qaeda–affiliated group had far fewer soldiers and resources than HTS, it presented a potential alternative that could have swayed many of HTS's sub-groups and commanders who disagreed with the leadership's new strategic direction. The emergence of Hurras al-Din illustrates how HTS, like Ahrar al-Sham in the past, had to navigate internal and external dynamics carefully between antagonistic demands for political opening and the necessary preservation of internal cohesion. HTS could not simply impose its political decisions over sub-brigades when the cost of defection was too low.

HTS placed strict conditions on the activities of Hurras al-Din. HTS leaders, including al-Jolani, insisted in private interviews that they prohibited Hurras al-Din from maintaining its own courts of justice, engaging in hostile domestic actions (including kidnappings), and planning foreign attacks.[50] Some of these claims are supported by independent sources (al-Sudani, & al-Urduni, 2019) and by HTS's highest religious authority, Abdullah al-Shami, who released a public communiqué to al-Qaeda that the agreement with Hurras al-Din prohibited the group from establishing checkpoints, forming courts of justice, and conducting security operations independently (Atun, 2020a). The Hurras al-Din leader, Abu Humam al-Shami, initially acknowledged real strategic differences with HTS, but argued that the group could play a role similar to that of al-Qaeda with the Taliban (Al-Shami, 1439). Tensions nonetheless remained high between the two groups. Hurras al-Din accused HTS of collaborating with Faylaq al-Sham to potentially unify all military forces under an army officer (al-Sudani & al-Urduni, 2019; al-Shami & al-Uraydi, 2019). Such a move could pave the way for the reintegration of these groups into the Syrian army in a reconciliation process, which Faylaq al-Sham vehemently denied (Faylaq al-Sham, 2019).

In the summer of 2020, HTS defeated Hurras al-Din in a swift operation that saw the seizure of Hurras al-Din's military strongholds, confiscation of its heavy weaponry, and takeover of its headquarters. This operation was a response to Hurras al-Din's attempts to ally with a former prominent HTS commander, Abd al-Malik al-Tilly, who formed the group al-Muqatilin al-Ansar. He had left HTS in opposition to its rapprochement with Turkey and its perceived acquiescence to the Russian-Turkish understanding. The renegades formed a new operation room called "Hold Fast" (Fa-Ithbatu) with smaller groups, including Tansiqiyat al-Jihad—which was formed by Abu al-'Abd Ashida, a former Ahrar al-Sham and then HTS commander—Jabhat Ansar al-Din, and Ansar al-Islam, to coordinate their military efforts against the regime (Tansiqiyat al-Jihad, Liwa al-Muqatilin al-Ansar, Ansar al-Islam, Jabhat Ansar al-Din, & Tandhim Hurras al-din, 2020). While this initiative emerged independently in Syria, it garnered explicit backing from al-Qaeda Central, underscoring their endorsement of the newfound alliance (Tandhim Qa'idat al-Jihad, 2020). HTS acted swiftly to prevent this new operation room from becoming a credible alternative on the ground by consolidating its military power. HTS's relatively easy subjugation of Hurras al-Din reveals its weaker institutionalisation and local anchorage compared to Ahrar al-Sham's, which fought with HTS for two years. Hurras al-Din was further weakened by repeated U.S. drone attacks against its prominent commanders, which limited its ability to organise and eroded its attractiveness for new members.[51] According to the head of HTS's military, Abul-Hassan al-Hamawi, the decision to take decisive action against Hurras al-Din was driven by an internal military necessity:

> We need a single military direction to prepare the defence of the province but Hurras al-Din was trying to destroy it. They would launch some uncoordinated attacks that subsequently justified Russian bombings against our defensive lines. They do not know how to deal with their regional environment. We gave them enough time but they refused to listen. So we went after them. They could not resist since they were not really organised. It was just a network of commanders without clear organisational structure.

HTS's crackdown on Hurras al-Din served as a template for addressing other smaller factions resistant to adopting the new military direction in the province. Two such groups were Junud al-Sham, led by a Chechen militant, Muslim al-Sishani, who participated in the two Chechen wars, and Jund Allah, founded by a Tajik militant, Abu Hanifa al-Adhari. HTS blamed al-Adhazi for excommunicating other factions and al-Shishani for providing protection to him.[52] Prominent groups of foreign fighters, notably the Turkistan Islamic Party and militants from Central Asia, voiced their support for HTS and criticised groups like Jund Allah for their radicalism, lack of effectiveness, and inability to collaborate with the mainstream opposition (al-Hizb al-Islami al-Turkistani, Jama'at tawheed wal-Jihad et al., 2021). By November 2021, HTS had confronted both groups, ultimately dismantling them due to their refusal to comply with its orders.

HTS also took decisive actions against IS networks in the region, which we detailed in a Crisis Group report (ICG, 2023a).[53] Following its retreat to Raqqa in 2014, IS was forced to leave Syria's northwest. The group started to reappear only after 2019, when individuals and small clusters started to find refuge in Idlib following the collapse of their territorial Caliphate in the east of the country. The more structured factions among them emerged from the south of the province, where they made strategic agreements with the regime, permitting their ingress into the province, according to interviews with HTS security officials, corroborated by various open sources. Other IS members began returning individually from the north. HTS improved its intelligence capabilities, effectively dismantling these nascent networks, which struggled to orchestrate any significant regional attacks. In lieu of direct assaults, IS attempted to forge alliances with dissidents from Hurras al-Din who formed Sarayat Abu Bakr al-Sadiq, and Sarayat 'Abdullah bin 'Omar Unais. One of their leaders published a document outlining HTS's apostasy, including forming alliances with Turkey and other "apostate" factions, the failure to implement Islamic law and its penal punishments, levying non-Islamic taxes, allowing non-Islamic subjects in education, and supporting the U.N. political process (al-Manhaj, 2020). According to HTS security commanders, IS proposed financial support in exchange for the ability to claim responsibility for armed attacks, but to no avail. In absence of operational ability, IS had more success safekeeping high-profile figures, including two of its leaders, Abdullah Qardash and Abul-Hussein al-Husseini, since their presence required a significantly reduced operational footprint, enhancing their ability to evade detection by HTS intelligence efforts (ICG, 2022).

A reconfiguration of HTS's internal structures helped its transformation. The group's membership grew significantly as individuals from other factions joined, many of whom were less religiously committed and ideologically indoctrinated by the group's religious scholars (Tsurkov, 2019a). Many internal opponents to the group's new direction were also killed, particularly among foreign fighters (Haid, 2017b), and internal opposition silenced. The institutionalisation of religious authority imposed a unique religious voice inside the group, through the Sharia council headed by Abu Abdullah al-Shami, containing any dissident voices, resulting in the expulsion of those who opposed the new strategic direction. HTS also reorganised itself militarily by creating new battalions, with the aim of centralising its military forces to better protect opposition-held areas. Like other groups, HTS recruited individuals aged 17 to 30, who were at most 20 years old when the uprising began. According to Abu Abdullah al-Shami, even the religious training of the new recruits is changing:

> We are now mobilising common Muslims (*'awaïs al-muslimin*) with whom we are no longer engaging in the theological debates that we used to, for instance on *al- wala' wal- bara* ("loyalty to Muslims and dissociation from non Muslims"). These require a higher level of intellectual awareness that was only possible when we were a smaller and more elitist group. Now we focus on the fundamentals in religion.

Both Ahrar al-Sham and HTS faced more hard-line foreign fighters and local commanders, but their responses differed significantly. Many of the same radical figures who opposed Ahrar al-Sham before joining HTS in opposition to Ahrar al-Sham's ties to Turkey subsequently expressed their opposition at the HTS leadership for developing similar ties. HTS was nonetheless more successful in constraining these figures for two reasons. First, it institutionalised internal authority and imposed administrative regulations, punishing dissenters with arrests when necessary. While Ahrar al-Sham also tried to institutionalise religious authority, as discussed in the next chapter, it lacked the same decisiveness and willingness to take direct action against dissenters. But institutional regulations and arrests alone do not explain the difference in outcomes. The key difference lies in how the two groups managed their factional orders. HTS punished defectors and tightly controlled all competing groups, from the pragmatic to the radical, in order to prevent the emergence of credible alternatives. This strategy ensured that dissidents had no other viable options and could either remain silent or withdraw, but could not join another group.

The battles that occurred between regime forces and the armed opposition from 2018 to 2020 shed light on the features of the latter following the control of the Salvation Government. The strategic threat posed by the regime's attacks in the south of the province forced all armed groups to establish cross-factional military defence in a shared military room called the Clear Victory operation room (al-Fath al-Mubin). In addition, new local forces were mobilised to provide additional defences to the second and third defensive lines in their respective villages, according to my field research in these communities in the Zawiyya mountains. The combination of light infantry troops and local fighters defending their homes facilitated the defence of the region despite heavy bombardments.

The local fighters' embeddedness in their communities also lessened Turkey's role, which initially involved only providing adequate weapons to the fighters.

The bi-polarisation of the remaining opposition did not entirely dissipate between 2019 and 2020. HTS and its supported government did not try to completely subjugate, let alone expel, other groups, including Ahrar al-Sham and other local armed groups. HTS instead sought to bring more military cohesion to their shared military operation room. The head of HTS's military forces, Abul-Hassan al-Hamawi, explained his rationale for not expelling Ahrar al-Sham after HTS took over:

> We are trying to unify the military forces but we cannot simply impose ourselves on other factions like Ahrar al-Sham. If we try to dissolve them, their soldiers will never join us. You cannot join the one who is imposing itself on you, it is a matter of dignity. So if we dissolve them their soldiers will leave and we will weaken the military defence of the region.

In the summer of 2019, Russian support for the Syrian regime's advances prompted a significant Turkish military intervention (ICG, 2020). By 2020, northwest Syria had become a major security concern for Turkey. To deter the regime and its allies from making further progress, Turkey deployed over 10,000 soldiers to the province. The cost, both politically and militarily, of continuing the Russian-supported military campaign became too high for Russia. As a result, Russia was forced to placate the regime's desire to continue its campaign, thereby preventing further military progress. But HTS's continued listing as a proscribed organisation linked to al-Qaeda and ISIS by the U.N. Security Council remains a real impediment to any direct engagement with the group. Turkey remains hesitant to engage HTS diplomatically, and Western countries have not specified the conditions under which HTS could potentially be engaged and removed from the Security Council listing of armed groups associated with al-Qaeda and ISIS—which would be unlikely because of a Russian veto—or individual countries' own terrorist listings (Khalifa & Bonsey, 2021).

In the absence of unification of all military forces under the HTS-supported Salvation Government, Turkey and HTS promoted the establishment of a military council that would integrate and restructure them into a single military structure. Turkey initially sought to rely on HTS's military strength to reorganise the defence of the province while diluting the group within a larger organisational structure that HTS does not fully control. To this end, Turkey formed a troika consisting of the military leaders of Ahrar al-Sham, Faylaq al-Sham, and HTS to lead a military council. HTS had also long believed in the creation of a military council that would more effectively defend the province and solidify its military preeminence over other groups, particularly Ahrar al-Sham.

The group accepted the troika formula, despite initially favouring its military leader Abul-Hassan to lead the council. The latter initially recalled:

> If we manage to unite all the military forces in a military council, we do not believe that we can mix the military brigades of different groups. That would create tensions and weaken us. It is better instead that each group [Ahrar al-Sham, Faylaq al-Sham, and HTS] creates a certain number of brigades [*liwa*] that perform all the military functions. Each brigade is responsible for a specific geographic area, which helps to cover all the frontlines and increase accountability. In addition, we think that this helps to create a healthy competition between the brigades, which will help them get better over time.

The formation of the military council was a significant development for Ahrar al-Sham. Until 2017, the group relied primarily on local military units. Then, it shifted towards creating centralised military forces that are not tied to specific geographic areas. The military council merges these two approaches. It aims to establish a number of military brigades linked to one another, most prominently Ahrar al-Sham, Faylaq al-Sham, and HTS, in addition to smaller independent organisations. Each brigade is responsible for a particular geographic area, rather than a specific type of mission (such as light infantry, tanks, or artillery). This approach has two advantages. First, it clarifies military responsibilities by ensuring that each brigade is entirely accountable for the defence of its respective area. Second, it leverages the local knowledge and embeddedness of these groups to improve military efficiency.

Many Ahrar al-Sham leaders, however, initially harboured suspicions towards HTS and feared that the military council could be a Trojan horse for HTS to assert its dominance by creating new structures that would subordinate Ahrar al-Sham's elite brigades. Ahrar al-Sham still agreed to participate in the military council on the condition that its brigades would remain loyal to its central leadership. To achieve this objective, Ahrar al-Sham emphasised the authority of its consultative council as the highest decision-making body within the movement. This message was indirectly directed towards Abu Mundhar, who served as the head of Ahrar al-Sham's military and represented the group within the military council troika. In October 2020, the leadership council of Ahrar al-Sham took action by demoting Abu Fares Dara', the head of one of its brigades (Ahrar al-Sham, 2020e). This decision triggered an internal rift between Ahrar al-Sham's consultative council and the head of its military wing, Abu Mundhar. Former Ahrar al-Sham leader Abu Yahiyya al-Hamawi commented on the situation, stating that at the time:

> The problems started with the council. We wanted to name reliable individuals to lead the new brigades. The problem is that Abu Mundhar, our military

leader, wanted to impose people who are closer to HTS. So we sacked him. Then he allied with a former Ahrar al-Sham leader, Hassan Sufan, who has long supported the idea of a military council. He saw this as an opportunity to stage a coup inside the group, which failed. We do not want a war with HTS now. Both HTS and Turkey need us for this project, so they need to preserve us. They need our special forces, the commandos (*mughawir*). Abu Mundhar and Hassan Sufan will not be able to lead them.

This episode further crippled Ahrar al-Sham as a cohesive movement. The decision of the consultative council to assert its authority over the military leader triggered internal opposition. Several Ahrar al-Sham brigades and leaders, including Abu Mundhar, released a communiqué (Ahrar al-Sham, 2020a), emphasising the urgent need to address the movement's paralysis and insisting on the appointment of Hassan Sufan, a former leader who had been isolated by the current leadership, as the new overall leader. Sufan stressed the importance of HTS's supported military council to address the substantial losses suffered during the recent Russian-supported military offensive (Sufan, 2020). Sufan emphasised the need for enhanced coordination among different factions in military matters and underscored the critical importance of military effectiveness (Sufan, 2020). He embraced the establishment of the military council to achieve these objectives, though he recognised that many in Ahrar al-Sham opposed either the idea or the practicalities of this council, especially as it could reinforce HTS. In response, the leader of Ahrar al-Sham announced the appointment of new heads of the brigades (Ahrar al-Sham, 2020e) and demoted Abu Mundhar (Ahrar al-Sham, 2020f) to stop the internal rebellion. Several military trainers and factions, such as the Homs Bloc, Ahrar al-Janub, and Katibat Mujahidi Ibn Taymiyya, emphatically asserted their unwavering allegiance to the old leadership (Ahrar al-Sham, 2020b, 2020d). But other brigades then opposed this decision and pledged their allegiance to Sufan instead as the new leader (Ahrar al-Sham, 2020c). Both sides fought for legitimacy, publishing videos of their troops to suggest that they each had the support of the majority of the movement. Some accused HTS of supporting this opposing faction, allowing it to seize some of the movement's headquarters in specific locations.

Ahrar al-Sham tried to reconstitute itself internally. In January 2021, Amer al-Shaykh was nominated as the new leader (Ahrar al-Sham, 2021b) with the responsibility of reconstituting the movement. Under Turkish pressure, both sides agreed to dissolve the consultative council (*majlis al-shura*) and establish a smaller leadership council (*majlis al-qiyada*), consisting of 12 members only, with an equal representation from each side (Ahrar al-Sham, 2021c). But, within two months, the council would be reduced to seven members, primarily aligned with Hassan Sufan (Ahrar al-Sham, 2021a). Some of the brigades aligned with the previous leadership, including Liwa Badr and Liwa al-'Abbas, decided to leave Ahrar al-Sham and join the Third Division of the Syrian National Army instead, which had become a key player in northern Aleppo by then (al-Jaysh al-Watani al-suri, 2021). By the end of the year, several brigades, including Liwa al-Iman and Liwa Khatab, advocated for a return to the previous situation, including the dissolution of the new leadership council. They named Abu Yusuf al-Hamawi as their new leader (Ahrar al-Sham, 2022c) with the support of the old leadership (Ahrar al-Sham, 2022b). Both sides started to claim that they represented Ahrar al-Sham as a movement, further weakening the group's general cohesion. By 2022, the movement was greatly weakened in the eyes of many members. Despite claims that factions previously positioned in Damascus and its Ghuta periphery were joining the group (Ahrar al-Sham, 2023b), a defector from a large brigade initially from Homs, representing up to a third of its forces, lamented to a newspaper (al-Kanj, 2021):

> We left Ahrar al-Sham because of all the rivalries at the leadership level. We had no more laws to follow and the movement turned into groups bickering over positions and interests, which made it lose its strength. Some members are loyal to Hayat Tahrir al-Sham [HTS], others support the Free Syrian Army (FSA)—so leaving Ahrar al-Sham and joining [other] factions was a given.

Another faction of Ahrar al-Sham that had previously left the group in 2017 to join al-Jabhat al-Shamiyya also found itself in conflict with their new group. They expressed discontent with what they perceived as a lack of proper integration and financial disagreements. As tensions escalated, this group decided to split from al-Jabhat al-Shamiyya, demanding the return of equipment and headquarters that they had brought with them when they joined (Ahrar al-Sham, 2022a). Clashes ensued between the two groups, prompting an Islamic Council-led committee to intervene and issue a ruling on the matter, which favoured al-Jabhat al-Shamiyya. The dissenting faction of Ahrar al-Sham refused to accept the ruling (Ahrar al-Sham, 2023a). Hassan Sufan, along with possible support from HTS, stood in solidarity with this faction, seemingly with the intention of weakening al-Jabhat al-Shamiyya in northern Aleppo. The older leadership of Ahrar al-Sham, on the other hand, supported the reconciliation council and urged this particular sub-group to remain within al-Jabhat al-Shamiyya (Ahrar al-Sham, 2023c). Despite their efforts, they ultimately resigned from the group, as they were unable to influence its course (Abu 'Ammar, Basha, Abu Yahiyya, al-Raqqa, 2022).

The consolidation of the military council by HTS in conjunction with Ahrar al-Sham granted them the authority to impose the Fath al-Mubin military operation room as the only institutional framework for military affairs in Idlib (ICG,

2023a). Starting from June 2020, all the other armed groups were required to adhere to the directives of the operation room and were strictly prohibited from acting independently from it (Hay'at Tahrir al-Sham, 2020a). Similarly, HTS forbade its members from joining or creating a new faction (Hay'at Tahrir al-Sham, 2020c). These measures sought to consolidate military decisions under the military council and prevent unauthorised actions by undisciplined armed groups. HTS used this system to control the small number of foreign-led brigades, which were given two options: either join HTS's own military forces by integrating into newly formed specialised brigades or at the very least abide to the orders of the shared operation room according to HTS's military leader and al-Jolani himself (ICG, 2023a).[54] This development accompanied the creation of a military academy by former officers to improve the training of the armed opposition. The institutionalisation of the military is a real step towards its professionalisation, though it is not yet fully completed. It nonetheless illustrates how the Syrian armed opposition increasingly tries to replicate the standards of a professional army (e.g., Kilcullen, 2020). The shared operation room has unified military decision-making but without unifying financial incomes as well, as each armed group within the operation room continues to receive its own independent sources of funding. According to the head of HTS's military, Abul-Hassan al-Hamawi:

> We have put a system in place for all the factions in the Fath al-Mubin operation room. Our objective is to unify military work, though this is only partial now. Each faction still maintains its own source of funding for instance, but we share our weapons during the battles. We also created a military academy with 30 colonels in 2021 to move from a revolutionary situation to real military work. The military academy is important to provide additional training that's more professional, for which we drew inspiration from different Western doctrines. The regime and its foreign supporters evolve, so we need to change too. All the frontline brigades now have the same capabilities and specialisations. Additional brigades that are centralised can also be sent to the frontlines to bring in additional support if needed.

HTS also recognises the importance of leveraging local communities' inherent drive to safeguard their regions, all while avoiding entanglement in factional politics that could arise from formal alliances. To achieve this, HTS encouraged the development of the popular resistance (*al-muqawama al-sha'biyya*) in the Jabal Zawiyya in particular. According to interviews on the front lines and with some of the popular resistance's coordinators, this military formation recruits local civilians who engage in part-time commitments, typically spanning a few days each month. They are intentionally not positioned at the forefront of direct confrontations against the regime and its foreign allies on the front lines. Rather, their primary role involves enhancing the overall defensive capabilities of the province by undertaking tasks such as trench excavation and secondary frontline patrolling. This supportive presence not only reinforces the main front-line fighters but also ensures the resilience of secondary defensive lines.

The armed opposition in Syria has remained divided into two sides since then. On one side, there is the Interim Government, consisting of remnants of the Free Syrian Army merged into the National Army, along with parts of Ahrar al-Sham. On the other side, there is Hay'at Tahrir al-Sham (HTS) and the remaining components of Ahrar al-Sham. Each side has something that its counterpart wants. The Salvation Government officially controls the province but has not transformed into a consensually accepted entity where all the factions (including HTS) would merge into a ministry of defence. HTS and its government continue their attempts to legitimise themselves internationally. They want to prove themselves as the last guarantor against an exodus of refugees in Europe and a spillover of foreign fighters. The Interim Government conversely enjoys international legitimacy but no real presence on the ground to truly matter.

Turkey maintains relations with both sides, with the ultimate objective of unifying local military forces to stabilise the territory, though this is not politically possible, because of HTS's continued designation by the U.N. as a group linked to al-Qaeda and ISIS (despite it no longer being the case). In the meantime, Turkey has increased its military commitment to the defence of the province by 2020, as it realised that the observation points authorised in the Astana agreements lacked the capacity to function as genuine defence lines unless reinforced with additional troops. By 2020, Turkey understood that the sole effective deterrent would entail a substantial deployment of soldiers exceeding 10,000 in number. While the armed opposition's professionalism and organisational capacity has significantly improved by 2024, the province of Idlib continues to be predominantly under their control, largely due to Turkey's military presence. Turkey's military forces serve as a significant deterrent to both Russia and the Syrian regime, making it improbable for any change in the ground situation without an unlikely Turkish military withdrawal (ICG, 2020).

Conclusion

During the first phase of the conflict, attempts to institutionalise the armed opposition were driven by military necessity, though most initiatives were undermined by foreign countries' meddling with the opposition. Their support for contending factions and failure to join a common initiative to institutionalise the armed opposition reinforced the armed opposition's internal divisions.

Syrian armed groups also tried to institutionalise cross-factional relations independently, with Ahrar al-Sham playing a leading role. Despite this, most initiatives failed, as Syrian armed groups were hesitant to unite with an al-Qaeda affiliate they did not trust. As Turkey and Russia became more directly involved in managing the conflict, political and military necessity imposed the internal and external institutionalisation of the armed opposition. Although Ahrar al-Sham was initially better positioned to take the lead, its internal institutional structure weakened as it started to face a more cohesive competitor, Jabhat al-Nusra. The latter successfully transformed into HTS and supported the creation of a local government that imposed itself over the province, but failed to achieve a consensus with other groups that would gain wider international legitimacy.

5
Politicising Jihad

Insurgencies cannot be won by military means alone; the achievement of long-term political objectives is crucial for armed groups' victory. The preceding chapters explored the emergence and expansion of Ahrar al-Sham and Jabhat al-Nusra, particularly how Ahrar al-Sham institutionalised itself both internally and externally to become a central player in the Syrian armed opposition. In this chapter, we take a step back with a cross-sectional analysis of the politicisation of the two groups, examining how Ahrar al-Sham's internal and external institutionalisation informed its politicisation over the years, up to Jabhat al-Nusra's transformation into HTS. This analysis situates the context in which new political and religious ideas develop and take over within armed groups. It suggests that armed groups' ideological construction is a relational process, with new ideas emerging in tandem with these groups' internal and external institutionalisation.

The Pre-War Roots of Jihadi Revisionism

Many Syrian armed groups, particularly Ahrar al-Sham, emerged from the Islamist social movement, which was mostly dormant in northwest Syria before 2011, where many Ahrar al-Sham's leaders originated. While the group has extended its reach throughout Syria in the years since, its leaders, cadres, and members primarily mobilised in the countryside of Idlib and Hama, especially around the al-Ghab plains, followed by Aleppo and Homs. These regions constitute the group's core popular incubator (*hadina sha'biyya*), which has remained central throughout the conflict, despite Ahrar al-Sham's various phases of expansion and retreat. Ahrar al-Sham reflects a largely latent Islamist social movement and the "radical milieu" – defined in social movement studies as armed groups' supportive environment – that formed around it in the early days of the armed opposition, which sustained the mobilisation of its early brigades.

This characteristic is a significant departure from most other Jihadi groups, which either emerged or were substantially moulded outside their domestic constituencies. The roots of Jihadi Salafism can be traced back to the mid-1970s, when Egyptian and Syrian groups developed this ideology in their respective countries and in prisons. During the Afghan War, these groups interacted and radicalised in a competitive social movement, which helped shape their ideology further (Lav, 2012; Hamid & Farrall, 2015; Drevon, 2022).[1] Many Salafi Jihadi groups that emerged in the Middle East and North Africa in the 1990s and 2000s were formed by individuals who embraced Salafi Jihadi ideas in exile before importing them into their home countries.[2] Algerian, Iraqi, Libyan, and Indonesian groups are examples of such organisations. Although these groups also radicalised because of their specific domestic environments, including repression and political exclusion (Hafez, 2003; Burgat, 2007), ideological developments in exile played a critical role in shaping the ideological construction and radicalisation of most Salafi Jihadi groups for the past three decades.

In interviews, Syrian Jihadis emphasise the domestic nature of their conflict with the regime. They contend that the Syrian conflict cannot be compared to resistance to foreign occupation, which they associate more closely with previous conflicts such as in Afghanistan and neighbouring Iraq. This is also stressed by HTS, whose top religious figure, Abu Abdullah al-Shami, argued:

> In 2011, the situation was substantially different from Iraq in 2003. The militarisation of the conflict in Syria involved a Muslim people fighting a popular revolution. This is very different from Iraq and its foreign occupation. Our jihad was a revolution. It was not solely a reaction to occupation. Our struggle therefore had to develop according to the local context and in line with local developments. We could not be differentiated or isolated from the reality around us.

Ahrar al-Sham emerged as one of the most successful groups during the early stages of the Syrian uprising, as its growth paralleled the reactivation of the Islamist social movement when militarisation became inevitable. The group's core membership originated primarily in the northwest region of Syria, which had a history of violence and opposition to the Syrian regime. This region played a critical role during the armed confrontation between Syrian Islamists and the Baath party in the 1970s. While the first conflict is often portrayed as a confrontation solely between the Muslim Brotherhood and the regime, a plurality of Islamist armed groups were involved at the time. The Brotherhood leadership was notably divided on the legitimacy of violence between Hama and Aleppo, with a more confrontational leadership in the former, where Ahrar al-Sham's current strongholds are located (Lefèvre, 2013: 89–96; Conduit, 2019: 105–111). Other organisationally distinct groups made common cause with the Brotherhood by the late 1970s, when the conflict intensified. Although many Brotherhood-affiliated families moved to Jordan and Iraq during the following decades, many others remained in Syria.

The group's popular incubator is grounded in this political tradition.³ Ahrar al-Sham draws its popular support from a tradition of opposition to the Syrian regime that is grounded in local politics rather than the internationalist ideology of Salafi Jihadi activists. The group is aligned with Syrians who reside in regions that have long resented the nature of the Syrian regime. This political stance can be traced back to the domestic conflict that engulfed Syria in the 1970s and continues to be the dominant narrative for Ahrar al-Sham's members and associates. In contrast, the Salafi Jihadi ideology that emerged from foreign jihads in Afghanistan and is historically associated with Palestinian and Egyptian ideologues such as Abu Muhammad al-Maqdisi, Abu Qatada al-Filistini, and Sayyed Imam al-Sharif, takes a back seat to the Syrian context. Former prison leader Rami Dalati reinforces this point, arguing:

> Many prominent Ahrar al-Sham members come from families affiliated to the Muslim Brotherhood in the past. Others were associated to the trend despite several divergences on particular positions, for instance on the legitimacy of party politics. Even somebody like Abu Khaled al-Suri, who was accused of being closely associated with al-Qaeda networks, was a son of the vanguard group (al-Tali'a), not al-Qaeda.⁴ Ahrar al-Sham youth were therefore not far from the pragmatism historically developed by the Brotherhood. The transition was not difficult. The youths wanted jihad without being al-Qaeda so what happened in Iraq in terms of excessive violence helped them to take distance from the organisation quickly. In reality, they previously only embraced Jihadi Salafism because they wanted jihad. But it was not their real skin.

But Ahrar al-Sham is not a Muslim Brotherhood offshoot. While many group leaders and members come from families associated with the Muslim Brotherhood, Ahrar al-Sham is not a spin-off of the organisation.⁵ The Muslim Brotherhood played a role in the early development of a certain tradition in political Islam, which influenced subsequent generations of Islamists. Even intellectuals associated with Jihadi Salafism, such as Abu Mus'ab al-Suri (2004) and the former Ahrar al-Sham and current HTS preacher Abu Fath al-Farghali (2020a), recognise this point.⁶ But most activists consider the Muslim Brotherhood an old organisation that has lost ground in both militant activism and the development of political Islam. Instead, the growth of new ideologies that have spread in the Muslim world swayed Ahrar al-Sham and its popular incubator. This is particularly true of the younger Islamist-leaning generations influenced by the diffusion of Salafism in the region. Salafism has shaped the mobilisation and socialisation of the Islamist social movement and has also determined its evolving religious language and approach.

Non-Jihadi Salafism swayed Ahrar al-Sham's popular constituency in north and northwest Syria for the past two to three decades. While this movement was largely confined in the underground, it resonated with local conservative families who were exposed to Salafi ideas through new means of communication and the small-network approach of its adherents. Prior to the uprising, small-scale networks of Salafi Muslims from different persuasions already engaged in political and theological debates, including discussions on the legitimacy of jihad in Iraq and the postponement of the application of Islamic law in the Muslim world (*irja'*), as suggested in chapter 2.[7] These debates had long divided Jihadi and non-Jihadi Salafis (Lav, 2012; Ismail, 2021).

The diffusion of Jihadi ideas in the 2000s influenced many youths who joined Ahrar al-Sham after 2011, despite the early wishes of its leaders to distance itself from this trend. Some leaders and members of the group viewed al-Qaeda favourably after the 9/11 attacks, seeing it as the sole opponent to American domination in the Middle East. The popularity of Jihadi Salafism in the region grew in reaction to the two successive American wars in Afghanistan and Iraq, as many local youths looked for a response to the new threat to the region (Drevon, 2017). However, it is important to note that, since the youths embraced these ideas individually or in small-group settings, their beliefs were not necessarily fully consistent with al-Qaeda's. Some individuals supported al-Qaeda's political agenda without embracing all of its theological or ideological tenets. For example, some supported al-Qaeda's opposition to a perceived American military hegemony in the region without accepting the group's opposition to Hamas. This view has been shared by a former leading member of Ahrar al-Sham who joined the group in its early days:

> I did identify with Jihadi Salafism as a student, when I was at the university. But being Salafi Jihadi was more complicated than some might assume. I was also close to Hamas as well for instance. I believed in the group's strategy in Palestine but I disagreed with it on other fronts. I knew that there were real divergences between the group and al-Qaeda, but it did not matter to me.

A senior Islamist prisoner who participated in the armed conflict with the regime in the late 1970s before becoming the highest religious reference of the Islamic Front spearheaded by Ahrar al-Sham, Abu al-'Abbas al-Shami, emphasised this diversity:

> I was incarcerated along with some 1100 prisoners. We were all caught between 2005 and 2006. We were from everywhere in Syria. Many prisoners were very simple, with little nuanced political understanding. They merely sympathised with the Iraqi resistance against foreign occupation. Others, increasingly,

adopted the ideas of al-Qaeda. But most of them evolved subsequently in prison when we were all together.

The conflict in Iraq was a catalyst for the mobilisation of numerous Syrian youths who were willing to fight American troops. The Syrian regime played a facilitating role by allowing them to transit through Syria during the initial years of the conflict. The regime believed that de-stabilising Iraq would prevent future wars that might also target Syria. Additionally, the Syrian regime saw the conflict in Iraq as an opportunity to eliminate local Islamist activists while simultaneously positioning them as bargaining chips with the American administration in the future. While some of the Syrian youths who travelled to Iraq to fight against the Americans were not necessarily aligned with al-Qaeda or its ideology, many became sympathetic to the armed resistance against the American presence in Iraq. As al-Qaeda's leader in Iraq, Abu Musab al-Zarqawi,[8] gained influence and control over the Iraqi armed factions, many of the Syrian youths who had joined the armed opposition gradually began to adopt his ideological positions. This created tension among supporters of the armed opposition, and even some of the founders of groups like Ahrar al-Sham, such as Khaled Abu Anas, who insisted:

> Personally, I did not want them to go to Iraq. I did not dissuade them but I did not encourage them either. I nonetheless insisted that they should not undertake suicide operations with [Zarqawi's] group Tawheed wal-Jihad.

In 2005, the Syrian regime's previously lenient policy towards those wanting to participate in jihad in Iraq ceased. Assad negotiated with the United States to crack down on networks supporting jihad within Syria. This resulted in widespread arrests across the country, targeting thousands of individuals suspected of supporting the insurgency in Iraq. This shift in policy was concurrent with Syria's changing regional and international environment, which was heavily influenced by events such as the assassination of former Lebanese Prime Minister Rafiq Hariri and the subsequent forced withdrawal of Syrian troops from Lebanon. Abul-Abbas al-Shami, a former prison leader, argued:

> We have to remember the context in 2005. After the assassination of Lebanese prime minister Hariri, an international investigation was ordered by the UN Security Council. The team had to find those responsible in the regime and among Hizbullah leaders. They had all the names, including Asef Shawkat [a Syrian official]. We all believed that the US and Syria had an agreement. They would not release the names publicly if the Syrian regime agreed to do something in exchange. The regime therefore closed the border with Iraq

and prevented the fighters from going. Many Islamists of all tendencies were arrested in Syria, including myself.

Many youths who were arrested in Syria had participated in the war or were associated with local supporting networks. For example, a Syrian whose cousin quickly rose in Ahrar al-Sham leadership after 2011 affirmed:

> My cousin was caught by the regime when repression started to target these supporting networks. He was not involved in Islamist militancy but was simply caught with them. Prison truly changed him, though. He got closer to Islamist prison leaders. He learnt a lot from them, during these close interactions. He quickly joined Ahrar al-Sham when he was liberated. Between them, they call themselves the graduates of Saydnayya [the main Syrian prison] as if it was a university!

The experience of imprisonment had a significant impact on Syrian Islamists, particularly on members of Ahrar al-Sham. The Islamist prisoners drew across various generations, ranging from those closely associated with the Muslim Brotherhood legacy to younger Jihadi Salafis swayed by al-Qaeda. While some prisoners had fought on the Iraqi front, many were arrested simply for sympathising with the cause. In Saydnayya Prison, in the north of Damascus, the prisoners engaged in lively discussions and debates on a range of issues that were prominent in the Islamist social movement at the time. One of the most significant challenges faced by Jihadi Salafis during the Iraq War was the imposition of harsh rulings on the local population, which forced many Sunnis and Iraqi tribes to collaborate with American forces to protect their communities (Benraad, 2011; Malkasian, 2017). This collaboration led to the formation of the so-called *sahwa* or revival movement, which Ahrar al-Sham has since argued should force the Islamists to forge their ties with their popular constituency to prevent similar setbacks (al-'Omar, 2016). Additionally, the prisoners realized that Salafi Jihadi theoretical tenets cannot be blindly applied without careful consideration. The excessive use of excommunication (*takfir*) by Salafi Jihadi groups resulted in many violations and killings of Muslims accused of heresy in Iraq, which made many sympathisers reluctant to repeat these actions. Even individuals later associated with Jabhat al-Nusra and its leadership have spoken publicly about these dynamics and their impact on the most effective strategic route to achieve Jihadi groups' objectives . Aside from these weighty issues, daily life in prison management was also a concern among the prisoners. Abul-'Abbas al-Shami recalled this aspect of their imprisonment:

> In prison we could administer ourselves. Prison authorities were at the door while we conducted our own affairs inside. We elected our representatives to

make decisions but ideological arguments plagued even administrative issues. Some of us wanted to create a council to represent us. I was part of the council and wanted to give a vote to every prisoner, including non-Islamists, atheists, and spies for Israel. There was no alternative. Some individuals, who were closer to al-Qaeda, refused the principle of elections. They said that this was democracy, but I insisted that elections were just a tool. I told them that we were not legislating on Islamic law. We were not changing religion. We were just simplifying administrative decisions. Moreover, we divided on the conflict with the regime. How could we end it? I believed that there could be nonviolent ways too. We could solve our issues politically. Most of those who joined Ahrar al-Sham were part of this group. Others, those closer to al-Qaeda's ideas whether organisationally or ideologically, only believed in violence. I told them that the regime had tanks, planes, etc. What can you do? We have to choose the most suited means to achieve our shared objectives. Their rationality is deficient. Al-Qaeda always thinks the same way. They think in military terms only, instead of complementary ways. But our interpretation (*ijtihad*) changes over time depending on the circumstances and our capacities

The contradictions between Salafi Jihadi ideology and its actual practices were laid bare in 2008, during a riot that erupted in the Saydnaya Prison. In July of that year, the military police conducted a security sweep of the prison, which resulted in a standoff between the Islamist prisoners and the authorities. The riot was fuelled by the deplorable conditions of prison detention. The situation escalated quickly, resulting in intense clashes between the incarcerated individuals and the prison authorities. During the chaos, the prisoners managed to overpower the guards, and despite the regime's control over the outside, they also managed to retain control over the prison by neutralising the military police. A tense siege ensued, accompanied by ongoing negotiations to resolve the situation, as the prisoners had taken officials and military police hostages (Saad, 2008). In the course of the crisis, the prisoners retrieved small weapons from the security guards and debated their next move. Rami Dalati, a member of the prisoners' negotiation committee that eventually reached an agreement with the prison authorities to end the crisis, recounted the events.

The prisoners divided along three lines regarding the use of weapons. The first group wanted to find a solution whatever the price might be. It included individuals of all persuasion, from the Muslim Brotherhood, independents, and common criminals. The second group insisted that we should use the weapons. We kill them and we die fighting. The third group said that we should only use the weapons for self-defence. The third group managed to convince parts of the second group of its ways. After 2011, most of the third group joined Ahrar al-Sham. A minority, among the survivors of the second group, joined IS. Maybe ten, nothing more. Those who switched side joined Jabhat al-Nusra!

Prison debates prior to the outbreak of conflict in 2011 generated new arguments and practical positions that challenged the excesses of Jihadi Salafism. As early as three years before their eventual release, leaders and members who would later join Ahrar al-Sham had already embraced an ideological revisionism that positioned them favourably to promote new reforms in the future. When the regime eventually released these prisoners between 2011 and 2012, the Islamist militants who formed the core of Ahrar al-Sham were keen to learn from the experiences of Iraq and avoid repeating its mistakes. Associates of Hassan Abud, Ahrar al-Sham's founding leader, confirmed that he was determined not to be associated with al-Qaeda in the new conflict with the regime.[9] This decision was in line with the trajectory that Ahrar al-Sham's core militants had already embraced, as many of them were already active outside the prison and eager to create a new project that would differ from both the Muslim Brotherhood and al-Qaeda. As Khaled Abu Anas argued:

> When we met with the others, we all wanted to create something new. Al-Qaeda was scary for many, so we had to take distance from this brand. We wanted to take what was good in all the previous Islamist experiences. In the Brotherhood, we would take the comprehensive vision (*shumuli*) and the organisational development. In al-Qaeda, we would take the fight (*al-qital*). We consider jihad and politics as complementary. For al-Qaeda, politics is the embrace of democracy so they reject it. For us, jihad and politics go together. We were the first organisation of this type.

The decision to distance themselves from al-Qaeda at the outset of the Syrian uprising was reinforced by the arrival of Syrian militants who had previously been involved in jihad abroad. These veterans of earlier conflicts joined Ahrar al-Sham early on, forming a network of like-minded militants who embraced armed jihad in Syria while expressing a distaste for al-Qaeda's influence. Abul-'Abbas al-Shami, the former prison leader who negotiated the end of the Saydnayya uprising, became the highest religious authority of the Ahrar al-Sham–supported Islamic Front. Iyad al-Sha'ar, a prominent leader of Ahrar al-Sham who had been active during the first war in Afghanistan alongside Abdullah 'Azzam, also played a significant role in the group's formation (see Tarsha, 2018 for more details). Sha'ar met Abu Anas through shared contacts and quickly assumed leadership of the group's military apparatus. Abu Anas was impressed by Sha'ar's close association with Abdullah 'Azzam in Afghanistan. According to Sha'ar and others, Ahrar al-Sham's early leaders were determined to distance themselves from al-Qaeda, as he explained:

> I am the one who chose the name Ahrar al-Sham, a name that was not directly Islamic. In the beginning of the uprising, here in Istanbul, I even wrote a political program on behalf of the group. I set-up many meetings with other sheikhs to convince early Ahrar al-Sham leaders of our ways. The programme was not immediately adopted however, but the youths later embraced these ideas.

Ahrar al-Sham found itself in a paradoxical situation at the start of the conflict. Many prominent leaders and former prisoners who were hostile to al-Qaeda still recognised that bin Laden's organisation enjoyed some level of popularity among their supporters. Ahrar al-Sham shared a similar frame of reference with al-Qaeda, stemming from the Salafi approach (and partly Jihadi) to Islam, despite real disagreements with al-Qaeda's long-term trajectory. The new conflict nonetheless presented a unique opportunity for Ahrar al-Sham to develop a new Islamist project that was not affiliated with either the Muslim Brotherhood or al-Qaeda. The new project would be Salafi, but only conditionally *mujahid*. In other words, Ahrar al-Sham would be a Salafi armed group engaged in jihad because of the circumstances. It would not be Jihadi, but *mujahid* (literally: engaged in jihad), since jihad is not be an end in itself but only a means to achieve specific political objectives.

The Structure of the War

Ahrar al-Sham's pre-war ideological debates positioned the group favourably to politicise during the conflict. Individual leaders who were long cognisant of the impact of radicalism, the negative legacy of al-Qaeda, and the trajectory of the Salafi Jihadi movement were likely to commit to translating pre-existing ideological debates into practice after the beginning of the conflict. This was particularly true as they joined like-minded activists who had previously been involved in jihad abroad and were determined not to repeat the same mistakes of the Jihadi movement. This network of entrepreneurs collectively formed Ahrar al-Sham's early core, which was tasked with mobilising and socialising a new generation of fighters that started to join them despite having no prior involvement in militancy, although they were often associated with the Islamist social movement.

However, while pre-war developments may set the stage for an armed group's ideological trajectory, in-war dynamics can also shape this early trajectory in unpredictable ways. Armed groups unable to maintain control over their mobilisation and socialisation processes may lose control over their members and see their ideological construction evolve in unintended ways.[10] This is particularly true when armed groups engage in competitive escalation with other groups, compartmentalise organisationally as they insulate themselves from their environments, and start to define violence as an objective in itself (Della Porta, 2013).

The nature of the Syrian uprising, being a domestic confrontation for political authority rather than a war against foreign occupation, shaped the initial perceptions of Ahrar al-Sham leaders. Like other armed groups, Ahrar al-Sham saw itself as part of the Sunni majority in opposition to a minority-led political-security apparatus. Other domestic conflicts like Algeria in the early 1990s, where there were no sectarian differences between the regime and the opposition, previously led to a violent spiral of radicalisation (e.g., Hafez, 2003; Burgat, 2007). Ahrar al-Sham leaders therefore emphasised the need to build stronger ties and embeddedness with the local Sunni communities from which they originated. Many leaders had participated in the conflict in Iraq or had connections to activists who had. They feared a repeat of the so-called Sunni awakenings (*sahwa*), when local Sunnis allied with U.S. forces – their former opponents – against al-Qaeda–allied groups that had antagonised them. Ahrar al-Sham leaders and members hence often referred to the cultivation of the group's popular incubator early on, epitomising their efforts to avoid repeating past mistakes. Ahrar al-Sham's religious scholars stressed the importance of paying attention to local populations, avoiding imposing harsh regulations, and refraining from excommunication (Al-Shar'i, 2013). Even Jabhat al-Nusra leaders believed that the revolutionary nature of the armed opposition differentiated their group from the Iraqi experiment, despite their common affiliation with al-Qaeda.[11] However, the differences between Ahrar al-Sham and Jabhat al-Nusra suggest that the revolutionary nature of the armed opposition alone cannot explain the diverging trajectories of all Syrian armed groups.

Ahrar al-Sham's perceptions of its popular constituency were informed not only by past experiences but also by new opportunities to cooperate with other Syrian actors from 2011 onwards. The widespread adoption of violence after 2011 was not limited to Islamist or sub-Islamist groups, as in previous conflicts involving Jihadis. Rather, the wide legitimisation of violence opened up new avenues for collaboration between Islamist and non-Islamist groups and allowed them to cater to a larger constituency beyond their immediate circles. This is in contrast to conflicts such as Algeria in the 1990s, where repression was more systematically focused on Islamist groups, leading to their isolation from society as they embraced violence and had little possibility of reaching out to other groups. The indiscriminate nature of violence in Syria created an opportunity for Ahrar al-Sham and other groups to form alliances and build stronger ties with local communities, which was a key factor in shaping their approach to the conflict.

Ahrar al-Sham's external ties outside Syria also informed its politicisation. Unlike other local factions, Ahrar al-Sham's early external connections allowed it to become a critical broker between various local, regional, and international actors supporting the uprising during its initial two years. This structuring positioning enabled Ahrar al-Sham to establish multiple ties with other groups, including Islamist movements and activists based in Istanbul, where Ahar al-Sham's political bureau was located. While foreign networks and militants are often associated with ideological radicalisation (e.g., Kilcullen, 2011; Bakke, 2014), this was not necessarily the case for Ahrar al-Sham. The group's leaders' interactions with other actors shaped their approach to the conflict. For instance, Iyad al-Sha'ar recognised that Hamas leaders based in Istanbul provided them with advice on the group's organisational structure and political program.[12] Despite differing ideological traditions with the Palestinian group, Hamas' careful balance of political and military objectives served as a valuable reference point. Other meetings included former Egyptian Islamist militants, including members of the ex-Jihadi group al-Jama'a al-Islamiyya. One of their leaders, Rifa'i Taha, offered advice and suggestions, and attempted to mediate the conflict with Jabhat al-Nusra by encouraging the latter to break ties with al-Qaeda, though his mission was aborted when he was killed in a U.S. drone attack in April 2016.[13]

Inside Syria, the fragmented nature of the armed opposition reinforced Ahrar al-Sham's politicisation. After three decades of repressive regime policies, the armed opposition was highly diverse and difficult to unify. The presence of numerous factions during the early phase of the conflict exacerbated internal tensions between local armed groups, which were often more practical than ideological in nature. For instance, they struggled with issues such as how to share war spoils (*ghanima*), how to manage the proliferation of checkpoints manned by different groups, and how to resolve family conflicts that could escalate into factional disputes. Additionally, the armed opposition's control of broad geographic areas necessitated more advanced military collaboration. As a result, large front lines with regime forces emerged, requiring new military approaches to counter the growing influence of external militias backed by Iran and its regional allies in support of the regime.

The seizure of large territories forced all the armed groups, including Ahrar al-Sham, to institutionalise internally and externally, as discussed in chapter 3. Ahrar al-Sham and other larger groups could no longer be a mere patchwork of local military units coordinating only small-scale military battles. They also had to confront economic and social challenges affecting civilians under their control, which necessitated the development of a local system of governance. Yet the armed groups lacked experience in governing civilians and did not have a clear practical programme to implement. Unlike ISIS, which previously governed

Sunni areas in Iraq with excessive violence and exerted hegemonic control, other armed groups shared power—sometimes uneasily—with one another and with competing local councils. Their attempt to govern Raqqa, where Ahrar al-Sham was dominant and which was the first Syrian provincial city under the armed opposition's control, was unsuccessful, as they were ill-prepared to rule the population and failed to recognise the threat posed by ISIS. In other cities, Ahrar al-Sham and other factions formed Islamic committees (al-Hay'at al-Islamiyya) to address local issues, police the areas, and provide assistance. They recognised the importance of collaborating with local groups, initiatives, and international organisations and NGOs.[14] These experiences informed their political perspectives, which revealed the need for local governance beyond the mere implementation of Islamic law in a post-Assad Syria.

Ahrar al-Sham's decision to institutionalise cross-factional alliances to support its organisational expansion also significantly bolstered its politicisation. The integration of more urban factions contributed significantly to the development of a more nuanced political understanding of reality, although these positions were not necessarily embraced by all the new sub-groups. For instance, Mujahidu Ashida, a group committed to stricter local practices,[15] opposed Ahrar al-Sham's politicisation and later severed ties with its leadership, citing a lack of trust in its religious council and the belief that the group was impeding cross-factional unity (Ashida, 2016b). However, the integration of significant factions like Liwa al-Haq (the Brigade of Truth) from Homs had a profound impact on Ahrar al-Sham's political development, too. As a faction made up of middle-class, educated Syrians, Liwa al-Haq's inclusion in Ahrar al-Sham reinforced its political construction. Although one of its three prominent commanders passed away shortly after joining Ahrar al-Sham, the two others, the Nahhas brothers Labib and Kanan, became leading reformists in Ahrar al-Sham's consultative council. Their formal inclusion in the group's organisational structures confirmed Ahrar al-Sham's willingness to collaborate with other actors, including foreign countries. The Nahhas brothers joined Ahrar al-Sham's political bureau with the responsibility of cultivating friendly relationships with foreign countries and conveying the group's stance to Western audiences. Labib al-Nahhas, the new head of Ahrar al-Sham's international relations, famously wrote two editorials for an American and a British newspaper in 2015 (al-Nahhas, 2015b, 2015c). In these articles, he criticised the stereotypical association of the Syrian opposition with al-Qaeda and argued that Syrian groups like Ahrar al-Sham were institutionalised armed groups with broad public support on the front-line against IS. These efforts were aligned with broader international attempts to legitimise the group, including vis-à-vis the United States, as an acknowledgement of its strength and potential (Akum, 2015).

The position of Western countries on the Syrian conflict also impacted Ahrar al-Sham's choices. Unlike previous conflicts, in which Islamists challenged ruling regimes, as in Algeria in the 1990s, Western countries did not stand in opposition to violent change in Syria. The nature and level of repression, in addition to their own antagonism of the Assad regime, instead legitimised their endorsement of violence, as in Libya beforehand. Though Western countries, especially after 2014, continued to reject any group associated with al-Qaeda or IS, as well as those advocating violence beyond Syria, they have also shown some willingness to engage with Islamists who disavow global jihad. In certain instances, they have even opposed the U.N. Security Council's designation of certain groups for their association with al-Qaeda, including Ahrar al-Sham (Nichols, 2016).

Ahrar al-Sham's transformation allowed it to become more than a military organisation. The group's involvement in wider political initiatives and negotiations with Syrian and foreign actors forced it to clarify its political positions. Ahrar al-Sham participated in a range of multilateral negotiations, from local cease-fires to international discussions on the future of Syria. The exigencies of the war and the changing political landscape compelled the group to engage in political discourse, despite internal hesitations about fully embracing the revolutionary agenda, including the symbolic flag and Arab penal code, as will be discussed later in this chapter.

Competition between Jihadi Groups

The Syrian conflict has been one of the most competitive wars for Salafi Jihadi groups worldwide. These groups have not only impacted the war in terms of military effectiveness by introducing new repertoires of violence, such as foreign fighters and suicide bombings, but also influenced international perceptions of the conflict. The regime exploited their presence to de-legitimise the popular uprising as an al-Qaeda or IS-led armed insurgency that threatened international peace and security. Although Ahrar al-Sham is not a Salafi Jihadi group per se, some of its early leaders were partially associated with this ideological trend in the past. This forced the group to clarify its political positions to both Syrians and foreign countries supporting the uprising. As a result, the group increasingly had to differentiate itself from other Salafi Jihadi armed groups and their political agendas. The competition with other Salafi Jihadi groups ultimately shaped how Ahrar al-Sham politicised during the war.

The competition among Jihadi groups in the Syrian conflict is not a new phenomenon. This trend has been plagued by internal divisions and competition since its coalescence in Afghanistan in the late 1980s (Gerges, 2011; Moghadam & Fishman, 2011). The crystallisation of Salafi Jihadi ideology in the context of war by poorly institutionalised groups exacerbated internal ideological debates and radicalised their social movement in exile (Drevon, 2022). As these groups participated in numerous other conflicts, especially Algeria in the 1990s, internal divisions worsened. Today, divisions over the trend's strategic priorities, balance between ideological fidelity and practical accommodation, and relations with one another strongly resonate with the Syrian conflict.

When the conflict erupted, Ahrar al-Sham leaders were aware that al-Qaeda had gained some popularity among Sunni youths who joined the rebellion. They acknowledged that many of them were not fully aware of al-Qaeda's past actions in Iraq and sympathised with the group's political agenda, as al-Qaeda had dominated the Salafi Jihadi trend since 9/11 (Drevon, 2017). Al-Qaeda had effectively monopolised armed resistance against foreign occupation through its actions against American forces and their allies in the region, and had come to represent the cultural idiom of Salafi armed jihad, including slogans, symbols, literature, and vocabulary.[16] As of 2011, Islamist militants involved in foreign jihad had failed to present a credible alternative, which made it difficult for them to disassociate themselves from al-Qaeda in the eyes of their followers. Khaled Abu Anas noted:

> Al-Qaeda could not use their traditional arguments against us. They could not accuse us, like the Muslim Brotherhood, of embracing democracy for instance. But, on the other hand, we did not have anything to differentiate ourselves either. al-Qaeda monopolised the field with its slogans, *nasheed* [a capella religious songs], and concepts. Many of our youths felt that they were part of that too. Many youths went for Jabhat al-Nusra when the group appeared publicly. Jabhat al-Nusra leaders also sent people to our youths to receive their allegiance. They had a lot of success. We could have disappeared. So we had to develop a distinctive identity, as Ahrar, not al-Qaeda. Our vision developed as a response.

Despite Ahrar al-Sham's early leaders' opposition to al-Qaeda's agenda, the latter's domination of the Jihadi trend meant that its worldviews and frames of reference were still prevalent. Ahrar al-Sham relied on shared literature and references, particularly in their training camps, which some Islamists close to Ahrar al-Sham and its leaders claimed was a reason for distancing themselves from the group. They did not perceive a clear enough distinction between Ahrar al-Sham and al-Qaeda, as argued by Rami Dalati:

> I did join Ahrar al-Sham in the beginning. When I was with them, I went to the training camps and I saw that all their literature and references were drawn from al-Qaeda despite the real opposition to the direction taken by the

organisation! I left for that reason though we continued to be in discussion over the years. Now, I believe that the group should be more open. That means that they have to become a modern movement that does not use this old terminology. No more amir, no more *kunya* [Islamic *noms de guerre*]. It does not sound right to continue using these terms.

Abu Fath al-Farghali, a former member of the Egyptian group al-Jama'a al-Islamiyya who identifies as Salafi Jihadi, equally perceived similarities between Ahrar al-Sham's early positioning and Jihadi Salafism. He pointed out that a prominent Ahrar al-Sham religious scholar, Abu Sarayya al-Shami, published a book in 2013 entitled *Lights on the Method of the Mujahid Group* (al-Shami, 2013), which very much aligned with the Salafi Jihadi trend. Abu Sarayya was a founder of the smaller group Harakat al-Fajr al-Islamiyya, which later joined Ahrar al-Sham during its transformation into a larger movement. According to al-Farghali (2020b):

When I entered Syria, I read the book authored by Abu Sarayya. I was told that it was the ideology of Ahrar al-Sham, and effectively it was at the time. I found that the book was entirely Salafi Jihadi. It was the ideology of al-Qaeda. It relied on their sheikhs like Abu Muhammad al-Maqdisi, Abu Qatada al-Falastini, Abu Yahiyya al-Libi, and Sayyid Imam. The main difference between them and al-Qaeda was international jihad (*al-jihad al-'alami*) [which the book did not condone]. Most ideas of Ahrar al-Sham were congruent with Jihadi Salafism on democracy, offensive jihad [*jihad al-talab*], and the return of the caliphate among other issues.

Competition within the same Islamist social movement can contribute to the radicalisation of armed groups. Fringe groups tend to develop uncompromising ideological frames to maintain the loyalty of their members and isolate them from their surroundings (Della Porta, 1995: 113–135). They create internal messages that define their conflict as an existential war against their opponents. The use of excommunication (*takfir*) illustrates this development in Islamist groups that gradually reject non-members as non-Muslims, as in Algeria in the late 1990s (Hafez, 2003: 109–198). Excommunicating non-members and deserters helps maintain internal cohesion and prevent dissent that could threaten group survival. Embracing radical ideas can also address critical organizational challenges by providing members with ideational incentives, ensuring soldiers are committed, and demonstrating credible behaviour externally (Walter, 2017).

It means that, although Ahrar al-Sham's leaders were already vying to distance themselves from global jihad in the beginning of the conflict, they were still apprehensive at being excommunicated by more radical groups. Many individuals who interacted closely with Ahrar al-Sham's leadership in the early stages of the conflict express regret over the group's concerns about how IS and Jabhat al-Nusra perceived it. They lament that Ahrar al-Sham's worry that these groups would excommunicate it hampered its ability to adopt a more assertive political stance during the first phase of the conflict, fearing that this would weaken its internal cohesion.[17]

The competition between Jihadi groups played out in two distinct phases. The first phase began with the split between IS and Jabhat al-Nusra. IS was threatened by the success and empowerment of its Syrian affiliate and attempted to reassert itself by forcibly announcing a public merger of the two entities in April 2013. But Jabhat al-Nusra leader al-Jolani refused to accept IS's control, hastening the split between the two groups. This initial separation was primarily driven by power dynamics, as the Syrians wanted to lead their armed opposition against the regime instead of submitting to the authority of their Iraqi commanders. Ideological differences nonetheless existed, such as Jabhat al-Nusra's decision to cease so-called martyrdom operations against targets near civilian gatherings, which IS promoted. Jolani also opposed sectarian warfare against religious minorities, and did not heed IS's orders to plan armed attacks against the mainstream Syrian opposition in Istanbul.[18] As time passed, substantial ideological differences crystallised, and the two groups began to follow divergent paths. IS succeeded in obtaining the allegiance of foreign fighters who were attracted more by the idea of an Islamic state than by mere opposition to the regime. In the east of the country, where Jabhat al-Nusra historically held extensive economic resources, especially the oil fields, IS imposed itself. Ahrar al-Sham also helped Jabhat al-Nusra survive. The group did not want to face IS alone, believing that balancing more radical groups against one another would prevent any of them from becoming a hegemon.[19]

The conflict with IS led to Ahrar al-Sham's first dissociation from Jihadi Salafism. After Jabhat al-Nusra's split from IS, a wider conflict between the mainstream Syrian opposition and the Iraqi group ensued, resulting in IS's expulsion from northwest Syria. This confrontation posed a challenge for Ahrar al-Sham, as its leaders realised that their soldiers were not always willing to fight fellow Muslims, regardless of their ideological and organisational differences. The shared symbols and concepts between Ahrar al-Sham and other Jihadi groups made cross-factional infighting difficult. To address this, Ahrar al-Sham resorted to both financial punishments and renewed ideological indoctrination. The group withdrew financial support from sub-factions that refused to fight and declared their neutrality instead. For example, it expelled a sub-group based in Damascus from its ranks for refusing to fight IS and demanded that the group return the weapons that belonged to Ahrar al-Sham (Ahrar al-Sham, 2015e). Second, Ahrar al-Sham decided to focus on ideological indoctrination by attacking the Islamic illegitimacy of IS, describing them as heretics (*khawarij*) and extremists (*bugha*) (al-Shami, 2014b; Tarsha, 2018). Khaled Abu Anas argued:

> We did not develop a proper ideological and religious approach against IS until the loss of Raqqa. We only reacted after. The risk was that, as they declared their Caliphate, many people left for them from Jabhat al-Nusra, the Free Syrian Army, even Suqur al-Sham. So we had to develop an approach against extremism in religion (*ghulu*) as well. It was difficult to fight them militarily as we could not fight other Muslims and many of our youths were not responsive to our call for action against them.

IS's new international prominence, which threatened to tarnish the reputation of Syrian Islamists, informed Ahrar al-Sham's embrace of the Syrian revolutionary agenda. As IS occupied areas previously held by Syrian factions and imposed harsh rules, the international community started to perceive the group as a real threat. This also furthered the regime's claims that only its military forces could prevent IS's expansion. The situation was particularly alarming for the Salafi factions with ambiguous relationships to transnational Jihadi groups, as they feared being associated with IS and potentially listed as terrorist groups. To prevent this, the Islamic Front (inclusive of Ahrar al-Sham), Ajnad al-Sham, Faylaq al-Sham, Jaysh al-Mujahideen, and Alwiya al-Furqan signed a revolutionary covenant of honour (*mithaq sharaf thawri*) in April 2014 to assert their inclusion in the Syrian mainstream armed opposition to the regime. A former head of Ahrar al-Sham's political bureau, Abu Khaled, explained:

> The covenant of honour was the outcome of regional developments. External actors expected a quick initiative from the factions to take a clear stance on what was happening with regards to the actions of groups like IS vis-à-vis Western countries.

The covenant of honour emphasised the political—and not religious—objectives of the revolution against the regime and IS's radicalism. It aimed to distance the Islamist factions from Salafi Jihadi internationalism by claiming that they were manned by Syrian fighters without foreign allegiance, and that their goal was to establish a just state that would respect the rights of all its citizens, including religious minorities. This position aligns with legitimacy-seeking groups that abide by International Humanitarian Law to legitimise themselves (Jo, 2015). Additional communiqués confirmed that Ahrar al-Sham did not have external relations with al-Qaeda but was only fighting for the self-determination of Syrians through various means, including military (Ahrar al-Sham, 2015d). The most controversial element for Salafi Jihadi groups like IS and Jabhat al-Nusra was the covenant's declaration that the signatories were willing to meet and cooperate with regional and international state supporters of the uprising, violating a central Salafi Jihadi ideological tenet (*'adam isti'ana bil-kuffar*) that Muslims "cannot seek the assistance of non-Muslims."[20] Ahrar al-Sham's leader, Hassan Abud, accompanied this overture with multiple interviews to Arab media in 2013 (Abud, 2013a, 2013b, 2014), triggering strong opposition from Salafi Jihadi intellectuals and groups unaffiliated with IS. Jabhat al-Nusra (2014) notably denounced collaboration with states at war with Islam, prioritisation of citizenship over religious brotherhood, and lack of commitment to a state ruled by Islamic law. According to Husam Tarsha:

> The signing of the covenant occurred because of the international context. Western countries did not differentiate the armed Islamist groups active in Syria. We were described as terrorists, which impacted our relations with other actors. We wanted to respond to that with an Islamic solution so we discussed with all the groups to find a way out. We released the communiqué in response. Jabhat al-Nusra attacked us at the time, claiming that we were renouncing the implementation of Islamic Law. But that was a lie. The covenant did not say that.

In 2015, Ahrar al-Sham started to be "revisionist," largely due to the group's development of political positions that deviated from major Salafi Jihadi ideological tenets (Heller, 2015). The group's covenant was a clear statement of its stance against elitist jihad (*jihad al-nukhba*), which is often associated with Jihadi Salafism. Instead, Ahrar al-Sham advocated for jihad of the Muslim community (*jihad al-umma*), which emphasises the central role of local communities. In distancing itself from groups it previously considered "brothers of the Salafi method" (*ikhwat al-manhaj*), Ahrar al-Sham changed its initial motto from a "project for the Muslim community" *(mashru' umma)* to one in support of "the people's revolution" (*thawrat al-sha'ab*). Although Ahrar al-Sham had begun to shift its focus before 2014, its conflict with IS forced the group to publicly clarify its political positions.

Some of the group's intellectuals, who were previously associated with the Salafi Jihadi trend, such as Abu Yazan al-Shami, expressed regret to the Syrian people for bringing ideological debates into their revolution. This was a significant move, considering Abu Yazan's past affiliation with the trend. While many Ahrar al-Sham leaders had not embraced Jihadi Salafism or distanced themselves from it before 2011, Abu Yazan was more closely associated with it. According to his friend Muhammad al-Amin, Abu Yazan was even offered the position of mufti for al-Zarqawi in Iraq in the 2000s (Heller, 2014). In 2014, Abu Yazan declared:

> Yes, I was Salafi Jihadi, and I was imprisoned in the regime's jails for it. Today, I ask for God's forgiveness and repent to Him, and I apologise to our people for involving them in Don Quixotic battles of which there was no need. I apologise for being apart from you for even a day, as when I exited my intellectual prison and mingled with you and with your hearts.

However, IS was not the only Salafi Jihadi contender that posed a lasting and threatening challenge to Ahrar al-Sham. After successfully evicting IS from opposition-held territories, Jabhat al-Nusra emerged as a significant player in the conflict. The split with IS led to the departure of most foreign fighters and the loss of critical oil resources in Deir al-Zor province. Jabhat al-Nusra reasserted itself in the next few months by reconfiguring its organisational structures and promoting more radical figures to leadership positions. For instance, the group's Sharia council head, Abu Maria al-Qahtani, who was relatively inclusive, resigned and was replaced by a more maximalist Jordanian, Sami al-'Uraydi, who is close to the Salafi Jihadi theologian Abu Muhammad al-Maqdisi. By the end of 2014, Jabhat al-Nusra became a target for U.S. forces and began to dismantle arguably corrupt or American-supported factions. The group notably attacked the Front of Revolutionaries and the Hazm movement, as mentioned in previous chapters. An audio leak in the summer of 2014 suggested that the group might be trying to set up an independent emirate in the northwest, though group members argue that the leak was rhetorical and did not reflect a real project. This accompanied the group's stronger local implementation near the border with Turkey, withdrawal from governing structures previously shared with other groups, and the creation of the group's own courts and social services (Lund, 2014c, 2015b).

The reassertion of Jabhat al-Nusra after its split with IS posed a lasting and significant threat to Ahrar al-Sham. While non-Islamist armed factions and Jabhat al-Nusra may have had limited overlap in their support bases, Ahrar al-Sham and Jabhat al-Nusra were part of an overlapping social movement, sharing ideational symbols and embracing similar politico-religious concepts and views.[21] Unlike other factions, Jabhat al-Nusra could not paint Ahrar al-Sham as a Western-supported project, given that both groups adhered to the Salafi approach to Islam, which precluded the type of argument used in the past against the Muslim Brotherhood, for instance.[22] This made the competition between the two groups a potential zero-sum game, with fears on both sides that they could lose popular support to the other. Ahrar al-Sham was a notable threat for Jabhat al-Nusra, since it specifically strived to create an Islamist project that could be an alternative to both al-Qaeda and the Muslim Brotherhood. Even Osama bin Laden recognised that his brand had become more toxic after 2011 and encouraged the use of alternative names such as Ansar al-Shari'a (supporters of sharia) (Zelin, 2012a). In Syria, the space for a Salafi armed alternative to al-Qaeda was particularly wide, as al-Qaeda was no longer a hegemon in its social movement.

A primary distinction between IS and Jabhat al-Nusra lay in their differing attitudes towards other groups. IS claimed to be the only legitimate Islamic state globally and denounced all other factions, which justified a full-scale military confrontation with the opposition. In contrast, Jabhat al-Nusra did not publicly excommunicate other Syrian groups and selectively targeted specific factions while remaining integrated into the mainstream opposition. This approach prevented all-out conflict with other factions and allowed for a more strategic use of military force.

Ahrar al-Sham opposed Jabhat al-Nusra on two fronts. First, it opposed Jabhat al-Nusra's external ties to al-Qaeda, which the regime and its allies used to denounce the armed opposition as an international threat. Even Western countries supportive of regime change, particularly the United States, strongly considered it a threat, leading to numerous drone attacks against prominent Jabhat al-Nusra leaders. Ahrar al-Sham therefore insisted that Jabhat al-Nusra renounce its foreign allegiance to al-Qaeda and fully embrace the Syrian revolution before agreeing to merge with the group. Although Ahrar al-Sham initially invited Jabhat al-Nusra to join the Islamic Front, the ties to al-Qaeda subsequently became a strong prerequisite to any unification of the Syrian opposition. Ahrar al-Sham gradually raised its demands against Jabhat al-Nusra, as stated by a prominent Ahrar al-Sham leader:

> We raised our demands when Jabhat al-Nusra appeared, and further raised them when IS appeared. We decided to discuss their concepts (*mafahim*) from within, with our own understanding despite a similar frame of reference. We had to correct what was wrong. It was really challenging for them. We came from the same positions and frame of references. We would say that we also want an Islamic state but differ from them in how to create it, as we believe in something more gradual.

Second, Ahrar al-Sham sought to distance itself from certain aspects of the Salafi approach to Islam. The group realised that it could not simply denounce Jabhat al-Nusra as heretics or extremists (*khawarij, baghi*) as they had with IS, to highlight their violations of Islamic orthodoxy in theological terms. The problem with Jihadi Salafism was more profound. It lays in its ideological foundation and recognised sources of authority. Ahrar al-Sham leaders recognised that the horizontal Salafi hierarchy, which eschewed clergies, had alienated Muslims from their scholars. The absence of hierarchy granted considerable influence to unaccountable independent intellectuals, such as Abu Muhammad al-Maqdisi, Abu Qatada, and others. As independent figures of authority, Salafi Jihadi intellectuals and thinkers were not bound by the organisational interests of specific groups and their constituents in armed conflicts. Therefore, Ahrar al-Sham leaders reflected on the role of Sunni 'ulama' and the schools of jurisprudence in Islam (*madhhab*) as well. They argued that the group began training its religious scholars in the Shafi'i and Hanbali schools of jurisprudence to reconnect young people with their scholars and reduce the influence of foreign intellectuals. Khaled Abu Anas contended:

> One of the core issue with the Salafi approach of al-Albani, *la madhhabiyya* [not referring to the classical schools of jurisprudence], is to cut our ties to the religious scholars (the "ulama"). We therefore wanted to revive the schools of jurisprudence (*madhhab*) and teach the Shafi'i and Hanbali schools. This is an answer to the centrality taken by the intellectuals (*munathirin*) like [Abu Basir] al-Tartusi, Abu Qatada, and Abu Muhammad al-Maqsissi. They are not 'ulama', just thinkers. They took the place of the "ulama" when the "ulama" stayed silent. But the risk is that our youths rely on them instead of relying on the "ulama."

But Ahrar al-Sham was not alone in revising its theological approach. Jabhat al-Nusra also recognised the need to revive Islam's schools of jurisprudence for similar reasons. HTS's chief religious authority, Abu Abdullah al-Shami, argued:

> Initially there were two positions in Jabhat al-Nusra. Some individuals opposed the schools of jurisprudence and others supported it. Abu Muhammad al-Jolani embraced it. This position now prevails in the group. We now train people on the schools of jurisprudence, even though we still believe in the Salafi (*athari*) religious creed. The Hanafi school of jurisprudence was historically adopted by the Ottoman administration but we have a preference for the Shafi'i school, as it is the school of the majority in Idlib.

Ahrar al-Sham rooted its political positions in established religious traditions to legitimise itself vis-à-vis its constituency and groups like Jabhat al-Nusra (Ahrar al-Sham, n.d.d, n.d.f, n.d.h, n.d.g). The group rejected labels such as "liberal," "democratic," or "modernist" and instead aligned itself with Islamic Law-Guided Public Policy (*siyasa al-shari'yya*), a tradition associated with the prominent modern Salafi scholar, Ibn Taymiyya (al-Shami, 2014a). Ahrar al-Sham argued that Islamic Law is built on constant (*thawabit*) principles that are valid across time and place, and that even jihad as armed struggle is only a means to an end. The group maintained that Islamic constants cannot be applied without consideration for the higher purposes of Islamic law (*maqasid al-shari'ya*) in the jurisprudence of objectives (*fiqh al-maqasid*), which helps to legitimise a degree of pragmatism in how Islamic Law is applied (Ahrar al-Sham, n.d.f, n.d.h). In other words, armed groups must evaluate their priorities in light of changing realities and the interests of the community.

Ahrar al-Sham argued that the current reality of the conflict in Syria required new choices from the armed opposition. The Muslim community is in a dire condition of subdual (*istid'af*), which necessitates working within the constraints of what is actually possible (*istita'*) (Ahrar al-Sham, n.d.d). As explained by Abu Yazan al-Shami, Muslims need a jurisprudence of renaissance (*fiqh al-nahda*) instead of a jurisprudence of empowerment (*fiqh al-tamkin*), which is often used by Islamists vying to impose their governance (Ahrar al-Sham, n.d.d). Creating a just Islamic state does not solely rely on a few victories, but also on preserving the gains of a Muslim community that faces a battle for survival. Armed groups do not choose their reality, including their position in the international political and economic systems. The characteristics of current conflicts, including military, economic, political, and media developments, is shaped by this external reality. Ibn Taymiyya and Ahmad Ibn Ahmad, both prominent medieval Muslim scholars revered by contemporary Salafis, acknowledged the need for prioritising enemies in their time. Ahrar al-Sham hence insisted that the Syrian revolution has to adapt its approach and discourse to succeed in the modern era, which is dissimilar to the medieval period (al-Minbar al-Fikri, n.d.). Ahrar al-Sham therefore contended that it is necessary to balance the positive and negative yield (*maslaha* versus *mafsada*) of their decisions. The group defended a step-by-step gradual approach that includes collaboration with other groups.

Similar views were articulated in public during an extensive conference held in 2016 in northwest Syria, where numerous leaders of Ahrar al-Sham, including 'Ali al-'Omar, delineated the lineage of Ahrar al-Sham to other Islamist movements. Al-'Omar connected Islamist movements to the 1924 end of the Muslim Caliphate and identified four main trends and their respective approaches to political action: the Muslim Brotherhood and its emphasis on politics, the Tabligh movement and its focus on individual proselytisation, the intellectual debates of Hizb ut-Tahrir, and the resort to weapons of the Jihadis. He added that Ahrar al-Sham views these approaches as complementary, not exclusive. Al-'Omar also stressed important lessons from the war in Iraq, where Jihadis were strong but behaved violently with civilians. Instead, he stressed the importance of responding to the people's demand and to fight alongside non-Salafi Muslims too. The immediate objective should be fighting the regime and creating a Muslim state gradually, not imposing harsh measures on the population (al-'Omar, 2016).

Ahrar al-Sham accordingly reviewed various conceptions embraced by other Salafi Jihadi groups. Drawing upon Islamic tradition, the group argued that IS's claims to a Caliphate were unfounded (al-Malik, 2014), especially since it had been seized through violent means from rival factions (Ahrar al-Sham, n.d.g; al-Minbar al-Fikri, 2014). However, the group did not stop there. It went on to repudiate the narrow conception of the "victorious sect" (*al-ta'ifa al-mansura*) favoured by Salafis to justify that only their approach to Islam is legitimate. Instead, it contended that the nature of the uprising against the attacking enemy (*al-'adu al-sa'il*) necessitates the unity of all, even those who do not subscribe to the same religious beliefs (Al-Shami, 2014b). In addition to these publications, the group produced a variety of studies examining Turkey and its governance system (Ahrar al-Sham, n.d.b), the political realities of the revolution (Ahrar al-Sham, n.d.f, n.d.g, n.d.h; al-Minbar al-Fikri, n.d), and the imperative to draw upon the group's popular base (*hadina sha'biyya*) in order to build a lasting political order (al-'Omar, 2016).

However, the adoption of new ideological positions alone was insufficient for Ahrar al-Sham to confront the challenge posed by Jabhat al-Nusra. IS isolated itself from the armed opposition by indiscriminately attacking all its components, Jihadis and non-Jihadis alike. Ahrar al-Sham could not simply denounce Jabhat al-Nusra in a similar manner, since the latter had established a strong presence within the armed opposition, often fighting alongside Ahrar al-Sham's own troops. Ironically, Jabhat al-Nusra would later adopt a similar religious and political rhetoric to justify its own political positions after 2017, when it transformed into HTS.

Ahrar al-Sham's Institutional Impediments to Politicisation

The structure of the conflict and the nature of Salafi Jihadi competition informed Ahrar al-Sham's political construction, yet these cannot be isolated from the broader institutional dynamics that govern the group's decision-making processes. Ahrar al-Sham's institutionalisation is unique in this regard, as the group was founded on multiple networks that institutionalised the ties connecting different units, rather than being centred on a single geographic area or local leader. This institutional setting proved appealing to many independent military units, which quickly joined the group and contributed to Ahrar al-Sham's transformation into the leading armed group of the Syrian conflict.

Ahrar al-Sham consolidated in two stages prior to the assassination of most of the group's leaders in September 2014. The initial formation of the group's leadership council was based on its constitutive military units, which got an equal role in the leadership. As new factions integrated into the group, negotiations occasionally took place to include their leaders into the council based on their strength, strategic importance, or particular attributes. The loose ties that connected Ahrar al-Sham leaders, stemming from their embeddedness in various social networks such as the Islamist social movement or prison networks, facilitated the consolidation process in a relatively smooth and organic bottom-up process. To clarify the prerogatives of the leader and the leadership council, as well as the conditions in which new members could be named, internal reforms were implemented in 2014 to review internal organisational procedures, considering the group's rapid expansion. Khaled Abu Anas, who advocated for a consensual leadership style, clarified the principles of the system, stating:

> We created the consultative council as a binding (*mulzima*) institution. The leader has some level of freedom but everything pertaining to strategic decisions requires a majority of the votes. The council chooses the leader (*amir*). It can also isolate him. This did happen in the past. In addition, the leader cannot get new people into the council. He can propose some names, based on their skills and abilities, but he still requires a vote.

In September 2014, a devastating explosion during a meeting in the province of Idlib claimed the lives of most of Ahrar al-Sham's leaders, including nearly all members of the leadership council.[23] Only a few individual leaders who did not participate in the meeting were sparred. While other Syrian groups previously split along pre-existing organisational divides when individual leaders disappeared, Ahrar al-Sham managed to survive and even resume its organisational expansion in the following months, despite the loss of key figures. A new leadership was quickly named, which included a general commander, head of military, and highest religious authority. The process of reconstruction was not without controversy, and it would go on to plague Ahrar al-Sham for the next two years and ultimately contribute to its downfall. Khaled Abu Anas, one of the main surviving founders, explained the challenges of this period:

> When other leaders were killed, remaining members wanted me to lead them but I refused. I chose Abu Jaber al-Sheikh. I knew him from the previous consultative council but as an individual, not a leader. When he took over, he excluded many people. The main issue was the inclusion of Abu Muhammad al-Sadeq, who was acting in isolation from others.

The reconstitution of Ahrar al-Sham's leadership after the assassination of most of its leaders in September 2014 was challenging, both ideologically and organisationally.[24] The new leadership included Abu Jaber al-Sheikh as the general leader, Abu Saleh Tahhan as the head of the military, and Abu Muhammad al-Sadeq as the highest religious authority. Without embracing al-Qaeda, these new figures were not aligned with the ideological revisionism of the previous leadership that they were replacing. Moreover, Abu Jaber did not support the broader union of all the opposition that had been discussed in the summer of 2014.[25] The new leaders were also in a minority position organisationally, as some were marginal figures within the group, and others had frozen their membership before September 2014. This organisational vulnerability led Abu Jaber to isolate prominent Ahrar al-Sham individuals, including several founding members, and to rely instead on a minority close to him (Abazeid, 2015a: 6–7). The reconstitution of the group's leadership caused controversy among group members and partially led to its downfall. Some individuals, including founding members, were marginalised and eventually left the group to create Jaysh al-Sham, under the leadership of Abu Abd al-Rahman al-Suri (Abazeid, 2015b). They considered themselves the true heirs of the group's assassinated leaders at the time.

Ahrar al-Sham struggled with institutional paralysis for the next two years, hindering its ability to fully embrace the revolutionary agenda. Despite real efforts to collaborate with other factions and foreign countries, internal strife hindered the group's progress. Two factions within the group vied for control over leadership and resource allocation, resulting in prolonged power struggles until January 2017. One faction aimed to steer the group's strategic direction towards pre-2014 revisionism, seeking to maintain the group's politicisation, while the new leadership was more circumspect. These disagreements prevented the group from achieving unity and coherence, stalling its politicisation.

The first transition of Ahrar al-Sham's leadership occurred a year after the election of Abu Jaber. The leadership council elected Abu Yahiyya al-Hamawi as the new consensual leader, who represented a compromise between the two factions vying for leadership control (Ahrar al-Sham, 2015a). Al-Hamawi used his administrative prerogatives as leader to restructure Ahrar al-Sham's organisational structures and sideline parts of the first faction. Hamawi gave Abu Jaber responsibility for the group's religious activities (Ahrar al-Sham, 2015f) and promoted him to the position of head of the committee for proselytisation and guidance, which now superseded the Sharia office (Ahrar al-Sham, 2016i). Al-Hamawi also reorganized the political council to design a political strategy (Ahrar al-Sham, 2015g). He ultimately dismissed Tahhan from the military leadership (Ahrar al-Sham, 2016j), but armed threats and the kidnapping of several prominent figures by Tahhan and his associates (e.g., Wikileaks Ahrar, 2016) led to Tahhan's appointment as symbolic deputy commander for military affairs (Ahrar al-Sham, 2016k). While the internal reconfiguration was welcomed by factions that had been marginalised after 2014, such as Jaysh al-Sham, which subsequently rejoined the movement (Ahrar al-Sham, 2016b), other issues remained, including the marginal position of Suqur al-Sham within the group. Despite the fact that its head became Ahrar al-Sham's deputy leader for political affairs, he was subsequently demoted (Ahrar al-Sham, 2016h). Suqur al-Sham did not become Ahrar al-Sham's central force, as initially planned, and a continuous game of musical chairs among an array of leaders continued, reflecting the group's internal balancing act.

The most significant internal disagreements within Ahrar al-Sham were between its religious and political offices. The revisionists acknowledged that appointing a single religious scholar as the leader after the assassination of the previous leaders was a mistake. Sadeq's beliefs were not in line with those of the assassinated leadership. He did not espouse al-Qaeda's ideology, and still aimed to strike a balance between populist and elitist approaches to jihad (al-Sadiq, 2015). However, his ideas did not align with the previous leadership's revisionism, and he attempted to exercise a veto over the group's strategic decisions. A group of Egyptian religious jurists who shared similar beliefs and worked to impede Ahrar al-Sham's politicisation supported Sadeq. The disagreement over the leadership of Ahrar al-Sham's religious bureau revealed two significant issues highlighted by the former religious authority of the Islamic Front, Abul-'Abbas al-Shami:

> Sadeq's position as mufti was authoritarian. I opposed the presence of only one main religious leader. An individual can make mistakes and not have a proper understanding of everything that is unfolding. The idea was therefore to create a Sharia Office, which is executive, and the Fatwa Council (*majlis al-fatwa*), which delivers religious positions. I only wanted Syrians in this council. Non-Syrians could give their advice and help, but decisions had to be taken by locals who have a better understanding of reality. Its members should be taken from those who have the necessary skills, making decisions with the majority of the votes.

In particular, the religious bureau was highly critical of Ahrar al-Sham's foreign policy initiatives, particularly its collaboration with Turkey. The office opposed the group's political bureau, which was the driving force behind Ahrar al-Sham's outreach to foreign countries, as well as the two editorials written by Ahrar al-Sham's head of international relations. This opposition ultimately led three prominent Egyptian religious scholars, Abu Fath al-Farghali, Abu Yaqthan al-Masri, and Abu Shu'ib al-Masri, to resign from the group.

The reorganisation of Ahrar al-Sham's religious bureau (*al-maktab al-shar'i*) into the guidance and proselytisation bureau (*maktab al-da'wa wal-irshad*) operating under a collective leadership of four individuals sought to address some of these issues. The key step was the dissolution of Sadeq's bureau (Ahrar al-Sham, 2015f) and its restructuring. This move did not signify a rejection of the group's Salafi or religious leanings, but rather aimed to align its religious edicts (*fatwa*) with the political decisions of the political office and leadership council. The institutionalisation of the group's figures of authority mirrored the institutionalisation of the religious sphere in Saudi Arabia after the death of the powerful mufti, Muhammad ibn Ibrahim Al al-Sheikh, in 1969 (Mouline, 2014). The guidance and proselytisation office's prerogatives were reduced in the leadership council, according to one of its members:

> There were differences in the consultative council. Some people are permanent, based on their status in the group and how they were previously included. But it was decided that others would just be temporary. For instance the head of the Shariʿa bureau would only be in the council based on his position, not as individual.

Still, Ahrar al-Sham's politicisation continued to be hindered by prolonged internal disputes. The group's relatively consensual organisational structure became an obstacle to the articulation of clear political positions on the Syrian conflict due to leadership contests. This inability to express clear stances was clear when the group considered participating in the Riyadh conference in December 2015 and later discussed a potential cease-fire. Although Ahrar al-Sham effectively participated in the Riyadh conference, it later claimed that it had to withdraw due to its dissatisfaction at factional representations and the lack of consideration for several objections previously expressed (Ahrar al-Sham, 2015c). The group's quasi-permanent ambiguity eroded its credibility among other Syrian groups, as well as foreign states such as Turkey and Qatar that supported the group but were constrained by its peculiar internal dynamics. Ahrar al-Sham's position was often not to take a position. Ahrar al-Sham's decentralised organisational structures, which initially helped the group expand quickly during the uprising, became an impediment during times of leadership contests.

In 2016, the institutional impediments that had hindered progress were overcome after Abu Yahiyya's term. In the next round of elections, the two contending factions presented their candidates. The revisionists were able to elect Ali al-'Omar as the head of the movement, in opposition to the minority's attempts to impose a new term for Abu Jaber (Ahrar al-Sham, 2016f). This reflected the internal balance in favour of ideological revisionism, but the minority did not accept the continued leadership of the revisionists as they had done the previous year. Eight members froze their membership in the leadership council (Ahrar al-Sham, 2016g) and announced the creation of a new military unit called Jaysh al-Ahrar (the Army of the Free Ones) (Ahrar al-Sham, 2016l). The new sub-group claimed to encompass 16 brigades merged for military efficiency. According to Ahrar al-Sham leaders and people close to them (Abu Sayyaf, 2016), these divisions reflected internal divergences over authority as much as real divergences in political preferences. Later, Abu Jaber (al-Shaykh, 2016c) denounced the revisionists' financial favours based on political alignments as well as numerous media leaks, thereby pressuring Ahrar al-Sham's leadership. Jaysh al-Ahrar sought to assert its internal military strength and suggest that the leadership council did not enjoy the local support of all group soldiers, especially its important military brigades. But the creation of the new sub-group failed, as numerous brigades published their own communiqués, asserting their support for the current leadership (Ahrar al-Sham, 2016g). Additionally, most religious scholars affiliated with Ahrar al-Sham denounced the creation of the new sub-group, emphasizing the importance of internal consensus and respect for the group's internal regulations (n.m., 2016a).

The contenders' refusal to abide by the group's internal consensus reached in the elections, as they did the previous year, was due to the changing dynamics of the war. In 2015, they accepted defeat in the hope of achieving future gains in the next round of elections. They believed that accepting defeat would allow them to re-empower themselves internally before potentially retrieving the leadership one year later. Leaving the group would have meant losing control over Ahrar al-Sham's resources and having to establish a new faction equipped primarily with limited military supplies and without Ahrar al-Sham's extensive ties and recognition in Syria and abroad. Thus, in 2015, it was better to remain a minority that could still control the whole group in the future while continuing to push for their political preferences from within. But the conflict reached a turning point in 2016. The armed opposition lost control over the city of Aleppo, and foreign support began to wane. Factional discussions with Jabhat al-Nusra favoured a union of the armed opposition under the same umbrella to survive the next stage of conflict. This presented a decisive choice to armed groups: prioritise a military solution with Jabhat al-Nusra or combine political and military means with the development of stronger ties to foreign actors like Turkey. This choice mirrored Ahrar al-Sham's internal divisions in terms of strategy priority rather than ideological divergences per se. The dissidents wanted to reassert military pre-eminence over the revisionist's political agenda. Although Abu Jaber ultimately argued that he just wanted reforms and unity in jihad, calling Jaysh al-Ahrar to rejoin Ahrar al-Sham, it did not happen (Al-Shaykh, 2016b).

Abu Fath al-Farghali, one of the Egyptian scholars who identifies as Salafi Jihadi, parted ways with Ahrar al-Sham due to disagreements with the political bureau, particularly the Nahhas brothers, and attributed the failure of the unification with Jabhat al-Nusra to them, as did many others in HTS. In a retrospective of the events, he accused the two brothers and the leaders of Ahrar al-Sham allied to them of compromising and surrendering, in line with the path of the Brotherhood. He noted that (al-Farghali, 2020b, 2020c: 186–187):

> When Abu Ammar Ali al-Omar took over Ahrar al-Sham I realised that the movement had reached a dead end. [. . .] Eight members of the leadership council also rejected the decision. We sat and realised that many brigades, which were important in the movement, wanted to leave also. If they left Ahrar al-Sham, some brigades will remain in their homes, join other factions, or remain independent. They will disintegrate and disappear so why not form an internal bloc? [. . .] After this session, we issued a statement in the name of Jaysh al-Ahrar. [. . .] The goal was to bring together those who wanted to leave the movement and were about to disperse or abandon jihad. [. . .] If Abu Ammar was able to carry out the duties of leadership efficiently, we would reintegrate Ahrar al-Sham.

After joining forces with former Jabhat al-Nusra (back then known as Jabhat Fath al-Sham) in a new organization called Ha'yat Tahrir al-Sham (HTS), Jaysh al-Ahrar's former leader, Abu Jaber, was appointed as the nominal head of the group. Ahrar al-Sham's former military commander, Tahhan, drew Ahrar al-Sham sub-groups closer to him. Additionally, three former Ahrar al-Sham religious scholars who had resigned from the group due to its politicization and ties to Turkey—Abu Fath al-Farghali, Abu Yaqthan al-Masri, and Abu Shuʻib al-Masri—joined HTS. They would ultimately become vocal critics of their former group. Yaqthan, in particular, became infamous for urging HTS soldiers to target Ahrar al-Sham members in the head when storming their checkpoints, though HTS denounced this call to violence (Hay'at Tahrir al-Sham, 2017f). Meanwhile, the leader of a small brigade previously affiliated with Ahrar al-Sham, Abu Abd Ashida, compared his former group to the Afghan mujahideen and their leader, Burhanuddin Rabbani, who failed to establish an Islamic state in Afghanistan after the war, while Ashida likened HTS to the Taliban (Ashida, 2017). However, in the following months, most former members of Ahrar al-Sham left HTS or were expelled for opposing the group's opening to Turkey. Jaysh al-Ahrar ultimately became an independent group in September 2017.

By January 2017, Ahrar al-Sham had successfully overcome the main institutional obstacle to politicisation with the departure of Jaysh al-Ahrar. This significant internal reorganisation paved the way for the adoption of the Syrian green revolutionary flag and the Arab penal code, which demonstrated the group's strong commitment to other opposition factions and foreign countries.[26] The group also collaborated with Geneva Call, a Swiss non-governmental organization (NGO), to create a military code of conduct aligned with international humanitarian law (Ahrar al-Sham, n.d.i). However, the two-year gap between the assassination of Ahrar al-Sham's collective leadership and its full embrace of political ideology resulted in a significant delay that could not be easily rectified. Additionally, notable disagreements still existed within the group, particularly on religious matters. According to Rami Dalati, who maintained close ties with the group prior to his passing:

> Diversity is good for movements but there are limits as to how much diversity can be tolerated. Here the movement ranges from Amr Khaled [a liberal preacher] to Jihadi Salafis. It means that it remains difficult to agree on important issues regarding the range of political positions that the movement can embrace and its shared religious foundations.

The Dual Deadlocks of Power Politics and HTS's Ultimate Ascent

The resurgence of Turkish and Russian predominance, both in terms of the political process and military developments on the ground, shaped the final phase of the conflict. As mentioned in the previous chapter, the Astana and Sochi processes designated four de-escalation zones to reduce hostilities in areas held by the armed opposition. These developments helped the regime recapture these areas through a combination of military force and "reconciliation" processes. While these processes officially sought to reintegrate former fighters into regime-held areas, many armed groups were subsequently arrested, killed, or sent to other front lines to fight against their former comrades. This situation highlighted the constraints on the strategies and independent agency of local Syrian armed groups, including Ahrar al-Sham, due to the dominance of Turkish and Russian interests in conflict management at the regional and international levels.

In 2016, Ahrar al-Sham began to pursue a closer relationship with Turkey, publicly supporting its military intervention in northern Syria and justifying collaboration with Turkish troops in a fatwa. The fatwa emphasised the need to understand the reality of the situation, which required fighting against IS, preventing the expansion of Kurdish groups, and establishing the presence of Islamist factions. However, Ahrar al-Sham did not explicitly endorse working alongside American troops (Ahrar al-Sham, 2016n). But the situation in 2017 was significantly different from that in previous years. Ahrar al-Sham's reputation had deteriorated among its external supporters, including Turkey, which no longer saw the group as reliable as before because of its continued internal frictions, notably reflected in its refusal to attend the Astana conference. Despite remaining popular in the province of Idlib, Ahrar al-Sham was increasingly overshadowed by Faylaq al-Sham, which had emerged as Turkey's preferred partner. Both Syrian armed groups and civilians began to look to Faylaq al-Sham to infer Turkish positions, as Turkish troops even entered the province of Idlib with Faylaq al-Sham's military convoys.[27] Rumours circulated that Faylaq al-Sham was planning to integrate all armed opposition groups, including Ahrar al-Sham, before reconciling with the Syrian army (al-Sudani & al-Urdini, 2019; al-Shami & al-Uraddi, 2019). Faylaq al-Sham denied these accusations (Faylaq al-Sham, 2019).

Two significant decisions following the departure of Jaysh al-Ahrar confirmed Ahrar al-Sham's politicisation. The first was the adoption of the Unified Arab Code, which the group had previously refused to endorse. This move was controversial within the group and resulted in some judges leaving, including Ibrahim Shasho, a future minister of the HTS-supported government. The adoption of the Unified Arab Code was a convenient way to unify the judiciary system in opposition-held areas, which some Ahrar al-Sham sub-groups justified as a means of ending judicial anarchy in the province (e.g., Maktab al-Shar'i li Jaysh al-Iman, 2017). The application of uncodified Islamic Law gave too much leeway to local judges and eroded the cohesion of the courts (see also Hussein, 2017d). Despite this, the move was still controversial for a Salafi group that rejected the theological legitimacy of the codification of Islamic Law, which Salafis denounced as un-Islamic positive law.

The second decision was the official adoption of the three-colour Syrian revolutionary flag, a move that had been previously adopted by some group leaders and was legitimised in an internal opinion presented by Husam Tarsha as early as 2012.[28] Ahrar al-Sham previously relied only on its own flag combined to the white Islamic flag with the Muslim testament of faith (*shahada*). The adoption of the flag was not as controversial as the Unified Arab Code, but it still sent a strong signal to the population and other factions that the group perceived itself as fully embedded in the mainstream opposition (Ahrar al-Sham, n.d.c). Other groups praised these choices, including the Islamic Council (al-Majlis al-Islami, 2017). Ahrar al-Sham complemented these major steps with minor ones, including the adoption of its own code of conduct of hostilities (Ahrar al-Sham, 2017e), which was later rendered fully compatible with International Humanitarian Law in agreement with other armed opposition groups.

These changes mattered, although some critics continued to point out the persistent role of internal lobby politics. Ahrar al-Sham has played musical chairs among a certain number of leaders who alternate positions on both political and military levels to balance different interests and visions, without bringing in new blood or reconstructing the movement's foundations. Many criticised this internal politics for preventing the group from truly reforming (Hussein, 2017a). A new leader, Hassan Sufan, claimed that he faced a deep state that opposed restructuring the group. Sufan attributed the group's internal inertia and paralysis to this deep state, which prevented any real internal reforms from taking place (Sufan, 2019). When he resigned in 2019, he insisted that he had advocated for the dissolution of the consultative council due to its unsuitability for responding to rapid development. He said that the movement remained entrenched in its internal structure, which reinforces the perception both internally and externally that the group struggles to reach decisions promptly, as it continually engages in bitter debates over every matter. The binding nature of the consultative council has created a weak leader, according to him, causing decision-making bottlenecks, obstructing progress, and undermining flexibility when agility is most needed. Sufan suggested instead that the consultative council's binding authority should be reserved for pivotal strategic issues, rather than applied on nearly all matters.

In spite of persistent internal disagreements, Ahrar al-Sham gradually consolidated its interactions with other groups, particularly as the conflict with HTS escalated. Initially, it formed an alliance with the Zinki Movement to counterbalance HTS's military might. Later on, it joined the National Front for Liberation , led by Faylaq al-Sham. By joining this alliance, Ahrar al-Sham somehow became part of what remained of the Free Syrian Army (FSA), more than seven years after its inception. It is nonetheless unclear whether Ahrar al-Sham still maintains a distinctive political agenda beyond the need to survive and safeguard the territory under the control of the opposition forces. One possibility that was floated was to hold a national conference that would culminate in the formation of a united government, bringing together all active opposition forces and local civil society. By presenting a unified front, the Syrian opposition could have bolstered its external legitimacy. Some Ahrar al-Sham leaders even suggested that all factions could dissolve their troops and integrate this new entity, including Ahrar al-Sham itself. For instance, Husam Tarsha argued at the time:

> Our ideas and specificities remains. The new developments in Syria and in the north do not mark the end of Ahrar al-Sham. We believe in the creation of a united army around shared political principles. This could pave the way to the dissolution of all the factions. As Ahrar al-Sham, we could dissolve our military forces into one national army and become a social movement and political party that works to achieve our political vision, as an Islamist movement, for the future of Syria, side by side with all the components of Syrian society.

However the rise of HTS ultimately allowed the group to impose the formation of its own supported government. HTS organised its own national conference, which paved the way for the formation of a government dominated by HTS. Following HTS's victories over Ahrar al-Sham and its allies, all of Idlib province came under the administrative control of the HTS-supported Salvation Government, putting an end to inter-factional fighting. Ironically, HTS followed Ahrar al-Sham's trajectory and managed to achieve its contender's objectives. HTS established a political bureau to develop more refined political positions, similar to Ahrar al-Sham's choices. Despite its early reservations as to Ahrar al-Sham's openness to Turkey, HTS later developed tactical ties with Turkey and sought to transform the relationship into a strategic partnership, as mentioned by the group's religious authority, Abu Abdullah al-Shami:

> We want strategic relations with Turkey. We believe that Turkey will always need to remain allied with the Europeans and the Americans. We do not deal with Turkey as a faction but in terms of the interests of the revolution and the liberated areas. Syria is important for Turkey, especially for its national security. What I want is to preserve the liberated areas. Moreover, we are not against contacts with other countries. But that is contingent on the interests of the revolution. All channels have to be clearly assessed first in light of our relation with Turkey. Now, we need a military victory to be translated politically as well.

Although the idea of a national army (*jaysh watani*) unifying all opposition groups—except for HTS and smaller units—seemed promising in theory, reality is quite different. The creation of the national army officially marked the unification of most groups under a single ministry of defence (Ahrar al-Sham. 2017a), but it did not fundamentally alter the practical organisation of its constituting groups. Numerous violations committed by members of the national army in armed operations in northern Syria alongside Turkey eroded its reputation. Additionally, the groups that composed the national army were primarily made up of younger Syrians who joined for financial reasons, with little connection to local communities. The army also suffers from endemic corruption (Tsurkov, 2019b). As a result, many consider the national army, at best, a Turkish proxy and, at worst, lawless bandits who have executed civilians (Hubbar, Shoumali, Gall, & Kingsley, 2019). The participation of some of these groups in Turkish-supported operations in Libya also contributed to negative perceptions,[29] although the Syrian National Army denounced it (al-Jaysh al-Watani al-Suri, 2019c). Despite attempts to normalize the army through various initiatives, including the creation of a code of conduct and support for the Geneva conventions (al-Jaysh al-Watani al-Suri, 2019a), and calling for good treatment of prisoners (al-Jaysh al-Watani al-Suri, 2019b), the national army has not crystallised as a national alternative to the regime's army due to the constraining regional circumstances under which these changes occurred. Efforts to overhaul the Syrian National Army, including initiatives such as centralising their funding, relocating barracks away from urban centers, and reinforcing the authority of the interim government's Ministry of Defense, are underway though progress has been sluggish and results are not consistently favourable.

Despite joining the national army, Ahrar al-Sham claims that its political views had not changed significantly. The group's head of international relations rejected criticisms that the national army would be corrupt, secular, or democratic (Tarsha, 2019). He warned against the excommunication of the new institution by Salafi Jihadi groups and stressed that joining the army did not mean embracing secularism. According to him, in the condition of jihad against the "aggressor enemy" (*al-'adu al-sa'il*), there was no requirement to adopt a specific religious (Salafi) creed. Joining the army was simply a means to achieve the revolution's interests without altering the group's stance on democracy and secularism. Moreover, democracy should be viewed as a tool of governance that is acceptable, rather than a philosophy that is rejected.

However, the transformation of HTS caught Ahrar al-Sham off guard. Despite HTS's hostile actions against other factions, it has ultimately followed a similar political trajectory as Ahrar al-Sham, which it describes as a failing project (Hay'at Tahrir al-Sham, 2017n). After becoming the hegemon of northwest Syria, HTS argued that it needs to limit the number of external enemies and reach out to others (Atun, 2020b) and began to use arguments similar to those that Ahrar al-Sham previously used to legitimise itself against other Salafi Jihadi groups. For example, the group's religious council resorted to the same tradition previously used by Ahrar al-Sham, Islamic Law-Guided Public Policy (*al-siyasat al-shar'iyya*), to similarly argue that it is necessary to prioritise enemies and neutralise antagonistic forces without making compromises on principles (Hay'at Tahrir al-Sham, 2018d; Hay'at Tahrir al-Sham, 2018f). HTS claims that its fundamental principles remained intact, such as the belief in God's sovereignty (*hakimiyyat Allah*) and rejection of democracy and secularism (Hay'at Tahrir al-Sham, 2017h). Still, the group also acknowledges that the external situation and challenges have changed significantly, and that it needs to adapt accordingly. Even the implementation of Islamic Law is linked to a group's strength according to HTS, which changes in contrast with the principles that do not (Atun, 2019). In this jihad, HTS argues that there should be no internal fight over religious creed, as this is a war for survival (Hay'at Tahrir al-Sham, 2017d), which means that fighting alongside non-Salafis is a non-issue. As an example, HTS said that it publicly supported the Southern Front, regardless of previous ideological differences, as they fought the same enemy (Hay'at Tahrir al-Sham, 2018b). In several communiqués, HTS added that as an independent organization, it does not threaten other states but rather seeks to develop balanced relations and collaboration with them for the purposes of regional stability (Hay'at Tahrir al-Sham, 2018a). This means that the group welcomes humanitarian work for neutral organizations (Hay'at Tahrir al-Sham, 2017m). These changes antagonised other Salafi Jihadi figures, as one of their leading theologians, Abu Muhammad al-Maqdisi, argued:

> Jolani played us. When he split with IS, I put all my weight in their favour. I released a communique telling the youth to join them. Most people who loved al-Qaeda joined them. Jabhat al-Nusra exploited the Salafi Jihadi trend for its military battles, as our youths were the fuel of the revolution. Lots of people were willing to join them and blow themselves up for the cause, from Europe, from Gulf countries, and elsewhere. But once they freed themselves from the allegiance, there were no more limits and our divergences became ideological. Now they say that all the fighters are mujahideen, even if they don't fight to implement Islamic law. This is not a change of tactic, this is ideological.

Without expressing the same antagonism, the former mufti of al-Qaeda, Abu Hafs al-Mauritani, states:

> I supported the split with a-Qaeda. It was a necessary step to alleviate the huge pressure on the group. But I think that the outcome is contrasted. HTS provides security, services to the population, and united many groups. But their security services have repressed al-Qaeda without dialogue. This is not the proper way of doing it. And they fail to implement proper Islamic behaviour locally (*hisba*). From what I can see, their rule is not consistent with Islamic Law.

HTS was able to successfully implement the internal changes that Ahrar al-Sham had attempted, but with more success in containing dissidence. One of the significant decisions HTS made was to institutionalise religious authority within its Sharia council. The goal was to prevent dissident voices from challenging the group's views and to prohibit members from expressing opinions outside of the council (Hay'at Tahrir al-Sham, 2019c), as well as from excommunicating any individuals or groups (Hay'at Tahrir al-Sham, 2017k, 2017l). Violating these rules could lead to punishment, as when prominent HTS members like Abu Abd Ashida were called to present themselves to a court after criticising the group (Hay'at Tahrir al-Sham, 2019b), or when others like the Egyptians Abu Yaqthan and Abu Shu'ib were expelled (Hay'at Tahrir al-Sham, 2019a). All three individuals were former Ahrar al-Sham members who had switched allegiance to HTS when they opposed the decisions of their former group. The institutionalisation of religious authority allowed HTS to impose its views as a matter of procedure rather than content. Rather than addressing the religious content of dissident voices, the group focused on their violation of institutional norms regarding the expression of religious views.

By 2024, Ahrar al-Sham had experienced a significant decline, leading to a repositioning of its role primarily as a military force aligned with HTS. The group has effectively splintered into several factions, each holding divergent perspectives on its relationship with HTS and their political agenda, as mentioned in the previous chapter. The dominant faction prioritises military efficiency in collaboration with HTS, recognising the loss of Ahrar al-Sham's independent political influence in the province.[30] Meanwhile, the older leadership still aspires to maintain a political voice, even though it has effectively relinquished control over the majority of ground troops. As a result, the group's status as an independent political project has virtually disappeared. While Ahrar al-Sham still possesses effective military capabilities, HTS now dominates the local administration and has established a new order in Idlib. HTS's new role has decisively marginalised Ahrar al-Sham, which was previously at the forefront of the political initiatives taken on behalf of the armed opposition in Syria, including diplomatic outreach to foreign countries. As a consequence, Ahrar al-Sham has become a relatively minor player within the province.

A comparison of Ahrar al-Sham's and HTS's trajectories shows a paradoxical outcome. Despite being best positioned to politicise, Ahrar al-Sham failed to achieve its objectives. Ahrar al-Sham started its project as an alternative to al-Qaeda and the Muslim Brotherhood that would position itself in the middle ground of Islamist politics. It created consensual and inclusive institutions that fostered internal dialogue and bolstered both internal and external support. The two most prominent state actors during the conflict, Qatar and Turkey, also supported the group. But, in spite of favourable circumstances, Ahrar al-Sham failed to impose itself due to its internal impotence after the killing of its leadership. Ahrar al-Sham's strategic choices certainly informed HTS's trajectory, but the latter was more successful despite its own sets of challenges. Jabhat al-Nusra lost most of its soldiers and resources when it split with IS. It was burdened by an allegiance to al-Qaeda that precluded significant external support from states but also underpinned numerous drone attacks against its leaders. Jabhat al-Nusra nonetheless succeeded with tighter internal organisational control but also selective attacks against several components of the mainstream armed opposition. The organisational choices and approach to other armed groups ultimately mattered more than these groups' respective ideologies. Jabhat al-Nusra and then HTS successes in containing its most threatening contenders and achieving their objectives positioned it as the dominant actor in the armed opposition. In contrast, Ahrar al-Sham's internal culture of consensus and cooperation with other groups prevented it from imposing itself, despite more favourable circumstances.

Conclusion

Ahrar al-Sham's ideological development during the Syrian conflict situates the roots of the group's politicisation within both pre-war and in-war contexts. Ahrar al-Sham did not emerge in a vacuum; the group is the heir to lasting debates among Jihadi groups that preceded its creation. Early leaders of Ahrar al-Sham had long debated the legacy of al-Qaeda and its negative impact on the Muslim world, reflecting on the excesses committed by al-Qaeda affiliates during the war in Iraq. However, Ahrar al-Sham's politicisation was not solely the product of pre-existing ideological debates. It was also the result of the group's external and internal institutionalisation, which promoted consensual decision-making and favoured a congruent outcome. This ideological-organisational leaning was favoured by the nature of the Syrian conflict and the nature of factional competition with other Salafi Jihadi armed groups, which further forced Ahrar al-Sham's differentiation from them. But the institutional context of Ahrar al-Sham's politicisation ultimately proved to be an impediment, as the group's consensualism prevented it from adapting quickly to unfolding events in Syria, particularly the resurgence of its main competitor, Jabhat al-Nusra, as it transformed into HTS.

6
Syria and the Future of Jihad

The politicisation of Ahrar al-Sham—and Jabhat al-Nusra / HTS in its own way—illustrates the potential long-term evolution of global jihad. These groups' trajectories expose the choices of other Jihadis after the failure of IS to achieve any lasting territorial strategic objective and al-Qaeda's strategic conundrum between transnationalism and localism. Too much attention focuses on these two, but all Jihadis do not have to follow the trajectory of the most extreme actors. The choices of armed groups like Ahrar al-Sham and HTS in Syria suggests the existence of other strategic choices, including towards their potential normalisation. These groups' repositionings during the Syrian conflict reveal important social movement dynamics that delineate the conditions in which Jihadi groups can politicise, become more mainstream, and perhaps even start to engage the international community. This perspective also helps to reassess the impact of post-9/11 political decisions and their consequences on Jihadi groups and their constituencies.

The Lessons from Armed Groups' Trajectories in Syria

Most Jihadi groups followed a relatively linear trajectory towards radicalism until 2011. These groups originate in the Egyptian and Syrian insurgents that sought to overthrow their governments in the 1970s. In the 1980s, these groups and their leaders immigrated to Afghanistan, where they joined forces with thousands of fighters from across the Muslim world, laying the foundations of what became known as the Salafi Jihadi trend. This movement dressed its opposition to existing Muslim regimes in a Salafi theological garb. The competitive conflicts that arose among these groups in the following years exacerbated internal competition and ideological divides, fuelling their radicalisation. Over time, successive generations of Jihadi Salafis became increasingly extreme in their objectives and ideological commitments. They even began targeting civilians within the Muslim community, such as Algerians in the 1990s and Shia Muslims in Iraq in the 2000s. While the initial goal of these groups was to change Muslim regimes through guerrilla warfare or military coups, this singularly transformed into a full-scale war against the United States and its allies by the 9/11 attacks.

IS's evolution after 2011 is the expected outcome of a long-standing historical pattern. Internal controversies over the proper approach to reviving the historical Caliphate have plagued Jihadis for decades. Medieval arguments justifying its gruesome killings and the re-institution of slavery are a natural extension of the Salafi Jihadi approach to religion and politics when it lost control over potential excesses. The role of foreign fighters and ideologues further validates existing research on their impact on armed groups' ideologies and behaviour, including the spread of new maximalist positions and repertoires of violence. IS is the pinnacle of the Salafi Jihadi trend, taking it to the most severe excesses possible by claiming to have revived the Muslim Caliphate, isolating itself from its potential allies, and insisting on being the only legitimate Muslim authority worldwide.

However, the Syrian war has also transformed the incubator of global jihad; IS's violence is more of an exception than the norm. Other groups have moved into a more pragmatic direction during the conflict, partially in response to IS's radicalism. They have come to realise that the uncontrolled implementation of Salafi Jihadi ideas can only lead to a stalemate, hindering the achievement of any lasting political objectives. This new direction is also a result of the structural configuration of the war. Unlike many conflicts against foreign occupation, the Syrian war is essentially a battle for domestic authority. As a result, the groups that emerged during the conflict understood that they had to win over the majority Sunni population while fighting against the ruling regime. They had new opportunities to reach beyond Islamist constituencies, as they were not specifically targeted by the regime's repression, since the latter never differentiated its targets, assaulting, besieging, and destroying Syrian cities without distinctions. This contrasts with previous conflicts, such as Algeria in the 1990s, where Islamists were specifically targeted and insulated themselves in response, often targeting non-affiliated civilians. Besides, Syrian Jihadi groups also reflected on past excesses that have plagued their movement, from Algeria to Iraq in the 2000s, and realised that radicalism hinders strategic victories. Many groups have recognised the need to make new strategic choices.

Ahrar al-Sham and HTS's trajectories challenge existing academic understandings of Jihadi Salafism, suggesting that Jihadi groups do not systematically radicalise and divide. Instead of adopting new maximalist positions, both groups distanced themselves from al-Qaeda and IS groups due to the nature of internal competition, IS's new views, and Western countries' more lenient positions on Islamists who agreed to distance themselves from global jihad. This marks a stark contrast with the Afghan jihad in the 1980s, where radical fringes radicalised the Jihadi movement as a whole. The Syrian jihad's trajectory suggests that the root cause of Jihadi radicalisation is not inherent to its ideological nature but is rather rooted in these groups' ability or failure to cultivate external strategic ties and institutionalise their relationships with other actors, including the population and other states. Such ties can constrain Jihadi groups and shape their ideological and behavioural evolution.

The Syrian conflict also provides insight into the impact of foreign fighters. While some of them promoted maximalist views and tried to impede Jihadi politicisation, even reinforcing IS's radicalism, others played a significant role in promoting a clear dissociation from al-Qaeda and embracing the revolutionary agenda of the armed opposition. These individuals encouraged the development of a pragmatic political project that offered a viable alternative to the maximalist positions of IS and, to a lesser extent, al-Qaeda. Many had participated in jihad before and were dissatisfied with the globalist choices of al-Qaeda, preferring to focus on local causes instead. Although less experienced foreign fighters were at the forefront of IS troops in Syria, many veterans of previous jihads who opposed al-Qaeda's direction sought to promote a new strategic direction for the Jihadi movement in Syria.

The impact of radicalism on the long-term efficiency of Jihadi groups is also questionable. While some have argued that Jihadi radicalism is a strength (e.g., Walters, 2017), the example of Ahrar al-Sham and HTS challenges this view. Although reliance on transnational Jihadi networks helped Syrian Jihadis mobilise and build organisational strength, international opposition to the Jihadis, often framed in counter-insurgency and counter-terrorism, also obstructed significant foreign support for the armed opposition, antagonised large parts of the population, and exacerbated internal infighting. The short-term success of IS is debatable, and it is unclear how the group can sustain itself in the long run without transforming into a more pragmatic actor able to build some level of international legitimacy, as the Taliban movement in Afghanistan is trying to do to some extent.

A major lesson of the Syrian jihad is that Jihadi politicisation is contingent on armed groups' ability to institutionalise their strategic relationships to other actors while preserving their internal cohesion. Foreign fighters disappointed with al-Qaeda's direction, Syrian pre-war debates, the structure of the armed opposition, and IS's radicalism provided the backdrop for Ahrar al-Sham's and HTS's politicisation, but this was not an easy process. Armed groups do not simply decide to embrace a new strategic direction. Both groups had to preserve their internal cohesion to prevent dissidence, maintain commander loyalty, and enforce new political decisions. Environmental factors largely defined their ability to institutionalise. Ahrar al-Sham's emergence as a de-centralised group facilitated its institutionalisation through bottom-up consensus. While this facilitated the group's internal institutionalisation, it also impeded decision-making, slowed down or prevented critical decisions, and eroded credibility with potential partners, including other states and the population, by demonstrating a lack of resolve during the conflict.

Similarly, HTS's predecessor, Jabhat al-Nusra, recognised the impasses encountered by IS's previous choices during the 2000s war in Iraq. Like Ahrar al-Sham, the group has politicised over the years, recognising the need to develop regional alliances with new strategic partners, particularly Turkey, and institutionalising its interactions with the population by establishing a civilian administration in northwest Syria. However, HTS's politicisation differs from Ahrar al-Sham's in one key aspect: Jabhat al-Nusra had historically centralised resources and decisions to a greater extent than did Ahrar al-Sham, facilitating the group's internal control. However, this was also accompanied by several attacks against other factions that it considered hostile, and at times, harsher local practices.

Ahrar al-Sham's attempt to reshape the strategic direction of global jihad beyond Syria initially aimed at setting up a new example for other Islamists, but it ultimately fell short on several levels. Ahrar al-Sham failed to become the dominant actor in the Syrian opposition, with HTS ultimately outmanoeuvring it. The marginalisation vis-à-vis HTS prevented it from proposing and implementing a clear political alternative on the ground, leaving its political project in question. At the same time, while the national focus of Ahrar al-Sham and HTS may have some potential for replication elsewhere, it is unlikely to appeal to foreign fighters who are mostly attracted to the internationalist dimension of jihad. Without a successful replicable model, Ahrar al-Sham's initial "project for the Islamic community" can only remain a motto.

The Future of Jihad

Ahrar al-Sham and HTS are the outcomes of significant structural changes that transformed the Jihadi movement after the 2011 Arab uprisings. The initially non-militarised revolts of civilians throughout the Arab world de-stabilised the established regional political order, leading to the downfall of authoritarian regimes such as Zine El Abidine Ben Ali in Tunisia and Hosni Mubarak in Egypt, while conflicts broke out in Libya and Syria. These uprisings shifted the strategic priorities of Jihadi groups in the Muslim world. While some groups in Algeria and Iraq already pursued domestic objectives in the 2000s, the new political opportunities to transform the Muslim world marginalised the importance of external armed attacks. The transnationalisation of the Jihadi movement in the 1990s was never meant to be an end in itself. Instead, the objective was to fight foreign countries supporting domestic Muslim regimes with the ultimate aim of toppling them. With the increase in domestic opportunities, targeting foreign enemies lost its relevance.

The death of Osama bin Laden in May 2011 had a significant impact on the Jihadi social movement, too. Bin Laden's leadership as a symbolic figure and central node trying to give strategic directives to affiliate groups left a void that his successor, Ayman al-Zawahiri, was unable to fill. In response, local groups sought to define their own alternatives, leading to the emergence of new entities such as Ansar al-Shari'a (the Partisans of Islamic Law), which aimed to distance themselves from al-Qaeda branding while pursuing similar local objectives. Over the next few years, local affiliates in Iraq and Syria further dissociated themselves from al-Qaeda by embracing their own strategic directions. As a result, the centre of power in the Jihadi social movement transformed, with a growing emphasis on local autonomy and de-centralised decision-making.

The structural changes in the Jihadi social movement resulted in its polarisation into three main directions. The most well-known of these is Islamic State (IS), which replaced al-Qaeda as the leading group in the Jihadi movement. IS has taken advantage of the relative marginalisation of al-Qaeda during the early days of the Arab uprisings to capitalise on the unpopularity of the Iraqi government and the war in Syria to expand its influence. Some of its commanders even went to Syria to form Jabhat al-Nusra, although IS later lost control of the new group's leadership. IS's strategic depth in Iraq allowed it to establish itself as a statelet in both Iraq and Syria. Its appeal, including the idea of a worldwide Caliphate, combined with its adept use of social media to mobilise unaffiliated Muslims, including converts to Islam, positioned it as the leading group worldwide. Many local insurgents in the Muslim world have affiliated with the organisation, especially in Africa, as they sought to capitalise on its successes in the Middle East. Unlike al-Qaeda, which was more selective in the recruitment of its members, IS has demonstrated its willingness to recruit a large number of individuals without imposing much control over their use of violence. This approach, combined with the simplicity of the group's core objective, has transformed the elitist legacy of al-Qaeda.

IS's brutality is both a strength and a weakness. This approach has allowed the group to mobilise a larger number of individuals, including those who are frustrated with the current political situation and seeking a tangible solution to their grievances. IS has achieved some undeniable successes. For example, it was able to consolidate its power in Iraq and Syria from 2014 to 2017 and expand its influence worldwide. IS continues to spread in many precarious environments, particularly in Africa, where its ideas continue to allure marginalised groups fighting primarily for local grievances. The practical revival of the Caliphate is a more palpable alternative to al-Qaeda's network of solidarity against Western intervention in the Muslim world. But it is unclear whether IS can achieve lasting political success beyond the mere de-stabilisation of weak states and arbitrary attacks against Western countries. It is doubtful that, in the current conditions of all-out war against everyone else, IS could impose a new reality on the international community and survive in the long run. While its ideology may be appealing to some, its brutal tactics have made it an international pariah, limiting its ability to achieve its objectives in a sustainable manner.

The second direction involves a genuine departure from Jihadi Salafism and its legacy. These groups have learned from the Arab uprisings that they must distance themselves from both IS and al-Qaeda by developing their own independent political projects. While they have not necessarily "moderated" or rejected their belief in the establishment of Islamic states in theory, they at least recognise the importance of engaging with their populations and the international system of states. While they may not align with groups such as the Afghan Taliban or Palestinian Hamas, they draw inspiration from them as viable Islamist alternatives. This evolution is a response to the challenges faced by al-Qaeda, which is mired in a deadlock as terrorist designations attract unwarranted international attention and targeted attacks, without any clear benefits or realistic strategic direction. Their dissociation from Jihadi Salafism is also a reaction to IS's radicalism, as the latter's harsh local governance and theology have shown their own limitations. Although IS successfully established local structures of governance, it has also faced significant popular opposition that questions the long-term viability of its prospects. Groups like Ahrar al-Sham and HTS, on the other hand, seek to become internationally manageable actors that could potentially be recognised internationally in the right circumstances, similar to groups like Hamas and the Taliban.

Al-Qaeda finds itself in a middle ground between these two directions. While the group rejects the extreme tactics employed by IS since 2011, it is not necessarily due to ideological differences, but rather a pragmatic understanding of their unpopularity within the Muslim world. Al-Qaeda has tried to become more flexible, but it has not officially abandoned its agenda of foreign operations. The group remains committed to its armed opposition to Western countries. Despite this, al-Qaeda has not openly embraced the attacks carried out by IS in Western countries, which it was the first to openly promote in the 1990s, without providing clear reasoning for this stance. The positions of prominent Salafi Jihadi theologians, such as Abu Muhammad al-Maqdisi and Abu Qatada al-Falastini, reflect these ambiguities. The latter has embraced a more populist and mass movement–oriented transformation of the Jihadi social movement, which is more tolerant of ideological divergences, including those with Muslim Brotherhood figures. Meanwhile, al-Maqdisi denounces IS but still believes that the purity of the religious creed should take precedence over any political pragmatism.

The al-Qaeda brand is toxic, and no longer beneficial to the groups that once supported it in the 2000s. More critically, the brand impedes some of these groups' transformation into legitimate political actors. If al-Qaeda merely seeks to promote the establishment of Islamic states in the Muslim world, then its leadership might be the greatest obstacle to achieving this objective. Besides, if al-Qaeda ceases to engage in armed attacks against Western countries, what purpose does the brand serve? Certainly, Osama bin Laden's initial aspirations extended far beyond the mere prevention of caricatures of the Prophet in Western countries, which has become one of al-Qaeda's focus over the years. Despite strong loyalty among its affiliates stemming from personal loyalty to its leadership over the years, many might realise that they cannot become local governments that are accepted regionally and internationally without rejecting their affiliation with al-Qaeda. This realisation can further erode the brand's reputation over time and render it more irrelevant than ever. Without providing any real value addition, al-Qaeda's return to its avant-garde elitist roots could also prove to be a daunting challenge.

A key question is whether other groups can follow the example set by Ahrar al-Sham and HTS and seek to normalise themselves. For instance, it might be in the interest of other Jihadis like Jama'a Nusrat al-Islam wal Muslimin (JNIM) in the Sahel and al-Shabaab in Somalia, who are the strongest al-Qaeda affiliates, to follow suit. But it is also unclear whether they could do so successfully. While Ahrar al-Sham and HTS are led by middle-class Syrians with higher education who recognised the limits of global jihad early on in the conflict, the situation in the Sahel and Somalia is significantly different. JNIM and al-Shabaab draw their memberships from significantly different societies, with their own socio-economic development and political awareness, though some of these groups' leaders are politicians in their own right too. More importantly, perhaps, both groups fight against a political order that Western countries want to uphold, in contrast with the latter's previous willingness to fight the Syrian regime. Additionally, no other state has the same kind of state leverage that Turkey has in Syria, where the armed opposition could not survive without Turkish political and military support. JNIM and al-Shabaab finally face the threat of IS, and any attempt to shift their strategy could result in internal divisions among their commanders. Both groups might remain stuck in the Jihadi paradox, as enduring insurgencies unable to achieve their strategic political objectives.

This understanding of how Jihadi groups balance their internal cohesion while institutionalising strategic relations with external actors also sheds light on the evolution of the Taliban. Although the Taliban is not a Jihadi group per se, drawing on the (non-Salafi and traditionalist) deobandi approach to Islam in the Afghan context, the group faces similar choices as a government. Unlike in Syria, where Turkey has significant leverage over Syrian armed groups, no foreign state has substantial leverage on the Taliban in Afghanistan, not even Pakistan. Additionally, there are no other armed groups with whom the Taliban must cooperate, and the population has limited ability to collectively resist its demands despite numerous attempts, the most successful of which being only at the local level. The Taliban can therefore prioritise its internal dynamics, which explains its most maximalist policies on women, for instance, reflecting the group's internal debates and power struggles. Yet the Taliban still seeks international legitimacy and normalisation despite being autocratic and unwilling to share power, signalling its politicisation.

While not Jihadi per se, Hamas also politicised as it institutionalised internally and externally, which can raise eyebrows given the intensity of the large-scale armed assault it launched on 7 October, 2023. Internally, Hamas has established a robust bureaucracy that assures the cohesion of the group beyond the Gaza Strip to encompass the West Bank under heightened Israeli control as well as Israeli prisons and the diaspora. Remarkably, the group has successfully navigated multiple leadership successions without dissent, overcoming numerous challenges over the years. Externally, since 2007, Hamas has effectively governed the Gaza Strip, anchoring its external institutionalisation within the local population. The group has solidified its ties to other factions through the creation of a shared military operation room and cultivated strategic relationships abroad. These international connections include associations with countries as diverse as Qatar and Turkey, both of which are closer to the United States and Europe, along with Iran. The intensity of Hamas's assault in October 2023 can legitimately challenge the notion that the group politicised due to its scale. However, the level of violence perpetrated by Hamas doesn't fundamentally deny the group's politicisation. Hamas remains a political organisation seeking to position itself as such both domestically and internationally, in contrast to IS and al-Qaeda's opposition to the international legal order. The willingness to make an array concessions and engage with other groups pragmatically is real. The unprecedented level of violence of the 7 October attack appears aimed more at disrupting the existing status quo through unprecedented force, which is not driven by radicalisation per se.

Regarding other Jihadis, it is highly unlikely that al-Qaeda and IS will reunify, given their current circumstances. The Syrian conflict has resulted in a strategic departure between the two groups that has only widened over time. Despite sharing some long-term objectives, their globalist views are at odds with each other. While it is possible for short-term, circumstantial cooperation in specific countries based on shared interests and interconnected members, it is implausible to result in a reunification. Though individuals, commanders, or even groups can change their allegiance, a reunification would ultimately require one leadership to submit to the other, which is not going to happen. Al-Qaeda is built on an enduring solidarity among its prominent leaders, which has been cemented over the past few decades. This solidarity has survived numerous challenges, and its resilience remained strong over the years despite considerable losses, though the absence of a clear leadership might bring the organisation to its end. On the other hand, IS has taken a new trajectory since declaring its caliphate. While an internal contest for the group's core leadership between geographic poles is possible, the strategic nature of the project is relatively consistent. Even in case of substantial losses, neither group is going to submit to the other once more.

Competition among the three directions is less intense when it comes to attracting foreign fighters. The groups that have distanced themselves from Jihadi Salafism have lost their appeal, and fighting for primarily local objectives without aligning with Salafi Jihadi globalism is a less potent alternative, especially as groups such as Ahrar al-Sham and HTS no longer seek to recruit foreign fighters. Both groups have transformed and instead seek to replicate state-like models, including the training of a combination of more professional soldiers with local fighters who can fight effectively in their respective areas. Conversely, al-Qaeda's more elitist approach and strategic deadlock is less able to capitalise on the emergence of new generations willing to fight for utopian purposes or direct action. The simplicity of IS's message and its adept use of social media have favoured the group's outreach worldwide, especially where it managed to exploit local grievances.

Revisiting the So-Called Global War on Terror and Its Lasting Consequences

The political upheavals that occurred after 2011 offer valuable historical insights into the decisions made in the aftermath of 9/11. The so-called global war on terror in the 2000s viewed non-state armed groups and states that collaborated with al-Qaeda as enemies, with no clear boundaries, drawing in countries as diverse as Afghanistan, Somalia, and Yemen. While the war's broad definition aimed to address al-Qaeda's international reach, its ill-defined nature bolstered the group's influence worldwide, elevating it to the forefront of Jihadi organisations that previously focused solely on domestic objectives.

In reality, al-Qaeda's decision to declare war on the United States was a significant departure from the strategies of other Jihadi groups. Until the 1990s, these groups focused on targeting their own countries or participating in classical jihad against non-Muslim foreign occupation. While critical of U.S. policies, they did not intend to engage in global conflict with American forces. Al-Qaeda, on the other hand, pushed for a strategic shift. The group believed that fighting domestic Muslim regimes was futile as long as they had American support. Attacking American forces in the region would increase the cost of American support for local regimes and ultimately force the United States to withdraw from the region, as happened after the 1983 Marine barracks bombing in Beirut or the United States' failure in Mogadishu in 1993. But virtually all other Jihadis and their sympathisers rejected this strategic choice before 9/11. Even prominent 9/11 hijackers were initially more interested in fighting Russian troops in Chechnya than attacking the American homeland.

The war on terror inadvertently boosted al-Qaeda's popularity and reputation. Prior to 9/11, the group had only a few hundred members and pursued an unpopular political agenda. But the U.S.-led wars in Afghanistan and Iraq thrust the group into the centre of new international conflicts, making it increasingly appealing to many Muslims who saw these wars as existential threats to the Muslim world. This was particularly true for the war in Iraq, which attracted thousands of young Muslim fighters driven by a desire to confront American troops, regardless of their initial ideological beliefs. Many of these fighters had limited understanding of Salafi Jihadi ideology and were motivated primarily by the need to defend the Muslim community against the new threat. By relentlessly focusing on al-Qaeda, the United States inadvertently bolstered the group's credibility and popularity, creating a self-fulfilling prophecy where it became the only viable option for those looking to resist American aggression. As a result, many local Jihadi groups that previously failed to achieve their national objectives began to affiliate with al-Qaeda, often strengthening their organisational capacity and increasing their visibility. This led to al-Qaeda–led Jihadi Salafism becoming the primary response to the new wars.

The Arab uprisings marked a significant turning point in the region. The widespread popular uprisings that de-stabilised the Arab world at the time showed that change was possible, despite al-Qaeda's claims that only force could compel these regimes to reform. In countries like Libya and Syria, local armed groups formed to topple regimes that had proven structurally unable to reform. These groups quickly realised that they could leverage foreign military support to tilt the balance of power in their favour. The emergence of these groups coincided with a shift in U.S. strategic priorities under President Barack Obama, who sought to reduce America's footprint in the Middle East and pivot towards Asia. In Afghanistan, this shift combined with the military stalemate to bolster support for direct negotiations with the Taliban. It was only the atrocities committed by ISIS—including the targeting of Kurdish forces, enslavement of Yazidi civilians, and execution of foreign hostages—that forced foreign countries to take military action against the group after 2014. It is questionable whether they would have done so otherwise.

The political changes that took place after 2011 created opportunities for new insurgent groups that were not affiliated with al-Qaeda or ISIS. Western countries, preoccupied with their own concerns, were less worried about the ideological orientation of these groups as long as they did not pose a direct threat. The incentives that prevailed in the early 2000s, when affiliation with al-Qaeda could enhance a group's credibility and effectiveness, had changed. Many groups could pursue their goals of establishing Islamic states without attracting the same level of international attention associated with the al-Qaeda franchise. The original vision of al-Qaeda was to fight the United States as a means of establishing local Islamic regimes. But in a new environment where groups could achieve their goals without being targeted by U.S. drone attacks, there was no need to remain affiliated with al-Qaeda. For example, Ahrar al-Sham and HTS can seek engagement on regional and international levels while maintaining their objective of establishing an Islamic state in Syria (which is very dissimilar to the views of al-Qaeda or ISIS anyway) without being targeted by Western countries. However, not all groups seized this opportunity, as many al-Qaeda franchises remained committed to the group. The lasting embeddedness of some of them in al-Qaeda networks, reflected in their organisational identity, made them reluctant to rescind their commitments in competitive environments. But many new groups chose not to join al-Qaeda, and sought their own paths towards achieving their goals.

But space remains tight for al-Qaeda affiliates that might renounce their allegiance to the organisation. The case of Jabhat al-Nusra / HTS is particularly noteworthy. Despite the group's efforts to distance itself from al-Qaeda, it remains listed by the U.N. Security Council as a group previously affiliated to the latter. Parts of the reason are inherent with sanction regimes, which imply that it is often easier to be listed than de-listed. While sanction regimes act primarily as deterrents and as a punisher, to discourage insurgents from affiliating with them and to prevent them from mobilising and funding, they lack flexibility once applied, hindering states' ability to respond to armed groups' strategic changes. They also obstruct the ability to provide the right incentives to armed groups to renounce some of their strategic commitments. These concerns are not merely related to foreign countries, as armed groups themselves might face strong internal obstacles to renounce international allegiances, as this can threaten their own organisational cohesion. However, foreign countries have a role to play in changing these groups' external incentives.

Jihadi groups closely observe one another's decisions and achievements. This previously contributed to the rise of al-Qaeda in the 2000s and, to some extent, IS after the establishment of the Caliphate in 2014. However, it can also influence armed groups in other ways. Successful engagement with certain groups based on the right incentives can have an impact on other armed groups in different regions. If armed groups perceive the benefits of an alternative approach, they could reject international attacks and renounce their affiliation with al-Qaeda or IS, too. These groups debate various tactical and strategic issues internally, and external incentives can sway them in one direction or another. While not every group will be responsive, a significant number may come to realise that their objectives can be better achieved without external affiliation.

The lack of clear objectives in the global war on terror has hindered its chances of success. Was the goal to end armed attacks against Western countries or Muslim regimes? To eradicate Islamist groups deemed too "radical"? To establish democratic regimes in the Muslim world? Military responses only could not achieve these objectives conjointly. Large-scale wars in Afghanistan and Iraq, as well as targeted killings of Jihadi leaders and commanders elsewhere, have killed off some of these groups' leaders and commanders, limiting some of their abilities to launch attacks abroad, while paradoxically expanding their reach. Before 9/11, al-Qaeda had only a few hundred members, but nearly 20 years later, al-Qaeda and IS enjoy the support of hundreds of thousands of Muslims worldwide. Military responses have limited these groups' ability to stage attacks in Western countries, but have not eradicated them. Instead of relying solely on brute force, including special forces, a combination of punishments and political incentives aligned with specific strategic objectives could yield more substantial outcomes. The recent partial Western retreat from the Muslim world, based on a recognition of its limitations, presents an opportunity to clarify its overall strategy.

Western countries need to clarify their strategic objectives. Deterring groups and individuals from directly attacking Western interests is a legitimate priority. But it's equally important to recognise that local armed groups fighting their own insurgencies do not necessarily represent a strategic threat, regardless of their ideological beliefs. Some of these groups can be offered an alternative. Many armed groups whose beliefs or practices are at odds with Western values do not pose a direct threat to Western interests. Negotiations with the Taliban, for instance, have shown that allowing non-internationalist Sunni alternatives to ISIS can be more effective than promoting only counter-narratives to "radicalism". The right incentives can shape the behaviour of armed groups beyond just military means. The same previously happened with Marxist-inspired insurgencies. This does not mean that these groups would cease to be a problem. Jihadis also want to impose their own societal views on the population, some of which strongly oppose them. They are also less willing, hitherto, to meaningfully share power with other actors. But these issues do not have to be faced militarily with drone strikes and foreign interventions.

Encouraging the politicisation of Jihadi groups requires a re-politicisation of Western approaches, too. Western countries should recognise that these groups are not merely security threats that have to be neutralised militarily. The securitisation of nearly all Jihadi groups, and the associated emphasis on their ideological commitments and the elimination of their leaders, has de-politicised counter-insurgency efforts. Counter-insurgency has either been conflated with counter-terrorism or used as a tool to isolate Jihadi groups from their constituencies. The amalgamation of counter-insurgency and counter-terrorism is not new, as it was in the 1970s, when armed groups formerly seen as insurgents began to be classified as "terrorists," with significant political implications.[1] But insurgencies also exploit legitimate grievances, unlike terrorists that states denounce as illegitimate, if not irrational or evil. After 9/11, al-Qaeda transformed from a network of hundreds of militants conducting high-profile attacks into a diffuse association of insurgent affiliates active across the Muslim world. Treating al-Qaeda and its affiliates only as "terrorist" groups with non-addressable ideological commitments excludes the possibility of dialogue and political transformation of at least some of these groups. These actors are considered only as security threats that can be neutralised through military-intelligence means designed to expose their organisational structures, detect critical nodes, and destroy them with sophisticated drone attacks. This makes counter-terrorism primarily a technical security issue. When counter-insurgency is considered, the primary objective is to isolate al-Qaeda affiliates from their constituency or to "take the fish out of the water," as Mao Zedong stated in his famous maxim. But little more is done to potentially engage some of these groups politically too, as Western countries did with other insurgencies in the past.

Western countries cannot do everything, but they can at least influence the international conditions that these groups face. Jihadi insurgencies are not solely a response to foreign policies, although these policies do play a role. Deep-seated grievances stemming from the historical construction of many Muslim states have been at the root of many of these insurgencies over the past few decades. But Western countries can still present a conditional set of incentives to encourage the politicisation of a substantial number of Salafi Jihadi groups. While it is unlikely that all of these groups will be receptive, many could be persuaded to do so. At the very least, Western countries can avoid exacerbating local conflicts and inadvertently bolstering the popularity of these groups or encouraging their international affiliation with groups such as al-Qaeda and IS. Globalist groups are unlikely to achieve their long-term strategic objectives. At best, they can destabilise local and international environments. Western countries could at least dissuade local groups from affiliating with them, offer existing franchises a way out, and focus on the most reluctant actors. Acknowledging past mistakes, such as the failure to meaningfully engage with Islamist groups that embraced the political process like Hamas after winning the 2006 Palestinian legislative elections, is also crucial.

ANNEX

Methodology and Sources

The Syrian conflict has received unparalleled global coverage due to various factors, including the proximity of Syria to Europe and the involvement of foreign fighters, including European nationals. This attention has generated extensive analysis and reporting from various sources, such as academics, journalists, think-tanks, and independent researchers. Social media has played a crucial role in disseminating information about the conflict, with armed groups and their supporters utilising online platforms to publish their statements, political positions, and engage in public debates. Unlike the al-Qaeda–affiliated groups that relied on obscure forums in the early 2000s, Syrian armed groups have effectively used social media to mobilise supporters and attract external support. A considerable amount of battle footage was also uploaded online, further amplifying the conflict's coverage and impact.

But the availability of considerable information comes with important trade-offs. In-depth historical analyses of long-term developments have often been overlooked in favour of the coverage of short-term events. Pressure to publish timely analysis drawn from extensive available data has paradoxically marginalised in-depth analyses, although extremely valuable studies have also been published. Many researchers have also been less critical about the information published by Syrian armed opposition groups than warranted. But armed groups themselves realised the benefits of publicising fake information about themselves to shape a larger narrative. For instance, many leaks and communiqués were published on social media by armed groups and their observers to suggest that they were getting the upper hand and to incite smaller factions to join in.[1] They often exaggerated their numerical strength to external observers to boost their credibility and gather more support. Despite the wealth of available data, extensive information is also still lacking. That was particularly the case in the beginning of the conflict, when many groups appeared and merged into other entities without any written trace of their existence.

One notable issue regarding the study of Salafi Jihadi groups and the availability of data concerns the disputed role of theology and ideology. Salafi Jihadi groups commonly emphasise their theological and ideological commitments, while their leaders are hardly accessible. A large corpus hence excessively relies on documents published by Salafi Jihadi groups, intellectuals, or theologians to explain their actions. Though many of these documents are extremely beneficial, particularly when insiders reveal information that they would not otherwise divulge, relying almost exclusively on them provides only a partial understanding of these armed groups' actions. Theological arguments, in particular, often mask very worldly issues, particularly power politics, under a religious garb that is more relatable to these groups' members and sympathisers. Focusing solely on theological arguments in a vacuum risks reifying them in isolation from their broader context. Moreover, primary sources released by external sources, particularly the American government, should be analysed reflectively, since researchers do not know the extent of information that is not released and why. The representativeness of the information is debatable, particularly when they align with the political agenda of the administration releasing the information. Salafi Jihadi groups' ideologies and primary sources are only one component of a broader analysis. I take ideological developments seriously but also consider them in the context of broader social-movement and group dynamics to alleviate most of these concerns.

Engaging in extensive field research and conducting numerous interviews over the years has underscored the critical significance of internal power dynamics, as opposed to ideological debates, in understanding the Jihadi groups' dynamics. While many research tends to concentrate on social media, this risks excessively prioritising ideology and intricate ideological debates. But I found that Jihadis, in private, dedicate a substantial amount of time to thinking of their organisational structure, power distribution, managing dissenting views on tactical and strategic matters, and orchestrating group reorganisation to align with leadership directives more than religion per se – like any other political entities. Among the multitude of communiques I have analysed, which total in the low thousands, a significant majority primarily concern internal restructuring, stances on current political developments, with minimal emphasis on theology or religion. This does not negate the importance of religion and theology; rather, it underscores that these elements do not invariably occupy the central focus of their concerns. Moreover, they can undergo reinterpretation based on the contextual exigencies faced by these groups, as happened repeatedly.

I do not attempt to cover every single detail and intricacy of the Syrian armed opposition. I decided to synthesise broader analytical patterns that align with my research objectives. While I may overlook some details, in particular the role of many marginal military units, this is necessary to maintain the overall clarity and coherence of the argument. My research does not intend to be the final word on the topic, but rather a contribution to the ongoing conversation about the conflict. Future researchers and journalists will add new insights and perspectives, particularly in areas where Ahrar al-Sham has been less present. Rather than attempting to explain every single choice of the armed opposition, I take a longer historical view to provide a nuanced understanding of the conflict's most important occurrences and turning points. Ultimately, I try to strike a balance between accessibility for a general audience interested in Jihadi armed groups and their evolution and a rigorous analysis of the available information.

Sources

I draw on extensive data from multiple sources, including field research, primary sources, and academic and journalistic analyses. The primary sources comprise a series of in-depth interviews conducted in Turkey and Syria since 2016. These interviews were crucial to the research, as they provided insights into the rationales behind Ahrar al-Sham and other groups' decisions, and expose their internal dynamics as well as the potential contradictions between leaders' intentions and these groups' actual impact. The interviews were conducted with a range of individuals associated with Ahrar al-Sham and other Syrian armed opposition groups that have allied or confronted the group in Syria. This included prominent Ahrar al-Sham leaders, commanders, and foot soldiers, as well as individuals who have left these groups and are no longer connected to them. To ensure the reliability and representativeness of the data, I selected a diverse range of interviewees. This included individuals who were previously associated with the group, independent Islamists, and those who were associated with other armed groups. Most people were interviewed over time, as the conflict unfolded, allowing for a dynamic assessment of their perspectives and reducing the risk of retrospective reinterpretations. I preferred this approach over conducting larger scale surveys, which may provide more insight into foot soldiers' perceptions but would not offer the same level of insights into the thinking processes of armed groups' leaders. The extensive interviews provided a more nuanced understanding of these groups' decision-making processes and allowed for a deeper analysis of their choices over time. While I do not cover all aspects of the Syrian conflict, the use of extensive data drawn from primary sources and field research offers a unique and valuable perspective on the evolution of Ahrar al-Sham and Jabhat al-Nusra.

I have conducted extensive field research in the opposition-controlled province of Idlib since 2019. Along with Dareen Khalifa from the International Crisis Group (ICG) and Patrick Haenni from Humanitarian Dialogue (HD), we were initially invited by HTS to visit the province and interview the group's leadership, as well as individuals associated with the HTS-supported government. Over the years, HTS facilitated multiple visits during which our team, typically composed of two to three people, addressed various issues, such as containing other Jihadi groups, including al-Qaeda and IS networks, and managing interactions between HTS and Syrian religious minorities. We interviewed the group's political, religious, military, and security leaders, which enabled us to understand the evolution of their positions as the conflict shifted from active front lines to conflict management between Turkey and Russia. These visits to the province also allowed us to establish a level of trust necessary to cover more sensitive issues. In addition, we met with various actors linked to the armed opposition, as well as independent civil society organisations, which provided us with a rich local perspective on ongoing events, and complemented the information provided by HTS. It was insightful to realise the strength of local civil society, which is often only analysed through the local councils, although many other associations are similarly active throughout the province. Although we could remain inside Syria for only a few days, up to a week at a time, the field research was still beneficial given the particular circumstances of the conflict.

At the start of my research, I received some assistance in identifying contacts, but I did not rely on research assistants to conduct the interviews. Instead, I personally conducted all of the interviews using the "snowball effect" method to expand my network of contacts. This approach allowed me to establish trust with interviewees over time and gain access to more detailed information. Building rapport and trust was critical in conducting these interviews. I conducted interviews over several years to understand these groups' understanding of the situation as the conflict unfolded.

I use extensive written sources to complement the field research and interviews. These sources include communiqués issued by the groups and their leaders, as well as online communication on platforms such as Twitter and Telegram. Additionally, analyses by armed group members and associated individuals offer critical internal perspectives on specific events. Although some of these sources may not be reliable due to the use of fake communiqués or anonymous pseudonyms to manipulate information, they still contribute to a richer analysis of the conflict. Most of these sources were gathered online, with some directly provided by Syrian armed groups. I cross-checked the reliability of these documents with other sources and my interviews with individuals associated with the groups. In addition to written sources, I also rely on the extensive coverage of the conflict by local Syrian researchers and journalists, as well as foreign researchers and journalists. These sources provided invaluable guidance for the interviews conducted over the past few years.

The two groups fit my objectives. Unlike other groups such as IS, whose leaders or commanders have rarely been interviewed outside of prison, Ahrar al-Sham's leadership was open and accessible. They welcomed external observers, including academics, journalists, and humanitarian organisations, to present and discuss their views. Its leaders were not only willing to share information but also open to improving their approach to the conflict. In addition, many leaders and members commuted regularly between Syria and Turkey, making it easier to conduct interviews. Ahrar al-Sham's institutional structure, which did not rely on a limited number of individuals, allowed for a comprehensive study of its internal organisation and constitution, making it easier to study the group as a political entity. Conducting field research with HTS inside Syria was also critical, as the group remains listed as a terrorist entity in Turkey, making it difficult to conduct interviews in foreign countries. The opportunity to conduct extensive interviews with the HTS leadership inside Syria allowed for a more thorough understanding of the group's perspectives on the conflict.

Methodological Choices

This book builds upon social movement studies. It is not sufficient to examine Jihadis' positions from their ideological writings, official statements, or even private interviews with their leaders. Jihadi leaders do not exist in a vacuum. Their beliefs and decisions are shaped by the dynamic and changing realities of the armed conflicts in which they fight, which they must interpret and navigate. I argue that armed groups' beliefs and behaviour consolidate at the crossroads of three levels of analysis, which form the foundations of the political process model in social movement studies (e.g., McAdam, 1982; McAdam, McCarthy, & Zaid, 1996; see also Wiktorowicz, 2004 for its relevance to Islamist movements). The first level is the macro-level environment, which is constituted by the state and political environment. The macro-level encompasses temporary and long-lasting features that affect the range of choices available to social-movement actors.[2] It includes "state and inter-state institutions (e.g., international organizations, formal channels of representation, the court system, etc.), non-state elite centres of power (e.g., parties, magnates, the media, moral authorities, etc.), and symbolic configurations (e.g., political legitimacy, trust of political institutions, public opinion, etc.)" (Alimi, Demetriou, & Bosi, 2015: 42). The second level is formed by Jihadi groups' intermediary, or meso-level, mobilising structures. These groups emerge from a broader social movement (with violent and non-violent components) and remain connected to a range of actors including competitors, opponents, and allies, among other armed groups and states. Jihadi groups must maintain their organisations, mobilise resources, and manage their external interactions with these actors amid changing environments. Last, Jihadi groups develop ideological principles that synthesize their understanding of their environments and guide their actions, which they communicate to their members and external actors. The interactions between these three levels of analysis shape Jihadi groups' trajectories, presenting constraints and opportunities that impact their evolution and inform the emergence and implementation of new political positions over time.

I chose to research specifically the meso-level of analysis. Like Thurston (2020), focusing on the meso-level helps to analyse Jihadis' internal dynamics, though field commanders—and not Jihadis as organisations—seem to be more important in his study of the Sahel. While the macro-, meso-, and micro-levels of analysis matter, this research specifically focuses on Jihadi groups' organisational structures and interconnections to other actors of the Syrian armed opposition. This perspective recognises the complex multi-level environments in which these groups operate, which shape their behaviours and ideas. I also argue that politicisation and radicalisation are not solely the product of macro-level variables such as state structures, economic inequality, and ethnic divisions. Focusing only on the macro-level would limit our understanding of the agency of armed opposition groups and fail to explain why different groups interpret the same macro-level factors differently. For example, it would fail to explain why some groups, like Ahrar al-Sham and HTS, politicised, while others, like ISIS / IS, radicalised during the same conflict. This research instead argues that both politicisation and radicalisation result from a combination of meso-level factors, including armed groups' organisational dynamics and evolving patterns of relations with other actors. Jihadi groups' organisational structures and interconnections mediate the impact of macro-level changes, which explains why different groups may react differently to the same external developments.[3] Additionally, these factors impact micro-level developments, including how individual Jihadis mobilise, socialise with the values and acceptable behaviour of their groups, and behave in armed conflicts. The behaviour of individual militants during armed conflicts, especially their use of violence, is indeed not only shaped by their personal choices but also by the organisational structures and networks to which they belong. These define, or may even fail to define, the scope of actions that are considered permissible or acceptable by their members.

My approach to Jihadi groups' organisational structures and their underlying networks additionally draws on social network analysis (SNA). SNA is increasingly popular for studying both real-life and online social networks, such as the real-life network connecting the 9/11 hijackers (Krebs, 2002). In addition to quantitative studies of network properties, SNA offers a qualitative perspective on the world through the relational ties that connect social actors.[4] This approach considers individual actors in relation to the content, direction, and type of connections linking them to one another. These relational ties serve as conduits for information, resources, and feedback mechanisms. For Jihadi groups, this perspective transcends a narrow focus on their "essential" or intrinsic properties, such as resources or ideologies, and instead promotes a more nuanced examination of the ever-evolving internal and external relational ties that shape their actions and interests. This perspective acknowledges that members of Jihadi groups can be embedded or connected to various networks, including the Islamist social movement, local communities, and other organisations. Both internal and external relational interactions shape Jihadi groups' perceptions, interests, and actions, regardless of their particular ideological preferences, and they play a vital role in structuring the development of their political preferences.

I finally build upon several sociological models of the emergence of social organisations (Padgett & Powell, 2012), which distinguish networks located at various levels, including local, regional, and international. These models have helped to graphically represent armed groups, such as the Haqqani network in Afghanistan (Rassler & Brown, 2011) and Palestinian armed groups in Lebanon (Parkinson, 2013, 2023; Hundman & Parkinson, 2019).[5] This conceptualisation recognises that members of armed groups are not just insurgents; they also come from specific geographic regions and families, as well as various intermediary social networks that include political groups, social movements, and politicised and non-politicised gatherings. This choice aligns with critical realism, which asserts that social structures, including Jihadi groups *as organisations*, have an independent causal impact on individuals. These structures are not simply the sum of their individual parts; they possess emergent properties that exert a distinct causal power

(Elder-Vass, 2010). This perspective contrasts with the mainstream reliance on methodological individualism in civil war studies, which focuses on the micro-level choices of rational individuals instead (Kalyvas, 2006; Balcells, 2017). In other words, the main difference between my approach and methodological individualism is the rejection of the latter view that the "influence of all social entities can be reduced to the influence of the individuals who are their members and that social entities as such have no causal significance over and above that of their aggregated members" (Elder-Vass, 2010: 144). This clarification is not just philosophical, as the research examines and compares the construction and impact of various meso-level social structures.

I used process tracing to reconstruct the organisational consolidation and political positioning of Syrian armed opposition groups over the years. By focusing on a single conflict, I could isolate macro-level variables and examine their internal dynamics and changing interactions with other actors. To reconstitute the emergence and subsequent evolution of the major Syrian armed groups, I systematically compared the trajectories of major armed groups as well as the evolution of their perceptions and actions over time, while also limiting biases and subsequent reinterpretations of past developments. Although I did not include most of the smaller units that quickly disappeared or were absorbed into larger units, to avoid delving into unnecessary details that would not alter the overall analysis, I examined the extent to which the developments of Ahrar al-Sham and HTS mirrored the evolution of other groups. Through this process, I was able to provide a comprehensive understanding of the choices of these armed groups and the resulting consequences.

My research, therefore, adopts a structuralist approach. Structuralist studies of armed conflicts typically involve a comparative analysis of cross-national factors that underlie civil wars. One prominent debate was the dominant "greed versus grievances" divide in the early 2000s, which questioned the macro-level factors that cause violence (Collier & Hoeffler, 2004; Cederman, Gleditsch, & Buhaug, 2013). The structuralist orientation of this research is narrower in scope. I acknowledge that armed groups encounter a diverse array of constraints and opportunities that they do not entirely control. Various factors, both domestic and international, along with these groups' own trajectories, significantly influence the choices of their leaders over time. Their agency is circumscribed by persistent structural constraints. Although I primarily focus on Ahrar al-Sham and Jabhat al-Nusra, I also compare these groups with other Syrian armed groups in order to (1) analyse the similarities and differences in the structural constraints faced by these groups and others, and (2) contextualize the decision-making capacity of their leaders within these constraints.

Notes

Chapter 1

1. The group was initially called Kata'ib Ahrar al-Sham (the Brigades of the Free Ones of the Levant) before renaming itself Harakat Ahrar al-Sham al-Islamiyya (the Islamic Movement of the Free Ones of the Levant), in 2013.
2. Its full name was Jabhat al-Nusra li-Ahl al-Sham min Mujahidi al-Sham fi Sahat al-Jihad (the Front of Support for the People of the Levant from the Muhajideen of the Levant in the Fields of Jihad).
3. The Salafi approach to Islam is defined by its specific understanding of the Islamic creed or core beliefs ('*aqida*) (Haykel, 2009; Meijer, 2009. See also Rougier, 2008). Jihadi Salafis are defined by their legitimisation of violence against Muslim leaders not applying Islamic law as well as Western countries denounced for their foreign policies (Wiktorowicz, 2006; Maher, 2016). This trend originated with the Egyptian and Syrian Jihadi groups active in the 1970s before expanding during the 1980s war in Afghanistan (Drevon, 2022). Ahrar al-Sham is Salafi but only partially Jihadi. Although some of its leaders and members were, at some point, closer to this ideological trend, this is not systematically true.
4. Kilcullen (2011), a counter-insurgency strategist who advised U.S. forces in Iraq and Afghanistan, explains how transnational combatants spread their ideas and practices, helping to transform local conflicts into a broader war with Western countries. See also Malet (2017), Byman (2019). On the role of Abdullah Azzam, see Hegghammer (2020).
5. See, e.g., Sageman, 2004; Moghadam, 2008; Kilcullen, 2011; Bakke, 2014; Lia, 2015; Mendelsohn, 2015; Warner et al., 2022.
6. I refer to these conflicts, including in Syria, as "armed conflicts" and not civil wars. The legal terminology describes these conflicts as "non-international armed conflicts," since they involve non-state armed groups; https://www.icrc.org/en/doc/resources/documents/article/other/armed-conflict-article-170308.htm.Though I draw on the literature on civil wars, this denomination is neither legal nor widely accepted by Syrians. Armed opposition groups refer to the conflict as a revolution, while the regime derides them as terrorists. Armed conflict is more neutral. It is also the term used in international humanitarian law.
7. See Drevon (2017).
8. This slogan was later replaced by "the people's revolution" (*thawrat al-sha'ab*) as the group continued its political maturation. See chapter 5.
9. Interviews with Abu Muhammad al-Jolani and Abul-Hassan al-Hamawi, respective general commander and military leader of HTS. Idlib. See also Drevn & Haenni, 2021; ICG, 2023.
10. Criticisms of the group's excessive violence were articulated by al-Qaeda's spokesman Adam Gadahn (Gadahn, 2011) in 2011, before its most publicised actions during the Iraqi and Syrian conflicts. Al-Qaeda leader Ayman al-Zawahiri (2017) added, in 2017, that the group was "struck with madness in excommunication and exceeded the limits of extremism."
11. See Brown, 2007; Fishman & Moghadam, 2010; Lahoud, 2010; Fishman, 2016; Drevon, 2022.
12. See Della Porta, 2013; Alimi, Bosi, & Demetriou, 2015.
13. Two major ideological concepts, the "(loyalty to Muslims and dissociation from non Muslims" (*al-wala' wal-bara'*) and "the non-reliance on the assistance of the infidels" ('*adam al-isti'ana bil-kuffar*), have justified Jihadi groups' opposition to external assistance by non-Muslims and Muslims who do not embrace the Salafi religious creed. See Wagemakers (2012: 147–165).
14. Interview with Abu Abdullah al-Shami, the higher religious authority of HTS. See also Drevon & Haenni, 2021.
15. Gerges, 2011: 34-42. It does not mean that there are no exceptions, including Islamic State (IS) (e.g., Hashim, 2018).
16. In some cases, like al-Qaeda in Afghanistan, Jihadis can rely in practice on personal allegiance combined with the intermarriage of their leaders and senior commanders to sustain themselves against the backdrop of strong ideological tenets.

17. The combination of ideological and personal differences is evidenced in primary testimonies by actors themselves (e.g., Hamid & Farrall, 2015) and in studies of their individual trajectories (e.g., Lia, 2009).
18. Interviews, Idlib.
19. See also Ashour (2021) for a focus on ISIS's military approach across provinces.
20. Which arguably characterise IS and al-Qaeda, respectively, according to Ahrar al-Sham and Jabhat al-Nusra / HTS leaders.
21. This theme has been central to my own discussions with an array of Islamist armed groups, including Ahrar al-Sham and Jabhat al-Nusra / HTS.
22. On the political thought of Ibn Tamiyya beyond excessive simplifications on the alleged association between the medieval scholar and modern violence, see Rapoport & Ahmed, 2010; Michot, 2011, 2012; Anjum, 2012; Hoover, 2019.
23. For instance, Gopal and Hodge argue that, in Syria, the margin of manoeuvre of foreign states was largely constrained by the nature of the pre-war networks upon which armed groups rely (e.g., Gopal & Hodge, 2021).
24. These two approaches are central to current debates on the prevention of violent extremism. They contend that *Jihadi* groups can be opposed through a combination of military means and de-legitimisation of their ideologies in alternative counter-narratives. They are more common than prospects of engagement and transformation, though exceptions exist (e.g., Dudouet & Göldner-Ebenthal, 2020).
25. Many Syrian opponents, especially those who oppose Jabhat al-Nusra / HTS, repeatedly emphasise Jolani's personality, including his pragmatism, to explain his group's actions. The leading Salafi Jihadi intellectual Abu Muhammad al-Maqdisi similarly denounces Jolani for exploiting the Jihadi trend to achieve his immediate military objectives, before rejecting it when convenient. Interview with Abu Muhammad al-Maqdisi.
26. For a similar approach, but more focused on Jihadi commanders than Jihadi organisations per se, see Thurston (2020).
27. Many groups remained in their localities throughout the conflict. They often switched loyalty without meaningful change. At best, they received additional material support and only changed their names as they joined the Free Syrian Army, Ahrar al-Sham, or Jabhat al-Nusra among other large entities. Interviews with several representative of smaller military brigades.
28. Embeddedness in local networks also shapes how external threats are framed and addressed by individuals (Shesterinina, 2016). Local ties play a crucial role in understanding the emergence of extreme patterns of violence, such as the genocide in Rwanda (Fuji, 2009). Rumors also wield a considerable influence over civilian perceptions of the strength of both the state and rebel forces, which are intricately woven into the ethnic demography and trusted network structures within villages (Lewis, 2020).
29. Most research on Jihadis focus on their leaders; see the books on Abu Mus'ab al-Suri (Lia, 2009), Abu Mus'ab al-Zarqawi (Warrick, 2015), Abdullah Anas (Anas & Hussein, 2019), Abdullah Azzam (Hegghammer, 2020), and Osama bin Laden (Scheuer, 2011).
30. Chapter 5 expends on this particular theme. This is very clear in the case of Hamas, which lost most of its leaders over time but survived thanks to its institutional strength (Gunning, 2007). On the impact of leadership decapitation, see also Jordan (2019) and Price (2019). See also Bacon & Grimm (2022) on the impact of new types of leaders on militant groups.
31. Jabhat al-Nusra is more difficult to judge, as it remained under the control of its founding leader. The group's institutionalisation became more evident when it started to rule northwest Syria (Drevon & Haenni, 2021).
32. This research largely aligns with Lacher's (2020) and Parkinson's (2023) emphasis on militant networks and their connections to local dynamics, but I focus more thoroughly on armed groups' organisational dynamics, a dimension that may not hold as much centrality in their contexts.
33. See chapter 4.
34. See Moloney (2007).
35. See Sageman (2004, 2008) and Hoffman (2008). See also Gartenstein-Ross & Barr (2018).
36. Armed groups occasionally decide to change their internal structuring by de-centralising their military forces, as the IRA in the 1980s, or conversely by reimposing a stronger internal hierarchy, like the FARC around the same time, depending on the circumstances. See Moloney (2007) and Gutiérrez-Sanín (2018).
37. Interviews with several local units that switched organisational affiliations over the years.

38. The comparison between Ahrar al-Sham and Jabhat al-Nusra suggests that they enjoyed relatively strong horizontal ties between their leaders, with Ahrar al-Sham benefiting from stronger ties to local communities at first. But they institutionalised very differently. Ahrar al-Sham generally integrated pre-existing factions into its early organisational structures while Jabhat al-Nusra promoted a more centralised process of consolidation. Both groups also developed diverging strategic relations to their external environments despite overlapping pre-war networks.
39. Asal et al. (2022) use a similar focus on armed groups' relation to the population and states to account for their use of violence.
40. The annex elaborates these methodological guidelines.
41. As mentioned by Lacher (2011) on Libya, "social embeddedness means that armed groups do not exclusively, or even primarily, follow their internal organizational logics, or the individual interests of their leaders. They also respond to obligations towards other members of the community they are embedded in." "This phenomenon is quite common during times of war, especially when armed groups emerge out of local communities without forming a formal hierarchy (or broadly replicating traditional village structures)." A study conducted by the International Committee of the Red Cross (ICRC) (2020) has identified numerous cases, including the Democratic Republic of Congo's Mai Mai group, where armed factions formed along these patterns. Daly's (2016) study of violence after civil wars is also relevant to the distinctions between the first and second ideal-types. She argues that armed groups that recruit locally can foster a stronger connection with their communities, which mitigates violence following the conclusion of conflicts, in contrast with groups that recruit non-locally.
42. This is despite real efforts to institutionalise them in a common framework when they regrouped to the north of Syria after 2018, under the Syrian National Army framework.
43. On these processes in social movement studies, see Della Porta (2013: 204–234).
44. Interview with Egyptian foreign fighters in Cairo.
45. I focus on relatively large entities. Smaller groups can also develop around an authoritarian strongman and cult-like dynamics instead of institutionalising internally. This was less the case in Syria, since these groups were not able to survive the loss of their leaders, contrary to more institutionalised armed groups.
46. I use "regime" instead of "government" or "state" to describe Syrian official authorities. Although the term "regime" often intends to erode the legitimacy of ruling authorities, this choice is purely factual. Regimes are a "set of rules, procedures, and understandings which govern relations between the state and society in a particular country" (Macridis, 1986). The Syrian conflict never opposed the government or the state to the opposition. The armed opposition is not fighting the Syrian state as a concept (with the potential exception of Kurdish armed groups, which are not my focus), nor is it merely changing the government or its president. The opposition is committed to the overthrow of the ruling regime and its replacement with its own political alternative.
47. Foreign jihadis, including Abu Muhammad al-Maqdisi, Abu Qatada al-Falastini, and others repeatedly tried to convince IS to cease its attacks against other armed groups, to no avail.
48. Relational approaches to radicalisation, such as Della Porta's (2013), highlight different mechanisms underpinning militants' growing insolation, such as competitive escalation with their opponents, activation of militant networks, organizational compartmentalization, action militarization, ideological encapsulation, and militant enclosure.
49. Salafism prioritises a strict adherence to what it considers how Islam was practiced during the time of the Prophet Muhammad and his immediate successors. Salafis reject religious innovations (*bida'*) that did not exist in the early days of Islam and emphasize instead the key importance of pure monotheism (*tawhid*). The foundational beliefs of Salafis, their creed (*'aqida*), hence set them apart from other Muslims due to their tendency to exhibit greater reluctance towards interpreting the meanings of God's attributes (*al-asma wa sifat*).
50. The separation of these trends is often a subject of debate, and research on Salafism regularly proposes new typologies. Yet, this separation in three main trends is valuable tools for understanding the broad spectrum of approaches to political action within Salafism. Salafis also commonly refer to these categories in practice, recognising their utility despite their inherent fluidity. So, while acknowledging that the distinctions between these trends are not always rigid and can vary depending on circumstances, we can still employ them to delineate general orientations within Salafist thought and practice.

51. This is the definition of Della Porta and Diani (2013) applied to Jihadi groups. I applied the term "Jihadi social movement" in another article (Drevon, 2017). In a similar vein, Hamming (2022) refers to the "Sunni Jihadi movement."
52. See also Wagemakers (2012) and Lav (2012).
53. Internal conflicts regarding tactical and strategic matters manifested through divergent perspectives between key figures. Abu Musab al-Suri and Abu Qatada al-Falastini held differing views on Algeria, while Khattab, a prominent Saudi militant, and bin Laden found themselves at odds about prioritising engagement in Chechnya over confronting the United States. Additionally, Abu Musab al-Zarqawi and abu Muhammad al-Maqdisi grappled with discord surrounding the excessive use of violence in Iraq. See also Moghadam & Fishman (2010).
54. Thurston (2017) argues that the GIA is really the first group that emphasises the primacy of Salafism.
55. See, e.g., Wickham, 2004; Clark, 2006; Schwedler, 2006, 2007; Wegner & Pellicer, 2009; Brown, 2012; Cavatorta & Merone, 2013; Pahwa, 2017.
56. This is not the case simply for Islamist groups, as the Provisional Irish Republican Army (IRA) demonstrates (Whiting, 2018).
57. Even in the case of Hamas and Hizbullah in Palestine and Lebanon, political integration was largely driven by a favourable political environment that changed their external incentives. See, e.g., Alagha, 2006; Gunning, 2007; Berti, 2013.
58. On the rationales for state support, see Bapat (2012) and Maoz & San-Akca (2012) for the relations between state rivalry and support for armed groups. See also Byman (2005) in the specific case of so-called terrorist groups.
59. Governance refers to the "range of structures and practices, both formal and informal, that rebels develop as part of a broader governance arrangement to interact with the civilian population and other unarmed actors" (Mampilly & Stewart, 2020: 3). See also Kasfir (2015) and Stewart (2021).
60. Most assumptions on the presumed connections between Ahrar al-Sham and al-Qaeda emphasise the role of an Ahrar al-Sham commander, Abu Khaled al-Suri, who was previously connected to a wide range of groups in Afghanistan, including al-Qaeda.

Chapter 2

1. Referring to non-Islamist Syrian armed groups as secular is a matter of debate. Most of these groups did not describe themselves as secular in Arabic (*'almani*). Although non-Islamist Syrian armed groups did not necessarily embrace Islamist political agendas, some of them opted for Islamic names and had conservative viewpoints, influenced by the composition of their membership, inter-factional competition, and the influence of their external backers. Self-identifying as secular can also pose a challenge for any opposition groups considering the Syrian regime's proclaimed commitment to secularism. See also Sakhi (2023 : 150–177), on the Free Syrian Army's religious trainings and use of clerics internally.
2. Gopal and Hodge (2021) differentiate several types of pre-war networks (including those linked to the Muslim Brotherhood, activist Salafis, loyalist Salafis, Jihadis, tribal, and liberal) underpinning the Syrian armed opposition and their consequences on their mobilisation after 2011.
3. See also Weismann, 2000, 2001; Lenfant, 2008; Al-Haj, 2013; Lefèvre, 2013: 3–42; Conduit, 2019: 21–40.
4. On the construction of the Syrian State before independence, including the role of France, see Provence, 2005; Van Dam, 2011; Neep, 2012; McHugo, 2014; Rey, 2018.
5. On the ramifications of pre-2011 regime-led large-scale violence as a governance mechanism, see Ismail (2018).
6. Some of the most important research on this topic was written by Batatu (1981, 1999).
7. For a historical retrospective of the role of minorities, see Van Dam (2011, 2017). See also Bou Nassif (2015)
8. On internal divergences between Alawis from "inside" and from the "coast," see Goldsmith (2015).
9. For recent studies on the group, see Pargeter (2011), Lefèvre (2013), Díaz (2017), and Conduit (2019). On the Syrian Sunni clergy more specifically, see Pierret (2013).
10. On the position of the Islamists on the failed uprising, see Larivière (2021).
11. For a list of notable Muslim Brotherhood members who went to Afghanistan, see Conduit, 2019: 232–237.

12. According to multiple interviews with a range of armed groups members, from Ahrar al-Sham, Jabhat al-Nusra, and also factions affiliated to the Free Syrian Army.
13. Egypt similarly had to accommodate Islamist charitable activities (Brooke, 2019), although the role played by the Muslim Brotherhood in Egypt was far more substantial than in Syria (e.g., Wickham, 2013).
14. On Islamic charities, clergies, and Islamic movement, see Lenfant (2008), Pierret & Selvik (2009), Donker (2013), Pierret (2013a, 2013b), Conduit (2019).
15. See Wagemakers (2012: 101–119) on additional differences between *sahwa* criticism and Salafi Jihadi positions, and Hassan (2016c) examines the impact on the *sahwa* on what would ultimately become IS.
16. Both are prominent medieval scholars favoured by contemporary Salafis.
17. Al-Albani is one of the three main Salafi religious scholars of the 20th century, known for his scholarship on hadith (Lacroix, 2009). Al-Tartussi is a Syrian thinker previously associated with Jihadi Salafism.
18. Tawheed is the concept of Islamic monotheism, which is arguably one of the core tenets of the Salafi approach to Islam (Maher, 2016; Wagemakers, 2016: 27–59).
19. Numerous interviews with Syrian militants active in a range of armed groups.
20. On Jihadi Salafism in Syria, see also Khatib (2018).
21. Interviews with former Islamist prisoners.
22. Numerous interviews with independent Islamists as well as members of Ahrar al-Sham and HTS suggest the existence of the two positions. Some individuals assert that they formed a small congregation of like-minded Islamists that met occasionally, while others posit that they never intermingled with anybody else.
23. This feature is similar to other countries in the region, including Jordan (Wiktorowicz, 2001). On the salience of Salafism in an armed conflict like Syria, see also Lund (2012) and ICG (2012).
24. Abu 'Isa is a militant who claimed that he re-created the historical Caliphate at the end of the war against the USSR in Afghanistan before traveling to London. *Irja* is a concept widely debated in Islamic law about the role of belief and deeds, and whether believing in Islam is sufficient to be considered Muslim.
25. On the influence of militant or *haraki* Salafism in Ahrar al-Sham, see Pierret (2016).
26. So-called *madkhali* Salafis might be more the exception than the rule, as they are loyal to Muslim rulers and strongly oppose any rebellion. The Syrian regime was also considered favourably by some mainstream Islamists for its position on the Palestinian issue.
27. These religious scholars are medieval scholars not necessarily associated with Salafism.
28. These two are arguably the most influential Salafi Jihadi scholars worldwide. On al-Maqdisi, see Wagemakers (2012).
29. On the early phase, see Abouzeid (2018), Yassin-Kassab & Al-Shami (2018), Mazhur (2021), Bishara (2022).
30. For first-hand testimonies, see Pearlman (2017). Pearlman (2016) also explores how civilians managed to overcome their fear and engaged in protests, despite the risks.
31. On revolutionary processes, see also Tilly, 1977; Skocpol, 1979; Goodwin, 2001. An important contribution of the study of revolution in its fourth wave is provided by Lawson (2019).
32. See for instance Simon (2023).
33. A comparison between Middle Eastern and North African regimes expose two central structural features underpinning the practicalities and outcomes of the Arab uprisings: (1) the presence of economic rents, and (2) a previous successful hereditary succession (Brownlee, Masoud & Reynolds, 2015). Other structural differences include the centralised versus decentralised nature of executive power in Egypt and Syria (Stacher, 2012).
34. See also Bou Nassif's work (2020) on how the Syrian regime implemented coup-proofing strategies in the 1960s, which left a substantial institutional imprint that significantly shaped the military's response to the 2011 population uprising. See also Droz-Vincent (2020).
35. For instance, in Egypt, the protestors largely drew on pre-existing networks that were previously involved in the 2000s, including in solidarity for the Palestinian cause (Gunning & Baron, 2015).
36. On Bashar al-Assad's regime, see Ziser (2007), Leverett (2005), Lesch (2013). On the marginalisation of the Baath Party, see Belhadj (2013).
37. The so-called Damascus Spring followed Bashar al-Assad's seizure of the presidency, when Syrian intellectuals promoted new forums to discuss political and social questions, and

expressed new political demands to the regime, including the end of the state of emergency, prisoner release, and the opening of political space

38. On the alliance with Iran, see Goodarzi (2009). See also Scheller (2014) on Syria's foreign policy. On the external dimension of the war, see Phillips (2016).
39. More on Russia's perceptions of Western interventions and policies in Charap, Treyger, & Geist, 2019; Hamilton, Miller, & Stein, 2020; Borshchevskaya, 2021.
40. See Abouzeid (2018).
41. Interviews with militants active early on in the conflict. Many videos were initially published on YouTube, though most were subsequently removed for featuring violence.
42. Veterans of other jihad, including Iraq, provided critical assistance in the growing sophistication of the insurgency, especially in the manufacturing of improvised explosive device (IED). Interviews with a range of insurgents.
43. On a similar explanation to the fragmentation of the insurgency, see Walther and Pedersen (2020). Fjelde and Nilsson (2018) add that stronger societal networks create structural barriers against the proliferation of many armed groups.
44. On Salafi internal debates on jihad in Syria, see Ismail (2021: 122–127).
45. On the role of connectivity between communities on insurgent mobilisation, see also Sarbahi (2021).
46. Interviews with several Ahrar al-Sham leaders and commanders.
47. On prison experience, see chapter 5.
48. Abul-Kheir is incidentally the brother of Abu Abdullah al-Shami, who was mentioned previously.
49. Interviews with armed groups commanders who split from several other factions for this reason.
50. Abu Anas mentioned that, initially, Ahrar al-Sham only had a Skype contact through its Ghouta sub-group, for instance.
51. Interviews with the heads of two small brigades that joined other groups before joining Ahrar al-Sham.
52. Many of these policies are examined by Balanche (2006a, 2011, 2018).
53. The next chapter expands on this.
54. By 2016, only a dozen armed opposition groups could be described as "power-brokers" in different regions. Their size and influence (Cafarella & Casagrande, 2016: 12–13) was substantially larger than the hundreds of groups that still remained after a few years of conflict (e.g., Cafarella & Casagrande, 2015: 4–7).
55. This is particularly the case of the early local brigades that often adopted the name Liwa Shuhada (the Brigade of the Martyrs of) followed by the name of their village.
56. This comparison explicitly focuses on the so-called dependent variable, since it aims to compare the trajectories of the most important groups instead of analysing the factors underpinning armed groups' survival or disappearance per se.
57. On the early armed groups, see also Hudhaifa (2021: 110–128).
58. On the rise and fall of the Faruq Brigades, its recomposition, and the role of foreign actors, see Abouzeid (2018).
59. See chapter 4.
60. Parts of Faruq later became the Hazm movement (Harakat Hazm), which received significant American support. See also Baczko et al., 2018: 112–117.
61. See chapter 3.
62. The group would ultimately, in 2019, be expelled by the successor of Jabhat al-Nusra, HTS, Cf. chapter 4.
63. Interviews with former members of Liwa Dawud.
64. Interview with a spokesman for the group conducted in Baab al-Hawa.
65. Interview with Islam Alloush.
66. Ibid.
67. The final section of this chapter expands on some of these debates.
68. The group's full name was initially Jabhat al-Nusra li Ahl al-Sham min Mujahidi al-Sham fi Sahat al-Jihad (the Front of Support of the People of the Levan from the Mujahideen of the Levant on the Fields of Jihad).
69. Interview with Abd al-Rahim 'Atun.
70. The interview was also published by International Crisis Group in Khalifa (2020).
71. Al-Jolani repeated this point in private interviews, which he mentioned in a public interview to al-Jazeera in 2013 as well.

72. The group started its military campaign with suicide bombings against Syrian security forces and intelligence offices in Damascus and Aleppo in early 2012, which resulted in civilian casualties as well.
73. One of them, Rami Dalati, argued that most former Islamist prisoners joined Ahrar al-Sham and not Jabhat al-Nusra or IS.
74. In his first televised interview, Jabhat al-Nusra leader Abu Muhammad al-Jolani (2013) argued that the expansion of the armed opposition to rural areas transformed the group, as it required a change of modus operandi.
75. For a study on its early days and internal Moroccan debates, see Caillet (2014).
76. Interview
77. The group was also connected to Egyptian militants, according to my field research in Cairo in 2012. See also the important coverage of European foreign fighters by Wassim Nasr, for example, France 24 2020, 2023.
78. Chapter 3.
79. Chapter 4.
80. Arab Sunni groups occasionally recruited among Kurds, including Ahrar al-Sham and its Kurdish sub-group.
81. Jabhat al-Nusra opened a political bureau only in January 2017, when it created HTS. Cf. chapter 5. On so-called rebel diplomacy, see also Huang (2016a).
82. See chapter 5.
83. This front is different from Jamal Maarouf's front, which emerged in 2013.
84. See chapter 3.
85. Abu Yazan al-Shami, a leading Ahrar al-Sham thinker, would later apologise for this. See chapter 5.
86. As in Ahrar al-Sham's first leader Hassan Abud's (2013b) first interview to al-Jazeera. The group's official position on Alawis does not mean that individual leaders did not express more hostile positions in a personal capacity. The term "Nusayri" originates from Ibn Nusayr al-Numayri, the initial inspiration behind this religious sect, though it carries a negative connotation.
87. According to interviews and leaks of internal documents.

Chapter 3

1. Many armed conflicts are described as either insurgencies or guerrilla operations, while in reality, they more closely resemble conventional warfare. This is partially informed by post–Cold War developments (Kalyvas & Balcells, 2010; Balcells & Kalyvas, 2013).
2. The next chapter considers the role of foreign support for the armed opposition more specifically.
3. More details are analysed in chapter 4.
4. Chapter 4 elaborates on this development.
5. On this issue, see also Goya, 2017; Charap, Treyger, & Geist, 2019; Hamilton, Miller, & Stein, 2020; Jones, 2020.
6. A recent testimony by a defecting Saudi major general argues that the Saudi Crown Prince Muhammad bin Salman encouraged the Russian intervention when he was the Minister of Defence (Borger, 2020).
7. On this theme, see Balcells & Kalyvas, 2013.
8. There were smaller armed opposition–held pockets, including in Qalamoun and Zabadani, which had an important role for the armed opposition considering their location. But this analysis does not examine them independently, as it primarily focuses on larger, more representative, regions to synthesise general patterns of development.
9. For a testimony of the early days of the armed opposition in al-Ghouta, especially its internal diversity and localism, see al-Dik & Bontemps, 2016.
10. Interview Islam Alloush.
11. Jaysh al-Islam also attacked other groups, such as Faylaq al-Rahman, but those were local entities without influence elsewhere, so they are not the focus of this analysis.
12. The main groups were Ajnad al-Sham, Faylaq al-Rahman, Ahrar al-Sham, Jabhat al-Nusra, and several smaller factions.
13. On Ahrar al-Sham, see also its partial integration in Faylaq al-Rahman (Salah, 2015) and joining of Liwa Fajr al-Umma (Ahrar al-Sham, n.d.a).
14. On the impact of geographic divisions between local factions and the regime's strategy, see chapter 4 and Lund (2018).

15. For a primary testimony on the siege, see al-Faris (2015).
16. Jabhat al-Nusra notably attacked Harakat Hazm in the enclave, a Free Syrian Army group that it accused of collaborating with the United States. Cf. chapter 4.
17. Cf. chapter 4.
18. Liwa Shuhada' al-Yarmouk formed in summer 2012. It was initially in the Southern Front before the exacerbation of tensions with other groups. The group gradually signalled pro-IS inclinations before excommunication of local institutions and developing its own IS-inspired model (Al-Tamimi, 2015b).
19. Interviews with several Ahrar al-Sham leaders. See also al-Jazeera (2016).
20. Interviews with humanitarian actors who were in Raqqa at the time.
21. Several interviews with Ahrar al-Sham leaders over the years.
22. On IS's governance strategy, see also Caris & Reynolds (2014) and Zelin (2016). See also Rosenblatt & Kilcullen, 2019.
23. See chapter 4.
24. Interviews with local witnesses.
25. Interviews with several former foreign fighters.
26. On the Kurdish experiment in Syria, see also ICG, 2014; Abdullah, Ayboga, Flach, Graeber, & Knapp, 2016; Schmidinger, 2018; Allsopp & van Wilgenburg, 2019; Haenni & Quesnay, 2020.
27. On the contested connection between the YPG and the PKK, see Haenni & Quesnay (2020).
28. On smaller scale local experiments, see e.g., Munif, 2017; Gopal, 2018.
29. The early presence of other groups like Jabhat Thuwar Suriyya and Ahfad al-Rasul in several Syrian regions in the first stage of the conflict does not contradict this argument, as these groups quickly overstretched, as argued in chapter 2.
30. Private discussion with Abu Maria al-Qahtani.
31. Chapter 4 expands on this theme.
32. See also Abdul-Ahad (2013).
33. Interview with Abu Abdullah al-Shami.
34. Interview with Abu Muhammad al-Jolani.
35. See also Khalifa (2020).
36. It will be followed by a strategy of territorialisation in 2017. Chapter 5. See also Berti (2020).
37. For instance, Sami al-'Uraydi became the group's new mufti at the time.
38. See also Jabhat al-Nusra's opposition to armed groups supported by the United States and the seizure of their equipment in Gutman (2015) and Torbati (2015).
39. See chapter 4.
40. See chapter 4.
41. See e.g., Baczko et al. (2018: 112–117). For an example of internal institutionalisation, in the case of Zinki, see Al-Tamimi (2020a, 2020b).
42. Other smaller military units like Tajamu' Fastaqim in Aleppo evolved similarly. These groups are not covered in this research, but one can also refer to Ibrahim (2021: 136–172) for additional details.
43. Chapter 4 expands on the last alliances.
44. On Jaysh al-'Izza's own system of alliance, see also Puxton (2017).
45. For a detailed study of armed groups' alliances, consolidation, and mergers during the conflict, see Ibrahim (2021).
46. For a first-hand testimony of these negotiations and their outcomes, see al-Atrash (2017).
47. Although al-Fajr al-Islamiyya is not solely composed of foreigners, as the group includes a substantial number of Syrians around Aleppo. More details on its politico-religious vision are available in its charter (jabhat ansar al-din, 2018).
48. For a brief retrospective of the Turkistan Islamic Party from Afghanistan to Syria, including the group's relation to the Taliban and al-Qaeda, see Hussein (2016b).
49. More information in chapter 4.
50. Interviews with commanders of local groups, and with humanitarian actors engaged in negotiations with them.
51. On the local councils, their divergences, and the impact of external Western assistance, see also Mukhopadhyay & Howe (2023). Interviews with local city councils.
52. On the local councils, see also Gharibah et al., 2017; Khalaf, 2015.
53. Interviews with a wide range of local council organisers.
54. Interviews with many civilians who played a role in local councils.
55. Interviews with locals living in Idlib province.

56. Interviews with local councils aligned with Jabhat al-Nusra.
57. Interviews with local humanitarian coordinators.
58. For a rare glimpse over the imposition of parts of Islamic law in Aleppo under the opposition, see Sly (2013).
59. An array of judicial edicts of the group's courts have been retrieved by Al-Tamimi (2015a).
60. Interview with a former judge involved in some of these mechanisms.
61. The positivisation of Islamic law corrupts it essence, in this view, since *shari'a* becomes akin to a positivist law (*al-qanun al-wad'i*) that Salafis consider human made and therefore non-Islamic. Ahrar al-Sham would nonetheless adopt the Unified Arab Code in 2017; cf. chapter 5.
62. Interview with a former judge.
63. Interview with Ibrahim Shasho.
64. This strategy is evident when tracing Syria's armed opposition alliance systems quantitatively, in which Ahrar al-Sham features prominently (see Gade et al., 2019).
65. The communiqué is available in Lund (2013a: 15).
66. Chapter 5. See also Tarsha, 2018.
67. Movement is here a reference to the group's use of *haraka* in Arabic to emphasise that Ahrar al-Sham was no longer an assortment of military brigades, as opposed to a larger entity pursuing complementary objectives, including non-military.
68. Interviews with several individuals close to Ahrar al-Sham.
69. See chapter 5.
70. Interviews.
71. Interviews with Syrians who lived under several armed groups as well as ISIS.
72. Interviews.
73. See al-Jazeera (2016).
74. Interviews with humanitarians in Aleppo.
75. Interview with several local armed group leader from Aleppo as well as civilians close to the armed opposition.
76. Cf. chapter 5.
77. See chapter 5.
78. See chapter 5.

Chapter 4

1. Interviews with a range of individuals who participated in the early militarization of the uprising among several armed opposition groups.
2. For example, a Dutch foreign fighter testified that he trained different groups before joining IS in 2014 (Nieuwsuur, 2014).
3. The first proposition to arm the opposition to the United States was even rejected (Simon, 2023).
4. For a more comprehensive analysis of the U.S. programme's assistance to different types of groups, see also Plana (2021).
5. See chapter 3.
6. According to Hasan Dugheim, who provided religious guidance to Free Syrian Army groups, ISIS initially claimed that they only opposed specific factions for being un-Islamic while claiming that the group did not attack other armed groups. A local member of Suqur al-Sham similarly argued that IS would tell them that they were brothers, and that ISIS only opposed other groups. ISIS's objectives were to target each group individually to impede or at least delay a collective backlash.
7. Several interviews with individuals involved in the provision of weaponry to armed opposition groups through the MOM in Turkey.
8. The group's new leadership notably refused to resume the initiative. Cf. chapter 5.
9. This group is different from Ahrar al-Sham's Syrian Liberation Front mentioned in chapter 2.
10. According to numerous interviews with armed groups members as well as humanitarians who worked in northwest Syria at the time
11. Interviews with armed groups commanders and judges who contributed to these mechanisms.
12. Interviews with local armed groups present in the northwest
13. Interviews with independent armed groups.
14. Interviews with an array of international organisations and NGOs.
15. Interview with a commander of a Free Syrian Army affiliated group.
16. For a discussion on possible means to alleviate the risks associated with the provision of MANPAD, see Groll (2016). The absence of provision of anti-aerial weapons is not merely

because of Jabhat al-Nusra's ties to al-Qaeda. A major reason is also a non-decisive commitment of Western countries to effectively topple the regime, as opposed to merely weakening it.
17. According to independent testimonies from local residents, stronger Islamic norms initially spread in the city of Idlib when the armed coalition took over. Most women started to wear the face veil, for instance. The situation would gradually change over time.
18. See also Lister (2016a) and Heller (2017a).
19. See also Bellamy (2022).
20. Interviews with commanders of independent armed groups.
21. A pro–al-Qaeda group that split from HTS. More information on the group's creation is in chapter 5.
22. For primary testimonies, see Harush, 2016; Muzmajir, 2016; al-Shaykh, 2016c; Al-Atrash, 2017.
23. Interviews with Islamists and non-Islamists commanders.
24. Many internal testimonies on these debates were retrieved and published online by Al-Tamimi. See the last part as well as links to previous documents in Al-Tamimi (2019).
25. For a primary testimony, see the views of Abu Abdullah al-Shami (Atun, 2016a).
26. Some simply split from Jabhat Fath al-Sham or remained in the group but refused to join HTS when it was created six month later (Hussein, 2016c; Lister, 2016d). Opponents include most Jordanians.
27. The following chapter explores these divisions in detail. See chapter 5.
28. The creation of Jaysh al-Ahrar is explored more thoroughly in the next chapter. See chapter 5.
29. Ahrar al-Sham denounced the war of communiqués launched to pressure the group (Ahrar al-Sham, 2017c).
30. On the role of the leadership council, see also Hussein (2017h).
31. Interview with a leading member of Ahrar al-Sham's Consultative Council.
32. On the SDF and IS in the East, see Haenni and Quesnay (2020).
33. On the PKK's strategies in Turkey and Syria, see ICG (2017).
34. See also the testimony of a local activist on the last days of al-Ghouta in Al-Shami (2018).
35. Several small factions, some of whom affiliated to the Free Syrian Army umbrella like Abdul Baset al-Sarout's group, insisted at the time that the factions in the north should open the front lines in support of the South, but large armed groups in the north (including Ahrar al-Sham and HTS) did not do so, as this could have endangered the whole province under their control.
36. See Arango (2017) and Chulov (2017).
37. On Turkish control in the north, see Stein, Abouzahr, & Komar (2017). On these groups, see also Tsurkov (2019b).
38. On Turkish policies in the northeast, especially after the American withdrawal announcement, see ICG (2019b).
39. Farghali's telegram channel. Farghali usually adopts more uncompromising ideological positions than does the HTS leadership. Abu Abdullah al-Shami, HTS's highest religious authority, recognised this point in an interview in Idlib, insisting that HTS's positions are expressed in its Sharia Council and that Farghali's positions are his own. See his interpretation to the nascent Turkish influence in Idlib in Heller (2020).
40. See chapter 5.
41. Interview.
42. On the group's short-lived history, see Abu Rumman & Abu Haniyeh (2021).
43. According to interviews with its organisers, HTS used its military domination to vet the participants in the conference.
44. Interview with several commanders of local armed groups.
45. Interview with a military commander who initially joined HTS.
46. Interviews with several Ahrar al-Sham's commanders.
47. Several groups of foreign fighters regularly expressed their support for HTS for unifying the opposition and bringing stability to the province (e.g., n.m. 2020).
48. A communiqué initially mentioned Ahrar al-Sham's dissolution from its strongholds in the southern province (Ahrar al-Sham, 2017d), though the group latter insisted that Ahrar al-Sham group was not dissolved, as only the fighters who refused to submit to HTS's authority left the area, before returning a few months later in the next round of fighting. This was confirmed by their own communiqués, which denounced HTS's seizure of their heavy weapons, and stated that they departed, as they refused to remain under HTS-supported government (Thuwar Sahl al-Ghab, 2019).
49. Interview.
50. Interview with Abu Muhammad al-Jolani.

51. Interview with individuals close to Hurras al-Din.
52. Interview with Abu 'Abdullah al-Shami.
53. On this theme, see also Zelin (2023).
54. Interview with Abul-Hasan al-Hamawi and Abu Muhammad al-Jolani.

Chapter 5

1. Abul-Waleed al-Masri and Leah Farrall (2015) portray the emergence of the "Jalalabad school" in exile during the early 1990s, which was detached from its natural constituency, prone to radicalism, and zealous about immediate military action.
2. On the ideological impact of foreign fighters, see Bakke (2014).
3. The impact of long-term historical legacies on political violence is rarely analysed as such in existing literature, which often focuses on immediate developments. But long-term economic and political transformations, let alone a history of violence in the past, can shape the trajectories of insurgencies that emerged only several decades later, as demonstrated in Europe (Sánchez-Cuenca, 2019).
4. This point is important since, as argued in note 12 of chapter 1, many analysts emphasised the role of Abu Khaled to denounce Ahrar al-Sham's alleged ties to al-Qaeda.
5. On the Muslim Brotherhood background of many early Ahrar al-Sham leaders, see also the documentary of al-Jazeera (2016).
6. Both review in a book and a series of videos the story of the Salafi Jihadi trend, and trace the influence and role of the Muslim Brotherhood, although they express a real opposition to the organisation.
7. See chapter 2.
8. The most comprehensive study is presented by Warrick (2015).
9. Interviews with his close associates.
10. On the association between armed groups' political indoctrination and their controlled use of violence, see Hoover Green (2017, 2018).
11. See also a rebuttal of Jihadi groups' extremism by a leading Jabhat al-Nusra leader (Al-qahtani, no date).
12. Interview with Iyad al-Sha'ar.
13. Taha is often wrongly considered close to al-Qaeda, or even a member of the organisation, while he never joined bin Laden according to my own interview with him and many of his associates in Egypt.
14. Interviews with Ahrar al-Sham bureaucrats who dealt with foreign organisations and humanitarians.
15. There is anecdotal evidence that this sub-group implemented, at least once, Islamic legal punishment on Syrians who missed the Friday prayer (France 24, 2014).
16. The impact and role of these cultural idioms is increasingly studied as such in the literature, see Hegghammer (2017).
17. Multiple interviews with Islamists and non-Islamists involved with the armed opposition.
18. Interview with Abu Muhammad al-Jolani.
19. Interviews with several Ahrar al-Sham leaders.
20. Wagemakers (2012: 147–164).
21. Jaeger et al. (2015) argue that, in the case of Palestine, outbidding between Islamist and non-Islamist factions do not target the same public.
22. Some of the main Salafi Jihadi arguments against the Muslim Brotherhood were articulated by al-Zawahiri (1988) himself.
23. The explosion prompted numerous accusations implicating foreign countries or groups like ISIS and Jabhat al-Nusra. However, evidence suggests that the presence of explosives within the compounds caused the explosion, rather than external involvement.
24. See also the testimony of Ahrar al-Sham's leaders (Tarsha, 2018), individuals close to the group (al-Shaykh, 2016e; Abu Sayyaf, 2016a; Al-Ghunami, 2017), and analysis (Abazeid, 2015a).
25. Abu Fath Farghali, who later left Ahrar al-Sham, says that he wrote an opinion against joining the initiative to Abu Jaber (al-Farghali, 2020b).
26. On the group's legitimisation of the flag, see Ahrar al-Sham (n.d.c).
27. Multiple interviews with Syrian analysts in the northwest.
28. Interview with Husam Tarsha.
29. On the participation of Syrian fighters in Libya, see Wehrey (2020).
30. Interviews with individuals close to the new leadership.

Chapter 6
1. See for instance Stampnitzky (2013).

Annex: Methodology and Sources
1. The most noticeable case occurred in January 2017, when HTS and Ahrar al-Sham were vying for the allegiance of one another's sub-brigades in an online battle of communiqués designed to suggest that each of them was about to prevail.
2. For important discussions on some of these characteristics, see McAdam, 1982; Meyer, 2004; Tarrow, 2011; Alimi, Demetriou, & Bosi, 2015.
3. For a recent review of organisational studies of political violence, see Phillips (2019).
4. This dimension has been relatively marginalised by the growing influence of quantitative research in SNA, though valuable exceptions exist (e.g., Parkinson, 2013; Kenney, 2018).
5. These studies build upon a pioneering research on the Renaissance in Florence (Padgett & McLean, 2006).

Bibliography

Primary Sources

I consulted hundreds of other communiqués and publications that I collected from most Syrian groups, but for sake of clarity, I only cite those that I directly mention in the book. Most communiqués have a name and a date, with limited exceptions. I used n.m. (no name), when the document has no name, and n.d. (no date), when it has no year.

Abu 'Ammar, 'A, Basha, J., Abu Yahiyya, M., al-Raqqa, A., 2022. n.m.
'Abud, H., 2013a. *hadith al-thawra . . . qa'id "Ahrar al-Sham" wa qama' muthaharat misr.* https://www.youtube.com/watch?v = gV84BDVX3XU.
'Abud, H., 2013b. *liqa al-yawm Hassan 'Abud.. Harakat al-Sham al-Islamiyya.* https://www.youtube.com/watch?v = vEFRdEPeE74.
'Abud, H., 2014. *liqa al-yawm ma' al-shaykh Hassan 'Abud hawul mithaq al-sharaf al-thawri.*
Abu Khalid, 2013. *nasiha li jama'a "Dawlat al-Islam fil-'Iraq wa al-Sham".*
Abu Saleh al-Uzbiki, Abd al-Rahman al-Masri, Abu Safiya., 2017. *bayan mawqif ('adad) min al-Muhajirin fi al-Sham.*
Abu Sayyaf, R., 2015. *bidayyat al-'amal al-'askari fi Dara'.* https://justpaste.it/pvom.
Abu Sayyaf, R., 2016a. *Jaysh al-Ahrar inshiqaq am 'itisam?* https://justpaste.it/11a3s.
Abu Sayyaf, R., 2016b. *Jund al-Aqsa wa khilaf fi kifiyya al-qada 'alayha.* https://justpaste.it/z7yr.
Ahrar al-Sham, 2013. *mithaq Harakat Ahrar al-Sham al-Islamiyya.*
Ahrar al-Sham, 2014. *i'dhar ila rabna.*
Ahrar al-Sham, 2015a. *bayan bikhusus ta'ayun qa'id jadid li Harakat Ahrar al-Sham al-Islamiyya.*
Ahrar al-Sham, 2015b. *bayan bi sha'n mashru' al-mantiqat al-amina fi shimal Suriyya.*
Ahrar al-Sham, 2015c. *bayan insihab min mu'tamar al-Riyadh.*
Ahrar al-Sham, 2015d. *bayan tawdihi hawul mawaqif Harakat Ahrar al-Sham.*
Ahrar al-Sham, 2015e. *qarar fasl.* In: Abazeid, A., 2015. *Ahrar al-Sham ba'd 'am tawil.* Markaz 'umran lil-dirasat al-istratijiyya, 50.
Ahrar al-Sham, 2015f. *qarar idari 67/a.*
Ahrar al-Sham, 2015g. *qarar idari 68/a.*
Ahrar al-Sham, 2015h. *ta'mim.*
Ahrar al-Sham, 2016a. *bayan bikhusus 'ilan tashkil Jaysh al-Fustat fi al-Ghuta al-Sharqiyya.*
Ahrar al-Sham, 2016b. *bayan indimam Jaysh al-Sham ila Harakat Ahrar al-Sham al-Islamiyya,* June 23.
Ahrar al-Sham, 2016c. *fatwa bikhusus qital Da'ish bil-tansiq ma' al-Jaysh al-Turki.*
Ahrar al-Sham, 2016d. *bayan majlis al-shura bi ta'ayun al-qa'id al-'am li Harakat Ahrar al-Sham al-Islamiyya.*
Ahrar al-Sham, 2016e. *bayan tawqihi bi sha'n taqrir al-'afu al-dawliyya 2.*
Ahrar al-Sham, 2016f. *madfa'iyya al-saha.*
Ahrar al-Sham, 2016g. n.m.
Ahrar al-Sham, 2016h. *qarar idari 82/a.*
Ahrar al-Sham, 2016i. *qarar idari 84/a.*
Ahrar al-Sham, 2016j. *qarar idari 86/a.*
Ahrar al-Sham, 2016k. *qarar idari 89/a.*
Ahrar al-Sham, 2016l. *qiyadat Jaysh al-Ahrar.*

Ahrar al-Sham, 2016m. *tarhib bi fak al-irtibak bi tandhim al-Qa'ida wa 'ilan Jabhat Fath al-Sham*.
Ahrar al-Sham, 2016n. *tawdih bi khusus i'tidat Jund al-Aqsa*.
Ahrar al-Sham, 2017a. *bayan bi khusus mubadara al-majlis al-islami al-Suri*.
Ahrar al-Sham, 2017b. *bayan dakhili min majlis shura ila abna Harakat Ahrar al-Sham al-Islamiyya bi khusus al-dhihab ila mu'tamar al-Astana*.
Ahrar al-Sham, 2017c. *bayan hawl baghi Ha'yat Tahrir al-Sham*.
Ahrar al-Sham, 2017d. *masa'il fi al-siyasat al-shar'iyya*. al-minbar al-fikri.
Ahrar al-Sham, 2017e. *mudhakirat ilzamiyya fi suluk al-muharib*.
Ahrar al-Sham, 2017f. *mubadara sadira 'an al-qiyadda al-'ama fi Harakat Ahrar al-Sham al-Islamiyya li inqadh wa tarshid masar al-thawra*.
Ahrar al-Sham, 2017c. n.m.
Ahrar al-Sham, 2017d. n.m.
Ahrar al-Sham, 2017e. n.m.
Ahrar al-Sham, 2020a. *bayan sadira 'an al-janah al-'askari li Harakat Ahrar al-Sham al-Islamiyya*.
Ahrar al-Sham, 2020b. *bayan sadir 'an hay'at al-'idad wal-tadrib fi Harakat Ahrar al-Sham*.
Ahrar al-Sham, 2020c. *bayan sadira 'an al-janah al-'askasi li Harakat Ahrar al-Sham al-Islamiyya*.
Ahrar al-Sham, 2020d. n.m.
Ahrar al-Sham, 2020e. *qarar idari*.
Ahrar al-Sham, 2020f. *qarar idari*.
Ahrar al-Sham, 2021a. *qarar i'adat haykil majlis al-qiyada*.
Ahrar al-Sham, 2021b. *qarar idari*.
Ahrar al-Sham, 2021c. *qarar tashil majlis al-qiyada*.
Ahrar al-Sham, 2022a. *bayan min qita' al-sharqi li Harakat Ahrar al-Sham al-Islamiyya*.
Ahrar al-Sham, 2022b. *bayan ta'id li-khutwa al-tati khataha alwiyya wa mujami' Harakat Ahrar al-Sham al-Islamiyya*.
Ahrar al-Sham, 2022c. n.m.
Ahrar al-Sham, 2023a. *bayan*.
Ahrar al-Sham, 2023b. *bayan tarhib bi indimam kawkaw min kata'ib Dimashq wal-Ghuta al-Sharqiyya li sufuf Harakat Ahrar al-Sham al-Islamiyya*.
Ahrar al-Sham, 2023c. n.m.
Ahrar al-Sham, n.d.a. *bayan bi indimaj Liwa Fajr al-Umma wa Harakat Ahrar al-Sham al-Islamiyya fi al-Ghuta al-Sharqiyya*.
Ahrar al-Sham, n.d.b. *haykaliya nitham al-hukm fi Turkiyya wa tatawro*.
Ahrar al-Sham, n.d.c. *hukm rafa' 'alam al-thawra al-suriyya*.
Ahrar al-Sham, n.d.d. *al-istid'af wal-tamkin bayna mu'tayat al-waqi'a wa ahkam al-din*.
Ahrar al-Sham, n.d.e. *qarar idari al-janah al-'askari*.
Ahrar al-Sham, n.d.f. *al-qawl al-mubin fi tartib maqasid al-shari'a wa maslaha al-nafs wa al din*.
Ahrar al-Sham, n.d.g. *shari'ya al-ghab*.
Ahrar al-Sham, n.d.h. *al-usul al-shar'iyya li-l'amal al-islami al-mu'asir*.
Ahrar al-Sham, n.d.i. *mudhakira ilzamiyya fi suluk al-muharib*.
Ahrar al-Sham, Jaysh al-Islam, Faylaq al-Rahman, al-Jabhat al-Shamiyya, Jaysh Yarmuk, Jaysh Idlib al-Hur, & Jaysh al-Nasr, 2017. *bayan mushtarak lil fasa'il al-thawriyya al-musalaha*.
Ansar al-Islam, JabhaT Ansar al-Din & tandhim Hurras al-Din, 2021. *bayan ta'sis ghurfa 'amaliyyat wa harid al-mu'minin*.
Ansar al-Tawheed, 2020. *bayan*.
al-Arjani, A., 2019. *""arabi 21" tuhawir qiyadiyan sabiqan bi "al-Nusra" hawl tajribato bi suriyya"* Arabi 21.
Ashida, A., 2016a. *asbab suqut Halab*. See also in English in https://justpaste.it/Aleppo_Fall.
Ashida, A., 2016b. *bayan min "Mujahidu Ashida"*.

Ashida, A., 2017. *i'tibaro bihayat burhan al-din rabani*. https://www.youtube.com/watch?v=t4xb7gyfAT0.
Assad, B., 2011. Interview with Syrian president Bashar al-Assad. *Wall Street Journal*, 31 January.
Atrash, H., 2017. *shahadat al-shaykh Husam al-Atrash shari' Harakat Nur al-Din al-Zinki*. https://justpaste.it/12ybv.
Atun, A., 2016a. *ta'sis Jabhat al-Nusra wa ahdath al-Sham min bidayat al-khilaf ila 'ilan al-Dawla*.
Atun, A., 2016b. *dawhat al-jihad*.
Atun, A., 2019. *al-ahkam thabita wal-qudra mutaghayra*.
Atun, A., 2020a. *radan 'ala bayan al-Qa'ida*.
Atun, A., 2020b. *tahdiw hawl liqa qiyadat Hay'at Tahrir al-Sham*.
Atun, A., n.d. *nasiha ila junud Hay'at Tahrir al-Sham*.
Al-Bayanuni, S., 2018. *hiwar London: halaqa khasa ma' al-ustadh 'Ali Sadr al-Din al-Nayanuni... juz al-thalith*. https://www.youtube.com/watch?v=wbFcvnjYHN8.
Bayraqdar, H., 2018. *al-marhala al-akhira allati marra biha Jaysh al-Islam*. https://justpaste.it/hamzabayraqdar.
Dar al-Qada, 2014. *dar al-qada fi kalimat: al-asas al-alti taqum 'alayha dar al-qada bi bilad al-Sham*. https://www.youtube.com/watch?v=BMk8Tmner2o.
al-Dik, M., & Bontemps, N., 2016. *A l'est de Damas, au bout du monde. Témoignage d'un révolutionnaire syrien*. Don Quichotte.
Droukdel, A., 2012. *tawjihat al-'ama bi khusus al-mashru' al-islami al-jihadi bi Azawad*. tandhim al-qa'ida bi bilad al-maghrib al-islami.
Al-Faris, W., 2015. *Homs: al-hisar al-'atheem tawthiq sab'amiya yawm min al-hisar*. Markaz al-'arabi lil abhath wa dirasat al-siyasiyat.
al-Farghali, A., 2020a. *al-tariq ila al-khilafa al-jil al-awal*.
al-Farghali, A., 2020b. *al-tariq ila al-khilafa al-jil al-khamis*.
al-Farghali, Y., 2020c. al-tariq ila al-khilafa tarikh al-harakat al-jihadiyya min al-ikhwan al-muslimin ila al-jihad al-Shami. dar al-kitab al-'alami.
Faylaq al-Sham, 2018. *bayan*.
Faylaq al-Sham, 2019. *bayan*.
Gadahn, A., 2011. Letter from Adam Gadahn. Reference Number: SOCOM-2012-0000004. Combating Terrorism Center at West Point. https://ctc.usma.edu/harmony-program/letter-from-adam-gadahn-original-language-2/.
Al-Ghunami, M., 2017. *ikhtiraq qiyyadat Ahrar al-Sham thum inhiyarha*. https://justpaste.it/19hud.
Hamawi, S., 2015. *shukran Jabhat al-Nusra*.
Hamid, M., & L. Farrall, 2015. *The Arabs at War in Afghanistan*. Oxford University Press.
Harush, A., 2016. *shahadat al-duktur Ayman Harush hawl natija mubadara ahl al-'ilm li tawhid al-fasa'il al-jihadiyya fi al-Sham*. https://justpaste.it/shahadetharoshahelalelm.
Al-Hay'at al-Shari'yya, 2014. *bayan al-ha'ya al-shar'iyya hawul al-Jabhat al-Islamiyya wa qiyyadatha*. https://justpaste.it/fib0.
Hay'at Tahrir al-Sham, 2017a. *bayan ham li thula min qiyyadat Hay'at Tahrir al-Sham*.
Hay'at Tahrir al-Sham, 2017b. *bayan ham li Jaysh al-Nusra Idlib*.
Hay'at Tahrir al-Sham, 2017c. *bayan indimam al-masha'ikh li-Ha'ya Tahrir al-Sham*.
Hay'at Tahrir al-Sham, 2017d. *bayan al-majlis al-shar'i al-'am hawl al-ahdath al-da'ira fi al-Ghuta al-Sharqiyya*.
Hay'at Tahrir al-Sham, 2017e. *bayan raqam 1 qiita' al-gharbi*.
Hay'at Tahrir al-Sham, 2017f. *al-haq ahaq an yutaba'*.
Hay'at Tahrir al-Sham, 2017g. *'idhar wa indhar li jama'at Liwa al-Aqsa*.
Hay'at Tahrir al-Sham, 2017h. *mabadi Hay'at Tahrir al-Sham*.
Hay'at Tahrir al-Sham, 2017i. *al-mawqif al-shar'i min al-tatawrat wa al-mustajidat al-akhira hiwal al-thawa al-suriyya*.

Hay'at Tahrir al-Sham, 2017j. *Russia muhtala la halifa.*
Hay'at Tahrir al-Sham, 2017k. *ta'mim.*
Hay'at Tahrir al-Sham, 2017l. *ta'mim (2 / 17).*
Hay'at Tahrir al-Sham, 2017m. *ta'qib 'ala al-tasrih al-sadir 'an munathamat wa hay'at Suriyya hawul al-tatawrat al-akhira.*
Hay'at Tahrir al-Sham, 2017n. *tawdih hawl al-ahdath al-jariyya ma' Ahrar al-Sham.*
Hay'at Tahrir al-Sham, 2017o. *tawdih wa rudud hawl mab'uth al-wilayat al-mutahida "maikl ratni".*
Hay'at Tahrir al-Sham, 2017p. *tawdih wa tabayun hawl al-tasrihat al-akhira.*
Hay'at Tahrir al-Sham, 2017q. *al-thawra mustamira.*
Hay'at Tahrir al-Sham, 2018a. *al-idarat al-amrikiyya al-jadida. al-kayyan bi makiyalin did al-thawra al-suriyya.*
Hay'at Tahrir al-Sham, 2018b. *al-janub yastansirna. da'wa lil 'amal.*
Hay'at Tahrir al-Sham, 2018d. *al-jihad wa al-siyasa al-shar'iyya bayna al-thawabit wa al-mutaghirat.*
Hay'at Tahrir al-Sham, 2018d. *satuksar hamlatihim wa yahzimun bi idhn illah.*
Hay'at Tahrir al-Sham, 2018e. *ta'mim.*
Hay'at Tahrir al-Sham, 2018f. *thawrat al-sham lan tamut.*
Hay'at Tahrir al-Sham, 2018g. *wa 'ala al-baghi tadawr al-dawa'ir.*
Hay'at Tahrir al-Sham, 2019a. *qarrar fasl.*
Hay'at Tahrir al-Sham, 2019b. *qarar.*
Hay'at Tahrir al-Sham, 2019c. *ta'mim.*
Hay'at Tahrir al-Sham, 2019d. *tawdih wa tarshid: 'ilan tashkil "lajna riqaba 'uliyya".*
Hay'at Tahrir al-Sham, 2020a. *hawl tawheed al-juhd al-'askari.*
Hay'at Tahrir al-Sham, 2020b. *itifaqiyya musku sirab jadid.*
Hay'at Tahrir al-Sham, 2020c. *ta'mim.*al-Hizb al-Islami al-Turkistani, Jama'at Tawheed wal-Jihad, et al., 2021. *kalimat wafa wa-nasiha.*
Hizb al-Turkistani al-Islami., 2018. *bayan bi-sha'n al-tatawrat al-akhira fi sahat al-sham.*
Hudhaifa, O., 2021. *al-waq'a al-suri taht al-mahjar dirasat maydaniyya.* Nebras.
Jabhat Ansar al-Din, 2018. *mithaq Jabhat Ansar al-Din.*
Jabhat Ansar al-Din, 2017. n.m.
Jabhat Fath al-Sham, 2016a. *bayan hawul ma'arik rif Halab al-shamali wa 'amaliyya dar' al-frat.*
Jabhat Fath al-Sham, 2017a. *tawdih hawl asbab indimam wa fasl "Jund al-Aqsa".*
Jabhat Fath al-Sham,. 2017b. n.m.
Jabhat Tahrir Suriya, 2018. *kalimat al-akh Hasan Sufan qa'id Jabhat Tahrir Suriyya bi khusus itifaq al-Fu'a wa Kafariyya.*
al-Jabhat al-Islamiyya, Ajnad al-Sham, Faylaq al-Sham, Jaysh al-Mujahideen, & Alwiya al-Furqan, 2014. *mithaq sharaf thawri lil-kata'ib al-muqatila.*
al-Jabhat al-Wataniyya lil Tahrir, 2018. n.m.
al-Jabhat al-Wataniyya lil Tahrir, 2019a. *bayan 'ilan al-nafir li sad 'udwan Ha'yat Tahrir al Sham.*
al-Jabhat al-Wataniyya lil Tahrir, 2019b. n.m.
Jabhat al-Nusra, 2014. *bayan 'ilami raqam 9 hawul mithaq al-sharaf al-thawri.*
Jabhat al-Nusra, 2015a. *bayan hawul al-ahdath al-akhira fi rif Halab al-Shamali.* https://justpaste.it/mwjt.
Jabhat al-Nusra, 2015b. *bayan raqam 1 sadira 'an dar al-qada bi rif Halab al-Gharbi.*
Jabhat al-Nusra, n.d. *nabdha 'ama na'qido wa nudin allah bi.*
 al-Jabhat al-Shamiyya, 2016. n.m.
Jabhat Tahrir Suriya, 2018. *ta'qib 'ala bayan al-ikhwa min al-Hizb al-Islami al-Turkistani hawl musharakatihim fi al-iqtital al-dakhili.*
Jami'a al-Duwal al-'Arabiyya, 1996. *mudhakirat al-tawdhihiyya lil-qanun al-juz'i al-'arabi al-muwahad.* https://da3msyria2.files.wordpress.com/2014/12/unified-arabic-criminal-law.pdf.

Jaysh al-Ahrar, 2018. *bayan raqam 6.*
Jaysh al-Badiya, 2018. *bayan ham min Jaysh al-Badiya.*
Jaysh al-Fath, 2016a. *bayan mubaraka.*
Jaysh al-Fath, 2016b. *bayan sadiq 'an al-quwa al-amniyya.*
Jaysh al-Malamih, 2018. *bayan Jaysh al-Malamih.*
al-Jaysh al-Watani al-Suri, 2019a. *bayan.*
al-Jaysh al-Watani al-Suri, 2019b. *bayan raqam 24.*
al-Jaysh al-Watani al-Suri, 2019c. *bayan bi khusur ma tadawal hawl taysir quwat min al-Jaysh al-Watani al-Suri ila Libya.*
al-Jaysh al-Watani al-Suri, 2021. *ila ri'asat arkan al-Faylaq al-Thalith wa fara' al-tandhim.*
al-Jazeera, 2016. *film Ahrar al-Sham.* https://www.youtube.com/watch?v = _lydv7dr6qE.
al-Jolani, A., 2013. *liqa al-yawm Abu Muhammad al-Jolani. al-Nusra was mustaqbal Suriyya.* https://www.youtube.com/watch?v = DIr1HoHJlQA.
Jund al-Aqsa, 2015. n.m.
Katibat al-Boukhari, 2018. n.m.
al-Majlis al-'Askari li Baldat Kafruma, 2019. *bayan sadir 'an al-majlis al-'askari fi Kafrruma.*
al-Majlis al-'Askari fi Kafr 'Uyud, 2019. *bayan sadir 'an al-majlis al-'askari fi Kafr 'Uyud.*
al-Majlis al-Islami, 2016. *bayan bifasil Jund al-Aqsa wa baghiha 'ala fasa'il al-jihad fi al-Sham.*
al-Majlis al-Islami, 2017. *bayan bi sha'n khutwat Harakat Ahrar al-Sham al-akhira.*
al-Majlis al-Islami,. 2019. *bayan bi sha'n 'amaliyyat (nab' al-salam) li iqama al-muntiqa al-amina.*
Majlis Shura Ahl al-'Ilm, 2019a. *bayan 94, bayan bi baghi wa 'udwan hay'at Tahrir al-Sham.*
Majlis Shura Ahl al-'Ilm fi al-Sham, 2019b. *bayan hukm dukhul al-quwat al-Turkiya li-shamal al-Suri wa ghairo.*
Majlis Shura Jaysh al-Ahrar, 2017. n.m.
Majlis Shura Sahl al-Ghab, 2017. *bayan raqam 3 sadir 'an al-majlis shura Sahl al-Ghab al-thawri.*
Maktab al-Shar'i li Jaysh al-Iman, 2017. n.m.
al-Malik, A., 2014. *ahkam al-imama al-'uthma.*
al-Manhaj, K., 2020. *al-ilmam bi ridat ta'ifa Hay'at Tahrir al-Sham.* Available in Al-Tamimi, Aymenn Jawad, 2020. *The Apostasy of Hay'at Tahrir al-Sham: Study by 'Khayal al-Manhaj'.*
al-Minbar al-Fikri, 2014. *shubuhat al-taghalub wa tatbiq shar'iyat al-ghab.*
al-Minbar al-Fikri, n.d. *al-thawra al-suriyya wa tahadiyyat al-marhalat al-rahina.*
al-Muhaysani, A., 2016. *hal fashala al-indimaj.*
Muzmajir, 2016. *mubadarat darar.* https://justpaste.it/qxi8.
al-Nahhas, K., 2015a. *ta'liqat hawl bayan Jund al-Aqsa bikhusus khurujhum min Jaysh al-Fath.* https://justpaste.it/abuazzam.
al-Nahhas, L., 2015b. I'm a Syrian and I fight ISIL every day: It will take more than bombs from the West to defeat this menace. *Daily Telegraph*
al-Nahhas, L., 2015c. The deadly consequences of mislabelling Syria's revolutionaries. *Washington Post.*
al-Nahhas, L., 2016. *""intisar" fawq al-rakam: awliyyat ma ba'd Halab".* Al-hayat.
n.m.,2016a. *'alaykum bil-sama' wal-ta'a.*
n.m,, 2016b. *fatwa bi sha'n tandhim Jund al-Aqsa.*
n.m., 2016c. n.m.
n.m., 2019. *bayan min muhajirin fi al-Sham al-mubaraka.*
n.m., 2020. *shukr wa ta'id.*
Nukhbat min al-Muhajideen al-Muhajarin fi Ard al-Sham, 2017. *bayan bara' muhajiri al-Sham mima iftarao 'alayhim ahl al-thulm wal-ijram.*
al-'Omar, 'A., 2016. *muhadarat al-qa'id al-'am li Harakat Ahrar al-Sham al-Islamiyya al-muhandis 'Ali al-'Omar.*
al-Qahtani, A., n.d. *madha khasara al-mujahidun 'indama dakhala al-ghula fi sufufihim.*
al-Sadiq, A., 2015. *harakat al-umma bayna al-nakhbawiyya wal-shu'ubiyya.* https://justpaste.it/ng38.

Saraqib, 2019. *bayan bi ism ahli saraqib wa fa'aliyatha al-thawriyya wal-madaniyya*.
Sarayat Kabul, 2018. *bayan ham min Sarayat Kabul*.
Sarayat al-Tamkin, 2018. n.m.
al-Shami, A., 2013. *adwat 'ala al-manhaj al-jama'a al-mujahida*.
al-Shami, A., 2014a. *masa'il fi al-siyasat al-shar'iyya*.
al-Shami, S., 2014b. *qiyadi sabiq fi Ahrar al-Sham yakshif kulis takhtit qiyadat al-ahrar li qital al-Dawla wasat rafd kathir min afradha*. https://justpaste.it/edsk.
al-Shami, A., 2018. *asbab suqut al-Ghuta al-Sharqiyya*. https://justpaste.it/guta.
al-Shami & al-Uraydi, 2019. n.m.
al-Sheikh, 2015. liqa al-yawm qa'id ahrar al-sham: iran hiya al-lati a'adat nitham bashar ila al-hayat. *al-jazeera*.
al-Shaykh, F., 2016a. *Ahrar al-Sham qad talfath infusiha al-akhira ba'd sa'aat ala hal balaghat*. https://justpaste.it/11l02.
al-Shaykh, A., 2016b. *ikhwani fi Jaysh al-Ahrar*. https://justpaste.it/12oxd.
al-Shaykh, A., 2016c. *istijaba li talab ba'd al-ikhwa bayan sabab al-ta'liq naqul*. https://justpaste.it/10x97.
al-Shaykh, A., 2016d. n.m. https://justpaste.it/ahl_al3elm.
al-Shaykh, F., 2016e. *nathara 'ala waqi'a Harakat Ahrar al-Sham al-Islamiyya*. Souriat.
Shehab al-Din, T., 2017. n.m.
Shishani, M., & Jazira, M., 2017. Full interview of Muslim Shishani with Muhammad Jazira. Chechene in Syria. http://www.chechensinsyria.com/wp-content/uploads/2018/06/Muslim-Shishani-interview-Muhammad-Jaz.pdf.
al-Sudani & al-Urduni., 2019. n.m.
Sufan, H., 2019. *risala dakhiliyya khasa min al-shaykh Abul-Bara Hassan Sufan ila kawadir wa junud Ahrar al-Sham al-Islamiyya*. https://justpaste.it/soufan.
Sufan, H., 2020. *tawdih min Hasan Sufan*.
Suqur al-Sham, Jaysh al-Islam, Jaysh al-Mujahideen, Fastaqim, & Jabhat al-Shamiya, 2017. *bayan mushtaraka min kubra al-fasa'il al-thawriya fi al-Shimal*.
al-Suri, A., 1991. *al-thawra al-islamiyya al-jihadiyya fi Suriyya*.
al-Suri, A., 2004. *da'wa al-muqawama al-islamiyya al-'alamiyya*, minbar tahweed wal-jihad.
Tajamu' Ahl al-'Ilm, 2016a. *bayan mubaraka*.
Tajamu' Ahl al-'Ilm, 2016b. *fatwa bi sha'n nazala al-rif al-Shamali bi Halab wa ma yata'alig biha*.Tandhim Hurras al-Din, 2018. *inqadhu fustat al-muslimin*.
Tandhim Hurras al-Din & Ansar al-Tawheed, 2018. *bayan 'ilan*.
Tandhim Qa'idat al-Jihad, 2020. *in allah aba 'ala qatl al-mu'min*.
Tansiqiyat al-Jihad, Liwa al-Muqatilin al-Ansar, Ansar al-Islam, Jabha Ansar al-Din, & Tandhim Hurras al-Din, 2020. *al-bayan al-ta'sisi, bayan raqam 1*.
Tarsha, H., 2018. *harakat ahrar al-sham-islamiyya al-nasha wal istimrar*. https://justpaste.it/2g47w.
Tarsha, H., 2019. *khawatir fi zaman al-taghayur (11) ma'alim al-mashru' al-islami al-watani... thibat al-mithaq watisaq al-muraja'at*.
Thuwar Kafr Halab, 2019. *bayan sadir 'an thuwar kafr Halab*.
Uraydi, S., 2012. *'aqidatna*.
Wikileaks Ahrar, 2016. *layla inqilab 'ala Ahrar al-Sham*. https://justpaste.it/wikiahrar.
Zayn al-Din, A., A. Harush, & M. 'Aloush, 2017. *mubadarat inqadh al-Shimal al-Suri*.
al-Zawahiri, A., 1988. *al-hasad al-murr*, al-tab' al-thani, al-fajr.
al-Zawahiri, A., 2013. *al-tawjihat al-'ama lil-'amal al-jihadi*. al-Sahab.
Zinki. 2019. n.m.

Secondary Sources

Abazeid, A., 2014. "*al-'Uraydi ba'd al-Qahtani: al-Nusra fi al-zaman al-jadid*". zamanalwsl.
Abazeid, A., 2015a. *Ahrar al-Sham ba'd 'am tawil*. Markaz 'umran lil-dirasat al-istratijiyya.
Abazeid, A., 2015b. *Jaysh al-Sham: harakiyya al-Shimal al-Suriyya al-mustadama*. markaz 'umran lil dirasat al-istratijiyya.

Abazeid, A., 2017. *kayf inharat Harakat Ahrar al-Sham?*. Shaam network.
Abazeid, A., & Pierret, T., 2018. Les rebelles syriens d'Ahrar al-Sham: ressorts contextuels et organisationnels d'une déradicalisation en temps de guerre civile. *Critique internationale* (1), pp. 63–84.
Abboud, S., 2015. *Syria*. Polity Press.
Abboud, S.N., 2018. *Syria: Hot Spots in Global Politics*. John Wiley & Sons.
Abd al-Haj, 2013. "al-hay'at al-shar'iyya diktatoriyya takfiriyya fi suriyya al-tha'ira". al-'arab.
Abdul-Ahad, G., 2013. How to start a battalion (in five easy lessons). *London Review of Books*, 35(4), pp. 13–14.
Abdullah, A., Ayboga, E., Flach, A., Graeber, D., & Knapp, M., 2016. *Revolution in Rojava: Democratic Autonomy and Women's Liberation in Syrian Kurdistan*. Pluto Press.
Abouzeid, R., 2018. *No Turning Back: Life, Loss, and Hope in Wartime Syria*. W.W. Norton & Company.
Abu Raman, M., 2013. *al-islamiyyun wa al-din wal-thawra fi suriyya*. Friedrich Ebert Foundation.Abu Rumman, M., & Abu Haniyeh, H., 2021. *Huras al-Din: The Rise and Fall of al-Qaeda in the Levant*. Friedrich-Ebert-Stiftung.
Adraoui, M.A., 2019. The case of Jabhat Al-Nusra in the Syrian conflict 2011–2016: Towards a strategy of nationalization?. *Mediterranean Politics*, 24(2), pp. 260-267.
Ahmad, A., 2015. "*ma hiyya al-hay'a al-islamiyya li idarat manatiq al-muharara.*" Al-Duwar al-Shamiyya.
Ahmad, A., 2017. *Jihad & Co.: Black Markets and Islamist Power*. Oxford University Press.
Ahmad, A., 2021. The long Jihad: The boom-bust cycle behind Jihadist durability. *Journal of Global Security Studies*, 6(4), p. ogaa048.
Ahmad, A., & O. Diallo, 2023. A winning team of losers: The logic of Jihadist coalitions in civil wars. *Journal of Global Security Studies*, 8(1), p. ogac029.
Akum, C., 2015. "*juhud dawliyya wa iqlimiyya li abraz "Ahrar al-Sham" kafasil mu'tadila*", al-sharq al-awsat.
Alagha, J.E., 2006. *The Shifts in Hizbullah's Ideology. Religious Ideology, Political Ideology, and Political Program*. Amsterdam University Press, Leiden/Amsterdam.
Albrecht, H., & Koehler, K., 2018. Going on the run: What drives military desertion in civil war? *Security Studies*, 27(2), pp. 179–203.
Alimi, E.Y., Bosi, L., & Demetriou, C., 2015. *The Dynamics of Radicalization: A Relational and Comparative Perspective*. Oxford University Press.
al-Kanj, Sultan, 2021. Defections threaten Ahrar al-Sham Jihadist movement in Syria. *Al-Monitor*, July 6, 2021.
Al Nofal, W., 2022. Mergers and tensions within the Syrian National Army: A 'struggle for existence'. Syria Direct.
Allsopp, Harriet, & Wladimir van Wilgenburg, 2019. *The Kurds of Northern Syria: Governance, Diversity and Conflicts*. I.B. Tauris.
Almustafa, Hamzah, 2020. From Arms to Talks: Transformations of Three Syrian Armed Islamist Movements, in *From Bullets to Ballots: Transformations from Armed to Unarmed Political Activism*, O. Ashour. Edinburgh University Press.
Almustafa, H., 2023. From Arm to Negotiations: Transformations within the Syrian Armed Islamist Movements (2011–2021): Ahrar al-Sham (The Islamic Movement of the Free Men of the Levant), Jaysh al-Islam (Army of Islam), and Failaq al-Sham (The Sham Legion). Doctoral dissertation.
Al-Tamimi, A.J., 2015a. Archive of Jabhat al-Nusra Dar al-Qa'a Documents. http://www.aymennjawad.org/2015/03/archive-of-jabhat-al-nusra-dar-al-qaa-documents.
Al-Tamimi, A.J., 2015b. Liwa Shuhada'al-Yarmouk: History and analysis. *Syria Comment*.Al-Tamimi, A., 2016. al-Qa'ida uncoupling: Jabhat al-Nusra's rebranding as Jabhat Fateh al-Sham. *CTC Sentinel*, 9(8), pp.16-20.
Al-Tamimi, A.J., 2017a. From Jabhat al-Nusra to Hay'at Tahrir al-Sham: Evolution. *Approach and Future, Konrad-Adenauer Stiftung/Al-Nahrain Center For Strategic Studies*, 29.

Al-Tamimi, A., 2017b. The Formation of Hay'at Tahrir al-Sham and Wider Tensions in the Syrian Insurgency. *CTC Sentinel*, *10*(2), pp.16-20.
Al-Tamimi, A. J., 2019. The Hay'at Tahrir al-Sham-al-Qaeda Dispute: Primary Texts (XI). www.aymennjawad.org/2019/02/the-hayat-tahrir-al-sham-al-qaeda-dispute-primary-10.
Al-Tamimi, A. J., 2020a. The History of Harakat Nour al-Din al-Zinki: Interview. https://aymennjawad.org/2020/01/the-history-of-harakat-nour-al-din-al-zinki.
Al-Tamimi, A. J., 2020b. The Internal Structure of Harakat Nour al-Din al-Zinki. https://aymennjawad.org/2020/01/the-internal-structure-of-harakat-nour-al-din-al.
Anas, A. and Hussein, T., 2019. *To the mountains: My life in Jihad, from Algeria to Afghanistan*. Oxford University Press.
Anjum, O., 2012. *Politics, Law, and Community in Islamic Thought: The Taymiyyan Moment*. Cambridge University Press.
Arango, T., & E. Schmitt, 2014. Escaped iInmates from Iraq fuel Syrian insurgency. *The New York Times*.
Arango, T., 2017. Big ransom and Syria deals win release of royal Qatari hunters. *The New York Times*.
Arjona, A., 2016. *Rebelocracy*. Cambridge University Press.
Arjona, A., Kasfir, N., & Mampilly, Z., eds., 2015. *Rebel Governance in Civil War*. Cambridge University Press.
Arquilla, J., & Ronfeldt, D., 2001. *Networks and Netwars: The Future of Terror, Crime, and Militancy*. Rand Corporation.
Asal, V., Phillips, B.J. and Rethemeyer, R.K., 2022. *Insurgent Terrorism: Intergroup Relationships and the Killing of Civilians*. Oxford University Press.
Ashour, O., 2009. *The De-radicalization of Jihadists: Transforming Armed Islamist Movements*. Routledge.
Ashour, O., 2021. *How ISIS Fights: Military Tactics in Iraq, Syria, Libya and Egypt*. Edinburgh University Press.
Atlantic Council, 2018. Breaking Ghouta. https://www.publications.atlanticcouncil.org/breakingghouta/wp-content/uploads/2018/09/20180924_breakingghouta_web.pdf.
Bacon, T., 2018. *Why Terrorist Groups Form International Alliances*. University of Pennsylvania Press.
Bacon, T. and Grimm, E., 2022. *Terror in transition: Leadership and succession in terrorist organizations*. Columbia University Press.
Baczko, A., Dorronsoro, G., & Quesnay, A., 2018. *Civil War in Syria: Mobilization and Competing Social Orders*. Cambridge University Press.
Bajis, M., 2015. talmih qiyadi fi "al-nusra" bitakfir Ahrar al-Sham yathir jadlan wasi'a. Arabi 21.
Bajis, M., 2016. ma hiya tafasil mubadara tawahud al-fasa'il? wa ma khilaf ma' Jabhat al-Nusra?. Arabi 21.
Balanche, F., 2006a. *La région alaouite et le pouvoir syrien*. Karthala Editions.
Balanche, F., 2006b. Les Alaouites: une secte au pouvoir. *Outre Terre*, *2*(14), pp.73–96.
Balanche, F., 2009. Clientélisme, communautarisme et fragmentation territoriale en Syrie. *A contrario*, 1(11), pp. 122–150.
Balanche, F., 2011. Géographie de la révolte syrienne. *Outre-terre*, 3(29), pp. 437–458.
Balanche, F., 2014a. Communautarisme en Syrie: lorsque le mythe devient réalité. *Confluences Méditerranée*, 2(89), pp. 29–44.
Balanche, F., 2014b. Insurrection et contre-insurrection en Syrie. *Géostrategic Maritime Review*, 2, pp. 36–57.
Balanche, F., 2015. "Go to Damascus, My Son": Alawi Demographic Shifts under Ba'ath Party Rule. *The Alawis of Syria: War, Faith and Politics in the Levant*, pp. 79–106. https://www.foreignaffairs.com/articles/syria/2017-08-02/end-cia-program-syria
Balanche, F., 2017. The end of the CIA program in Syria. *Foreign Affairs*.
Balanche, F., 2018. *Sectarianism in Syria's civil war*. Washington Institute.

Balcells, L., 2017. *Rivalry and Revenge*. Cambridge University Press.Balcells, L., & Kalyvas, S., 2013. Technology of Rebellion in the Syrian Civil War. *The Political Science of Syria's War*, pp.11–12. https://pomeps.org/technology-of-rebellion-in-the-syrian-civil-war

Balcells, L., & Kalyvas, S., 2022. Revolution in civil war: The "Marxist Paradox". *Available at SSRN*.

Balcells, L., Chen, C., & Pischedda, C., 2022. Do birds of a feather flock together? Rebel constituencies and civil war alliances. *International studies quarterly*, 66(1), p.sqab095.

Bakke, K.M., 2014. Help wanted? The mixed record of foreign fighters in domestic insurgencies. *International Security*, 38(4), pp. 150–187.

Bakkour, S., 2023. The last Jihadist battle in Syria: Externalisation and the regional and international responses to Hayat Tahrir al-Sham in Idlib. *Religions*, 14(9), p. 1098.

Bamber, M., & Svensson, I., 2022. Resisting radical rebels: Variations in Islamist rebel governance and the occurrence of civil resistance. *Terrorism and Political Violence*, pp. 1–21.

Bapat, N.A., 2012. Understanding state sponsorship of militant groups. *British Journal of Political Science*, 42(1), pp. 1–29.

Barany, Z., 2011. Comparing the Arab revolts: The role of the military. *Journal of Democracy*, 22(4), pp. 24–35.

Bareesh, M., 2020. How and why Idlib defied its Jihadi overlords, *Carnegie Endowment*. https://carnegie-mec.org/2020/05/15/how-and-why-idlib-defied-its-jihadi-overlords-pub-81811

Barnard, A., 2019. Inside Syria's secret torture prisons: How Bashar al-Assad crushed dissent. *The New York Times*.

Barnard, A., & Shoumali, K., 2015. US weaponry is turning Syria into proxy war with Russia. *The New York Times*. Baron, X., 2013. *Aux origines du drame syrien: 1918–2013*. Tallandier.

Batatu, H., 1981. Some observations on the social roots of Syria's ruling, Military group and the causes for its dominance. *Middle East Journal*, 35(3), pp. 331–344.

Batatu, H., 1999. *Syria's Peasantry, the Descendants of Its Lesser Rural Notables, and Their Politics*. Princeton University Press.

Bauer, S., 2019, May/June, Behind the lines. Mother Jones. https://www.motherjones.com/politics/2019/06/behind-the-lines-syria-part-one/

Belhadj, S., 2013. *La Syrie de Bashar al-Asad: Anatomie d'un régime autoritaire*. Belin.

Bellamy, A.J., 2022. *Syria Betrayed: Atrocities, War, and the Failure of International Diplomacy*. Columbia University Press.

Benraad, M., 2011. Iraq's tribal "Sahwa": Its rise and fall. *Middle East Policy*, 18(1), p. 121.

Bergen, P.L., 2011. *The Longest War: The Enduring Conflict between America and Al-Qaeda*. Simon and Schuster.

Berti, B., 2013. *Armed Political Organizations: From Conflict to Integration*. Johns Hopkins University Press.

Berti, B., 2020. From cooperation to competition: Localization, militarization and rebel co-governance arrangements in Syria. *Studies in Conflict & Terrorism*, 46(2), pp. 1–19.

Biddle, S., 2022. *Nonstate Warfare: The Military Methods of Guerillas, Warlords, and Militias*. Princeton University Press.

Bishara, A., 2022. *Syria 2011–2013: Revolution and Tyranny before the Mayhem*. Bloomsbury Publishing.

Black, I., 2013. Syria crisis: Saudi Arabia to spend millions to train new rebel force. *The Guardian*.

Blanford, N., 2013. The Battle for Qusayr: How the Syrian regime and Hizb Allah tipped the balance. *CTC Sentinel*, 6, pp. 18–22.

Blaydes, L., 2010. *Elections and Distributive Politics in Mubarak's Egypt*. Cambridge University Press.

Borger, J., 2020, August. Saudi strongman 'encouraged' Russia intervention in Syria, lawsuit claims. *The Guardian*.

Borger, J., & Inzaurralde, B., 2015. West 'ignored Russian offer in 2012 to have Syria's Assad step aside'. *The Guardian*Borshchevskaya, A., 2021. *Putin's War in Syria: Russian Foreign Policy and the Price of America's Absence*. Bloomsbury Publishing.

Bosi, L., & Ó Dochartaigh, N., 2018. Armed activism as the enactment of a collective identity: The case of the Provisional IRA between 1969 and 1972. *Social Movement Studies*, 17(1), pp. 35–47.

Bou Nassif, H., 2015. 'Second-Class': The grievances of Sunni officers in the Syrian armed forces. *Journal of Strategic Studies*, 38(5), pp. 626–649.

Brooke, S., 2008. Jihadist strategic debates before 9/11. *Studies in Conflict & Terrorism*, 31(3), pp. 201–226.

Brooke, S., 2019. *Winning Hearts and Votes: Social Services and the Islamist Political Advantage*. Cornell University Press.

Brown, V., 2007. *Cracks in the Foundation: Leadership Schisms in al-Qa'ida from 1989–2006*. Military Academy West Point NY Combating Terrorism Center.

Brown, N., 2012. *When Victory is Not an Option: Islamist Movements in Arab Politics*. Cornell University Press.

Brownlee, J., Masoud, T.E., & Reynolds, A., 2015. *The Arab Spring: Pathways of Repression and Reform*. Oxford University Press, USA.

Burgat, F., 2007. *L'islamisme en face*. La découverte.

Burgat, F. and Paoli, B., 2013. *Pas de printemps pour la Syrie: les clés pour comprendre les acteurs et les défis de la crise (2011-2013)*. La découverte

Burns, W.J., 2019. *The Back Channel: American Diplomacy in a Disordered World*. Oxford University Press.

Byman, D., 2005. *Deadly Connections: States that Sponsor Terrorism*. Cambridge University Press.

Byman, D., 2019. *Road warriors: Foreign fighters in the armies of jihad*. Oxford University Press.

Cafarella, J., 2014. Jabhat al Nusra in Syria. *Institute for the Study of War*. https://www.understandingwar.org/sites/default/files/JN%20Final.pdf

Cafarella, J., & G. Casagrande, 2015. Syrian opposition guide. *Institute for the Study of War*, 7, pp. 1–45.

Cafarella, J., & Casagrande, G., 2016. *Syrian armed opposition powerbrokers*. Institute for the Study of War.

Caferalla, Jennifer, Heras, Nicholas, A., & Casagrande, Geneviève, 2016. "Al Qaeda is gaining strength in Syria". *Foreign Policy*.Caillet, R., 2014. L'influence de la guerre en Syrie sur le courant Jihadiste marocain. *Religioscope. Études et analyses*, 33. https://www.religion.info/2014/04/29/influence-de-la-guerre-en-syrie-sur-le-courant-jihadiste-marocain/

Carenzi, S., 2020. A downward scale shift? The case of Hay'at Tahrir Al-Sham. *Perspectives on Terrorism*, 14(6), pp.91-105.Callimachi, R & Schmitt, E., 2015. "Iran Released Top Members of Al Qaeda in a Trade", *The New York Times*.

Caris, C.C., & Reynolds, S., 2014. ISIS governance in Syria. *Middle East Security Report*, 22, pp. 4–41.Cavatorta, F., & Merone, F., 2013. Moderation through exclusion? The journey of the Tunisian Ennahda from fundamentalist to conservative party. *Democratization*, 20(5), pp. 857–875.

Caves, J., 2012. *Syrian Kurds and the democratic union Party (Pyd)*. Institute for the Study of War.

Clark, J.A., 2006. The conditions of Islamist moderation: Unpacking cross-ideological cooperation in Jordan. *International Journal of Middle East Studies*, 38(4), pp. 539–560.

Cederman, L.E., Gleditsch, K.S., & Buhaug, H., 2013. *Inequality, grievances, and civil war*. Cambridge University Press.

Cesari, J., 2014. *The awakening of Muslim democracy: Religion, modernity, and the state*. Cambridge University Press.

Charap, S., Treyger, E., & Geist, E., 2019. *Understanding Russia's Intervention in Syria*. RAND.

Chivers, C.J., 2015. Behind the black flag: The recruitment of an ISIS killer. *The New York Times*

Chivers, C.J., & Schmitt, E., 2013. Arms airlift to Syria rebels expands, with aid from CIA. *The New York Times*
Chollet, D., 2016. Obama's red line, revisited. *Politico Magazine*
Christia, F., 2012. *Alliance Formation in Civil Wars*. Cambridge University Press.
Chulov, 2017. Qatari royal family members used as leverage in Syrian population swap. *The Guardian*.
Clark, J.A., 2006. The conditions of Islamist moderation: Unpacking cross-ideological cooperation in Jordan. *International Journal of Middle East Studies*, 38(4), pp. 539–560.
Cohen, D.K., 2016. *Rape during Civil War*. Cornell University Press.
Collectif., 2022. *Syrie, le pays brûlé (1970–2021) Le livre noir des Assad*. Seuil.
Collier, P., and Hoeffler, A., 2004. Greed and grievance in civil war. *Oxford economic papers*, 56(4), pp. 563–595.
Conduit, D., 2019. *The Muslim Brotherhood in Syria*. Cambridge University Press.
Courbage, Y., 2007. La population de la Syrie: des réticences à la transition (démographique). *La Syrie au présent. Reflets d'une société. Arles, Sindbad-Actes Sud*, pp. 177–213.
Cunningham, K.G., 2014. *Inside the Politics of Self-determination*. Oxford University Press.
Dagher, S., 2014. Syrian bomb plot marked deadly turn in civil war. *The Wall Street Journal*.
Dagher, S., 2019. *Assad or We Burn the Country: How One Family's Lust for Power Destroyed Syria*. Hachette UK.
Daher, J., 2019. *Syria after the Uprisings: The Political Economy of State Resilience*. Pluto Press.
Daly, S.Z., 2016. *Organized Violence after Civil War: The Geography of Recruitment in Latin America*. Cambridge University Press.
Daoudy, M., 2020. *The Origins of the Syrian Conflict: Climate Change and Human Security*. Cambridge University Press.
De Châtel, F., 2014. The role of drought and climate change in the Syrian insurgency: Untangling the triggers of the revolution. *Middle Eastern Studies*, 50(4), pp. 521–535.
Delanoë, I., 2018. What Russia gained from its military intervention in Syria. OrientXXI.
Della Porta, D., 1995. *Social movements, political violence, and the state: A comparative analysis of Italy and Germany*. Cambridge University Press.
Della Porta, D., 2013. *Clandestine political violence*. Cambridge University Press.
Della Porta, D., & Diani, M., 2013, *Social Movements: An Introduction*. Wiley.
Della Porta, D., Fillieule, O., and Reiter, H., 1998. Policing protest in France and Italy: From intimidation to cooperation?. *The Social Movement Society. Contentious Politics for a New Century*, pp. 111–130.
Della Porta, D., & Fillieule, O., 2004. Policing social protest. *The Blackwell Companion to Social Movements*, 217, p. 241.
Della Porta, D., Donker, T.H., Hall, B., Poljarevic, E., & Ritter, D.P., 2017. *Social Movements and Civil War: When Protests for Democratization Fail*. Routledge.
DeVore, M.R., 2012. Exploring the Iran-Hezbollah relationship: A case study of how state sponsorship affects terrorist group decision-making. *Perspectives on Terrorism*, 6(4/5), pp. 85–107.
Diani, M., 2003. Leaders or brokers? Positions and influence in social movement networks. In Diani, M. and McAdam, D., *Social Movements and Networks: Relational Approaches to Collective Action*, pp. 105–122.
Diani, M., & McAdam, D., 2003. *Social Movements and Networks: Relational Approaches to Collective Action*. Oxford University Press.
Díaz, N.R., 2017. *The Muslim Brotherhood in Syria: The Democratic Option of Islamism*. Routledge.
Donker, T.H., 2013. Islamist social movements and the Syrian Authoritarian Regime. In: Heydemann, S. and Leenders, R. eds., 2013. *Middle East Authoritarianisms: Governance, Contestation, and Regime Resilience in Syria and Iran*. Stanford University Press. pp. 107–124.
Donker, T.H., 2018. Dschihadismus und governance in Nordsyrien (Jihadism and governance in north-Syria). *Mittelweg 36*, vol 27(2), pp. 58–85.

Donker, T.H., 2019. Between rebellion and uprising: Intersecting networks and discursive strategies in rebel controlled Syria. *Social Movement Studies*, 18(1), pp. 17–35.
Doornbos, H., & Moussa, J., 2016a. Present at the creation. *Foreign Policy*, 18(1), pp. 17–35.
Doornbos, H., & Moussa, J., 2016b. The greatest divorce in the Jihadi world. Foreign Policy.
Drevon, J., 2015. The emergence of ex-Jihadi political parties in post-Mubarak Egypt. *The Middle East Journal*, 69(4), pp. 511–526.
Drevon, J., 2016. Embracing Salafi Jihadism in Egypt and mobilizing in the Syrian jihad. *Middle East Critique*, 25(4), pp. 321–339.
Drevon, J., 2017. The Jihadi social movement (JSM): Between factional hegemonic drive, national realities, and transnational ambitions. *Perspectives on terrorism*, 11(6) pp. 55–62.
Drevon, J., 2020. Can (Salafi) jihadi insurgents politicise and become pragmatic in civil wars? Social movement restraint in Ahrar al-Sham in Syria. *Third World Thematics: A TWQ Journal*, 5(3–6), pp. 189–205.
Drevon, J., 2021. Ahrar al-Sham's politicisation during the Syrian conflict. In: Bano, M., *Salafi Social and Political Movements: National and Transnational Contexts*, pp. 222–246.
Drevon, J., 2022, *Institutionalising Violence: Strategies of Jihad*. Oxford University Press.
Drevon, J., & Haenni, P., 2021. How global Jihad relocalises and where it leads. The case of HTS, the former AQ franchise in Syria. *The Case of HTS, the Former AQ Franchise in Syria (January 2021). Robert Schuman Centre for Advanced Studies Research Paper No. RSCAS*, 8, pp. 1–43.
Drevon, J., & Haenni, P., 2022. Redefining global Jihad and its termination: The subjugation of al-Qaeda by its former franchise in Syria. *Studies in Conflict & Terrorism*, pp. 1–16.
Droz-Vincent, P., 2020. *Military Politics of the Contemporary Arab World*. Cambridge University Press.
Dudouet, V., & Göldner-Ebenthal, K., 2020. Challenges and opportunities for conflict resolution with Salafi Jihadi armed groups—Policy Brief 10, Berghof Foundation.
Dukhan, H., & Hawat, S., 2014. The Islamic State and the Arab tribes in eastern Syria. *Caliphate and Islamic Global Politics*, pp. 60–66.
Eisenstadt, M., 2018. "Has the Assad regime 'won' Syria's civil war?". Washington Institute for Near East Policy.
Elder-Vass, D., 2010. *The Causal Power of Social Structures: Emergence, Structure and Agency*. Cambridge University Press.
Everton, S.F., 2012. *Disrupting Dark Networks* (Vol. 34). Cambridge University Press.
Farrall, L., 2011. How Al Qaeda works—What the organization's subsidiaries say about its strength. *Foreign Affairs.*, 90, p. 128.
Fishman, B., 2016. *The Master Plan: ISIS, Al Qaeda, and the Jihadi Strategy for Final Victory*. Yale University Press.
Fishman, B., & Moghadam, A., 2010. Self-Inflicted Wounds: Debates and Divisions within al-Qa'ida and Its Periphery. *WestPoint, CT: Combating Terrorism Center*.
Fjelde, H., & Nilsson, D., 2012. Rebels against rebels: Explaining violence between rebel groups. *Journal of Conflict Resolution*, 56(4), pp. 604–628.
Fjelde, H., & Nilsson, D., 2018. The rise of rebel contenders: Barriers to entry and fragmentation in civil wars. *Journal of Peace Research*, 55(5), pp. 551–565.
Ford, R.S., & El Yassir, A., 2015. Yes, talk with Syria's Ahrar al-Sham'. *Middle East Institute*, 15(7), p. 15.
France 24. 2014. aswat al-shabakat - musalahun mu'aradun yaljadun rijalayn fi Halab litakhalufuma 'an al-salah. https://www.youtube.com/watch?v = FQPXweuQEoY.
France 24, 2020. Syrie : "Le prédicateur français Omar Omsen est sur zone depuis sept ans" https://www.youtube.com/watch?v=6HMcnIyJJNI&t=2s
France 24. 2023. Exclusif : un jihadiste français tué à Idleb par l'armée syrienne • FRANCE 24 https://www.youtube.com/watch?v=KOnqjlZ9US4
Fujii, L. A., 2009. *Killing Neighbors: Webs of Violence in Rwanda*. Cornell University Press.

Furlan, M., 2020. Understanding governance by insurgent non-state actors: A multi-dimensional typology. *Civil Wars*, 22(4), pp. 1–34.

Furlan, Mart., 2022. From Jihad-making to state-building: Understanding governance by Salafi-Jihadist insurgents, Doctoral dissertation. University of St Andrew.

Gade, E.K., Gabbay, M., Hafez, M.M., & Kelly, Z., 2019. Networks of cooperation: Rebel alliances in fragmented civil wars. *Journal of Conflict Resolution*, 63(9), pp. 2071–2097.

Gade, E.K., Hafez, M.M., & Gabbay, M., 2019. Fratricide in rebel movements: A network analysis of Syrian militant infighting. *Journal of Peace Research*, 56(3), pp. 321–335.

Gartenstein-Ross, D., & Vassefi, T., 2012. Perceptions of the "Arab Spring" within the Salafi-Jihadi movement. *Studies in Conflict & Terrorism*, 35(12), pp. 831–848.

Gartenstein-Ross, D. and Barr, N., 2018. How Al-Qaeda Works: The Jihadist Group's Evolving Organizational Design. *Current Trends in Islamist Ideology*

Gerges, F.A., 2011. *The Far Enemy: Why Jihad Went Global*. Cambridge University Press.

Gerges, F.A., 2017. *Isis: A History*. Princeton University Press.

Ghadban, O.A., 2022. A tale of two revolutions: The sociopolitical dynamics of the Syrian revolution. Master's thesis. Marmara Universitesi.

Gharibah, M., Hajjar, B., Hilal, L., Sharbaji, M., von Burg, C., & Santschi, M., 2017. Perceptions of Governance—The Experience of Local Administrative Councils in Opposition-held Syria. Swiss Peace. https://www.swisspeace.ch/articles/perceptions-of-governance-the-experience-of-local-administrative-councils-in-opposition-held-syria

Giovanni, J., 2016. *The Morning They Came for Us: Dispatches from Syria*. W.W. Norton & Company.

Giustozzi, A., 2019. *The Taliban at War: 2001–2018*. Oxford University Press.

Giustozzi, A., 2020. A struggle for power: Al Nusra and Al Qaida in Syria. *Studies in Conflict & Terrorism*, 44(1), pp. 1–25.

Glasman, W., 2013. Les ressources sécuritaires du régime. In: Burgat, F. and Paoli, B. *Pas de Printemps pour la Syrie. Les clés pour comprendre les acteurs et les défis de la crise (2011–2013)*. pp. 33–53

Göldner-Ebenthal, K., and Elsayed, A., 2019. Salafi Jihadi armed groups and conflict (de-) escalation. The case of Ahrar al-Sham in Syria. Berlin: Berghof Foundation.

Goldsmith, L.T., 2015. Alawi diversity and solidarity. In: Kerr, M. and Larkin, C., *The Alawis of Syria: War, Faith and Politics in the Levant*, pp. 141–158.

Goodarzi, J.M., 2009. *Syria and Iran: Diplomatic Alliance and Power Politics in the Middle East*. I.B. Tauris.

Goodwin, J., 2001. *No Other Way Out: States and Revolutionary Movements, 1945–1991*. Cambridge University Press.

Gopal, A., 2018. Syria's last bastion of freedom. *New Yorker*.

Gopal, A. and Hodge, J., 2021. Social networks, class, and the Syrian proxy war. *New America*. pp. 1–69. https://d1y8sb8igg2f8e.cloudfront.net/documents/Social_Networks_Class_and_the_Syrian_Proxy_War.pdf

Goya, M., 2017. *Etoile rouge: Enseignements opérationnels de quatre ans d'engagement russe en Syrie*. Amazon Media.

Granovetter, M.S., 1973. The strength of weak ties. *American Journal of Sociology*, 78(6), pp. 1360–1380.

Grant-Brook, W., 2023. The state in Idlib: Hay'at Tahrir al-Sham and complexity amid the Syrian civil war. In Fraihat, I., and Alijla, A., *Rebel Governance in the Middle East*, pp. 51–86. Singapore: Springer Nature Singapore.

Groll, E., 2016. The U.S. wants to design safer anti-aircraft missiles for Syria's rebels. *Foreign Policy*.

Gunaratna, R., 2002. *Inside Al Qaeda: Global Network of Terror*. Columbia University Press.

Guardian. 2011. "Extraordinary rendition: a backstory"

Gunning, J., 2007. *Hamas in Politics: Democracy, Religion, Violence*. Hurst.

Gunning, J., 2009. Social movement theory and the study of terrorism. In: Jackson, R., Smyth, M. B., and Gunning, J. *Critical Terrorism Studies: A New Research Agenda*, pp. 156–177.

Gunning, J. and Baron, I.Z., 2014. *Why occupy a square?: People, protests and movements in the Egyptian revolution*. Oxford University Press.

Gutiérrez-Sanín, F., 2018. The FARC's militaristic blueprint. *Small Wars & Insurgencies*, 29(4), pp. 629–653.

Gutman, R., 2015. What really happened to the U.S. train-and-equip program in Syria? McClatchy Washington Bureau.

Haddad, B.S., 2011. *Business Networks in Syria: The Political Economy of Authoritarian Resilience*. Stanford University Press.

Haddad, B., & Wind, E., 2014. The fragmented state of the Syrian opposition. In: Kamrava, M., *Beyond the Arab Spring: The Evolving Ruling Bargain in the Middle East*, pp. 397–435.

Haenni, P. and Quesnay, A., 2020. *Survivre à la disparition de l'Etat islamique: la stratégie de résilience du mouvement kurde syrien*. European University Institute.

Haer, R., 2015. *Armed Group Structure and Violence in Civil Wars: The Organizational Dynamics of Civilian Killing*. Routledge.

Hafez, M.M., 2003. *Why Muslims Rebel: Repression and Resistance in the Islamic World*. Lynne Rienner Publishers.

Hafez, M.M., 2019. Not my brother's keeper: Factional infighting in armed Islamist movements. *Journal of Religion and Violence*, 7(2), pp. 189–208.

Hafez, M.M., 2020. Fratricidal rebels: Ideological extremity and warring factionalism in civil wars. *Terrorism and Political Violence*, 32(3), pp. 604–629.

Hafez, M.M., Gabbay, M., & Gade, E.K., 2021. Consolidation of nonstate armed actors in fragmented conflicts: Introducing an emerging research program. *Studies in Conflict & Terrorism*, pp. 1–21.

Haid, H. 2017a. "Who Is Assassinating Hay'at Tahrir Al-Sham's Leaders?". Chatham House.

Haid, H. 2017b. "Why Ahrar al-Sham Couldn't Stand Up to HTS's Attack in Idlib". Chatham House.

Haid, Haid, 2021, The "lesser evil": The Evolution of Jabhat al-Nusra's Governance Strategy in Syria. Doctoral dissertation.

Al-Haj, A., n.d., *thawahir al-islam al-siyasi wa tayarato fi suriya isti'ada khiyar al-dimuqrati*.

Al-Haj, A., 2013. *al-salafiyya wal-salafiyun fi suriya: min al-islah ila al-jihad*. Al-Jazeera Center for Studies.

al-Haj Saleh, Y., 2017. *Impossible Revolution: Making Sense of the Syrian Tragedy*. Trans. Ibtihal Mahmood. Chicago, IL: Haymarket Books.

Hamilton, R., Miller, C., & Stein, A., 2020. *Russia's War in Syria: Assessing Russian Military Capabilities and Lessons Learned*. Foreign Policy Research Institute.

Hamming, T.R., 2020. The Al Qaeda–Islamic State rivalry: Competition yes, but no competitive escalation. *Terrorism and Political Violence*, 32(1), pp. 20–37.

Hamming, T., 2022. *Jihadi Politics: The Global Jihadi Civil War, 2014–2019*. Hurst Publishers.

Hammond, J., 2018. Maps of mayhem: Strategic location and deadly violence in civil war. *Journal of Peace Research*, 55(1), pp. 32–46.

Hashim, A., 2018. *The Caliphate at War: The Ideological, Organisational and Military Innovations of Islamic State*. Oxford University Press.

Has, K., 2019. Turkey, Russia, and the Looming S-400 Crisis. *Middle East Institute*. https://www.mei.edu/publications/turkeyrussia-and-looming-s-400-crisis.

Hassan, H. 2016a. "Ahrar Al Sham and the myths that surround it". *The National*.

Hassan, H. 2016b. Jihadist Legacy Still Shapes Ahrar al-Sham. *Tahrir Institute for Middle East Policy*.

Hassan, H., 2016c. *The Sectarianism of the Islamic State: Ideological Roots and Political Context*. Carnegie Endowment for International Peace.

Hassan, H., 2017. The complex backstory of the Qatari hostage deal. *The National*.

Hassan, H., 2019. Sunni Jihad is going local. *The Atlantic*.

Haykel, B., 2009. On the nature of Salafi thought and action.In: Meier, R., *Global Salafism: Islam's New Religious Movement*, pp. 33–57.
Hazen, J.M., 2013. *What Rebels Want: Resources and Supply Networks in Wartime*. Cornell University Press.
Hegghammer, T. ed., 2017. *Jihadi Culture*. Cambridge University Press.
Hegghammer, T., 2009. Jihadi-Salafis or revolutionaries? On religion and politics in the study of militant Islamism. In: Meier, R., *Global Salafism: Islam's New Religious Movement*, pp. 244–266.
Hegghammer, T., 2010. The rise of Muslim foreign fighters: Islam and the globalization of Jihad. *International Security*, 35(3), pp. 53–94.
Hegghammer, T., 2020. *The Caravan: Abdallah Azzam and the Rise of Global Jihad*. Cambridge University Press.
Heller, S., 2014. Muhammad al-Amin on Ahrar al-Sham's Evolving Relationship with Jabhat al-Nusrah and Global Jihadism. Jihadologie.
Heller, S., 2015. Ahrar al-Sham's revisionist Jihadism. *War on the Rocks*.
Heller, S., 2016a. How Ahrar al-Sham has come to define the kaleidoscope of the Syrian civil war. *War on the Rocks*.
Heller, S., 2016b. Keeping the lights on in rebel Idlib. *The Century Foundation*,
Heller, S., 2016c. The home of Syria's only real rebels. *The Daily Beast*.
Heller, S., 2017a. Aleppo's bitter lessons. *The Century Foundation*
Heller, S., 2017b. The strategic logic of Hayat Tahrir al-Sham. *Perspectives on terrorism*, 11(6), pp 140–153.
Heller, S., 2017c. Turkey through the Syrian looking glass. The Century Foundation.
Heller, S., 2020. Leak reveals Jihadists' weakening grip in Syria's Idlib. *War on the Rocks*.
Heydemann, S., 2007. *Upgrading Authoritarianism in the Arab World*. Saban Center for Middle East Policy at the Brookings Institution.
Hinnebusch, R.A., 1990. *Authoritarian Power and State Formation in Ba'thist Syria: Army, Party, and Peasant*. Westview Press.
Hinnebusch, R., 2004. *Syria: Revolution from Above*. Routledge.
Hinnebusch, R., 2012. Syria: from 'authoritarian upgrading' to revolution?. *International Affairs*, 88(1), pp. 95–113.
Hinnebusch, R., 2013. Documenting the roots and dynamics of the Syrian uprising. *Middle East Journal*.
Hinnebusch, R., 2014. Historical sociology and the Arab Uprising. *Mediterranean Politics*, 19(1), pp. 137–140.
Hinnebush, R., 2015. Syria's Alawis and the Ba'ath Party. In: Kerr, M. and Larkin, C., *The Alawis of Syria: War, Faith and Politics in the Levant*, p.107.
Hinnebusch, R., & Zinti, T., 2015. *Syria from Reform to Revolt: Volume 1: Political Economy and International Relations*. Syracuse University Press.
Hinnebusch, R., & Imady, O., eds., 2018a. *The Syrian Uprising: Domestic Origins and Early Trajectory*. Routledge.
Hinnebusch, R., & Imady, O., 2018b. Introduction: Origins of the Syrian Uprising: From structure to agency. In: *The Syrian Uprising, Hinnebusch & Imady*, pp. 1–11. Routledge.
Hinnebusch, R., 2019. What went wrong: Understanding the trajectory of Syria's conflict. In: Matar, L. and Kadri, A., *Syria: From National Independence to Proxy War* pp. 29–52. Palgrave Macmillan.
Hisham, M., & Crabapple, M., 2018. *Brothers of the Gun: A Memoir of the Syrian War*. One World.
Hodgson, G.M., 2015. On defining institutions: Rules versus equilibria. *Journal of Institutional Economics*, 11(3), pp. 497–505.
Hoffman, B., 2008. The myth of grass-roots terrorism-why Osama bin Laden still matters. *Foreign Aff.*, 87, p.133.
Hokayem, E., 2017. *Syria's Uprising and the Fracturing of the Levant*. Routledge.

Hoover, J., 2019. *Ibn Taymiyya*. Simon and Schuster.
Hoover Green, A., 2017. Armed group institutions and combatant socialization: Evidence from El Salvador. *Journal of Peace Research*, 54(5), pp. 687–700.
Hoover Green, A., 2018. *The Commander's Dilemma: Violence and Restraint in Wartime*. Cornell University Press.
Huang, R., 2016a. Rebel diplomacy in civil war. *International Security*, 40(4), pp. 89–126.
Huang, R., 2016b. *The Wartime Origins of Democratization: Civil War, Rebel Governance, and Political Regimes*. Cambridge University Press.
Huang, R., Silverman, D., & Acosta, B., 2022. Friends in the profession: Rebel leaders, international social networks, and external support for rebellion. *International Studies Quarterly*, 66(1), p. sqab085.
Hubbard, B., 2015. In Syria, potential ally's Islamist ties challenge US. *The New York Times*
Hubbar, B., Shoumali, K., Gall, C., and Kingsley, P., 2019, "Syrian Arab Fighters Backed by Turkey Kill Two Kurdish Prisoners", *The New York Times*
Human Rights Watch, 2013. *Attacks on Ghouta Analysis of Alleged Use of Chemical Weapons in Syria*. Human Rights Watch https://www.hrw.org/sites/default/files/reports/syria_cw0913_web_1.pdf.
Human Rights Watch, 2013. "You Can Still See Their Blood": Executions, Indiscriminate Shootings, and Hostage Taking by Opposition Forces in Latakia Countryside. Human Rights Watch. https://www.hrw.org/report/2013/10/10/you-can-still-see-their-blood/executions-indiscriminate-shootings-and-hostage.
Humanitarian Dialogue, 2014. Local Administration Structures in opposition-held areas in Syria, Research report. Pp. 1–27.
Hundman, E., & Parkinson, S.E., 2019. Rogues, degenerates, and heroes: Disobedience as politics in military organizations. *European Journal of International Relations*, 25(3), pp. 645–671.
Huntington, S.P., 1968. *Political Order in Changing Societies*. Yale University Press.
Hussain, M., 2015. Al Qaeda Syria boss says that his "So-Called Khorasan Group Doesn't Exist". *The Intercept*.
Hussein, A., 2015. *"Jaysh "al-Muhajireen wal-Ansar".. la yuwali "al-Nusra" wa al yuba'y' "Da'ish"*. Al-mudun.
Hussein, A., 2016a. *"Abu Firas al-Suri.. rajul "al-Nusra" al-muthir lil-jadal"*. al-mudun.
Hussein, A., 2016b. *""al-Hizb al-Islami al-Turkistani": al-mahata al-shamiyya"*. al-mudun.
Hussein, A., 2016c. *""Jabhat Fath al-Sham" : inshiqaq ghayr muqalaqa"*. al-mudun.
Hussein, A., 2017a. *""Ahrar al-Sham" wa lu'bat al-tawazunat: i'adat haykaliyya la i'adat al-bina'"*. al-mudun.
Hussein, A., 2017b. *"b a'd hazimat "al-Ahrar": madha kasabat wa madha khasarat "Tahrir al-Sham"""*. al-mudun.
Hussein, A., 2017c. *"Hassan Sufan wa dawla "Ahrar al-Sham" al-'amiqa"*. al-mudun.
Hussein, A., 2017d. *""itimad "Ahrar al-Sham" li "qanun al-'arabi".. khutwa bayna al-kufr wal islam?"*. al-mudun.
Hussein, A., 2017e. *""Katibat al-Bukhari" al-Uzbiki: dahiyya al-sira' bayna "Da'ish" wa "al-Qa'ida""*. al-mudun.
Hussein, A., 2017f. *"li madha anharat "Harakat Ahrar al-Sham"""*. al-mudun.
Hussein, A., 2017g. *"li madha najahat "al-Zinki" fi muwajaha "Tahrir al-Sham"""*. al-mudun.
Hussein, A., 2017h. *"majlis shura ahl al-'ilm fi al-Sham": al-ba'th 'an al-dhat"*. al-mudun.
Hussein, A., 2017i. *""nazila" al-tadakhul al-Turki. bayna "al-wala lil kuffar" wa "al-mudtar lil-mahthur"?"*. al-mudun.
Hussein, A., 2018a. *""Jaysh al-Islam": su'al al-masir ba'd al-hijra ila al-Shamal"*. al-mudun.
Hussein, A., 2018b. *"mawaqif "al-muhajiriin" min al-iqtital bayna "Tahrir al-Sham" wa "Tahrir Suriyya"""*. al-mudun.
Hussein, A., 2018c. *""Suqur al-Sham": 'awda muqatil am intifada jarih?"*. al-mudun.
Hussein, T., 2020. The caliph of Lisson Green. *Newlines Magazine*.

Hyyppä, T., 2023. Council in war: Civilocracy, order and local organisation in daraya during the Syrian War. *Small Wars & Insurgencies*, *34*(1), pp. 52–80.
Ibrahim, Abdulla, 2021. Process of Rebel Groups Consolidation in the Syrian Civil War (2011–2021). Dissertation. Geneva Graduate Institute.
ICG (International Crisis Group), 2012. Tentative Jihad, Syria's Fundamentalist Opposition., *Middle East Report N°131*. International Crisis Group.
ICG (International Crisis Group), 2014. Flight of Icarus? The PYD's precarious rise in Syria. *Middle East Report, No. 151*. International Crisis Group.
ICG (International Crisis Group), 2015. New Approach in Southern Syria. *Middle East Report N°163*. International Crisis Group.
ICG (International Crisis Group), 2016. Steps toward Stabilising Syria's Northern Border. *Middle East Briefing N°49*. International Crisis Group.
ICG (International Crisis Group), 2017. The PKK's Fateful Choice in Northern Syria. *Middle East Report N°176*. International Crisis Group.
ICG (International Crisis Group), 2018. Syria's Idlib Wins Welcome Reprieve with Russia-Turkey Deal. *Statement*. International Crisis Group.
ICG (International Crisis Group), 2019a. Addressing the Rise of Libya's Madkhali-Salafis. *Middle East and North Africa Report N°200*. International Crisis Group.
ICG (International Crisis Group), 2019b. Steadying the New Status Quo in Syria's North East. *Middle East Briefing N°72*. International Crisis Group.
ICG (International Crisis Group), 2019c. The Best of Bad Options for Syria's Idlib. *Middle East Report N°197*. International Crisis Group.
ICG (International Crisis Group), 2020. Silencing the Guns in Syria's Idlib. *Middle East Report N°213*. International Crisis Group.
ICG (International Crisis Group), 2022. A Death In Idlib: The Killing of the Top ISIS Leader and Its Impact, *Q&A*. International Crisis Group.
ICG (International Crisis Group), 2023a. Containing Transnational Jihadists in Syria's North West, *Middle East Report N°239*. International Crisis Group.
ICG (International Crisis Group), 2023b, Gulf Arab Reconciliation Hides Simmering Tensions, *Commentary*. International Crisis Group.
ICRC, 2020. The Roots of Restraint in War. ICRC.
Ignatius, D., 2015. A new cooperation on Syria. *The Washington Post*, p. 21.
Ingram, H.J., Whiteside, C., & Winter, C., 2020. *The ISIS Reader: Milestone Texts of the Islamic State Movement*. Oxford University Press.
Ishiyama, J., 2016. Introduction to the special issue "From bullets to ballots: The transformation of rebel groups into political parties". *Democratization*. 23(6), pp, 969–971.
Ishiyama, J., & Batta, A., 2011. Swords into plowshares: The organizational transformation of rebel groups into political parties. *Communist and Post-Communist Studies*, *44*(4), pp. 369–379.
Ismail, R., 2021. *Rethinking Salafism: The Transnational Networks of Salafi'Ulama in Egypt, Kuwait, and Saudi Arabia*. Oxford University Press.
Ismail, S., 2018. *The Rule of Violence: Subjectivity, Memory and Government in Syria* (Vol. 50). Cambridge University Press.
Al-Jabassini, A., 2019. From rebel rule to a post-capitulation era in Daraa southern Syria: The impacts and outcomes of rebel behaviour during negotiations. *Robert Schuman Centre for Advanced Studies Research Paper No. RSCAS*, *6*. pp 1–39
Jackson, A., & Amiri, R., 2019. *Insurgent Bureaucracy: How the Taliban Makes Policy*. United States Institute of Peace.
Jackson, A., 2021. *Negotiating Survival: Civilian-Insurgent Relations in Afghanistan*. Oxford University Press.
Jackson, K., 2014. The Forgotten Caliphate. *Jihadica*. www. jihadica. com/the-forgotten-caliphate (accessed December 31, 2014).

Jaeger, D.A., Klor, E.F., Miaari, S.H., & Paserman, M.D., 2015. Can militants use violence to win public support? Evidence from the second Intifada. *Journal of Conflict Resolution*, 59(3), pp. 528–549.
Jo, H., 2015. *Compliant Rebels*. Cambridge University Press.
Jones, S.G., 2017. *Waging Insurgent Warfare: Lessons from the Vietcong to the Islamic State*. Oxford University Press.
Jones, S.G., 2020. *Moscow's War in Syria*. Center for Strategic and International Studies.
Juneau, T., 2020. Iran's costly intervention in Syria: A pyrrhic victory. *Mediterranean Politics*, 25(1), pp. 26–44.
Kalyvas, S.N., & Balcells, L., 2010. International system and technologies of rebellion: How the end of the Cold War shaped internal conflict. *American Political Science Review*, 104(3), pp. 415–429.Kalyvas, S.N., 2006. *The Logic of Violence in Civil War*. Cambridge University Press.
Kalyvas, S.N., 2015. Is ISIS a Revolutionary group and if Yes, What are the Implications?. *Perspectives on Terrorism*, 9(4), pp. 42–47.
Kalyvas, S.N., 2018. Jihadi rebels in civil war. *Dædalus*, 147(1), pp. 36–47.
Kaplan, O., 2017. *Resisting War: How Communities Protect Themselves*. Cambridge University Press.
Kasfir, N., 2015. Rebel Governance—Constructing a Field of Inquiry: Definitions, Scope, Patterns, Order, Causes In: Arjona, A., Kasfir, N. and Mampilly, W., *Rebel Governance*, New York: Cambridge University Press, pp. 21–46.
Kenney, M., 2018. *The Islamic State in Britain: Radicalization and Resilience in an Activist Network*. Cambridge University Press.
Kerr, M., & Larkin, C., eds., 2015. *The Alawis of Syria: War, Faith and Politics in the Levant*. Oxford University Press.
Keser, A., & Fakhoury, F., 2022. Hay'at Tahrir Al-Sham (HTS) from an insurgent group to a local authority: Emergence, development and social support base. *Studies in Conflict & Terrorism*, pp. 1–21.
Khaddour, K., 2015. Assad's officer ghetto: Why the Syrian army remains loyal. *The Carnegie Middle East Center*. http://carnegie-mec.org/2015/11/04/assad-s-officer-ghetto-why-syrian-army-remains-loyal-pub-61449.
Khalaf, R., 2015. Governance without government in Syria: Civil society and state building during conflict. *Syria Studies*. pp. 1–50.
Khalifa, Dareen, 2020. "The Jihadist Factor in Syria's Idlib: A Conversation with Abu Muhammad al-Jolani". International Crisis Group, *Commentary*.
Khalifa, Dareen, 2023. Idlib and the Hayat Tahrir al-Sham Conundrum in Syria. In *The Rule Is for None but Allah*, Cook, Joana & Maher, Shiraz. Hurst.
Khalifa, Mustafa, 2008. al-qawqa'.
Khalifa & Bonsey, 2021. In Syria's Idlib, Washington's Chance to Reimagine Counter-terrorism, International Crisis Group.
Khatib, L., 2012. *Islamic Revivalism in Syria: The Rise and Fall of Ba'thist Secularism*. Routledge.
Khatib, L., 2018. The pre-2011 roots of Syria's Islamist militants. *The Middle East Journal*, 72(2), pp. 209–228.
al-Khatib, K., 2018. ""*Faylaq al-Sham*": *al-hiyad al-sa'b ka khiyar istratiji?*". al-mudun.
Kilcullen, D., 2011. *The Accidental Guerrilla: Fighting Small Wars in the Midst of a Big One*. Oxford University Press.
Kilcullen, D., 2016. *Blood Year, Islamic State and the Failures of the War on Terror*. Black Inc.
Kilcullen, D., 2020. *The Dragons and the Snakes: How the Rest Learned to Fight the West*. Oxford University Press.
Koehler, K. and Albrecht, H., 2021. Revolutions and the military: Endgame coups, instability, and prospects for democracy. *Armed Forces & Society*, 47(1), pp.148-176.
Koontz, K., & Waters, Gregory, 2023. "Shabiha Forever": Assad's Creation, Control, and Use of Militias Since 2011. Harmoon Centre.

Krause, J., 2018. *Resilient Communities: Non-violence and Civilian Agency in Communal War*. Cambridge University Press.
Krause, P., 2017. *Rebel Power: Why National Movements Compete, Fight, and Win*. Cornell University Press.
Krebs, V.E., 2002. Mapping networks of terrorist cells. *Connections*, 24(3), pp. 43–52.
Kriesi, H., ed., 1995. New Social Movements in Western Europe: A Comparative Analysis (Vol. 5). University of Minnesota Press.
Kubari, A., & Drevon, J., 2018. Administering a borderland at war: Bab al-Hawa in Syria. In: Yousuf, Z. 2019 Borderlands and peacebuilding*Conciliation Resources*. pp 42–47.
Kujan, A., 2016. ""*Jund al-Aqsa*". *salafiyya jihadiyya ta'iha bayna "Da'ish" wa "al-Qa'ida*"". enabbaladi.
Lacher, W., 2020. *Libya's Fragmentation: Structure and Process in Violent Conflict*. Bloomsbury Publishing.
Lacroix, S., 2009. Between revolution and apoliticism: Nasir al-Din al-Albani and his impact on the shaping of contemporary Salafism. In: Meijer, R., 2011. *Global Salafism: Islam's New Religious Movement*, pp. 58–80.
Lacroix, S., 2011. *Awakening Islam*. Harvard University Press.
Lahoud, N., 2010. *The Jihadis' Path to Self-Destruction*. Hurst & Co.
Landis, J., 2012. The Syrian uprising of 2011: Why the Asad regime is likely to survive to 2013. *Middle East Policy*, 19(1), pp. 72–84.
Larivière, G., 2021. The Islamic Revolution in Syria from the Rebels' Perspective. Master's dissertation. McGill.
Larson, J.M., & Lewis, J.I., 2018. Rumors, kinship networks, and rebel group formation. *International Organization*, 72(4), pp. 871–903.
Lav, D., 2012. *Radical Islam and the Revival of Medieval Theology*. Cambridge University Press.
Lawson, G., 2015. Revolution, nonviolence, and the Arab uprisings. *Mobilization: An International Quarterly*, 20(4), pp. 453–470.
Lawson, G., 2019. *Anatomies of Revolution*. Cambridge University Press.
Leader Maynard, J., 2019. Ideology and armed conflict. *Journal of Peace Research, 56(5)*, pp. 635–649.
Ledwidge, F., 2017. *Rebel Law: Insurgents, Courts and Justice in Modern Conflict*. Oxford University Press.
Leenders, R., 2012. Collective action and mobilization in Dar'a: An anatomy of the onset of Syria's popular uprising. *Mobilization: An International Quarterly*, 17(4), pp. 419–434.
Leenders, R., & Giustozzi, A., 2019. Outsourcing state violence: The National Defence Force, 'stateness' and regime resilience in the Syrian war. *Mediterranean Politics*, 24(2), pp. 157–180.
Leenders, R., & Giustozzi, A., 2022. Foreign sponsorship of pro-government militias fighting Syria's insurgency: Whither proxy wars?. *Mediterranean Politics*, 27(5), pp. 614–643.
Lefèvre, R., 2013. *Ashes of Hama: The Muslim Brotherhood in Syria*. Oxford University Press.
Lefèvre, R., 2014. A Revolution in Syria's Muslim Brotherhood?. *Carnegie Endowment*.
Lefèvre, R., 2017. Syria. In: , Hamid, S. and McCants, W. eds. Rethinking Political Islam Oxford University Press.
Lefèvre, R., & El Yassir, A., 2013. Militias for the Syrian Muslim Brotherhood. Carnegie Endowment.
Lefèvre, R., & El Yassir, A., 2014. The Sham Legion: Syria's Moderate Islamists. Carnegie Endowment.
Lenfant, A., 2008. L'évolution du Salafisme en Syrie au XXe siècle. In Rougier, B., *Qu'est-ce que le Salafisme*, pp. 161–178.
Lesch, D.W., 2013. *Syria: The Fall of the House of Assad*. Yale University Press.
Leverett, F., 2005. *Inheriting Syria: Bashar's Trial by Fire*. Brookings Institution Press.
Lewis, J.D., 2013. Al-Qaeda in Iraq resurgent. *Middle East Security Report*.

Lewis, J.I., 2017. How does ethnic rebellion start?. *Comparative Political Studies*, 50(10), pp. 1420–1450.

Lewis, J.L., 2020. *How Insurgency Begins: Rebel Group Formation in Uganda and Beyond.* Cambridge University Press.

Lia, B., 2009. *Architect of Global Jihad: The Life of Al Qaeda Strategist Abu Mus' ab al-Suri.* Columbia University Press.

Lia, B., 2015. Understanding Jihadi proto-states. *Perspectives on Terrorism*, 9(4), pp. 31–41.

Lia, B., 2016. The Islamist uprising in Syria, 1976–82: The history and legacy of a failed revolt. *British Journal of Middle Eastern Studies*, 43(4), pp. 541–559.

Lia, B., & Hegghammer, T., 2004. Jihadi strategic studies: The alleged al qaida policy study preceding the Madrid bombings. *Studies in Conflict & Terrorism*, 27(5), pp. 355–375.

Lidow, N.H., 2016. *Violent Order: Understanding Rebel Governance through Liberia's Civil War.* Cambridge University Press.

Lister, C., 2015a. al-Qa'ida plays a long game in Syria. *CTC Sentinel, September.* pp 13–18.

Lister, C., 2015b. *The Syrian Jihad: Al-Qaeda, the Islamic State and the Evolution of an Insurgency.* Oxford University Press.

Lister, C., 2015c. Why Assad is losing. *Foreign Policy*Lister, C., 2016c. Profiling Jabhat al-Nusra. Brookings Institution.

Lister, C., 2016d. The dawn of mass jihad: Success in Syria fuels al-Qa'ida's evolution. *CTC Sentinel, September.* pp. 13–20.

Lister, C., 2016e. The Free Syrian Army: A decentralized insurgent brand. *The Brookings Project on US Relations with the Islamic World Analysis Paper*, (26). pp. 1–44.

Lister, L., 2016a. "Aleppo has fallen: But the conflict is far from over (pt.1)". *Huffington Post.*

Lister, L., 2016b. "Aleppo has fallen: Armed opposition seeks to redefine itself". *Huffington Post.*

Livny, A., 2020. *Trust and the Islamic Advantage: Religious-based Movements in Turkey and the Muslim World.* Cambridge University Press.

London, D., 2020. Rethinking US Counterterrorism Strategy. *Middle East Institute.*

Lund, A., 2012. *Syrian Jihadism.* Swedish Institute of International Affairs.

Lund, A., 2013a. Syria's Salafi insurgents: The rise of the Syrian Islamic Front. *UI Occasional Papers*, 17. pp. 1–51.

Lund, A., 2013b. Showdown at Bab al-Hawa. *Carnegie Endowement.*

Lund, A., 2013c. The Curious Case of the Commission for the Protection of Civilians. Carnegie Endowment.

Lund, A., 2014a. Does the "Southern Front" exist?. *Carnegie Middle East Center.*

Lund, A., 2014b. Syria's Ahrar al-Sham leadership wiped out in bombing. *Carnegie Institute Endowement for International Peace.*

Lund, A., 2014c. Syria's al-Qaeda wing searches for a strategy. *Carnegie Endowment for International Peace.*

Lund, A., 2014d. The Mujahideen Army of Aleppo. *Syria in Crisis.*

Lund, A., 2014e. The Revolutionary Command Council: Rebel unity in Syria?. *Syria in Crisis.*

Lund, A., 2014f. What is the 'Khorasan Group' and why is the US bombing it in Syria?. *Carniege Endowment for International Peace.*

Lund, A., 2014g. Who and What Was Abu Khalid Al-Suri? Part I.

Lund, A., 2015a. CHASING GHOSTS. In: Kerr, M. and Larkin, C., *The Alawis of Syria: War, Faith and Politics in the Levant*, p. 207.

Lund, A., 2015b. The Nusra Front's internal purges. *Syria in Crisis. Carnegie Endowment for International Peace*, 7.

Lund, A., 2016. Into the Tunnels: The Rise and Fall of Syria's Rebel Enclave in Eastern Ghouta. New York: The Century Foundation.

Lund, A., 2017. The Syrian rebel who tried to build an Islamist paradise. *POLITICO Magazine*, March, 31.

Lund, A., 2018. Assad's divide and conquer strategy is working. *Foreign Policy, March 28.*

Macridis, R.C., 1986. *Modern Political Regimes: Patterns and Institutions.* Scott Foresman.

Maher, S., 2016. *Salafi-Jihadism: The History of an Idea.* Oxford University Press.

Malek, A., 2017. *The Home That Was Our Country: A Memoir of Syria.* Hachette UK.

Malkasian, C., 2017. *Illusions of Victory: The Anbar Awakening and the Rise of the Islamic State.* Oxford University Press.

Malthaner, S., 2011. *Mobilizing the Faithful: Militant Islamist Groups and their Constituencies* (Vol. 4). Campus Verlag.

Malthaner, S. and Waldmann, P., 2014. The radical milieu: Conceptualizing the supportive social environment of terrorist groups. *Studies in Conflict & Terrorism*, 37(12), pp.979-998.

Mampilly, Z.C., 2012. *Rebel Rulers: Insurgent Governance and Civilian Life during War.* Cornell University Press.

Mampilly, Z., & Stewart, M.A., 2020. A typology of rebel political institutional arrangements. *Journal of Conflict Resolution*, 65(1), p. 0022002720935642.

Mantoux, S., 2017. "Le Parti islamique du Turkestan, bras armé ouïghour d'al-Qaïda en Syrie". France Soir.

Maoz, Z., & San-Akca, B., 2012. Rivalry and state support of non-state armed groups (NAGs), 1946–2001. *International Studies Quarterly*, 56(4), pp. 720–734.

Marsh, K., & Chulov, M., 2011. Assad blames conspirators for Syrian protests. *The Guardian*, 30 March.

Martínez, J.C., & Eng, B., 2018. Stifling stateness: The Assad regime's campaign against rebel governance. *Security Dialogue*, 49(4), pp. 235–253.

Matesan, I.E., 2020. *The Violence Pendulum: Tactical Change in Islamist Groups in Egypt and Indonesia.* Oxford University Press.

Mazur, K., 2015. Ordering Violence: Identity Boundaries and Alliance Formation in the Syrian Uprising. Doctoral dissertation. Princeton University.

Mazur, K., 2019. State networks and intra-ethnic group variation in the 2011 Syrian uprising. *Comparative Political Studies*, 52(7), pp.995–1027.

Mazur, K., 2021. *Revolution in Syria: Identity, Networks, and Repression.* Cambridge University Press.

Mazzetti, M., Goldman, A., & Schmidt, M.S., 2017. Behind the sudden death of a $1 billion secret CIA war in Syria. *New York Times*

McAdam, D., 1982. *Political Process and the Development of Black Insurgency, 1930–1970.* University of Chicago Press.

McAdam, D., McCarthy, J.D., & Zald, M.N., eds., 1996. *Comparative Perspectives on Social Movements: Political Opportunities, Mobilizing Structures, and Cultural Framings* (p. 1). Cambridge, UK: Cambridge University Press.

McHugo, J., 2014. *Syria: From the Great War to Civil War.* Saqi Books.

McLauchlin, T., 2018. The loyalty trap: Regime ethnic exclusion, commitment problems, and civil war duration in Syria and beyond. *Security Studies*, 27(2), pp. 296–317.

Mendelsohn, B., 2015. *The al-Qaeda Franchise: The Expansion of al-Qaeda and Its Consequences.* Oxford University Press.

Mendelsohn, B., 2018. *Jihadism Constrained: The Limits of Transnational Jihadism and What It Means for Counterterrorism.* Rowman & Littlefield.

Mendelsohn, B., 2019. Why do armed nonstate groups use foreign volunteers? The case of the Islamic State. *Orbis*, 64(1), pp. 111–130.

Meng, A., 2020. *Constraining dictatorship.* Cambridge: Cambridge University Press.

Mercy Corps, 2018. Preliminary Impact Assessment: Consolidation of HTS Control in Opposition-Controlled NW Syria. Mercy Corps.

Meijer, R., 2009. Global Salafism: Islam's New Religious Movement. London: Hurst.

Metelits, C., 2009. *Inside Insurgency: Violence, Civilians, and Revolutionary Group Behavior.* New York University Press.

Meyer, D.S., 2004. Protest and political opportunities. *Annual Review of Sociology.*, 30, pp. 125–145.

Michot, Y., 2011. Ibn Taymiyya's "New Mardin Fatwa". Is genetically modified Islam (GMI) carcinogenic?. *The Muslim World, 101*(2), pp. 130–181.
Michot, Y., 2012. *Ibn Taymiyya: Against Extremisms*. Dar Albouraq.
Mironova, V., 2019. *From Freedom Fighters to Jihadists: Human Resources of Non-State Armed Groups*. Oxford University Press.
Mitton, K., 2015. *Rebels in a Rotten State: Understanding Atrocity in the Sierra Leone Civil War*. Oxford University Press.
Moghadam, A., 2008. *The Globalization of Martyrdom: Al Qaeda, Salafi Jihad, and the Diffusion of Suicide Attacks*. Johns Hopkins University Press.
Moghadam, A., & Fishman, B., eds., 2011. *Fault Lines in Global Jihad: Organizational, Strategic, and Ideological Fissures*. Taylor & Francis.
Moghadam, A., 2017. *Nexus of Global Jihad: Understanding Cooperation among Terrorist Actors*. Columbia University Press.
Mohamedou, M.M.O., 2008. *Understanding Al Qaeda: The Transformation of War*. Pluto Press.
Mohamedou, M.M.O., 2017. *A Theory of ISIS*. Pluto Press.
Moloney, E., 2007. *A Secret History of the IRA*. Penguin UK.
Mosinger, E.S., 2018. Brothers or others in arms? Civilian constituencies and rebel fragmentation in civil war. *Journal of Peace Research, 55*(1), pp. 62–77.
Mouline, N., 2014. *The Clerics of Islam: Religious Authority and Political Power in Saudi Arabia*. Yale University Press.
Al-Mudun, 2017. "qararat Turkiyya taghrbal "al-zinki" 'izl qada al-saf al-awwal wa 'ala ras'hum "tawfiq shehab" wa "al-atrash".
Muhammad, M., 2019. "Jaysh al-'Izza" min al-ta'sis ila al-izdihar... hadina sha'biyya muhaba wa sumud usturi fi waj al-nitham". Sham.
Mukhopadhyay, D., & Howe, K., 2023. *Good Rebel Governance: Revolutionary Politics and Western Intervention in Syria*. Cambridge University Press.
Münch, P., 2018. Forces of heresy versus forces of conservation: Making sense of Hezb-e Islami-ye Afghanistan's and the Taleban's positions in the Afghan insurgency. *Small Wars & Insurgencies, 29*(4), pp. 709–734.
Munif, Y., 2017. Participatory democracy and micropolitics in Manbij: An unthinkable revlution. *The Century Foundation*.
al-Musa, 'A., 2020. "Faylaq al-Sham... al-tahawalat wa shabakat al-'alaqat wa halat al-farida fi al-'askara. Syria.tv.
Mustafa, M., 2012. *Jabhat al-Nusra li-ahl al-Sham: min al-ta'sif ila al-inqisam*. Arab Center for Research & Policy Studies.
Neep, D., 2012. *Occupying Syria Under the French Mandate: Insurgency, Space and State Formation* (Vol. 38). Cambridge University Press.
Nichols, N., 2016. U.S., Britain, France block Russia bid to blacklist Syria rebels. *Reuters*.
Nieuwsuur, 2014. Dutch former Royal Netherlands Army soldier trains jihadists in Syria. https://www.youtube.com/watch?v=nWua3exa6rw.
O'Bagy, E., 2013. *The Free Syrian Army*. Institute for the Study of War.
Al-'Omari, A., 2016. "Ahrar al-Sham bil-Ghuta tarfud qarar qiyyadatha al-indimaj bi Jaysh al-Islam". Arabi 21.
Oweis, K.Y., 2013. Insight: Saudi Arabia boosts Salafist rivals to al Qaeda in Syria. *Reuters*.
Padgett, J.F., & McLean, P.D., 2006. Organizational invention and elite transformation: The birth of partnership systems in Renaissance Florence. *American Journal of Sociology, 111*(5), pp. 1463–1568.
Padgett, J.F., & Powell, W.W., 2012. The problem of emergence. In: Padgett, J.F. *The Emergence of Organizations and Markets*, pp. 1–29.
Pahwa, S., 2017. Pathways of Islamist adaptation: The Egyptian Muslim Brothers' lessons for inclusion moderation theory. *Democratization, 24*(6), pp. 1066–1084.
Panebianco, A., 1988. *Political Parties: Organization and Power*. Cambridge University Press.

Paoli, B., 2011. Et maintenant, on va où?: les alaouites à la croisée des destins. In Burgat, F. and Paoli, B. *Pas de printemps pur la Syrie. Les clés pur comprendre les acteurs et les défis de la crise*, 2013, pp. 134–143.

Pargeter, A., 2011. *The Muslim Brotherhood: The Burden of Tradition*. Saqi Books.

Parkinson, S.E., 2013. *Reinventing the Resistance: Order and Violence among Palestinians in Lebanon*. University of Chicago.

Parkinson, S.E., 2023. *Beyond the lines: Social networks and Palestinian militant organizations in wartime Lebanon*. Cornell University Press.

Parkinson, S.E., & Zaks, S., 2018. Militant and rebel organization (s). *Comparative Politics*, 50(2), pp. 271–293.

Pearlman, W., 2011. *Violence, Nonviolence, and the Palestinian National Movement*. Cambridge University Press.

Pearlman, W., 2016. Narratives of fear in Syria. *Perspectives on Politics*, 14(1), pp. 21–37.

Pearlman, W.R., 2017. *We Crossed a Bridge and It Trembled: Voices from Syria*. Custom House.

Pearlman, W., 2020. *Mobilizing from Scratch: Large-Scale Collective Action without Preexisting Organization in the Syrian Uprising*. Comparative Political Studies.

Peçanha, S., & Watkins, D., 2015. ISIS' territory shrank in Syria and Iraq this year. *The New York Times*.

Pedahzur, A., & Perliger, A., 2006. The changing nature of suicide attacks: a social network perspective. *Social Forces*, 84(4), pp. 1987–2008.

Petersen, R.D., 2001. *Resistance and Rebellion: Lessons from Eastern Europe*. Cambridge University Press.

Phillips, B., 2019. Terrorist organizational dynamics. In: *The Oxford Handbook of Terrorism*, Chenoweth, E., English, R., Gofas, A., & Kalyvas, S.N. eds., 2019.. Oxford University Press. pp. 385–400.

Phillips, C., 2016. *The Battle for Syria: International Rivalry in the New Middle East*. Yale University Press.

Phillips, D.L., 2020. *Frontline Syria: From Revolution to Proxy War*. Bloomsbury Publishing.Pierret, T., 2013. *Religion and State in Syria: The Sunni Ulama from Coup to Revolution* (Vol. 41). Cambridge University Press.

Pierret, T., 2015a. Crise et déradicalisation: les rebelles syriens d'Ahrar al-Sham. *Confluences Méditerranée*, (3), pp. 43-49.

Pierret, T., 2015b. Les salafismes dans l'insurrection syrienne: des réseaux transnationaux à l'épreuve des réalités locales. *Outre-Terre*, (3), pp. 196-215.

Pierret, T., 2016. Logics of fragmentation and realignment. In: *Salafism after the Arab Awakening*, Cavatorta, F., & Merone, F., 2015. Hurst. pp. 137–154.

Pierret, T., & Selvik, K., 2009. Limits of "Authoritarian Upgrading" in Syria: Private welfare, Islamic charities, and the rise of the Zayd Movement. *International Journal of Middle East Studies*, 41(4), pp. 595–614.

Pischedda, C., 2018. Wars within wars: Why windows of opportunity and vulnerability cause inter-rebel fighting in internal conflicts. *International Security*, 43(1), pp. 138–176.

Pischedda, C., 2020. *Conflict among Rebels: Why Insurgent Groups Fight Each Other*. Columbia University Press.

Plana, Sara, 2021. The Proxy Paradox: Explaining (Lack of) Control Over State-Sponsored Proxy Armed Groups. MIT Doctoral dissertation.

Popovic, M., 2018. Inter-rebel alliances in the shadow of foreign sponsors. *International Interactions*, 44(4), pp. 749–776.

Provence, M., 2005. *The Great Syrian Revolt and the Rise of Arab Nationalism* (Vol. 22). University of Texas Press.

Puxton, M., 2017. "Jaysh al-Izza: comment l'Armée syrienne libre tente d'exister face aux groupes dJihadistes et Salafistes". France Soir.

Quesnay, A., 2017. "La révolution syrienne est une révolution acéphale". Lundimatin.

Quesnay, A., & Roussel, C., 2013. Avec qui se battre? Le dilemme kurde. . In Burgat, F. and Paoli, B *Pas de printemps pour la Syrie. Les clés pour comprendre les acteurs et les défis de la crise (2011–2013), Paris, La Découverte*, pp. 151–155.Qutrib, H.I., 2016. "Useful Syria" and demographic changes in Syria. *King Faisal Center for Research and Islamic Studies*. Working paper 26, pp. 1–22.
Randall, V., & Svåsand, L., 2002. Party institutionalization in new democracies. *Party Politics*, 8(1), pp. 5–29.
Rapoport, Y., & Ahmed, S., 2010. *Ibn Taymiyya and His Times*. Oxford University Press.
Rassler, D., & Brown, V., 2011. The Haqqani Nexus and the Evolution of al-Qa'ida. Harony Program. The Combating Terrorism Center, West Point. https://ctc.westpoint.edu/the-haqqani-nexus-and-the-evolution-of-al-qaida/
Revkin, M.R., 2020. What explains taxation by resource-rich rebels? Evidence from the Islamic State in Syria. *Journal of Politics*, 82(2), pp. 757–764).
Rey, M., 2013. La révolte des quartiers: territorialisation plutôt que confessionnalisationIn . In Burgat, F. and Paoli, B: *Pas de printemps pour la Syrie, les clés pour comprendre les acteurs et les défis de la crise (2011–2013), París, la Découverte*, pp. 86–87.
Rey, M., 2018. *Histoire de la Syrie XIX-XXIe siècle*. Fayard.
Rhodes, B., 2018. Inside the White House during the Syrian 'Red Line' crisis. *The Atlantic*.
Rida, N., 2016a. *"mubadara li hal "Harakat Ahrar al-Sham" wa damha li"Fath al-Sham".. wa qiyadat tarfudha"*, al-sharq al-awsat.
Rida, N., 2016b. *"sira'at dakhil harakat "Ahrar al-Aham" tahsam masirha qariban"*, al-sharq al-awsat.
Ritter, D.P., 2015. *The Iron Cage of Liberalism: International Politics and Unarmed Revolutions in the Middle East and North Africa*. Oxford University Press.
Rosenblatt, N., & Kilcullen, D., 2019. How Raqqa Became the Capital of ISIS. New America.Rougier, B. 2007. Everyday jihad: the rise of militant Islam among Palestinians in Lebanon. Harvard University Press.
Rougier, B., 2008. *Qu'es-ce que le Salafisme*. Presses Universitaires de France.
Rougier, B., 2015. *The Sunni Tragedy in the Middle East: Northern Lebanon from al-Qaeda to ISIS* (Vol. 60). Princeton University Press.
Roy, O., 2016. *Le djihad et la mort*. Le Seuil.
Ryan, M.W., 2013. *Decoding Al-Qaeda's Strategy: The Deep Battle against America*. Columbia University Press.
Saad, H., 2008. Police kill 9 inmates during prison riot in Syria. *The New York Times*.
Sadaki, Y., 2016. The MOC's Role in the Collapse of the southern Opposition. *Atlantic Council*.
Sageman, M., 2004. *Understanding Terror Networks*. University of Pennsylvania Press.
Sageman, M., 2008. *Leaderless Jihad: Terror Networks in the Twenty-first Century*. University of Pennsylvania Press.
Sakhi, M., 2023. *La révolution et le djihad—Syrie, France, Belgique*, La découverte.
Salah, H., 2015. *"al-qiyadat al-muwahada bil-Ghuta tu'akid inha wujud Ahrar al-Sham"*, arabi 21.
Salehyan, I., 2007. Transnational rebels: Neighboring states as sanctuary for rebel groups. *World Politics*, 59(2), pp. 217–242.
Samaan, M., & Barnard, A., 2015. Assad, in rare admission, says Syria's army lacks manpower. *New York Times*, 26(7), p. 15.
San-Akca, B., 2016. *States in Disguise: Causes of State Support for Rebel Groups*. Oxford University Press.
Sánchez-Cuenca, I., 2019. *The Historical Roots of Political Violence: Revolutionary Terrorism in Affluent Countries*. Cambridge University Press.
Saouli, A., 2018. The tragedy of Ba'thist state-building. In: Imady, O., Hinnebusch, R. *The Syrian Uprising* pp. 12–29. Routledge.
Sarbahi, A., 2021. The structure of religion, ethnicity, and insurgent mobilization: Evidence from India. *World Politics*, 73(1), pp. 82–127.

Scheller, B., 2014. *The Wisdom of Syria's Waiting Game: Foreign Policy under the Assads.* Hurst.
Scheuer, M., 2011. *Osama Bin Laden.* Oxford University Press.
Schmidinger, T., 2018. *Revolution, War and the Future of Syria's Kurds.* Pluto Press.
Schneider, T., 2018. The Fatemiyoun Division. Afghan fighters in the Syrian civil war. *Middle East Institute.*
Schubiger, L.I., & Zelina, M., 2017. Ideology in armed groups. *PS: Political Science & Politics, 50*(4), pp. 948–952.
Schulhofer-Wohl, J., 2020a. On-Side fighting in civil war: The logic of mortal alignment in Syria. *Rationality and Society, 32*(4), pp. 402–460.
Schulhofer-Wohl, J., 2020b. *Quagmire in Civil War.* Cambridge University Press.
Schwab, R., 2018. Insurgent courts in civil wars: The three pathways of (trans) formation in today's Syria (2012–2017). *Small Wars & Insurgencies, 29*(4), pp. 801–826.
Schwab, R., 2021. " Let's Fight Each Other Another Day": How Armed Opposition Groups Managed Challenges to Cooperation and Postponed Conflict in Syria's Multiparty Civil War (2012–2019). Doctoral dissertation, Johann-Wolfgang-Goethe-Universität zu Frankfurt am Main.
Schwab, R., 2023. Same same but different? Ideological differentiation and intra-Jihadist competition in the Syrian civil war. *Journal of Global Security Studies, 8*(1), p. ogac045.
Schwedler, J.M., 2006. *Faith in Moderation: Islamist Parties in Jordan and Yemen.* Cambridge University Press.
Schwedler, J., 2007. Democratization, inclusion and the moderation of Islamist parties. *Development, 50*(1), pp. 56–61.
Scott, W.R., 2013. *Institutions and Organizations: Ideas, Interests, and Identities.* Sage Publications.
Seurat, L., 2022. *The Foreign Policy of Hamas: Ideology, Decision Making and Political Supremacy.* Bloomsbury Publishing.
Seurat, M., 2015. *Syrie, l'État de barbarie.* Presses universitaires de France.Seymour, L.J., 2014. Why factions switch sides in civil wars: Rivalry, patronage, and realignment in Sudan. *International Security, 39*(2), pp. 92–131.
Shapiro, J.N., 2013. *The Terrorist's Dilemma: Managing Violent Covert Organizations.* Princeton University Press.
Al-Shar'i, A., 2013. *al-sahwa: nashatha, asbabha, wa mu'alajata* (no more indications in terms of edition).
al-Sharq al-Awsat, 2013. *"tandhimat madaniyya tuwaji "dawlat al-'iraq wal-sham al-islamiyya" fi al-raqqa. wa ta'tarid 'ala intihakatha.*
Shesterinina, A., 2016. Collective threat framing and mobilization in civil war. *American Political Science Review,* 110(3), pp. 411–427.
Simon, Steve., 2023. *Grand Delusion: The Rise and Fall of American Ambition in the Middle East.* Penguin Press.
Sindre, G.M., 2018. From secessionism to regionalism: Intra-organizational change and ideological moderation within armed secessionist movements. *Political Geography,* 64, pp. 23–32.
Skocpol, T., 1979. *States and Social Revolutions: A Comparative Analysis of France, Russia and China.* Cambridge University Press.
Sly, L., 2015, "The rise and ugly fall of a moderate Syrian rebel offers lessons for the West", *The Washington Post*Sly, L., 2013. Islamic law comes to rebel-held Syria. *The Washington Post*
Söderberg Kovacs, M., & Hatz, S., 2016. Rebel-to-party transformations in civil war peace processes 1975–2011. *Democratization, 23*(6), pp. 990–1008.
Soliman, Nagwan, 2020, Studying the Ideational Frame and Methods of Action of an Islamist Revolutionary Movement from Social Movement Studies' Perspective. Doctoral dissertation. European University Institute.
Solomon, E., 2017. The rise and fall of a US-backed rebel commander in Syria. *Financial Times.*
Sosnowski, M., 2023. *Redefining Ceasefires: Wartime Order and Statebuilding in Syria.* Cambridge University Press.

Stacher, J., 2012. *Adaptable Autocrats: Regime Power in Egypt and Syria*. Stanford University Press.
Staggenborg, S., 2013, Institutionalization of social movements In: *The Wiley-Blackwell Encyclopedia of Social and Political Movements*, McAdam, D., 2013. Malden: Blackwell.
Stampnitzky, L., 2013. *Disciplining Terror: How Experts Invented 'Terrorism'*. Cambridge University Press.
Staniland, P., 2014. *Networks of Rebellion: Explaining Insurgent Cohesion and Collapse*. Cornell University Press.
Stanton, J.A., 2016. *Violence and Restraint in Civil War: Civilian Targeting in the Shadow of International Law*. Cambridge University Press.
Stein, A., 2022. *The US War against ISIS: How America and Its Allies Defeated the Caliphate*. Bloomsbury Publishing.
Stein, A., Abouzahr, H., & Komar, R., 2017. How Turkey Is governing in northern Aleppo. Syria Deeply.Stewart, M.A., 2017. Civil war as state-making: Strategic governance in civil war. *International Organization*, 72(1), pp. 205–226.
Stewart, M.A., 2021. *Governing for revolution: social transformation in civil war*. Cambridge University Press.
Svensson, I., & Nilsson, D., 2018. Disputes over the divine: Introducing the religion and armed conflict (relac) data, 1975 to 2015. *Journal of Conflict Resolution*, 62(5), pp. 1127–1148.
Svensson, I. and Finnbogason, D., 2021. Confronting the caliphate? Explaining civil resistance in jihadist proto-states. *European Journal of International Relations*, 27(2), pp. 572-595.
Svensson, I., Finnbogason, D., Krause, D. and Hawach, N., 2022. *Confronting the Caliphate: Civil Resistance in Jihadist Proto-States*. Oxford University Press.
Syria TV, 2019. al-jolani yatahadath 'an turkiyya wa sharq al-frat wa mustaqbal Idlib. Syria TV. https://www.youtube.com/watch?v = 0kKFyYDeCMM.
Szekely, Ora, 2016. *The Politics of Militant Group Survival in the Middle East: Resources, Relationships, and Resistance*. Palgrave.
Szekely, O., 2023. *Syria Divided: Patterns of Violence in a Complex Civil War*. Columbia University Press.
al-Tahrir, F., 2017. "min al-alf li lya'.. "khat inha al-ahrar"". Shaam.
Tamm, H., 2016. Rebel leaders, internal rivals, and external resources: How state sponsors affect insurgent cohesion. *International Studies Quarterly*, 60(4), pp. 599–610.
Tarrow, S.G., 2011. *Power in Movement: Social Movements and Contentious Politics*. Cambridge University Press.
Tawil, C., 2011. *Brothers in Arms: The Story of Al-Qa'ida and the Arab Jihadists*. Saqi.
Tawil, C., 2011. *Brothers in Arms: The Story of Al-Qa'ida and the Arab Jihadists*. Saqi.
Thurston, A., 2017. Algeria's GIA: The first major armed group to fully subordinate Jihadism to Salafism. *Islamic Law and Society*, 24(4), pp. 412–436.
Thurston, A., 2020. *Jihadists of North Africa and the Sahel: Local Politics and Rebel Groups*. Cambridge University Press.
Tilly, C., 1977. *From mobilization to revolution*. McGraw-Hill.
Toft, M.D., & Zhukov, Y.M., 2015. Islamists and nationalists: Rebel motivation and counterinsurgency in Russia's north Caucasus. *American Political Science Review*, 109(2), pp. 222–238.
Tol, G., 2022. *Erdoğan's War: A Strongman's Struggle at Home and in Syria*. Oxford University Press.
Torbati, Y., 2015. U.S.-trained Syrian rebels gave equipment to Nusra: U.S. military. *Reuters*.
Tsurkov, E., 2019a. Idlib faces a fearsome future: Islamist rule or mass murder. *Foreign Policy*.
Tsurkov, E., 2019b. Who are Turkey's proxy fighters in Syria?. *The New York Review of Books*.
Tsurkov, E., 2020. The Syrian mercenaries fighting foreign wars for Russia and Turkey. *The New York Review of Books*.
Ucko, D.H., 2022. *The Insurgent's Dilemma: A Struggle to Prevail*. Oxford University Press.
Üngör, U.Ü., 2020. Shabbiha: Paramilitary groups, mass violence and social polarization in Homs. *Violence: An International Journal*, 1(1), pp. 59–79.

United Nations–Secretary-General, 2013. *Report of the United Nations Mission to Investigate Allegations of the Use of Chemical Weapons in the Syrian Arab Republic on the alleged use of chemical weapons in the Ghouta area of Damascus on 21 August 2013. UN Doc.* A/67/997-S/2013/553. United Nations. Available: https://undocs.org/A/67/997.

Van Dam, N., 2011. *The Struggle for Power in Syria: Politics and Society under Asad and the Ba'th Party.* IB Tauris.

Van Dam, N., 2017. *Destroying a Nation: The Civil War in Syria.* Bloomsbury Publishing.

Van Ostaeyen, Pieter, & Van Vlierden, Guy, 2017. The Role of Belgian Fighters in the Jihadification of The Syrian War. European Foundation for Democracy.

Vickers, M.G., 2023. *By All Means Available: Memoirs of a Life in Intelligence, Special Operations, and Strategy.* Books on Tape.

Viterna, J., 2013. *Women in War: The Micro-Processes of Mobilization in El Salvador.* Oxford University Press.

Voller, Y., 2022. Rethinking armed groups and order: Syria and the rise of militiatocracies. *International Affairs*, 98(3), pp. 853–871.

Wagemakers, J., 2012. *A Quietist Jihadi: The Ideology and Influence of Abu Muhammad al-Maqdisi.* Cambridge University Press.

Wagemakers, J., 2016. *Salafism in Jordan: Political Islam in a Quietist Community.* Cambridge University Press.

Wagemakers, J., 2017. Revisiting Wiktorowicz: Categorising and defining the branches of Salafism. *Salafism after the Arab Awakening. Contending with People's Power.* Cavatorta, F., & Merone, F., *Oxford: Oxford University Press.* pp. 7–24.

Walter, B.F., 2017. The extremist's advantage in civil wars. *International Security*, 42(2), pp. 7–39.

Walther, O.J., & Pedersen, P.S., 2020. Rebel fragmentation in Syria's civil war. *Small Wars & Insurgencies*, 31(3), pp. 445–474.

Warner, J., O'Farrell, R., Nsaibia, H. and Cummings, R., 2022. *The Islamic State in Africa: The Emergence, Evolution, and Future of the Next Jihadist Battlefront.* Oxford University Press.

Warrick, J., 2015. *Black Flags: The Rise of ISIS.* Anchor.

Warrick, J., 2022. *Red Line: The Unraveling of Syria and America's Race to Destroy the Most Dangerous Arsenal in the World.* Anchor.

Watts, C., 2016. Deciphering competition between al-Qaida and the Islamic State. *CTC Sentinel*, 9(7), pp.1-6.

Wedeen, L., 2015. *Ambiguities of Domination: Politics, Rhetoric, and Symbols in Contemporary Syria.* University of Chicago Press.

Wedeen, L., 2019. *Authoritarian Apprehensions: Ideology, Judgment, and Mourning in Syria.* University of Chicago Press.

Wegner, E., & Pellicer, M., 2009. Islamist moderation without democratization: The coming of age of the Moroccan Party of Justice and Development?. *Democratization*, 16(1), pp. 157–175.

Wehrey, F., 2012. Saudi Arabia reins in its Clerics on Syria. Carnegie Endowment.

Wehrey, F., 2020. Among the Syrian militiamen of Turkey's intervention in Libya. *The New York Review of Books.*Weinstein, J.M., 2006. *Inside Rebellion: The Politics of Insurgent Violence.* Cambridge University Press.

Weismann, I., 2000. *Taste of Modernity: Sufism, Salafiyya, and Arabism in Late Ottoman Damascus.* Brill.

Weismann, I., 2001. Between Sufi reformism and modernist rationalism: A reappraisal of the origins of the Salafiyya from the Damascene angle. *WELT DES ISLAMS*, 41(2), pp. 206–237.

Whiting, M., 2018. *Sinn Féin and the IRA: From Revolution to Moderation.* Edinburgh University Press.

Wickham, C.R., 2004. The path to moderation: Strategy and learning in the formation of Egypt's Wasat Party. *Comparative Politics*, 36(2), pp. 205–228.

Wickham, C.R., 2013, *The Muslim Brotherhood: Evolution of an Islamist Movement*, Princeton University Press.
Wieland, C., 2021. *Syria and the Neutrality Trap: The Dilemmas of Delivering Humanitarian Aid Through Violent Regimes*. Bloomsbury Publishing.
Wiktorowicz, Q., 2001. *The Management of Islamic Activism: Salafis, the Muslim Brotherhood, and State Power in Jordan*. SUNY Press.
Wiktorowicz, Q., ed., 2004. *Islamic Activism: A Social Movement Theory Approach*. Indiana University Press.
Wiktorowicz, Q., 2006. Anatomy of the Salafi movement. *Studies in Conflict & Terrorism*, 29(3), pp. 207–239.
Woldemariam, M., 2018. *Insurgent Fragmentation in the Horn of Africa: Rebellion and Its Discontents*. Cambridge University Press.Yassin-Kassab, R., & Al-Shami, L., 2018. *Burning Country: Syrians in Revolution and War*. Pluto Press.
Yazbek, S., 2016. *The Crossing: My Journey to the Shattered Heart of Syria*. Random House.
al-Zarier, B., Rateb, A., & Adely, T., 2017. Idlib's rebel court system in disarray, says former judge. Syria Direct.
Zelin, A.Y., 2012a. Know your Ansar al-Sharia. *Foreign Policy*.
Zelin, A.Y., 2012b. Rally'round the Jihadist. *Foreign Policy*.
Zelin, A.Y., 2016. The Islamic State's territorial methodology. *The Washington Institute for Near East Policy*, (29), pp. 2–3.
Zelin, Aaron, 2022. The Age of Political Jihadism: A Study of Hayat Tahrir al-Sham. Washington Institute.
Zelin, Aaron, 2023, Jihadi 'Counterterrorism:' Hayat Tahrir al-Sham Versus the Islamic State, *CTC Sentinel* 16(2).
Ziser, E., 2007. *Commanding Syria: Basher Al-Asad and the First Years in Power* (Vol. 60). IB Tauris.

Maps

Map of the original 12 Turkish observation posts, https://upload.wikimedia.org/wikipedia/commons/thumb/1/18/Turkish_Observation_Points_in_Idlib.svg/800px-Turkish_Observation_Points_in_Idlib.svg.png.
Situation in Syria (August 2012), https://commons.wikimedia.org/wiki/File:Situation_in_Syria_(August_2012).svg.
Situation in Syria (June 2013), https://commons.wikimedia.org/wiki/File:Situation_in_Syria_(June_2013).svg.
Situation in Syria (2014), https://commons.wikimedia.org/wiki/File:Situation_in_Syria_(2014).svg.
Situation in Syria (August 2015), https://commons.wikimedia.org/wiki/File:Situation_in_Syria_(August_2015).svg.
Situation in Syria (September 2017), https://commons.wikimedia.org/wiki/File:Situation_in_Syria_(September_2017).svg.

Index

For the benefit of digital users, indexed terms that span two pages (e.g., 52- 53) may, on occasion, appear on only one of those pages.

Tables are indicated by an italic *t* following the paragraph number/page number.

Abdullah al-Shami, 38, 39, 67–68, 105–6, 127, 128–30, 152–53, 154–55, 164, 183, 194–95
Abdullah Azzam, 21–22, 55, 170–71
Abu Anas, Khaled, 36–37, 40, 47–48, 52, 53–54, 55, 73, 104–5, 167, 170–71, 176, 178–79, 182–83, 185–86
Abu Fath al-Farghali, 143–44, 165, 177, 188, 190–91
Abu Hafs al-Mauritani, 3, 197
Abu Humam al-Shami, 152–53
Abu 'Isa al-Sheikh, 104–8
Abu Jaber al-Sheikh, 123, 132, 186–88, 189–90, 191
Abu Julaybib, 86–87
Abu Khaled al-Suri, 105–6, 117–18, 165
Abu Maria al-Qahtani, 67, 181
Abu Muhammad al-Jolani, 1, 3, 6, 23–24, 66–67, 92, 93, 130, 132, 148, 149, 150, 151, 152–53, 159–60, 178, 183, 197
Abu Muhammad al-Maqdisi, 21–22, 40, 67, 89, 129, 165, 177, 182–83, 196–97, 205
Abu Muhammad al-Sadeq, 186–87, 188–89
Abu Mundhar, 157–58
Abu Mus'ab al-Zarqawi, 167, 180–81
Abu Omar al-Shishani, 92–93, 153–54
Abu Qatada, 21–22, 40, 152, 165, 177, 182–83, 205
Abu Saleh Tahhan, 186–88, 191
Abu Shu'ib al-Masri, 188, 191, 197
Abu YahiyYa al-Hamawi, 144, 157–58, 187–88, 189–90
Abu Yaqthan al-Masri, 188, 191, 197
Abu Yazan al-Shami, 180–81, 184
Abud, Hassan, 53–54, 55, 57, 85, 104, 170, 179–80
Abul-'Abbas al-Shami, 104, 188
Abul-'Abd Ashida, 125, 153, 174, 191, 197
Abul-Khayr al-Masri, 128–30
al-'Adl, Sayf, 127, 129–30
Afghanistan, 1–2, 21–22, 35, 36, 165, 166, 170–71, 200, 202, 206–7, 208, 209, 211

Ahfad al-Rasul, 63–64, 71*t*
Ahrar al-Sham, 17–19, 55–56, 70–73, 74–75, 100–2, 105–8, 110–11, 117–19, 132–33, 148–49, 156–57, 158–60, 163, 173–75, 177–79, 183–85, 187–88, 189–95, 197–99
Ajnad al-Sham, 121, 179
Alawi, 33–35, 43–44, 58–59, 62, 74, 78, 81, 91
Aleppo, 12, 34–35, 36–37, 39, 50–51, 54, 60, 63–64, 65, 78, 81, 92–93, 96, 98–99, 102, 104, 105–6, 113–14, 117–18, 122, 124–26, 130, 138, 146, 158–59, 163, 164, 190
Alloush, Zahran, 66, 84–85, 105
Ansar al-Din, 96, 132, 144–45, 147, 153
Ansar al-Islam, 153
Ansar al-Tawheed, 147, 151–52
al-Assad, Hafez, 33–34, 35–36
Astana Process, 133–34, 136, 138, 143, 148, 161, 192–93

Baab al-Hawa, 76–77, 107, 114, 133, 144, 150
Baath Party, 33–34, 41, 43, 44, 60, 62, 164
bin Laden, Osama, 3, 4–5, 23, 36, 171, 181–82, 204

Caliphate, 1–2, 18, 40, 81, 94, 135, 177, 179, 184–85, 201, 204–5, 207–8, 210–11
Chechnya, 1, 21–22, 36, 68–69, 150, 208–9
CIA, 38–39, 116
Commission for the Protection of Civilians, 69, 94–95

Damascus, 33, 34, 38–39, 41–42, 44, 56, 59–62, 66, 67–68, 78–81, 84–85, 91, 102, 105, 133–34, 139, 168
Daraa, 41, 43, 45–46, 62, 139
Dar al-Qada, 93–94, 98–99
de-escalation zones, 133–34, 138, 140, 192
Democratic Union Party, 69–70
Droukdel, Abdelmalek, 20

Egypt, 20–22, 41, 42, 43, 44, 45, 47, 203

Fath al-Islam, 38–39
Fath al-Mubin, 155–56, 159–60
Fath Halab, 122
Fath Intifada, 38–39
Faylaq al-Sham, 94–95, 97, 121, 123–24, 130, 145, 147, 152–53, 156–57, 179, 192–93, 194
foreign fighters, 1–2, 60–62, 85–86, 87–88, 90–91, 92–93, 150, 153–55, 201, 202, 203, 208
Free Syrian Army (FSA), 1–2, 13, 47, 50, 51, 52, 56, 57, 99, 117–18, 119, 126, 159, 194
FSA. *See* Free Syrian Army

Ghab plains, 54, 57, 117–18, 145, 146, 149
Ghouta, 59–60, 66, 80–81, 84–86, 88–89, 90, 133–34, 138
GIA, 21–22

Hama, 34–35, 39, 50–51, 53–54, 60, 62, 65–66, 76–77, 78, 163
Hamas, 25, 41, 60, 166, 173, 205, 207
al-Hamawi, Saleh, 89, 93–94
Harid al-Mu'mineen, 147
Hazm (movement), 94, 97, 120, 181
High Negotiations Committee, 124
Hilf Nusrat al-Islam, 147
Hizbullah, 41, 78, 124–25, 146, 167–68
Homs, 45–46, 50–51, 59–62, 63–64, 76–77, 78–81, 83–84, 85–86, 106, 113–14, 133–34, 139, 141, 163, 174
HTS (Hay'at Tahrir al-Sham), 3–4, 17–19, 23–24, 131–34, 143–46, 147, 148, 149–55, 156–58, 159–62, 191, 194–95, 196–98, 203
Hudud, 74, 94, 98–99
Hurras al-Din, xxiii, 127, 147, 152–54. *See also* al-Qaeda

Idlib, 36–37, 39, 40, 50–51, 55, 60, 64–65, 81, 86, 97, 98–99, 104, 121–24, 133–34, 138, 140, 141, 146, 147–49, 150–51, 154, 159–60, 163, 183, 186, 192–93, 194–95, 198
Interim Government, 46, 161
IRA, 9
Iran, 41, 44–45, 78, 81, 124–25, 133–35, 138–40, 173, 207
Iraq, 35, 37, 38–40, 52–53, 66–67, 76–77, 78–79, 83, 87–88, 134–35, 139–40, 163–68, 172, 176, 178–79, 180–81, 184
Islamic Front, 104–6, 117–18, 146, 170–71, 179, 182

Islamic State (ISIS IS), 18, 38, 60, 65, 66, 67, 68–69, 78, 79, 80–81, 85, 86–89, 92–94, 95–97, 103–4, 108–9, 111, 114, 115–16, 117–18, 119–20, 123–24, 126, 128, 135, 141, 146, 150–52, 154, 156, 161, 169–70, 173–75, 177–80, 181–82, 184–85, 192–93, 197, 198, 201, 202, 204–5
al-Itilaf. *See* Syrian National Coalition

Jabhat al-Nusra, 38–39, 64–65, 66–68, 70–72, 79, 85–131, 136–38, 144–45, 147, 152, 168, 172, 176, 177–80, 181–84, 190–91, 197, 198, 203, 210
al-Jabhat al-Wataniya lil Tahrir. *See* National Front for Liberation
Jabhat Ansar al-Din, 96, 132, 144–45, 153
Jabhat Fath al-Sham, 129–32, 136–38, 151–52, 191
Jabhat Tahrir Suriya, 146. *See also* Syrian Liberation Front
al-Jama'a al-Islamiyya, 173, 177
Jama'a Nusrat al-Islam wal Muslimin (JNIM), 20–21, 206
Jaysh al-Ahrar, 130–31, 132, 144–45, 150, 189–92, 193
Jaysh al-Badiya, 147
Jaysh al-Fath, 94–96, 121–24, 125–26, 127–28
Jaysh al-Islam, 66, 71t, 73–74, 84–85, 89, 90t, 104–6, 117, 130, 132, 138
Jaysh al-'Iza, 65–66, 71t, 95, 148
Jaysh al-Malahim, 147
Jaysh al-Mujahideen, 95–96, 117–18, 132, 179
Jaysh al-Muhajireen wal-Ansar, 68–69
Jaysh al-Sham, 186–88
Jaysh al-Sunna, 121, 132
Jaysh al-Suqur, 108
Jaysh al-Watani-al-Suri. *See* Syrian National ArmyJaysh Fustat, 85
Jaysh Halab, 122
Jaysh Yarmuk, 138
Jisr Shughur, 45–46, 96
JNIM. *See* Jama'a Nusrat al-Islam wal Muslimin
Jordan, 35, 38–39, 43, 62, 68–69, 76–77, 80–81, 83, 86–87, 89–91, 117, 120, 135, 139, 152, 164, 181
Jund al-Aqsa, 92–93, 97, 121, 123–24, 130–31, 147, 151–52
Jund Allah, 153–54
Junud al-Sham, 68–69, 153–54

Kata'ib al-Faruq, 63–64, 73–74
Katibat Khalid bin Walid, 63–64

Libya, 42, 48, 49, 50–51, 68–69, 118–19, 141, 163–64, 175, 195–96
Liwa al-Haq, 104, 106, 121, 130, 132, 174
Liwa al-Islam. *See* Jaysh al-Islam
Liwa al-Muqatilin al-Ansar, 153
Liwa al-Tawheed, 55, 63–64, 65, 73–74, 95–96, 117
Liwa Shuhada al-Yarmuk, 138
Local councils, 97–98, 173–74

al-Mahdi, Abd al-Razzaq, 144–45
Majlis Shura Ahl al-'Ilm, 131–32, 136–38
Majlis Shura al-Mujahideen, 68–69, 92–93
MANPAD, 123
Military council, 156–58, 159–60
Military operation command (MOC), 86
Mosul, 79, 83, 87–88
Mujahidu Ashida, 174
Muslim Brotherhood, 22–23, 33, 34–36, 37, 39, 48, 49, 69, 94–95, 164, 165, 170

al-Nahhas, Labib, 123–24, 174, 190–91
National Front for Liberation, 147, 194

Pentagon, 115–16, 136–38
People's Protection Unit. *See* YPG
Petraeus, David (General), 115–16
PKK, 69–70, 88, 134–35, 136–38, 151

al-Qaeda, 1–3, 4–5, 18–19, 20, 37, 38–39, 54, 55, 67, 92–94, 105–6, 117–18, 120, 123, 127–30, 147, 152–54, 165, 166–67, 168–69, 170–71, 176–77, 181–82, 197, 198
Qatar, 74–75, 118–19, 121, 139–40, 189, 198, 207

Raqqa, 60, 62, 87, 109, 135, 151–52, 154, 173–74
Riyadh conference, 124, 189
Russia, 42, 44–45, 58–59, 81, 121, 122, 123–26, 128, 129–30, 132–39, 148, 156, 158, 161, 192

Sahwa, 36–37, 168, 172
Salvation Government, 3, 148–49, 155–57, 161, 194–95
Sarayat Abu Bakr al-Sadiq, 154
Sarayat Kabul, 147
Saudi Arabia, 36, 48, 84–85, 94–95, 114–16, 124, 139–40, 151, 153, 188–89
Saydnayya (prison), 53, 54, 168–71
SDF. *See* Syrian Democratic Forces
al-Shabaab, 206

Shabiha, 45–46
Shari'a Politics, 5, 19–20, 183–84, 196–97
al-Siyasat al-shar'iya. *See* Sharia Politics
Soleimani, Qasem, 81
Sotchi, 140
Southern Front, 86–87, 117
Sufan, Hassan, 105–6, 157–59, 193–94
Supreme military council, 114–15
Suqur al-Sham, 65, 73–74, 95–96, 98, 104, 105–6, 107–8, 117, 123–24, 127–28, 130, 132, 148–49, 150–51, 179, 187–88
Syrian Democratic Forces, 81, 88, 134–35
Syrian Islamic Front, 102, 104, 117
Syrian Islamic Liberation Front, 73–74, 95–96, 104, 117
Syrian Liberation Front, 95–96, 146, 147. *See* Jabhat Tahrir Suria
Syrian National Army, 141, 158–59, 195–96
Syrian National Coalition, 46
Syria Revolutionary Front, 120

Taha, Rifa'i, 173
al-Tali'a al-Muqatila, 34–35
Taliban, 68–69, 152–53, 191, 202, 205, 206–7, 211
Tansiqiyat al-Jihad, 153
Terrorist (listing), 22–23, 27, 105–6, 111, 118–19, 120, 127, 128, 130, 148, 156, 179, 180, 205, 211–12
al-Tilly, Abd al-Malek, 153
TIP. *See* Turkistan Islamic Party
TOW (anti-tank weapons), 115–16
Turkey, 51, 52–53, 62, 68–69, 74–75, 76–77, 78, 83, 88, 90–91, 94–95, 107, 114–16, 117–19, 123–25, 132–38, 140–45, 148–49, 151, 153, 154–56, 157–58, 161, 185, 188, 189, 190, 191, 192–93, 194–96, 198, 203
Turkistan Islamic Party, 68–69, 96, 150, 153–54

Unified Arab Code, 99, 152
Unified Military Command Council, 84–85
al-'Uraydi, Sami, 67, 93–94, 181
U.S. 38–39, 66–67, 86, 88, 115–16, 120, 135, 153, 173, 181, 208–10

YPG, 69–70, 77–78, 81, 88, 108–9, 115–16, 125, 134–35, 141, 151

al-Zawahiri, Ayman, 20, 67, 92–93, 105, 117–18, 123, 127, 128–30, 204
Zinki Movement, 65, 95–96, 123–24, 132, 144–45, 146–47, 149, 150, 194

www.ingramcontent.com/pod-product-compliance
Ingram Content Group UK Ltd.
Pitfield, Milton Keynes, MK11 3LW, UK
UKHW042158220126
467240UK00011B/79